Crude Oil, Crude Money

Great Uncle Harry

Crude Oil, Crude Money

Aristotle Onassis, Saudi Arabia, and the CIA

Thomas W. Lippman

BLOOMSBURY ACADEMIC
NEW YORK • LONDON • OXFORD • NEW DELHI • SYDNEY

BLOOMSBURY ACADEMIC
Bloomsbury Publishing Inc
1385 Broadway, New York, NY 10018, USA
50 Bedford Square, London, WC1B 3DP, UK
29 Earlsfort Terrace, Dublin 2, Ireland

BLOOMSBURY, BLOOMSBURY ACADEMIC and the Diana logo
are trademarks of Bloomsbury Publishing Plc

First published in the United States of America by ABC-CLIO 2019
Paperback edition published by Bloomsbury Academic 2024

Copyright © Thomas W. Lippman, 2019

For legal purposes the Acknowledgments on p. xi constitute
an extension of this copyright page.

All rights reserved. No part of this publication may be reproduced or
transmitted in any form or by any means, electronic or mechanical,
including photocopying, recording, or any information storage or retrieval
system, without prior permission in writing from the publishers.

Bloomsbury Publishing Inc does not have any control over, or responsibility for,
any third-party websites referred to or in this book. All internet addresses given
in this book were correct at the time of going to press. The author and publisher
regret any inconvenience caused if addresses have changed or sites have
ceased to exist, but can accept no responsibility for any such changes.

Library of Congress Cataloging-in-Publication Data
Names: Lippman, Thomas W., author.
Title: Crude oil, crude money : Aristotle Onassis, Saudi Arabia,
and the CIA / Thomas W. Lippman.
Description: Santa Barbara, CA: ABC-CLIO, [2019] |
Includes bibliographical references and index.
Identifiers: LCCN 2018058730 (print) | LCCN 2019009928 (ebook) |
ISBN 9781440863950 (ebook) | ISBN 9781440863943 (print)
Subjects: LCSH: Petroleum industry and trade—Political aspects—Saudi
Arabia. | Onassis, Aristotle Socrates, 1906–1975. | United States. Central
Intelligence Agency. | United States—Relations—Saudi Arabia. | Saudi
Arabia—Relations—United States.
Classification: LCC HD9576.S332 (ebook) | LCC HD9576.S332 L57 2019 (print) |
DDC 338.2/72820953809045—dc23
LC record available at https://lccn.loc.gov/2018058730

ISBN: HB: 978-1-4408-6394-3
PB: 979-8-7651-2105-4
ePDF: 978-1-4408-6395-0
eBook: 979-8-2160-6875-4

To find out more about our authors and books visit www.bloomsbury.com
and sign up for our newsletters.

Contents

Notes on Language and Usage — vii

Cast of Characters — ix

Acknowledgments — xi

Introduction — xiii

Chapter 1	The Reign of Big Oil	1
Chapter 2	Signs of Trouble	17
Chapter 3	Intrigue on the Riviera	32
Chapter 4	Onassis in the Dock	46
Chapter 5	The Shot Heard 'Round the World of Oil	54
Chapter 6	Oil and the Cold War	66
Chapter 7	The CIA Is on the Case	76
Chapter 8	A Two-Tier Strategy	88
Chapter 9	The World vs. Onassis	96
Chapter 10	Too Many Moving Parts	110
Chapter 11	Onassis "in the Doghouse"	121
Chapter 12	Power Struggle in the Kingdom	133
Chapter 13	Don't Embarrass the King	142
Chapter 14	The Revenge of Spyridon Catapodis	152

Chapter 15	The Power of the Press	159
Chapter 16	Impasse	169
Chapter 17	Dark Days for Onassis	178
Chapter 18	New Issues Emerge	186
Chapter 19	New Crisis, Old Cases	196
Chapter 20	The Suez Crisis	204
Chapter 21	The End of the Affair	216

Notes   229

Select Bibliography   255

Index   257

Notes on Language and Usage

English-Language Quotations and Spelling

Quotations from British government documents and texts by British writers appear throughout this book. In general, these are used with their original spellings, as in "realise" for "realize" and "honour" for "honor." The British also used plural verbs for collective nouns, such as government. These are retained in quotations in the text.

Many quotations are from diplomatic cables that were written in a peculiar truncated style intended to reduce cable costs. In these, direct articles and prepositions were generally omitted. I have quoted most of them as they appear in the original documents, but for clarity I have taken the liberty of adding some of the omitted words in square brackets.

Official documents and diplomatic messages routinely capitalized common nouns such as government and king. They are quoted here as they appear in the original.

Some documents capitalized all the letters of the acronym Aramco, the Arabian-American Oil Company. In this book, only the first letter is capitalized.

Arabic Words and Names

There is no standard transliteration into English of Arabic words and names; the Arabic alphabet contains letters for which there is no English equivalent. Standard Arabic is written without vowels, so the transliterator has to surmise them. The name Gorgoni, for example, is sometimes spelled Gargani in English. Often, the spelling depends on whether the first transliteration was to English or French. This book uses the transliterations that have become standard in the U.S. news media. However, in quoted material, the transliteration used in the original document is retained. Thus, the name

Faisal, for example, sometimes appears as Feisal or Feysal, Jeddah as Jidda. Therefore, the same name may be spelled differently in different sections of the text, but there will be only one listing in the index. Some Arab men used "Mohammed" as the English version; others used "Muhammad." Where an individual's preferred English spelling of his or her name is known, it is used in this text. Arabic words that are not translated, such as *baksheesh*, are italicized.

Cast of Characters

These are the most prominent actors in this story, appearing frequently. This is by no means a complete list of all people mentioned or quoted.

The Saudis

Saud bin Abdul Aziz, second king of Saudi Arabia. Enthroned November 9, 1953

Faisal bin Abdul Aziz, King Saud's brother, Crown Prince and foreign minister

Abdullah Sulaiman al-Hamdan, known as Abdullah Sulaiman, longtime minister of finance in the royal Saudi government

Mohammed Surur, succeeded Abdullah Sulaiman as minister of finance in September 1954

Abdullah Alireza, head of prominent merchant family based in Jeddah. Appointed minister of commerce by King Saud in spring of 1954

Yusuf Yassin, Syrian-born deputy foreign minister

The Greeks

Aristotle Socrates Onassis, international shipping tycoon and renowned playboy, citizen of Argentina, resident of Paris

Stavros Niarchos, international shipping tycoon, Onassis's brother-in-law and implacable rival

Spyridon Catapodis, small-time shipowner, well-connected Riviera lounge lizard

Spyros Skouras, shipping-fleet owner and president of 20th Century Fox film studio

The Americans

Dwight D. Eisenhower, president of the United States, 1953–1961

John Foster Dulles, secretary of state in the Eisenhower administration

Allen Dulles, John Foster's brother, director of the Central Intelligence Agency

George Wadsworth, U.S. ambassador to Saudi Arabia, 1953–1958

Fred J. Davies, chief executive, Arabian-American Oil Co. (Aramco)

George W. Ray Jr., Aramco general counsel

William Owen, Aramco lawyer, antitrust specialist

William A. Eddy, Aramco's representative in Beirut, former assistant secretary of state for intelligence and research

Robert A. Maheu, private investigator, employed by both Stavros Niarchos and the Central Intelligence Agency to thwart Onassis

Leon Turrou, former FBI agent, confidant of Onassis in Paris

J. Paul Getty, oil tycoon, owner of Pacific Western Oil Co.

Edward Bennett Williams, prominent Washington lawyer

Henry A. Byroade, career diplomat, assistant secretary of state for Near East Affairs

John Jernegan, deputy assistant secretary of state for Near East Affairs

Parker T. "Pete" Hart, career diplomat, director of State Department Bureau of Near East Affairs, former consul in Dhahran, Saudi Arabia

Acknowledgments

A book such as this would not be possible without the assistance of the researchers and document specialists of the National Archives of the United States. I am grateful to the Archives staff in Washington, D.C.; College Park, Maryland; and Kansas City, Missouri, and to their colleagues at the Eisenhower Presidential Library in Abilene, Kansas, for their prompt and patient responses to my requests.

I am especially indebted to Valoise Armstrong, of the Eisenhower Library staff, who unearthed material I needed, and to Sydney Soderberg, who sorted and organized those files.

The indefatigable researchers at the independent, nonprofit National Security Archive in Washington, D.C., are a national treasure. One of them, my daughter-in-law Autumn Kladder, deserves a special word of thanks.

I am grateful also for the prompt assistance I received from the staff of the Minnesota Historical Society in St. Paul.

The late Timothy J. Barger, a true "Aramco brat" whose father was chief executive of the oil consortium in Saudi Arabia, provided indispensable material from his personal library. So did the family of Abdullah Sulaiman, Saudi Arabia's longtime finance minister and a major character in this book.

My wife, Sidney, edited the manuscript in draft and improved it immensely, as did my agent, Janet Reid.

I thank them all.

Introduction

The Cold War was fought on many fronts.
  Sometimes it was an actual shooting war, such as the large-scale, extended military engagements in Korea, Vietnam, Angola, and Afghanistan. In other dangerous episodes, such as the Berlin blockade and the Cuban Missile Crisis, the great global contest for power and influence that pitted the United States and its allies against the Soviet Union and its communist partners took the form of direct confrontation that carried the threat of all-out war. But the Cold War was also a struggle of ideology and economics. Most of it was fought in the shadows, by diplomats, spies, agents of influence, arms dealers, propagandists, and other civilians whose preferred weapons were money, threats, favors, blackmail, and political pressure. The details of these skirmishes, and of the efforts of diplomats to manage them, were largely unknown to the public until secret documents were declassified decades afterward.
  Perhaps the least likely theater of this hidden war was the Kingdom of Saudi Arabia, the vast, thinly populated monarchy that spans the Arabian Peninsula from the Red Sea to the Persian Gulf. In the mid-20th century, Saudi Arabia appeared well-insulated from the tensions of the Cold War. It was rigorously anti-communist; it had no diplomatic or economic relations with the Soviet Union or any other communist nation nor did it have communist neighbors. Never having been occupied or colonized, it had no cadres of resentful nationalists who might have been receptive to Soviet blandishments. The Soviet troops who had imposed Moscow's will on prostrate Eastern Europe after World War II were thousands of miles from the Arabian Peninsula.
  Saudi Arabia was firmly aligned with the United States because a group of giant American companies had an exclusive contract to develop its immense reserves of crude oil, the kingdom's only source of the revenue it needed for development. As different as Saudi Arabia was from the United States in

every aspect of government and organization of human society, the two countries were locked together by mutual need: the United States, land of the automobile, needed the kingdom's petroleum, and the impoverished kingdom needed the technology, investment capital, and military assistance that only the Americans could provide. This peculiar marriage of convenience, forged during World War II, has endured to the present day, but only after surviving many stern and angry tests, one of which erupted out of the blue in January 1954. The catalyst was a Greek shipping magnate named Aristotle Socrates Onassis.

Even at that time, years before he married Jacqueline Kennedy, Onassis was one of the most famous people in the world, a renowned playboy whose personal life fascinated the tabloid press while his business dealings were chronicled in the *Financial Times* and the *Wall Street Journal*. He was the biggest and boldest of the cutthroats known as "Greek shipping tycoons," the hedge fund billionaires of their day. Born in 1906 in a Greek community in Ottoman Turkey, he was legally a citizen of Argentina but in truth a citizen of the world, a resident of Paris who was equally at home in New York and on the French Riviera. Before shipping, he had made a fortune in tobacco. He later created Olympic Airways, Greece's flagship carrier for four decades. His tempestuous affair with the opera star Maria Callas riveted the gossip columns for years. Even in 2016, 41 years after his death, *Vanity Fair* was reporting on his long-ago affair with Jackie Kennedy's sister, Lee Radziwill.[1]

His flamboyant lifestyle and scandalous romances contributed to a shady reputation—a reputation that was damaged further when a long investigation by the Federal Bureau of Investigation (FBI) resulted in his indictment on charges of defrauding the U.S. Navy. But Onassis operated in a milieu of money, intrigue, and power where public opinion meant little unless it interfered with business deals. By the middle of the 20th century, he seemed to have it all—money, fame, women, a yacht the size of a football field. Then in 1954 he made a mistake: he tried to buy his way into the growing oil bonanza in Saudi Arabia. He secretly signed a contract with the Saudi royal government that would give his ships the right to transport almost all the oil exported from the kingdom, at rates he would control. It was a bold move that would have reshaped the global oil market and the international shipping business and would have made Onassis vastly wealthier than he already was, but it brought down on him the wrath of the most powerful enemies he ever faced. For reasons he never fully understood, he became a collateral casualty of the Cold War.

The murky international drama that unfolded after revelation of the contract featured freewheeling business operators, cautious diplomats, and unscrupulous self-promoters. The story had elements of comic opera, but the stakes were high: access to oil, containment of communism, the end of colonialism, and the future of the global maritime industry. In this contest, there were five major centers of power, as the Arabs call them. Two of these were joined in defending the contract: Onassis and a handful of his friends in business and politics, and King Saud bin Abdul Aziz and his ministers. On the other side in opposition were the four major U.S. oil companies that controlled the Saudi oil fields; the operators of every major shipping fleet in the noncommunist world, except that of Onassis himself, and the governments of the countries in which those fleets were based; and the U.S. administration of President Dwight D. Eisenhower, including the State Department of John Foster Dulles, the Central Intelligence Agency of Dulles's brother, Allen, and the U.S. Navy.

The opposition of the oil companies and shipping interests was easy to understand, but why would Eisenhower and his national security team care about a business deal with no ideological component between non-Americans in some far-off country? If the oil companies opposed the contract, they would not seem to need the government's help: they were vast corporations with deep pockets. They could hire as many lawyers as they needed and litigate in as many countries as necessary for as long as it took. But to officials in Washington, the Onassis agreement with Saudi Arabia was not just a business contract and not just about money. The Dulles brothers, patrician stewards of the Eisenhower administration's foreign and national security policies, saw the tanker deal as a challenge to a global economic and security order that they were committed to defend. They saw it as a breach of faith by Saudi Arabia, which was dependent on the United States for its development and its security—a breach of faith that could encourage nationalistic upheaval throughout the Arab world and create opportunities for the Soviet Union to spread influence.

In the 1950s, the United States dominated the global economy; American companies, along with British Petroleum, were the preeminent powers in the international oil trade. The Democratic administration of President Harry S. Truman, concerned about the monopolistic appearance of control of the petroleum industry by the giant companies known collectively as Big Oil, had encouraged smaller, independent operators to seek opportunities in the Middle East. In Eisenhower's Republican administration, by contrast, the Dulles brothers valued stability and wanted to keep the existing oil order in place. In their view, the Onassis deal could be a precursor to nationalization of the Saudi oil industry, and that contagion would spread across the region. They feared a recurrence of the oil crisis that had erupted three years earlier in Iran, just across the Persian Gulf from Saudi Arabia, which had provoked an international uproar by nationalizing its oil industry. In Egypt, across the Red Sea from Saudi Arabia, Gamal Abdel Nasser, a fiery Arab nationalist, had overthrown a British-dominated monarchy and was forcing British troops to leave his country. Washington was watching apprehensively as postcolonial societies all across Asia and Africa sought to escape the economic and political domination of the great powers.

President Eisenhower was sympathetic to the aspirations of colonized and newly independent peoples, but fear of communist expansion sometimes overrode those sentiments. Eisenhower's national security advisers saw Onassis's contract with the Saudis as a potential Cold War gift to the Soviet Union, which after the 1953 death of Joseph Stalin was beginning to court favor throughout what came to be known as the Third World. To Eisenhower and his national security team, expansion of Soviet influence was a critical threat to U.S. interests; arrangements that appeared to threaten the existing order—such as the Onassis deal—had to be stopped.

The Central Intelligence Agency (CIA) was already hostile to Onassis because its operatives had discovered that he had used a fleet of Liberty Ships, U.S.-built navy-surplus vessels that he had bought after World War II, to carry cargo to North Korea and China during the Korean War. Anger about that was still fresh in Washington when news of his Saudi Arabia deal broke. The FBI, which had suspected for years that Onassis had defrauded the navy in the purchase of those ships, viewed his Saudi Arabia deal as a threat to the oil supply of Western Europe, which was still recovering from World War II. A senior FBI official who visited the Saudi oil fields in the spring of 1954 concluded that the Onassis contract could lead to the "diversion of the oil to Soviet-bloc interests" and possibly to war.[2]

The Onassis deal became a flashpoint amid the turbulent events that roiled the Middle East in the 1950s as the United States and the Soviet Union maneuvered for advantage at a time of rising nationalism and anti-colonialist sentiment among the Arabs.

In July 1954, President Eisenhower and the members of his National Security Council gathered at the White House for a broad review of the threat of Soviet expansionism in the Middle East. The president signed off on general statements of policy about countries and issues, and on several "Specific Courses of Action." One of those was a blunt directive that the United States take "all appropriate measures" to ensure that the Onassis contract never took effect.[3] The State Department and the CIA were already looking for ways to do that and now had specific authorization from the president to act forcefully. The White House directive did not indicate what measures would be "appropriate."

Saudi Arabia was weak, thinly populated, and underdeveloped, but neither the oil companies nor the U.S. government could simply bully the kingdom into doing their bidding. Exxon, Chevron, Texaco, and Mobil, the giant companies that owned the Arabian American Oil Company, or Aramco, were in a delicate position.[4] They wanted the tanker contract cancelled, but they did not want to embarrass or humiliate King Saud because he held the ultimate weapon: he could revoke the American companies' concession and give it to some rival company or group from another country. The oil executives wanted the king to save face so that he would not turn against them.

Similarly, the U.S. government wanted to break the Onassis contract, but it did not want an open breach with Saudi Arabia, a critical supplier of an increasingly essential commodity and a bulwark of anti-communism with which relations were already strained because of disputes over other issues. United in their objective, the U.S. government and Big Oil were also united in their desire to leave no fingerprints.

The result was a protracted international struggle waged on the surface by diplomats and oil executives but behind the scenes by shady characters, self-appointed mediators, Riviera playboys, brand-name lawyers, anonymous go-betweens, and a few unscrupulous Saudis. The contract itself and Washington's distress about it were reported in the press at the time, but the campaign to break the deal, and CIA's involvement in it, were clandestine.

Equally invisible to the public was the high-stakes maneuvering within the Saudi royal court, where a new king was struggling to consolidate his authority. When the contract was signed, Saud had been on the throne only two months after succeeding his father, King Abdul Aziz al-Saud, who was a giant of Arab history as the founder of modern Saudi Arabia and the dominant force in his country for decades. Saud proved woefully unable to match his father's abilities.

I came across the basic elements of this tale while I was writing a biography of Abdullah Sulaiman, who for decades was the right hand man of King Abdul Aziz. It was Sulaiman, in his position as minister of finance, who negotiated and signed the contract with Onassis that triggered these events. Family records, correspondence, translations of Arabic-language books about him, and other documents were made available by his son.

The full story can now be told because other key documents, from the White House, the State Department, the CIA, the FBI, the oil companies, the British Foreign Office, the Saudi government, and individuals who were involved, have been declassified and made public. There are also extensive court records. There are no known documents about the Onassis deal from the Soviet Union or any other communist country because the Kremlin and its satellites had nothing to do with it, except in overheated imaginations in Washington. The Soviet Union, recovering from severe damage to its oil fields and pipelines during World War II, was more than self-sufficient in oil, and, in the Middle East, was pursuing targets that seemed much more promising than Saudi Arabia.

CHAPTER ONE

The Reign of Big Oil

The world of energy passed a critical milestone late in 1948. At about the time that Harry S. Truman was winning election to a full term as president, the United States became a net importer of crude oil and petroleum products. The United States was one of the world's largest producers of oil, as it is today. But just as U.S. officials had foreseen during World War II, the lines delineating its output and its rapidly growing demand crossed a few years after the war. Crude oil became the world's most important commodity, and not just in the United States. Oil supplanted coal to become the fuel of the world's commerce, powering the ships, motor vehicles, airplanes, and railroads that moved all other goods transported in a growing global economy.

Oil fueled the reconstruction of Europe and Japan out of the ruins of war; in the United States, it was the energy source for a booming economy of industrial expansion, family cars, suburban living, and long-haul trucks. For other commodities, there were alternatives: wheat could be replaced by other grains, lumber by other building materials. For oil, there was no substitute. Access to worldwide oil resources became an economic and strategic imperative for the United States.

The importance of oil was matched by the cost and difficulty of obtaining it. Oil cannot be dug from the ground with hand tools, like some other minerals. Nor can it be grown from seeds. Finding and producing oil requires knowledge of geology, substantial investments of capital, and access to drilling and refining technology that were far beyond the means of most of the countries where extensive reservoirs of "black gold" were to be found.

Except in Mexico, which nationalized its oil industry in 1938, the oil business almost everywhere in the noncommunist world was controlled by a small number of well-endowed international corporations. These companies were based in the United States and Western Europe, but they operated wherever oil reservoirs happened to be, from Venezuela to Iraq to Indonesia. These powerhouse corporations were known colloquially as the Seven Sisters: Standard Oil Company of New Jersey (now known as Exxon), Standard Oil Company of California (or Chevron), Socony-Vacuum Co. (known as Mobil), and Texaco, Gulf Oil, Royal Dutch Shell, and British Petroleum (known as BP). All were vertically integrated, that is, engaged around the world in every aspect of the petroleum business: exploration and production, shipping, refining, and retail marketing.

Within a few years after World War II, these companies owned or controlled more than half the world's production outside communist countries, including 99 percent of the output in the Middle East; about 57 percent of the world's refining capacity; about two-thirds of the privately owned tanker fleets; all major pipelines in the noncommunist world outside the United States; and a dominant share of retail outlets worldwide.[1]

By its nature, vertical integration on this global scale was detrimental to most of the producing countries because they were largely foreclosed from setting prices or marketing their own oil outside their borders.

These giant companies were competitors, but in some places they also operated in partnership with each other. The most lucrative and productive of those partnerships was in Saudi Arabia, which had the biggest of all pools of crude oil. The desolate terrain of eastern Saudi Arabia became one of those places where the interests of U.S. national security and the economic well-being of the noncommunist world converged with the interests of powerful American corporations.

That convergence resulted in a long-standing conundrum within the U.S. government, regardless of who was president. The oil companies were major international power players who sometimes made their own arrangements with foreign governments without regard to U.S. foreign policy and who sometimes cooperated with each other in ways that were clearly monopolistic, but they were also indispensable pillars of the free world's industrial economy. U.S. government policy alternated between attacking them in antitrust legal cases and acting strongly to protect their interests abroad, sometimes pursuing both approaches simultaneously.

An article about the history of oil development in the Middle East published by BP noted that after the war

> The region was important for two reasons. It formed a geographical barrier to the spread of communism as the Cold War began to identify new ideological battlefronts around the globe. Just as importantly, the region was set to play a leading role in the geopolitics of the Oil Age. Middle Eastern reserves had transformed the world energy outlook. Everette deGolyer, an American geologist advising the U.S. government, remarked in 1944: "The centre of gravity of world oil production is shifting from the Caribbean

area to the Persian Gulf area." He had good reason to believe it. Major discoveries by the British-controlled Anglo-Iranian Oil Company in Kuwait and Qatar just before the outbreak of war had been matched by the immense potential of a 1938 discovery in Saudi Arabia by a subsidiary of Standard Oil of California and the Texas Company.[2]

The oil from those giant Mideast fields was pumped through pipelines to the nearest coastline, usually the Persian Gulf. From there to Europe, the United States, and Japan, it was transported by tanker ships. Tankers became the feeding tubes of the postwar Western economy. The more oil the world consumed, the more tankers were needed and the larger they became.

In Saudi Arabia, and throughout the Middle East, the oil in the ground belonged to the host country, but the host country lacked the technology and capital to develop the fields and facilities needed to produce and transport it. It was standard practice in the region for the host country to negotiate an agreement with a European or U.S. oil company or consortium by which the country and the company would split the proceeds. By the time Saudi Arabia got into the business, oil production was well established in some nearby countries, most of it controlled by British interests.

These agreements with international companies, known as concessions, pumped cash into countries that had little else, but they gave the oil companies an advantage because their executives decided how much oil would be produced. Thus, they had de facto control over the price and over how much revenue the host countries would receive.

While the oil companies were installing the vast and hugely expensive infrastructure of oil production and transportation in countries that had no other source of capital, the host governments had little choice but to leave in place concession terms that sometimes gave the companies more revenue than the producing countries earned. But as oil flows increased and the companies amortized their investments, the host countries began to seek better terms for themselves. Their people, better educated and increasingly trained in oil field operations, sought greater opportunities in their home industries. The oil companies naturally wanted to maintain the favorable terms that were in place.

The Original Aramco Concession

King Abdul Aziz al-Saud, who had unified the tribes of Arabia into a new country known as Saudi Arabia in 1932, was a deeply pious adherent of a form of Sunni Islam known to Westerners as Wahhabism, which was generally xenophobic and disdainful of foreigners and unbelievers. He reluctantly allowed foreign oil workers into his realm only because he lacked other sources of revenue for development or even basic sustenance. Before oil, the chief source of revenue was a tax on Muslims from other countries making the annual pilgrimage to Mecca; that traffic shriveled during the worldwide Great Depression in the 1930s, rendering the new kingdom nearly destitute.

The king authorized his finance minister and chief operating officer, the crafty Abdullah Sulaiman, to negotiate a concession agreement with Standard Oil Company of California, or SoCal, now known as Chevron. The crucial first article of the deal they struck in 1933 gave the company "the exclusive right, for a period of sixty years from the effective date hereof, to explore, prospect, drill for, extract, treat, manufacture, transport, deal with, carry away and export petroleum, asphalt, naphtha, natural greases, ozokerite, and other hydrocarbons, and the derivatives of all such products."[3]

SoCal obtained its concession after arduous negotiations with Finance Minister Sulaiman, who was the most powerful man in Saudi Arabia aside from King Abdul Aziz himself. "Wearily the duelists fought it out" in those negotiations, the renowned author Wallace Stegner wrote in his account of the deal. The bargaining went on for more than three months—on one side, impatient Americans; on the other, the king's representatives who were, in Stegner's words, "hardheaded, smart, patient, tenacious, wary . . . bargainers worthy of anyone's steel."[4]

Stegner recognized one of the unlikely but inescapable truths about this agreement between a giant corporation from the United States, the world's greatest industrial and economic power, and Saudi Arabia, which was at the opposite pole of human development. This was that the relationship was not as unequal as it might seem because each side had something the other very much wanted. Different as they were culturally as well as materially, they needed each other. The Americans were not colonizers; they entered Saudi Arabia by invitation, not at gunpoint. They were welcome, but if they incurred the king's disfavor, they could be replaced at any time by some company or syndicate from Europe.

The first geologists set sail from the United States a few months after the contract was signed. When they arrived in the kingdom, they camped on the Persian Gulf coast in a harsh, unforgiving landscape where the 20th century had not yet arrived. Saudi Arabia, officially created just the year before, was one of the poorest and least developed countries in the world. In a nation the size of Western Europe, basic features of modern life—electricity, paved roads, telephones, hospitals, radios, even schools—hardly existed outside of Jeddah, the ramshackle commercial and diplomatic capital on the Red Sea coast. And Jeddah was inaccessible to the oil workers because it was on the opposite side of the country from the oil fields on the Gulf coast, 750 roadless miles away in a country with no airports. The royal capital, Riyadh, in the desert in the middle of the country, was also inaccessible because foreigners were generally not permitted to go there. The oil camp's sole

The Reign of Big Oil

connection to the outside world was through Bahrain, the tiny British-controlled island sheikhdom a few miles off the Saudi coast.

SoCal was taking a massive gamble. In the midst of the Depression, the company was about to spend untold millions of dollars in the expectation, or rather the hope, of finding useful amounts of crude oil. Its competitors had locked in assured sources of supply around the world, but SoCal was "crude short"—if it wanted to grow and compete with the other majors, it needed urgently to expand its controlled reserves. In Saudi Arabia, the quest was more expensive than it might have been elsewhere because while the oil turned out to be close to the surface and relatively easy to extract, the kingdom was devoid of modern technology and commerce. Every tool and implement, every vehicle and length of pipe and wire that the geologists and drillers would need, as well as their food and housing, had to be imported. In the harsh landscape, the early geologists camped in tents, accompanied by suspicious local guides whose language few of them knew. The temperature regularly rose above 100 degrees. Dhahran, the small city SoCal built to house its American workers and, eventually, their families, was constructed from scratch.

Chevron's explorers drilled one dry hole after another for four years. Then in 1938, two years after Texaco acquired a half interest in the venture, the well known as Dammam No. 7 finally delivered oil in commercially viable quantities, lifted from 4,727 feet below the desert surface. The first cargoes of crude were exported the following year from a shipping terminal the oil company built at Ras Tanura, on the Persian Gulf coast. Further development of the oil fields was stalled by World War II, when shipping lanes were closed and equipment unavailable, but production soared after the war. By 1954, the most productive oil fields ever discovered were delivering growing quantities to a consuming world where the automobile was king. Output escalated from 164,229 barrels per day in 1946 to 844,642 barrels by the beginning of 1954, and no end to the expansion was in sight.[5]

Almost all that oil was exported because undeveloped Saudi Arabia had little domestic use for it. The kingdom's dependence on the revenue from those exports was nearly total, but the dependence ran both ways. The United States and the industrialized West needed the oil as much as Saudi Arabia needed the money. The U.S. government was not a direct participant in the Saudi oil commerce, except as a purchaser of fuel for the navy, but as Stegner noted in his history of this venture, the commodity's centrality to the economy gave Washington "the inevitable political responsibilities of massive involvement."[6]

In the late 1940s, as the enterprise grew and required more capital, SoCal and Texaco took in two more major U.S. oil companies as partners—Exxon and Mobil—and named the consortium Arabian American Oil Company, or Aramco.

An American who worked for Aramco at the time described it as "in effect the neurotic child of four parents, subject to the whims, qualms, and jealousies of each."[7]

It was true that the partners had different corporate cultures, but in the big picture their interests were aligned, and the interests of the U.S. government and these giants of corporate America now converged: the flow of U.S.-controlled crude oil must be maintained because it was central to the American economy and way of life. The Aramco operation became the focus of U.S. strategic policy in the region, and the oil industry became inextricably intertwined with Cold War security issues.

History has demonstrated that concerns about access to oil were unwarranted. Even if Saudi Arabia had turned communist overnight, it would still have exported oil into the world market because that was the country's only source of revenue. The same was true of Iraq, Kuwait, and Iran. Since the beginning of the petroleum age in the 19th century, no nation that has been a major producer of oil has voluntarily cut off its exports, regardless of what kind of government was in charge. If a country such as Saudi Arabia refused to sell to the United States, as happened during the Arab oil embargo of 1973, it would still have to sell to other consuming countries. The oil those consumers would have bought elsewhere would thereby become available to the United States instead. Refining processes and shipping patterns would have been disrupted at least briefly, but overall world supply would not be much diminished. In the atmosphere of the Cold War, no one in the United States or other industrialized countries was willing to take that gamble.

The Truman "Denial Plan"

In the judgment of President Truman's national security and intelligence teams, the importance of securing access to Persian Gulf oil for the United States and its allies was matched by the urgency of denying access to that oil to the Soviet Union and its satellites. The Soviet Union was rich in oil resources and in normal circumstances more than self-sufficient, but its fields had been severely damaged in the war. Production in 1945 was only 60 percent of what it had been in 1941, and after the war Moscow faced the burden of supplying oil to its satellites in Eastern Europe.[8] U.S. strategy dictated that the Soviets not be allowed to gain any form of control over Gulf production that could help them or jeopardize the flow of oil to the West.

"The lessons of World War II, the growing economic significance of oil, and the magnitude of Middle Eastern resources all served, in the context of the developing Cold War with the Soviet Union, to define the preservation of access to that oil as a prime element in American and British—and Western European—security," the oil historian Daniel Yergin wrote.[9]

It became official U.S. policy to ensure that if the United States and its allies did not have access to Gulf oil neither would anybody else. On January 10, 1949, Truman approved a plan developed by his National Security Council (NSC) for the "Removal and Demolition of Oil Facilities in The Middle East."

The plan, known as NSC 26/2, said that "the interests of the United States dictate that prior to the occupation of the Saudi Arabian oil fields and facilities by an enemy, the refinery and other surface facilities, stocks and equipment or such portions thereof as would render them unusable by the enemy, should be removed or destroyed." The wells themselves should be plugged but not destroyed, so that they could be reactivated once the United States regained control.

The State Department had recently opened a consulate in Dhahran to serve the fast-growing U.S. oil community and the personnel of a nearby military airfield that the king had allowed the United States to build and operate. To implement the Denial Plan, the department was instructed to direct its diplomats there to seek the acquiescence of the Saudi government.[10] Until that point, the Saudis knew nothing about this plan by a foreign country they thought was friendly to seize control of their most valuable national asset.

The NSC advised the president that "the materials [to be] used for the demolitions should be located in the oil fields without delay in such quantities or in such additional increments as will not arouse suspicion." The plan also called for "all military forces of the United States stationed in Saudi Arabia and all facilities at their disposal" to be made available to implement it. The NSC planners anticipated that Britain could be persuaded to do the same in Kuwait, Abu Dhabi, and Bahrain.

Separately, in April 1951, the Truman administration adopted a "Strategic War Plan" developed by the Central Intelligence Agency that laid out who would be responsible for doing what in the event of war with the Soviet Union. The spy agency assigned to itself the duty to "ensure the availability to the Western world, and the denial to the USSR and satellites, of the strategically important resources of the area."[11] By that summer of 1951, Aramco had managers throughout its facilities who were briefed on the plan and prepared to implement it, and the CIA had five operatives working under Aramco cover at headquarters in Dhahran.[12]

A State Department report to the White House on implementation of these plans, dated April 7, 1952, recommended "further development of Aramco-type Denial Plans to Kuwait, Kuwait Neutral Zone, Bahrain, and Qatar."[13] (The Neutral Zone was an area between Kuwait and Saudi Arabia that was not part of either country.) But then Aramco withdrew its cooperation because the State Department and CIA refused to tell the Saudis about it and the company did not want to do so on its own.[14] British oil companies operating in other Gulf countries also refused to participate; like Aramco, they feared that even if they did not tell the host countries, the plans would leak out and the angry host countries would revoke their concessions over this slight to their sovereignty.

As the issue of oil company participation demonstrated, the intent of the "Denial Plan" was clear, but efforts to turn it into an operational document raised as many questions as they answered. What if the Saudi government refused? How would the plan be implemented in the oil installations of Kuwait, Bahrain, and Abu Dhabi, where the British were responsible for security? Could the installations be destroyed by air attacks, or would ground troops have to go in? If by air, from which airfield? What would happen if local citizens tried to interfere? How could the hundreds of Americans working in the oil fields be protected and evacuated?

Wilbur Crane Eveland, a longtime CIA operative in the Arab world, asked what would happen if the plan were implemented but then "the threatened Russian attack didn't materialize and the Arabs, embittered by our destruction of their vast resources, invited the Soviets in as friends and not enemies? Could we then face international opinion and justify taking back what we'd destroyed?"[15]

Arguments about such questions, and inconclusive discussions with the British, went on through the rest of Truman's time in office and into Dwight D. Eisenhower's first year as president.

In March 1953, shortly after Eisenhower took office, the State Department reported to the White House that the supply of oil, especially from the Middle East, had become vastly more crucial to the United States and its allies than it had been at the time the Denial Plan was first adopted. A department memo summarized the developments:

a. The United States has increasingly become a net importer of petroleum (now about 600,000 barrels per day);
b. The use of petroleum in Europe and other free world areas has increased greatly;
c. Exploration of oil resources in the Middle East has proved [that there are] vast additional reserves;
d. United States and United Kingdom investment in oil producing, transporting (pipelines), and refining facilities has been greatly augmented;
e. Iran has nationalized its oil industry; Iranian oil exports have been totally eliminated since July 1951 [because of a boycott organized by the British, whose assets Iran had expropriated];
f. Middle East oil production in areas of United States responsibility has been doubled.

In Bahrain, Kuwait, and Qatar, the State Department memo said, explosives to be used in implementing denial plans had been purchased but not deployed. In Saudi Arabia, the memo said, the "last resort" Denial Plan was well advanced: "Explosives have been placed in three oil field magazines in Saudi Arabia in sufficient quantity to support the demolition plans for the producing areas and the refinery. Security considerations precluded storage of explosives at pipeline stations; a stock of explosives that can be flown to some of these stations is available. Company management has developed concern over the presence of these explosives on its premises, but no secure method of removing them has been suggested."[16]

The biggest issue, the memo said, is that "none of the four oil companies involved in this project"—that is, the Aramco parent companies—"will accept the responsibility for carrying out denial." Because the issues of responsibility and notification to the host governments had not been resolved, the State Department recommended a top-to-bottom review of the Denial Plan, which the National Security Council duly undertook. The result was a revised version of NSC 26/2, designated NSC 5401.

It reaffirmed that "the interests of the United States and the free world indicate that, in the event of war, oil wells, surface oil stocks, other petroleum facilities, and certain accessory equipment in the Middle East should be denied to the USSR by action prior to any occupation by its forces of the area. . . . Although Denial Planning should be carried on continuously, such planning does not lessen the importance of keeping the Middle East from communist domination by such forcible action as may be feasible in accordance with approved U.S. policy."[17]

NSC 5401 was "no passive policy statement," Eveland wrote.

> It contained plans for the military and the CIA to ensure that Middle East oil fields would be denied [to] an invading Soviet army. If necessary, the oil fields would be totally demolished. This was essentially a navy-instigated policy, based on the recognition that even as access to this petroleum had enabled the Allies to win Word War II, so the West's naval and ground forces were now similarly dependent on Middle Eastern oil. Since Western and indigenous forces were incapable of stopping a conventionally mounted Russian strike into the area, should it be executed in concert with a land attack on NATO's forces by the Warsaw Pact nations, we'd have to deny the Soviets Middle eastern oil until our military could recover the area.[18]

The Neutral Zone and J. Paul Getty

In the late 1940s and early 1950s, relations between the Saudis and their American patrons deteriorated because of multiple irritants, not just oil.

The Saudi government's chief interlocutor with oil companies was the veteran finance minister, Abdullah Sulaiman. In addition to haggling with

Aramco on money and on issues such as working conditions for Arab employees, he represented the Saudi government in separate negotiations with other oil companies about drilling concessions offshore, in potentially rich fields beneath the waters of the Gulf. Aramco claimed the undersea area as part of its 1933 concession, but the finance minister argued that Aramco's claim was limited to the three-mile limit of territorial waters and that the government still maintained full control of minerals under its continental shelf.

After months of discussion and consultation between various oil companies and the British and U.S. governments, Aramco and the Saudi government reached an agreement in principle in September 1948 that confirmed Aramco's rights to the offshore areas. In return, Aramco relinquished rights in the Saudi Arabian portion of the Saudi-Kuwaiti Neutral Zone, a land area of about 2,000 square miles, originally delineated by the British, in which the two countries ruled jointly and their Bedouin subjects were allowed to roam freely regardless of official nationality.

With the encouragement of the U.S. government, which was concerned about the appearance of a "Big Oil" monopoly in the region, a group of smaller American companies known as American Independent Oil Company, or AMINOIL, purchased the oil rights in Kuwait's share of Neutral Zone with what Daniel Yergin called "a bid that stunned the oil industry: $7.5 million in cash, a minimum annual royalty of $625,000, 15 percent of the profits—and a million-dollar yacht for the Amir of Kuwait."[19] That became the baseline for bidders seeking the oil rights in the Saudi area of the Zone—that is, on land that was administered by Saudi Arabia but outside the Aramco concession area.

The highest bidder turned out to be Pacific Western Oil Company, which was controlled by J. Paul Getty. That is the same billionaire J. Paul Getty whose refusal to pay ransom for his kidnapped grandson was recounted in the 2017 movie "All the Money in the Word."

His company offered even better terms for the Saudi part of the Zone than AMINOIL had given to Kuwait: a considerably higher royalty rate than Aramco was paying, plus 12.5 percent of gross proceeds from sales of natural gas, 20 percent of the profits from a refinery to be built in the Neutral Zone, stipulated amounts of gasoline and kerosene from the refinery, the right to buy one-quarter of the shares of any subsidiary company formed to operate in the Neutral Zone, and significant contributions to Saudi education in and outside the country.[20] By itself, this deal represented a triumph for Abdullah Sulaiman, but it also opened the door for an attempt by the Saudi government to force Aramco to renegotiate the original 1933 concession terms. Twenty years on, those terms were short-changing the kingdom.

The oil company and the U.S. government were making more money off Saudi Arabia's oil than the kingdom itself was: in 1949, for example, Aramco paid $38 million to the Saudi government and $43 million in U.S. income tax.[21] Getty's Neutral Zone bid demonstrated that the market was willing to pay more. There was no good reason why Saudi Arabia should not get at least the same terms as Kuwait or, better still, the same terms as Venezuela, which a few years earlier had extracted from the oil companies operating there a straightforward split of the revenue, half and half—an arrangement known as a "Fifty-Fifty agreement."[22]

Sulaiman's suspicion that the oil company was not fully meeting its obligations or dealing in good faith—suspicion shared by the king—was reinforced by Chevron's decision to take on new partners in the Aramco venture.

In 1948, Standard of New Jersey (later Exxon) and Socony-Vacuum of New York (Mobil) bought shares, joining Chevron and Texaco in the ownership consortium. These were large international companies, but they had no experience in Saudi Arabia; none of their people had been in the kingdom during the long years of looking for oil and keeping the venture alive during the war. The Saudis believed that these new partners wanted to limit Aramco's expansion because they saw the Saudi company as competition for their own subsidiaries in other countries. Obviously, the less Aramco grew, the less the kingdom's revenue would grow.

Sulaiman was also pressing the company to reduce its hiring of South Asian workers and to take on more Saudis, as required by Article 23 of the 1933 concession agreement. He listed his hiring preferences: (1) Saudi Arabs, (2) Palestinian refugees, (3) citizens of Arab League member countries, and (4) citizens of other Muslim countries such as Pakistan.[23] But as the end of the war approached and rapid expansion loomed, the oil company began hiring hundreds of Italians, who were refugees from Eritrea. According to Stegner, these Italians "were welcomed by the Saudi Arab government only because it had been assured that no qualified Saudis were available," but their arrival increased pressure on Aramco to train and promote more Saudis.[24]

The Minister's hiring preference for Palestinian refugees was another symptom of the difficulties that entered the relationship with Aramco at about this time. Aramco was a U.S. company, and the United States in the early 1950s was in disfavor throughout the Arab world because of Truman's recognition of the new state of Israel in 1948. Aramco and its parent companies had opposed Truman's decision to accept creation of a Jewish state in what had been part of Palestine, but that did not entirely insulate them against the anti-American sentiment that was growing across the Arab world.

Another irritant was growing Saudi dissatisfaction with the implementation of Truman's Point Four program, named for the fourth point in his inaugural address of 1949, which was a foreign aid program that offered technical and organizational help to developing countries. More tension would soon rise over the U.S. government's reluctance to support Saudi Arabia in a long-running territorial dispute with Britain over a remote stretch of land known as the Buraimi Oasis, in what is now the emirate of Abu Dhabi, largest of the United Arab Emirates.

King Abdul Aziz had rebuffed appeals from other Arab leaders to revoke the American oil concession over the Palestine issue, but the cumulative effect of all these difficulties was to stiffen the resolve of Finance Minister Sulaiman to make Aramco pay more.

The oil company proposed "an equal participation in net profits after foreign taxes," but Sulaiman understood that an equal share of after-tax profit was not the same as an equal share of gross revenue, which is what he wanted. Difficult negotiations unfolded over many months in 1950, complicated by arguments about which currency would be used for payment, but in the end Sulaiman had the leverage to get what he wanted. When the oil company balked at increasing its payments for oil, he demanded that it pay for other things, such as construction of a new pier at the commercial port of Dammam and construction of a railroad from Dammam to Riyadh, the royal capital deep in the interior. In December 1950, Aramco accepted the inevitable, agreeing to a deal similar to the one in Venezuela: a 50–50 split of profits from oil exploitation, paid in the form of a 50 percent tax. The tax was calculated on profits after all other money paid to the government, including royalties and duties, had been deducted. The agreement was retroactive to the beginning of 1950.[25]

A Giant Tax Break

The results were dramatic. Aramco's payments to the Saudi government jumped from $39.2 million in 1949 to $56.7 million in 1950 to $966 million in 1954.[26] This amounted to a virtual tidal wave of money for a country that had been among the world's poorest just a decade earlier, but it hardly cost the Aramco companies anything because, as they had anticipated, the U.S. Treasury Department allowed Aramco to declare its payments to Saudi Arabia to be a tax, as specified in the text of the new agreement and a royal decree ratifying it, rather than royalties. This legal distinction allowed the four members of the consortium to offset the tax payments to Saudi Arabia against their domestic tax obligations.

"The 50% Saudi Arab income tax on petroleum producers, like other similar taxes enacted by other oil producing countries at about the same time, was recognized by the U.S. Internal Revenue Service as an income tax which was allowed as a credit against U.S. income taxes on income generated by sales in Saudi Arabia," Aramco vice president Joseph J. Johnston told a U.S. Senate subcommittee that investigated this arrangement years later. This was not a special benefit for Aramco, he said; it was in keeping with the practice of many U.S. companies operating in many countries.[27]

In those same hearings, the senators heard a vigorous defense of the policy from George McGhee, a petroleum geologist from Texas who turned to a career in diplomacy and became assistant secretary of state for Near East Affairs. At the time of the tax agreement, he said, "The Middle East was perhaps the most critical area in the world in the contest between ourselves and the Soviets." Policy was driven by the fear of "some nationalist leader particularly in the countries where there were kings and sheikhs, who might seize power as Nasser did later." He said the income tax arrangement was justified because "the ownership of this concession was a valuable asset for our country," and the government shared Aramco's concern about the possibility of nationalization.[28]

In effect, American taxpayers subsidized the Fifty-Fifty Agreement, not that Sulaiman or the king cared whose money it was. In Saudi Arabia, the distinction between public revenue and regime revenue meant little anyway.

By 1953, according to a State Department memo, "The net transfer [was] probably in the neighborhood of two hundred million dollars a year"—more than $1.8 billion in today's dollars.[29] Not all of that was attributable to Aramco; as Aramco's Johnston had noted, other U.S. companies operating abroad had adopted similar taxation arrangements. The State Department official who wrote that memo, Henry Byroade, noted that while these tactics were legal, the Treasury Department was unhappy over the lost revenue, but he recommended that no change be made lest the foreign governments force the oil companies to reincorporate in the producing states.

The amount of tax obligation the oil companies could offset was inflated by a peculiarity of the companies' pricing agreements with the producer countries: they paid tax to the host country on the basis of a negotiated price known as the "posted price." The actual price was often lower—Aramco sold oil to its parent companies at a discount, reducing the kingdom's royalty revenue—but that did not reduce their taxes.

Like the Denial Plan, this de facto subsidy was a strong signal of the U.S. government's commitment to guarantee the supply of oil from the region. It also augmented the international clout of the major oil companies. As Anthony Sampson put it in his landmark book about these companies, "Thus the role of the oil companies in foreign policy was firmly underlined: they were given private privileges to enable them to be the paymasters of the Arab states. It was from the State Department's point of view a neat, even brilliant solution for they could overtly support Israel and covertly support the Arabs, effectively bypassing Congress" by eliminating the need for appropriated aid funds to bolster the Arab governments. "But it was a solution which also served greatly to increase the power of the oil companies, to which the government had virtually delegated part of its foreign policy."[30]

Finance Minister Sulaiman's relentless determination to get the best possible deal for Saudi Arabia did not endear him to Aramco, even though the tax arrangements protected the parent companies' profits.

In July 1953, Raymond A. Hare, then finishing an assignment as U.S. ambassador to Saudi Arabia, sent an extensive report to Washington about an unpleasant conversation he had with Sulaiman. The subject was the government's constant haggling with Aramco.

Hare bluntly reminded Sulaiman that Saudi Arabia had nothing before the oil company came. "One would have to admit that prior to the coming of Aramco and exploitation of Saudi oil resources," he said,

> Saudi Arabia had been little more than a geographical expression. Other countries of the area such as Egypt, Syria, Lebanon, Iraq, etc., had experienced long periods of development in various fields of activity. They had communications, schools, hospitals, industries, roads, and the various other attributes of a normally modern state, but Saudi Arabia had had none of these. It had been an economic vacuum and, being so, had been a mere skeleton without flesh. All that had been changed by oil and Saudi Arabia was now in the process of building itself up to a position similar to that of its neighbors. Flesh was being put on the bone.

Sulaiman, who had been in the royal government since before the creation of the kingdom in 1932, knew all that, of course, but like most Saudis he did not like to be reminded of it.

The inescapable conclusion he came to from this history, Hare continued, was that

> dependent as it is on a single source of income, a strong Aramco means a strong Saudi Arabia; a weak Aramco means a weak Saudi Arabia. And in this latter connection, I had been both surprised and somewhat concerned to note what had appeared to be a recent tendency in certain circles in the Saudi Arabian Government to treat Aramco as something to be attacked rather than something to be supported. It was, of course, to be assumed that problems would arise from time to time where Aramco and the government might have different ideas but these were not serious if the two parties settled such differences in a spirit of cooperation. It was quite a different thing when a policy was followed of nagging at Aramco and seeming to want to weaken it. Such a policy could only end in hurting both the Government and Aramco and do no one any good.

The minister "agreed fully that a strong Aramco meant a strong Saudi Arabia," Hare reported. "The trouble seemed to be that Aramco was resorting to undue haggling when clear-cut action was required. A case in point was the payment for services rendered by the Government on Tapline," the Trans-Arabian Pipeline, which carried some Saudi oil overland to a port on the Mediterranean, "where Aramco had been bargaining with the Government for some time and the matter still remained unsettled. Also Aramco did not seem to appreciate the necessity of getting along with the Ministry of Finance which was the Ministry under whose jurisdiction it came. As a consequence many of its problems were being brought before other authorities and the situation was getting steadily more complicated and difficult."[31]

Aramco executives went so far as to discuss with State Department officials at the consulate in Dhahran the possibility of forcing the minister out of the government. William A. Eddy, who had been the senior U.S. diplomat in Saudi Arabia in the mid-1940s and was now working for Aramco, complained in a 1951 letter to his wife that Sulaiman, "who is again drinking heavily, told the King a pack of lies and the King told Ray Hare that Aramco has been insulting him, deceiving him, and that 'all those with whom he has been dealing recently in the company must leave Saudi Arabia.'"[32]

It is highly unlikely that Sulaiman ever "told the King a pack of lies"; Eddy's intemperate language reflected growing anger within Aramco at Sulaiman not only over money but also over his efforts to win better working and living conditions for the company's Arab workers. For the Saudis, Aramco's hard line and the deteriorating relationship with the United States created an environment conducive to an effort to chip away at Aramco's position.

Shortly before leaving Saudi Arabia at the end of his tour that summer, Hare tried again to calm these waters. By that time, Finance Minister Sulaiman, though still in the government, was falling from royal favor for reasons mostly unrelated to Aramco. He had been removed from the Saudi price negotiation team, so Hare met with two other senior members of the royal entourage, Yusuf Yassin and Khalid Bey Gorgoni. They were among the Levantine Arabs whom King Abdul Aziz had imported early in his reign to perform secretarial and administrative tasks of which few Saudi Arabs were then capable and who became part of the king's inner circle. The king and his family had their roots in the Nejd, a region of central Arabia where few people were educated or trained in management.

The ambassador said that he had "talked this matter over at length with Aramco officials and knew that they really wanted to reach a reasonable settlement, and I felt certain that, if the Saudi Government afforded an opportunity, the matter could be adjusted."

Perhaps so, Yassin responded, but Aramco still insisted on paying its royalties, as opposed to its taxes, on the basis of the discounted price rather than the posted price. Any court would find that tantamount to robbery, he said, and "this situation would no longer be tolerated." Yassin complained that an Iraqi government delegation had recently been in Riyadh and complained that the oil company there, Iraq Petroleum, was also seeking to pay on the basis of the discounted price, citing Aramco as an example.

"As a consequence, the Saudi and Iraqi Governments had decided that this practice must stop and they also intended approaching the Governments of Kuwait and Qatar to elicit their cooperation," he said. Furthermore, Yassin told Hare, "The attitude of the Aramco representatives had been abrupt and discourteous in their negotiations. They did not seem to understand where their best interests lay."

"I was not just trying to defend Aramco," Hare said he told Yassin, "although as Ambassador I was naturally very much interested in the welfare of such an important American enterprise; I was also thinking of the welfare of Saudi Arabia itself. As the time for my departure from Saudi Arabia neared, I hoped that I could feel that this matter would be settled in a broad and constructive spirit."

To that, Yassin responded that he was "certain that Saudi Arabia would reciprocate any goodwill shown by Aramco," which Hare "interpreted to mean that such good-will could be shown by full compliance with Saudi demands." Hare said he knew from experience that Yassin's comments were an accurate reflection of the views of the king, the crown prince, and "others in the Saudi hierarchy."[33] That did not bode well for the oil company's position.

CHAPTER TWO

Signs of Trouble

By the time Eisenhower became president in January 1953, Dhahran had become a thriving modern town where Aramco's American workers and their families lived much as they had at home. It was like an American suburb, a self-governing enclave complete with baseball games, theatrical performances, dances, television, and bicycles ridden by women, all prohibited everywhere else in Saudi Arabia. Saudi Arabia itself was being transformed, from a semi-primitive land of herders and fishermen into a modernizing state with roads, telephones, indoor plumbing, and electricity in the cities, all made possible by oil money, although it remained extremely rigid and conservative in social matters.

The oil enterprise was prospering and the Aramco people had reason to be proud of themselves. They had created something out of nothing and were lifting Saudi Arabia out of backwardness. They were educating and training Saudi workers. Aramco built schools and clinics. Most of the Americans saw themselves as doing well by doing good and believed they had established a relationship of trust and respect with their hosts.

In reality, relations between the Saudi government and the oil company, and between Saudi Arabia and the United States, were deteriorating.

The company's senior executives were well aware that despite their efforts, labor unrest was festering among the Saudi workers, who were unhappy about living conditions, food, and lack of promotions. While the American workers and their families lived in modern comfort, the Arab workers—without their families—were housed in palm-frond huts known as *barastis*. The Americans called these "coolie camps." An Aramco program to help the Saudi workers obtain modern housing was in its infancy. The company was hiring hundreds of Saudi workers each month, but the turnover rate approached 70 percent.

The Saudi government and some of the most vocal workers believed that Aramco was not living up to Article 23 of the concession contract, which specified that Aramco "shall employ Saudi nationals as far as practicable," nor was it promoting Saudis above manual labor positions, even after they had been trained for higher-level work. Article 23 did not specifically require Aramco to provide job training, but the government insisted that was the only way to develop a qualified Saudi workforce.[1]

During that same period, developments in the international oil and currency markets showed that Aramco was paying a bargain price for its oil and that the Saudi government had strong arguments for raising it.

In March 1945, as oil production was set to surge with the coming end of the war, a State Department analysis had showed that the Saudi government was receiving a fixed amount of royalty per barrel, and thus did not benefit from increases in the market price. The posted price-discount price disparity was already in effect. The government's oil revenue had declined sharply during the war. Before the war, Aramco had paid royalties amounting to 32 percent of its gross revenue, but by 1944 that figure had declined to 22 percent, and output had been curtailed by wartime shipping constraints. Government revenue "could be considerably increased by an adjustment of the rate basis of royalty payments," the State Department said.[2]

As a practical matter, that meant that the U.S. government would not object, and might actually approve, if the Saudis woke up and began to press Aramco to pay more, which they soon did.

In the first week of January 1954, King Saud, who had succeeded his father on the throne two months earlier, paid his first visit to Dhahran. Accompanied by an enormous entourage, he arrived on the new railroad that Aramco had built to link the oil fields to Riyadh, and stayed for several days of feasts and ceremonies. All appeared to be harmonious.[3]

Aramco's leadership knew, however, that the government, in the persons of Abdullah Sulaiman and Yusuf Yassin, was increasingly unhappy with the company because of the second- or even third-class status of its Arab workers. As early as 1948, at a company retreat in Pennsylvania, the company's Government Relations Department circulated papers making clear that trouble was brewing. "The company today is faced with a problem of great magnitude and of far reaching importance: It is not in good standing with the Saudi Arab government," one of those papers said. Sulaiman and Yassin, on a recent visit to Dhahran, had "pressed the point that living conditions of the Arab employees must approach [those] provided for the Americans." Another urgent issue was creating family housing areas for Arab workers, most of whom lived bachelor lives in their *barastis*.[4]

Most of the rank-and-file U.S. workers, living with their families in the homey comfort of their suburban-style community, were unaware of these ominous warnings. Secure in their desert enclave, most of them believed that they were bringing nothing but benefits to the local people, for whom Aramco provided education, basic health care, transportation, and more money than their parents could have imagined.

This, the Americans thought, insulated Aramco against the accusation leveled at big international corporations in other parts of the developing world that they were exploiting the indigenous population. "Set against the popular picture of the big bad oil industry," wrote one American who arrived in the year of the Pennsylvania conclave, "our little band of altruistic executives clinging to their shining doctrine amid the Stygian night of Middle Eastern politics suggested a troop of boy scouts set adrift in a brothel."[5]

These oblivious Americans failed to recognize that the Middle East's concession agreements were anachronistic and would be obvious targets of the post-independence era of Arab nationalist sentiment that was developing around them—sentiment that had been spurred by the creation of Israel with Great Power support in 1948.

The first serious challenge to the dominance of big foreign oil companies in the Gulf region developed in 1951, not among the Arabs but across the Gulf in Iran. With a young and untested Shah Mohammed Reza Pahlavi occupying the Peacock Throne, the government of Prime Minister Mohammed Mossadegh seized the initiative. Parliament voted to nationalize Iran's oil industry, which was controlled by the British company Anglo-American Petroleum, later renamed British Petroleum (BP).

Mossadegh was a quirky leader whose French was better than his Farsi and who sometimes received official visitors in his pajamas, but he was also a fierce nationalist and a charismatic foe of British domination. His political alliance with the Tudeh, Iran's communist party, set off alarms in Washington and London.

The ensuing chaos lasted two years. Nationalization backfired because British interests organized a successful worldwide boycott of Iranian oil, cutting off Iran's major source of revenue and emptying the imperial treasury. The Shah dismissed Mossadegh, then reinstated him and fled the country. As the Soviet presence in Tehran increased, the United States and Britain agreed that Mossadegh had to go. In 1953, the Central Intelligence Agency orchestrated a coup in which Mossadegh was ousted, and restored the Shah to the throne. The United States, eager to see Iranian oil exports resume and to stabilize the country to thwart the communists, assembled a group of seven international companies to resume Iranian production, in nominal partnership with the Iranian National Oil Company. Iran owned the oil, but its industry was once again in the hands of foreign operators.[6]

In Washington and in European capitals, fear that the nationalistic fever displayed in Iran would spread to the other major producer states in the region, especially Iraq and Saudi Arabia, now entered into policy calculations, with good reason. Shortly after the events in Iran, it was Aramco's turn to confront a disruption of its comfortable position.

A Legendary Arab Dies

The door opened in late 1953 with the death of King Abdul Aziz, the leader who had created Saudi Arabia out of a patchwork of nomadic tribes and oasis villages and had welcomed the U.S. company into his otherwise xenophobic realm.

Abdul Aziz, often referred to by Americans as Ibn Saud, was renowned for his piety, his courage in battle, his shrewd assessments of character, and his dedication to Arab independence. After his warriors seized the holy cities of Mecca and Medina and a majority of the world's Muslims grudgingly accepted his authority over those sacred sites, his stature among the Arabs was unrivaled. But he made one unwise choice that would haunt his country for a decade after his death: he designated his eldest son, Prince Saud, as his successor.

Saud was duly enthroned on November 9, 1953, in accordance with his father's wishes. Unfortunately for his country, he was not the man his father was; he lacked his father's wisdom, political judgment, self-control, and understanding of people. The old king would have done better to choose one of his many younger sons, Prince Faisal, to follow him as ruler; Faisal became crown prince instead. Saud's weaknesses, profligacy, and blunders would cost the country dearly over the next 10 years as the kingdom largely squandered what should have been a decade of growth and progress. Talent and energy that could have been spent on development were consumed instead by a power struggle between Saud and the ascetic, disciplined Faisal.

Saud was well-intentioned and ambitious, but the other adjectives usually applied to him were much less flattering: incompetent, wasteful, impetuous, and priapic. "His mental equipment wasn't very good," the U.S. diplomat Parker T. Hart said of Saud. "He just never understood anything complex. He oversimplified and made the wrong judgments. Complicated matters annoyed him because he couldn't understand them."[7] Clinton Pelham, British ambassador to the kingdom at the time, described Saud as "more figurehead than ruler." Pelham reported that Saud "has many of the regal attributes—dignity, generosity, piety," but "a true understanding of affairs, he almost certainly lacks."[8]

On the Web site of the King Saud Foundation in Jeddah, established to honor him, this is his entire biography: "The 2nd King of Saudi Arabia, after the unifier King Abdulaziz, King Saud was born in Kuwait in 1902, fought from the age of 13, he was then Crown Prince for 20 years, and then King for 11. And he died in Athens in 1969."[9]

Saud was clumsy, and nearsighted to the point that even with glasses he could not read ordinary print. Workers at Aramco derided him as "banana nose," but it was not only his physical attributes that Americans found unsatisfactory. He was generous to a fault. Whereas his father had been circumspect in handing out money to supplicants, Saud was frivolous, throwing cash around as if it were sand. According to Parker Hart, when Saud traveled to other countries he took with him a groom from the royal stables who "gave everybody all the money the King wanted given. On royal air trips he handed out bunches of hundred dollar bills to members of the household as they got off the plane. As princes, merchants, relatives, contractors, and servants helped themselves to cash, Saud built ever more lavish palaces for himself, all the while traveling around the country taking young brides." The king, Hart said, ordered the construction of lavish palaces that neither he nor anyone else actually occupied.[10]

The only endeavor in which Saud performed better than his father was having children, of whom he fathered more than 100.

The intelligence agencies in Washington, in a collective report, told the White House and State Department that King Saud "lacks the prestige, skill, and strength of character of his father. . . . His administration is weakened by inefficiency and corruption, an extreme dependence on oil royalties for its revenue, and failure to recognize growing resentment of the profligacy of the royal family and government officials."[11]

During Saud's reign, according to the knowledgeable British writers David Holden and Richard Johns, "with truth at a premium and dishonesty in the chair, those with the glibbest tongues climbed fastest up the ladder of success. None climbed faster than a certain Id bin Salem, a native Nejdi of no previous royal connection who started life as a mechanic in the palace garage. He became the royal pimp and supplier of alcohol. . . . To foreign diplomats, Aramco men and, not the least, senior princes like Feisal and Muhammad, he seemed to be virtually the unofficial premier, supervising Saud's appointments, monitoring his conversations, and authorizing his signature."[12]

This Id bin Salem was the "groom from the royal stables" referred to by Parker Hart. The only apparent source of his influence was that he was born in the Nejd, the region of northern Arabia that was the ancestral home of the al-Saud, rather than in Syria or Palestine like the administrators and advisers whom King Abdul Aziz had imported.

"The king was stupid. He was controlled by two of his wives and by Id bin Salem, controller of the privy purse," said Mike Ameen, who was Aramco's representative in Riyadh at the time. "I had to deal with that little bastard." Ameen died at age 94 in 2018, but when I spoke to him in 2016 he was blunt and vulgar as ever. He said Crown Prince Faisal "knew how they were controlling the king with booze and pussy."[13] Ameen could be crude, but he was so great a figure in Aramco's history that when he reached his 80th birthday, the U.S. Department of Energy sponsored a party for him in Texas.

Such was Saud's incompetence that his brothers eventually would oblige him to share power with Faisal, who became prime minister in 1958. Saud was forced to abdicate and go into exile in 1964.

"Saud ibn Abdul Aziz reigned for barely a decade," the acerbic historian J. B. Kelly wrote, "during which time he managed to dissipate the entire fund of political capital which his father had bequeathed to him, as well as to bankrupt the Saudi treasury."[14]

Nasser, the New Voice of the Arabs

Saud took the throne at a time of deteriorating relations between the United States and Saudi Arabia, and between Aramco and the Saudi government. Saud also began quickly to feel rhetorical pressure from the new nationalist leader of Egypt, Gamal Abdel Nasser, who had overthrown the monarchy in 1952. Nasser soon began criticizing the royal regimes of the oil states, accusing them of living in luxury while other Arabs were poor. (His targets included Iraq, which at the time was still a monarchy.) At first Saud's defense against that criticism was to profess support for Nasser's nationalist ideas. In March 1954, he went to Cairo, where he gave an interview in which he said that "our foreign policy is based on the interest of the Arabs in general. We are in agreement with Egypt on her foreign policy." Asked by Egypt's official news agency about his country's dependence on the United States, he replied, "We strive to maintain good relations with all governments reciprocating such a desire. We welcome cooperation with any state, provided that it does not encroach on our independence and sovereign rights or cause any damage to an Arab country. On this basis we deal with America or any other state when we accept or reject cooperation."[15]

Saud may have been an inarticulate bumbler, but he instinctively understood the temper of the times in his part of the world. A form of aggressive nationalism was brewing even inside the Saudi oil industry, in the person of a rising young radical named Abdullah Tariki, who would become the kingdom's chief oil policy official and a founder of the Organization of Petroleum Exporting Countries (OPEC). As the U.S. intelligence community said in a collective "National Intelligence Estimate" in January 1953, "Throughout the area, many proponents of change have a similar negative and emotional attitude. There is a general disposition to eliminate the powers that be, with little regard or thought for what comes after." A principal cause of that attitude, the intelligence report said, was "a desire to eliminate foreign influence. The Middle Eastern governments and people are basically suspicious of Western motives and tend to become increasingly nationalist and neutralist."[16]

A British diplomat reported to London that 1954, under King Saud, was the first year of the kingdom's "deplorable maturity . . . I am struck most by the appalling growth of Saudi vanity and arrogance. By bribing unscrupulously and by playing on Washington's fear of communism in this country, the Saudi rulers have in the past year achieved a position in the Middle East which they conceitedly regard as that of a major power."[17]

Aramco's Workers Strike

The royal government, in the person of finance minister Abdullah Sulaiman, now joined by the aggressive Tariki, had been trying for years to extract higher payments from Aramco.

The structural breakthrough in Venezuela that gave the host country there a half share in the proceeds from its fields had prompted Saudi Arabia to seek and achieve a similar agreement. But even after the Fifty-Fifty Agreement went into effect, retroactive to the beginning of 1950, the amount of the government's half share depended on the price Aramco charged, and on that there was no agreement. The oil companies in Venezuela were paying the tax on the posted, or official, price. Aramco paid it on the discounted price of the oil it sold to its parent companies, which was most of its output. As contentious negotiations dragged on, unrest broke out among Aramco's Arab workers, who actually went on strike briefly in 1945, 1947, and 1953.

Ali al-Naimi, Saudi Arabia's oil minister from 1995 to 2016, was in the early years of his career at Aramco during the 1945 strike. The strike "had its roots," he recalled in a memoir, "in nearly a decade of mounting labour tension between the oil company and its Saudi employees. In July 1945, Saudis walked off the job at Ras Tanura refinery for several days. Aramco increased wages modestly, particularly for low-level workers, and operations resumed. Just a month later, however, as many as 9,000 workers in Ras Tanura as well as in Dhahran, the heart of our operations at the time, downed tools." There was another brief walkout in 1947.

Naimi said that many of the "well-meaning Americans" could not understand what the workers were complaining about—they thought they had created a benevolent environment. "Had we not been living in our own goat-hair tents just a few years earlier?" In truth, he said, "Their major complaints involved working conditions, pay, living arrangements, and the fact that foreign workers, notably Italians who arrived during the war, were treated better than Saudis."[18]

The 1953 strike, according to the Central Intelligence Agency, "gave evidence of a considerable increase in group-consciousness among the [Arab] employees of Aramco and the USAF [U.S. Air Force] Dhahran airbase in Eastern Saudi Arabia, where tribal values are being more quickly destroyed than in other parts of the country. Another strike, perhaps accompanied by violence, is a strong possibility."[19]

Under the circumstances, Saud and his advisers thought they had had ample reason to want to break Aramco's iron grip on all aspects of their oil industry. The royal government remained chronically short of money, no matter how much oil Aramco produced, because the king allowed numerous princes to help themselves to as much cash as they wanted.[20]

What better way for the king to stand up to Washington, break away at least in part from Aramco, ingratiate himself with Nasser, and get more money, than to somehow undermine Aramco's complete control of all aspects of Saudi Arabia's oil industry and bring in some form of competition?

The problems in the kingdom's relations with Washington had emerged well before Saud succeeded his father. King Abdul Aziz and his government had been unhappy that President Truman recognized Israel when it proclaimed its independence in 1948. Government ministers under Abdul Aziz and Saud were dissatisfied with the operations of Truman's Point Four technical assistance program (which Saud would terminate in the summer of 1954). And they felt aggrieved that the United States had done little to support their claims to the Buraimi Oasis. That was a territory at the point where Saudi Arabia, Oman, and the Emirate of Abu Dhabi converge that had long been subject to conflicting assertions of sovereignty. Aramco supported the Saudi claim because its geologists believed there was oil under Buraimi, which, if Buraimi were Saudi, their company would have the right to extract. And if they did that, royalties from Buraimi production would accrue to the Saudi government. Aramco went so far as to provide the transportation when a small Saudi military force entered the territory in 1952. The British, however, claimed control of Buraimi as part of their protectorate in Abu Dhabi.[21]

Winston Churchill, who had returned as British prime minister in 1951, "well understood the area's strategic value for Britain's national security," as the security analyst Rachel Bronson wrote. "He adopted an unyielding stance on Buraimi both to secure British access to oil and to stanch the more general deterioration of world-wide colonial holdings." King Abdul Aziz, on the other hand, "was still testing the outer boundaries of his national conquest and argued that the remote area was, and had always been, loyal to Riyadh."[22]

Under Eisenhower, as under Truman, the United States was sympathetic to Saudi Arabia's Buraimi claims but—to the great frustration of Prince Faisal, an aggressive advocate of the Saudi position—Washington declined to get involved, desiring not to alienate either of two friendly countries. Following a meeting in Washington in March 1953 between Faisal and Under Secretary of State Walter Bedell Smith, Secretary Dulles told Ambassador Raymond Hare that "after careful consideration United States Government had concluded it should not change its previous stand in favor [of] arbitration as best machinery for settling Buraimi and other boundary problems. [The] United States Government had no desire [to] mediate or arbitrate in such disputes."[23]

As Joseph Kéchichian put it in his biography of Faisal, "America was not about to set aside its peerless 'special relationship' with the United Kingdom for a land dispute that most State Department officials found incongruous and absurd."[24] The United States stood by when British troops eventually expelled all Saudi forces from the oasis, adding to the growing list of Saudi grievances against Washington.

A few months before his death, King Abdul Aziz wrote a long, sorrowful letter to Eisenhower about the British military action, saying he was disappointed that the United States failed to intervene forcefully when "British officials in the Persian Gulf area suddenly made a cruel and reprehensible attack upon our subjects by bombing peaceful women and children, continuing the attack against them for several days until they killed a number of them and left others homeless, and occupying their country." He accused Britain of abrogating a "standstill agreement" that had been reached through U.S. diplomatic efforts. He appealed to Eisenhower, a "warrior and honest man," for a new effort.[25]

Eisenhower responded that he and Secretary Dulles had analyzed all aspects of the competing claims to Buraimi and concluded that they should be settled through international arbitration. "I feel confident," the president wrote, "that upon careful review of the facts, Your Majesty will conclude that the United State has not failed in its duties as a true friend of Saudi Arabia."[26]

The Eisenhower administration's efforts to enlist a group of oil companies to restore production in Iran became another irritant to Riyadh. On April 3, 1954, the New York newspaper *Journal of Commerce*, which specialized in news about trade, energy, and shipping, published an article explaining how resumption of exports from Iran would inevitably cut into sales by Saudi Arabia. The piece was written by "W. N. Jablonski." This was the legendary Wanda Jablonski, the best-informed oil reporter anywhere, who long used her initials to disguise the fact that she was female.

The article reported that even without Iranian production, Saudi Arabia's share of oil exports from the Gulf region, while increasing in absolute numbers, was declining as a percentage of the regional total because of an aggressive sales push by Kuwait. It said that King Saud, "already irked" by those numbers, was "likely to take a dim view of the fact that the four companies that own Aramco are also members of the proposed consortium." If that consortium succeeded in Iran, it would further erode Saudi market share.

Inside the Elite

Dependent though they were on the United States, the Saudis, like other non-Americans, generally failed to understand the close, durable ties that bound the U.S. foreign policy establishment and the country's elite leaders in business and the law; these relationships were reflected in U.S. government policy, regardless of which party was in power. Often, the business and legal elite and the senior foreign policy officials were the same people, moving seamlessly in and out of government with changes in administrations. The effort to form a consortium to take over the Iranian industry reflected that closeness. So did the Buraimi dispute, which was not just a minor conflict over a few oases and sand dunes in a remote part of the world. Wilbur Crane Eveland, in his classic book about dubious U.S. intrigues and maneuvers in the region, recounted an incident that showed how U.S. politics, big oil, and major international banks were entangled in the Buraimi conflict.

On his way to Damascus, Syria, not long after King Saud took the throne in Riyadh, Eveland, then a CIA agent, traveled on the private plane of John J. McCloy, the chairman of Chase National Bank. McCloy was a classic example of the influential lawyer who moved all his life between the corporate and political worlds. He had been the U.S. military governor in West Germany after World War II and at one time was president of the World Bank. He was an adviser to every president from Franklin D. Roosevelt to Ronald Reagan. His legal clients included 23 oil companies. He was chairman of so many boards and foundations that one political writer dubbed him "chairman of the Establishment."[27]

Eveland's seat on his plane had been arranged by Sam Kopper, a former State Department Arabist now working for Aramco; at the same time Kopper was helping Adlai Stevenson, the Democrat whom Eisenhower had beaten in the 1952 election, with position papers on the Middle East, in preparation for another campaign against Eisenhower in 1956.

McCloy told Eveland that the profligate Saud was constantly asking Chase Bank for loans against future oil royalties, and that the British objected because they were disturbed by Saud's political flirtation with Nasser. Now, McCloy said, the British, through their control of the Arab monarchies along the Persian Gulf, "were creating border incidents on Saudi Arabia's eastern flanks, which showed promise of leading to major tribal wars. McCloy therefore was going to see King Saud to explain the extent to which his foolish policies were making it difficult for Chase to continue the very loans upon which Saud was almost dependent." He was referring to Saud's "foolish" fiscal policies, not to his policy on Buraimi, which the Aramco partner companies supported.

Eveland said he "now understood why Aramco's management had sent Sam Kopper to follow McCloy's activities closely."[28] It was that kind of cross-pollination within the U.S. establishment that would resurface again and again during the events of the next two years.

"Minister of Everything"

Resolving all the issues confronting Saudi Arabia in 1953 and 1954 would have been difficult even for a competent leader supported by reliable assistants, but Saud was not competent and he was beset by palace intrigue. His most pressing domestic concern, other than the chronic shortage of cash, was deciding what to do with the finance minister, Abdullah Sulaiman.

Sulaiman had entered into royal service as a young man even before the kingdom was officially created, and had been King Abdul Aziz's most trusted adviser in the three decades before his death. His official title was minister of finance, but he was popularly known as "minister of everything" because at one time or another he was involved in almost every aspect of domestic governance, from training the armed forces to managing the pilgrimage to Mecca to stabilizing the currency. It was he who signed the original concession contract with Standard Oil Company of California in 1933 and negotiated the Fifty-Fifty Agreement, but by early 1954 he was in disfavor with the new king and especially with Crown Prince Faisal.

Physically, Sulaiman was slowing down: time and the incalculable amounts of energy he had expended in serving King Abdul Aziz and steering the exchequer through the leanest years had taken their toll. He was plagued by chronic digestive ailments. Many accounts of the time say he also consumed too much alcohol, as indicated by Bill Eddy's vituperative 1951 letter.[29] He would have continued to give whatever he had left if Saud had confidence in him, but it was soon apparent that he did not.

One reason for that was that the minister, who had been overworked for decades, was simply no longer able to shoulder as much responsibility as in the past. Another was that times were changing. Saudi Arabia in the early 1950s was no longer a country that could be run in the old tribal fashion, with one man making all decisions and a few loyal followers carrying them out. Saudi Arabia did not yet have paper currency, but payments in coin and handouts of cash were relics of simpler times; the country was entering a new era of bank transfers and contracts with foreigners.

British ambassador Clinton Pelham reported to London that Sulaiman "came to symbolize in the eyes of the younger men who now fill the ministerial posts all that was unsatisfactory in the old regime."[30]

On top of that, King Saud and Crown Prince Faisal carried a grudge about the minster's role in a key episode of the postwar period: one of Abdullah Sulaiman's most ambitious and most complicated efforts to increase the kingdom's revenue and manage its development had ended in acrimonious failure. This failure was not his fault, or at least not entirely, but there was no escaping his responsibility for having created the situations in which the failure occurred. This episode came to be known as the GOVENCO Affair, and it irrevocably undermined the senior princes' faith in him.

Big Deals, Unhappy Outcomes

For more than three decades after World War II, the government of Saudi Arabia was besieged by European and U.S. entrepreneurs who wanted a piece of the economic action. This parade of outsiders seeking to cash in on the kingdom's new wealth began while Abdul Aziz was still on the throne.

In Sulaiman's final years of service to his royal patron, it was part of his duties to evaluate these various business proposals and decide whether the kingdom would benefit from accepting them. That had been fairly easy to do in the years when projects involved a single, uncomplicated task, such as building a road or importing automobiles. But after the war, as the economy of Saudi Arabia grew and foreign interest expanded, the development proposals—many of them unsolicited—became more ambitious, more complicated, more difficult to evaluate, and much harder to supervise as projects went ahead. These deals were risky in themselves, and loaded with potential danger to the minister's reputation and his standing with Abdul Aziz, Saud, and Faisal. Because of the Saudis' relative lack of sophistication and experience with the outside world, it was sometimes difficult for Sulaiman and his colleagues to assess the reputations, intentions, and trustworthiness of the Americans and Europeans who approached the kingdom with big promises. They understood Aramco and its purpose, but they did not understand these newcomers.

One of the most ambitious proposals came from the American Eastern Co., a shipping and trading company founded in New York in the 1920s "for the purpose of introducing American products and know-how into the Near and Middle East," as it described itself. American Eastern had operational bases in Egypt and Lebanon; as World War II ended, its president, Marcel Wagner, spotted a new opportunity in Saudi Arabia. Wagner wanted to get in on the ground floor of the potential bonanza in the kingdom, a country that was soon to have substantial revenue but had little economic infrastructure outside of Aramco. To expedite entry into Saudi Arabia, Wagner enlisted as a partner a mining engineer from Vermont named Karl Twitchell. To the Saudis, Twitchell was perhaps the most esteemed American because it was he who had toured the country at Abdul Aziz's request years earlier to search for water and minerals, traveling more than 1,500 miles through the roadless hinterlands.[31] Asking nothing for himself, Twitchell earned the king's trust and persuaded him to open the country to oil development.

Wagner and Twitchell proposed to create a Saudi Arabian American Development Co., or SAADCO, to be incorporated in the kingdom under Saudi law, for "construction and operation of public works, including power, light, water, drainage, sewage and transportation systems, roads, ports and port installations," agricultural and industrial projects in the private sector, and the purchase and distribution of machinery and equipment. In effect, SAADCO would be the primary contractor for almost all of the country's development projects and would be responsible for managing them after construction or installation. The company's proposal was in the form of a draft charter, written by Twitchell, to be signed by the king if he approved.

According to the terms Twitchell negotiated with Sulaiman in preparing this proposal, the company's capital would be in riyals, the Saudi currency.

Initially, SAADCO would own 55 percent of the shares and the government 45 percent; after 20 years, 20 percent of the company shares would be offered for sale to Saudi citizens. For its first 10 years, the company would have four permanent directors: Wagner, Twitchell, Abdullah Sulaiman, and Ibrahim Shakir, a businessman closely tied to the finance minister. SAADCO would act as the parent company of a number of smaller companies aimed at specific segments of Saudi development, including a shipping company.

As part of this grand scheme, Twitchell wrote to Sulaiman, "We feel confident that a national merchant marine can be developed which would give Saudi Arabia added prestige, would assure independence in shipping, and would further the existing cordial relationship between our two countries." The Saudi government would hold an initial 15 percent of the stock and would receive more if the company proved successful. Vessels owned by the company would carry freight between Saudi Arabia and other ports in the region. "Subjects of the government would be trained and used in the operations of the company to the extent that they are capable of filling available positions," Twitchell wrote. The proposed company would have an exclusive franchise for 60 years, would be fully exempt from taxes, and would pay reduced customs fees.[32]

This was a good example of the kind of unsolicited proposal that the Saudis could not fully understand: the concept of stock ownership was unknown to all but a few of them. In the end, nothing came of the SAADCO proposal or the shipping plan at the time, largely because of fierce opposition from the British, whose companies would be shut out of potentially lucrative projects, and from prominent Saudis who would not benefit; but the idea of a national shipping fleet, controlled by the Saudis, was in play, and the State Department was not averse to it.

In a "Dear Marcel" letter to Wagner on February 21, 1945, State's Gordon Merriam relayed comments from William A. Eddy, then U.S. minister in Jeddah, on the American Eastern proposal regarding the "steamship service."

"It is my own conviction," Eddy said, "that the proposal for a steamship line, under the Saudi Arabian flag, promises great advantage to Saudi Arabia and to American trade," though it would not in any way be a U.S. government enterprise. A copy of this note was sent to Finance Minister Sulaiman.[33]

Even though SAADCO never went into business, the company's argument about the need for a single entity to organize and carry out multiple development projects across the vast country was valid because the Saudis lacked such capabilities, so Sulaiman continued his quest to find such a partner. His failure to do so, and the embarrassment that resulted from his final attempt, would severely damage his standing with the royal court.

In October 1951, he signed a two-year contract with Michael Baker Jr. International Inc., effective at the beginning of 1952, to carry out a wide range of development projects. Baker, known as MBJI, was an ambitious

Pennsylvania engineering and consulting company founded in 1946. It was growing rapidly in 1951 but had little if any experience at managing complicated projects outside the United States, let alone serving as the de facto public works department for an entire undeveloped country.

According to the company history formerly posted on its Web site, "In 1951, Michael Baker was made the consulting engineer and construction administrator for Saudi Arabia. This post entailed the design of harbor facilities, customs buildings, major highway systems, airports, water supply and electrical systems, a private hospital for the royal family, a $30-million air base, and additions to the royal palaces. Baker also acted as purchasing agent for the King, and his firm was responsible for maintenance work in the King's harem, a signal honor."[34]

To ensure that it would get paid, MBJI insisted on the establishment of a U.S. bank account into which the Saudi government would deposit $500,000 for Baker's use and replenish it monthly. The government, however, could spare only $100,000 for the account, and Baker faced the additional problem of finding suitable personnel for its operations.

A team from the U.S. Export-Import Bank, sent to assess the situation, issued a very negative report after its visit to Saudi Arabia in June 1952. In the first place, the team was critical of bank-funded activities in the kingdom, concluding that "a very good case could be made that no credits at all should be extended to the Saudi Arabian Government" because the government exerted little control over spending.

The report noted that a previous contractor had left three projects unfinished: expansion of Jeddah harbor beyond the pier, Jeddah airport, and a Jeddah-Mecca road. But it was also critical of MBJI, noting that the company's top two operations officials were not engineers and had no background in construction. Changes would need to be made before the company would be allowed to work on Ex-Im Bank projects, not just in Saudi Arabia but anywhere: "In other words, Baker would have to make good or get out," as one chronicler of this episode put it. MBJI promised to make the necessary administrative changes, but in the end, the job was just too big for the company.

Overall, the work of Baker's firm proved even less satisfactory to the government than that of its predecessor had been—another blot on Sulaiman's copy book—so Sulaiman ended Baker's contract and turned to a new European enterprise. Two German firms formed a partnership called the Government Engineering Company of Saudi Arabia, or GOVENCO. Abdullah Sulaiman gave GOVENCO a contract to complete all the projects left unfinished by Michael Baker and to undertake the planning, design, and construction of additional projects.[35]

But the Baker story did not end there. Michael Baker personally appealed the cancellation of his company's contract to Saud, then still crown prince.

He apparently won Saud's support because shortly afterward Baker's company told the U.S. embassy that the new contract with GOVENCO had been cancelled and Baker would continue its work. Sulaiman then told MBJI once again to hand over its installations to GOVENCO. It is inconceivable that the minister would have done that if he had not consulted King Abdul Aziz and if the king had not decided to overrule Prince Saud.

MBJI then appealed to Prince Saud again, an end run that apparently angered Sulaiman, who knew that the king would back him up: he informed Baker that his company's work in the kingdom was now terminated because of delays in completing projects and unduly high administrative costs. This squabble was another cause of Prince Saud's disenchantment with Sulaiman and increased the pressure on Sulaiman to deliver some big success.

To limit demands on GOVENCO by various princes and business leaders, Sulaiman had set up an arrangement by which only he or a deputy designated by him could deal directly with the company. That may have seemed like a good idea but it backfired on him when the deal went bad. Because of his tight control, he personally took a good bit of the blame as GOVENCO's fortunes in the kingdom declined even more rapidly than those of its predecessors. When the company fired its purchasing manager, the man retaliated by going to Prince Faisal with allegations of bribery and corruption. The prince took control of the contract and ordered an investigation, directed by another brother, Prince Sultan. On August 4, less than a year after the contract had been signed, Abdullah Sulaiman informed GOVENCO that its operations would have to cease. On August 7, a royal decree annulled the contract.

Compounding the embarrassment at the royal court, the U.S. embassy reported in late August that GOVENCO had a silent partner, a Saudi, who had been convicted of corruption in a religious court. Shortly thereafter, the company's resident managers were also convicted. Sulaiman's strategy of assuming full control of the contract thus backfired on him.

After that fiasco and the death of his great friend and protector King Abdul Aziz, Sulaiman's standing with the royal family was precarious. He had served King Abdul Aziz for his entire adult life, but that mattered little to Saud and Faisal. The crown prince especially was weary of Sulaiman and of his failed grand schemes. Sulaiman needed a big success to reclaim the family's confidence and secure his position. Suddenly, from a completely unexpected source, he got an opportunity to take on the most lucrative target of all, the American-controlled oil business.

CHAPTER THREE

Intrigue on the Riviera

The power play that Abdullah Sulaiman and the Saudis pulled on Aramco in January 1954 was not their idea. It originated in September 1952 when a man named Spyridon Catapodis happened to go to Baghdad, Iraq, on a business trip. Before he went there, Saudi Arabia and the transportation of oil were not on his agenda.

Catapodis was a minor-league shipowner and, by all accounts, a pushy, loud-mouthed social climber. The British journalists David Holden and Richard Johns described him as "a Greek living in the south of France who, amongst other dubious activities, pimped for prominent Saudis."[1] A team of British journalists wrote that he was "the quintessence of the Mediterranean demimonde. . . . He owned a villa in Cannes and, more important, a yacht—a necessary possession for anyone with pretensions to the good life on the coast. His circle of acquaintances was wide; barmen and croupiers in Monte Carlo, Nice and Cannes remember him with pleasure and affection. His bulky, flannel-clad form had graced the *Salles privées* for many years. His histrionic gestures belonged between the chandeliers and thick pile carpeting of five-star hotels. Raconteur, gambler, and inveterate middleman, he lived by an abundant supply of wits."[2]

A longtime resident of Cannes, Catapodis had managed to run his business during World War II without interference from France's Vichy government. He acquired a small fleet of nondescript cargo ships, which he made available to ingratiate himself with the Americans when they landed in southern France in 1944. As his prosperity and visibility grew, it was only natural that he came to know, at least casually, another ship-owning Greek denizen of Riviera watering holes: Aristotle Onassis, who had a residence in Antibes.

Catapodis went to Iraq, a major oil-producing state, in hopes of selling to the government some war-surplus Liberty ships he had acquired from the United States. While there, by his account, he "learned that the Iraqi government was likewise interested in forming a tanker fleet of about 150 to 200 thousand tons for operation under the Iraqi flag to transport the 12½ percent of oil produced in Iraq which the government has the right to dispose of under its agreement with the oil concessionaire companies."[3]

As an operator of dry-cargo ships, Catapodis had no tankers, but he knew someone who did—Onassis, who "indicated his willingness to provide the necessary tanker tonnage," Catapodis said.

To meet Onassis formally and discuss business, Catapodis went through Costas Gratsos, another Greek wheeler-dealer. Gratsos was close to Onassis; one British biography described Gratsos as "Onassis's house intellectual, the only man in the Onassis entourage who could not only effectively execute the boss's orders but also come up with new ideas."[4]

Onassis told Peter Evans, a British writer whom he commissioned to write his biography, that he had first met Catapodis in London in the 1930s. According to Evans, Catapodis was "essentially a middleman and a fixer. He was also a compulsive gambler." Onassis's wife, Christina, disliked Catapodis, partly because of his "unsavory sexual reputation," but in her dislike "she underestimated his usefulness to Onassis."[5]

Nothing came of the Iraq discussions because of a change of government in Baghdad, but the idea of creating a tanker fleet for one of the oil-producing states was now in play.

When Onassis and Catapodis met in August 1953 to discuss whether the Iraq deal could be revived, the focus of their conversation quickly turned to Saudi Arabia, where it would fit nicely with the proposal that Karl Twitchell had floated a few years earlier to create a "national merchant marine." Onassis ventured the opinion that "a great deal of money could be made if I could obtain an agreement from the Saudi Arabian government, whereby a fleet of tankers would be placed at their disposal under the Saudi Arabia flag," according to Catapodis. The two devised a plan by which Onassis would create a fleet of tankers that would fly the Saudi flag, and train Saudis to operate them, in exchange for the right to use those ships to transport most, if not quite all, Saudi oil exports.

That conversation set off six months of scheming, deceit, and greedy demands. The deal that resulted would disrupt Aramco, threaten long-established global shipping practices, divide the royal court of Saudi Arabia, and anger the government of the United States, but at that moment nobody in those organizations and businesses had any inkling of what was about to happen.

Unfortunately for Catapodis, he had chosen the wrong partner. If he lived in an environment that valued probity, rectitude, and discretion, he would not have joined up with Onassis, whose flamboyant style, flexible loyalties, and questionable business tactics ensured that he would encounter hostility from the United States and from rival shippers.

Catapodis also apparently failed to recognize the extent to which Onassis would face relentless opposition from his greatest personal and business rival, Stavros Niarchos. Neither he nor Onassis understood the extent to which the interests of national security and big business converged in Washington.

A Nautical Fraternity

Onassis was usually described in breathless media reports as a "Greek Shipping tycoon," but he was both more and less than that: more, because his business interests and connections extended well beyond the shipping business, and less, because while he was Greek and a tycoon, he also remained something of an outsider to the established ship-owning class.

When he first arrived in Argentina, he was penniless and stateless. Later, according to a definitive study by Gelina Harlaftis, "Despite his marriage into an old shipping family, traditional top Greek shipowning families still regarded Onassis as a newcomer and excluded him. Prior to 1946, he was an ambitious small-to-medium shipowner, and it was clear that he was not part of the Greek shipowning inner circle."[6]

The "old shipping family" into which he married was that of Stavros Livanos, described by Assistant U.S. Attorney General Warren E. Burger in 1953 as "a British subject of Greek origin who is known in the shipping trade as 'Stormy Weather' Livanos. He had two daughters, one of which is married to Stavros Niarchos and the other to Aristotle Socrates Onassis."[7] That was true as far as it went, but it hardly did justice to the intensity of Onassis's rivalry with Niarchos, another shipping magnate.

Through their marriages to the Livanos sisters, Onassis and Niarchos were brothers-in-law, at least until they shed those wives to pursue other, more glamorous, women, but they were far from friendly with each other. Onassis, already famous, became a household name in the United States in the 1960s when he married Jacqueline Kennedy, the widow of President John F. Kennedy. Niarchos had his own celebrity bride, the auto heiress Charlotte Ford. His name lives on in New York, where a public library branch on Fifth Avenue and a gallery in the Museum of Modern Art were funded by his foundation.

Onassis and Niarchos were bitter rivals throughout their adult lives, competing to have the biggest ships, the flashiest yacht, and the most celebrity friends. The one endeavor in which Niarchos clearly surpassed Onassis was the collection of art. He began buying works by well-known artists in 1949, and in 1956 purchased the extensive collection of the Hollywood actor

Edward G. Robinson. When "The Niarchos Collection" was shown at London's Tate Gallery in 1958, the museum said it contained "a large proportion of works of the highest quality," including paintings by Van Gogh, Matisse, Gauguin, and El Greco.[8]

When Niarchos died, his obituary in the *New York Times* on April 18, 1986, said he had "spent much of his life battling his archrival Aristotle Onassis for supremacy on the high seas, in conspicuous consumption, and at the altar," and had "built a personal fortune estimated at $4 billion." It said that in the years after World War II, Niarchos and Onassis "began a rivalry that amounted to a global game of one-upmanship. If Mr. Onassis built a 30,000-ton ship, Mr. Niarchos was sure to respond with one of 31,000 tons." When Niarchos in 1956 launched the world's biggest tanker, the one it surpassed belonged to Onassis.

"And Mr. Niarchos," the *New York Times* said, "who became a hero in Greece by building the country's first shipyard after the war, found himself upstaged when Mr. Onassis became an even bigger hero in the jet age by creating Olympic Airways." Each owned his own Greek island.

The Greek Network

Warren Burger's 1953 memo to Federal Bureau of Investigation (FBI) director J. Edgar Hoover, prepared in the course of a federal investigation of Onassis's business deals, noted that the Livanos family "operates a great deal of shipping under various names using Greek, Panamanian, Honduran, Liberian, and American registration."[9] That was typical of the Greek maritime clans: their operations ranged far from the port of Piraeus, and many were not residents or even citizens of Greece. When Onassis took up residence in Argentina, more than 6,000 Greeks lived there, including not just shipowners but also operators of wine, carpet, and tobacco industries.

A long article distributed by the North American Newspaper Alliance in 1966 described the international Greek network in illuminating detail:

> Many of the Greeks are relatives, either by marriage or by blood, but when it comes to business the relationship does not prevent them from trying to cut each other's throats. Some of them are international playboys and their luxurious living and lavish spending is the theme of society gossip columns all over the world.
>
> A few of them, mostly industrialists, are patriotic citizens living permanently in Greece who, while making their pile in that country, are sincerely trying to help Greece and their countrymen. But most of the largest shipping tycoons have long forgotten the country of their birth to adopt foreign citizenships of convenience and hoist foreign flags that would give them tax advantages or enable them to hire cheaper labor.

Most prominent members of "The Greeks" and best known in international financial circles are the shipping tycoons who, collectively, control several million tons of shipping, from whalers to the world's largest supertankers.

Of that group, the article said, Onassis and Niarchos were the "undisputed leaders."[10]

That was the context of the bitter rivalry between them, both striving to own the most and biggest ships, show off the richest and most socially prominent wife or lover, and have the most luxurious yacht. It would hardly have surprised those who knew them both that Niarchos would want to do whatever he could to torpedo any deal that would bring new power or wealth to Onassis.

As a lifelong social climber, Onassis reveled in the company of celebrities, to whom he was gracious and charming. But he beat his first wife in drunken rages, and according to one of his biographers, "He possessed a volatile temper, especially when he'd had too much to drink and [had a] habit of smashing plates and making scenes in restaurants."[11] Even his indulgences were large-scale: he smoked three packs of cigarettes a day, giving his voice a husky quality, and was a prodigious drinker.[12]

According to Gelina Harlaftis, Onassis was a caring and generous boss who inspired loyalty among his employees. "In the Piraeus shipping market to the present day, he is regarded as a model employer," Harlaftis wrote. "He was known for his generosity, and he often visited his ships wherever he could. In 1947, he wrote, 'I always had much higher victualing and wage costs than anybody, to the point to be regarded an ignoramus and a fool.' Onassis built sound human and professional relations with top executives and office employees alike, as well as with the seamen of his ships; mutual loyalty characterized his relations with most of his Greek employees."[13]

That benign assessment was hardly universal. When a group of colonels took over the Greek government in 1967 and established a military dictatorship, Onassis collaborated with them and "ended up glamorizing one of the most unlovely regimes in Europe," his British biographers wrote. They quoted Helen Vlachos, a renowned newspaper publisher who opposed the new regime, as saying that "with the coming of the Colonels, the worst traits of both the top star shipowners and all of the discreetly following tribe came out into open. Their grabbing instincts were sharpened by the Great Junta Sale," a selloff of state assets. One prominent politician said that "Onassis has always been an exploiter of labor, and exploitation of labor is going to intensify in Greece under the fascist regime."[14]

Onassis himself told Peter Evans, the British journalist whom he hired to write his life story, "There is no right and wrong. There is only what is possible."[15]

Gossip columnists loved Onassis because he provided a constant stream of good copy. In addition to his very public affair with Maria Callas, he had a brief fling with Eva Peron, according to several accounts. He even showed up posthumously in a Hollywood movie. The actor Anthony Quinn portrayed an unmistakably Onassis-like character in a 1978 film, "The Greek Tycoon."

The British ambassador to Saudi Arabia at the time of the tanker deal, Clinton Pelham, referred to him as "the notorious Mr. Onassis."[16]

FBI Scrutiny

The FBI file on Onassis contains this report from the Defense Department's Office of Naval Intelligence about his early years as a tobacco dealer in Buenos Aires, before he got into the shipping trade:

> Onassis's father, a tobacco merchant, consigned a quantity of leaf to A. Onassis for sale in the Argentine. This consignment was followed by others and a business grew, Onassis obtaining a contract for the supply of Turkish leaf to Piccardo & Company.
>
> The tobacco was sent via Genoa, where it was transshipped, and it appears that Onassis hit upon the idea of spraying the bales with salt water during their stay at Genoa, the resultant collections from [insurance] underwriters for sea damage forming a welcome addition to legitimate trading profits.

In addition, this FBI "Summary of Information" said, Onassis obtained an appointment as Greece's honorary consul in Argentina. "This appointment is reported to have become extremely lucrative," the report said, "since, as Consul, Onassis was able to obtain substantial sums of currency at official rates and sold the same in the Black Market, which at that time was flourishing."[17]

When Onassis applied for a visa to the United States in 1942, the U.S. Embassy in Buenos Aires advised Washington that "Onassis possessed fascist ideas and was considered shrewd and unscrupulous."[18] But after the FBI looked into that and several similar allegations that Onassis had sentiments potentially inimical to the United States, the agency's records show that such charges were never confirmed and the Bureau found no reason to consider Onassis dangerous or subversive.

When Onassis bought the famous casino in Monte Carlo in early 1953, *TIME* reported on the deal:

> Aristotle Socrates Onassis is a Greek-born Argentine who water-skis in the best international circles and includes among his friends Prince Rainier III, Poo-Bah of the tiny principality of Monaco and its famed Monte Carlo

Casino. At 47, Onassis has homes in Paris, New York, Montevideo and Antibes, owns or controls a fleet of 91 tankers and whaling ships worth an estimated $300 million, and he has a pretty 23-year-old wife. But he didn't get all this by breaking the bank at Monte Carlo—quite the opposite. Last week 'Ari' Onassis let it be known that, for $1,000,000, he had bought the 75-year-old Casino lock, stock and roulette table, and with it the purse strings of Monaco.[19]

A chart of data at Lloyd's Register of Shipping showed that at the time of his conversations with Catapodis, Onassis and companies he controlled operated 88 ships, including 41 tankers and a whaling fleet, in 10 countries.[20] That fleet seemed to position him as a knowledgeable ship operator and a logical candidate for Catapodis's plan. But his record on business matters and his notorious personal life ensured that the U.S. Navy and the international oil companies that owned Aramco would not want to be dependent on him for the transportation of their oil. Neither he nor Catapodis nor the Saudis to whom they would present the plan understood that.

Old Money, Saudi Style

Onassis was apparently familiar with the terms of Aramco's concession agreement because he said he believed it contained a loophole that would allow the development of a deal such as the one Catapodis had discussed with Iraq. Catapodis responded that he would "explore the possibilities of negotiating such an agreement" with the Saudis. If he succeeded, according to Catapodis, Onassis promised to "give me a share of profits amounting to about a million dollars a year free of tax."

Neither man had connections in Saudi Arabia, but through the Riviera social network Catapodis knew just the right man to approach: Mohammed Alireza, a prominent Saudi businessman from one of the kingdom's most influential non-royal families. Mohammed Alireza at the time was president of the Saudi Arabia Chambers of Commerce and Industry, the most important business organization in the kingdom. He had the Ford Motor Company franchise in Saudi Arabia, and his family held the contract to operate the port of Jeddah.

By Saudi standards, the Alirezas were old money—pillars of a mercantile and trading fraternity that dominated commerce in much of the Arabian Peninsula even before the kingdom was created, and still does so today. They were rich before oil was discovered. Mohammed's brother Ali had been a member of Prince Faisal's official delegation when the prince, as foreign minister, met with President Eisenhower at the White House in March 1953.[21]

Mohammed Alireza, like many ambitious young Arabian men of his generation and class, had little formal education, but he had spent time in British-dominated Bahrain and India and was fluent in English and Hindi, as well as Arabic. A biographical sketch of him compiled by Aramco's research department described him as "blue-eyed, big, and hearty," and said he "shows up regularly at British and American diplomatic functions." His blue eyes, unusual in an Arab, made him a dashing figure "who thinks of himself as Douglas Fairbanks playing a Saudi merchant."[22]

Like many of the kingdom's prosperous businessmen, Alireza was well connected at the royal court. But according to the Aramco files, Alireza's "politics are chameleonic. He never takes any action or stance which might endanger his business interests." Despite his long-standing connections to Aramco officials, the oil company's researchers noted, "It is no secret that several members of the family feel that Aramco has treated them badly by not giving them a monopoly or two on some of the services Aramco has paid others for."[23] In short, he was the perfect person to team up with Onassis to take on Aramco.

As was common among prosperous Saudis, Mohammed and Ali Alireza fled the heat of Arabia in the summer for more congenial environments in Europe. They, too, were in Cannes at the time Catapodis was talking to Onassis. With a letter of introduction from one Count Maximilian de Pulaski, secretary of his yacht club (who claimed to have invented water skiing), Catapodis arranged to meet the Alirezas at the Hotel Martinez.[24] In that initial conversation, he told them he was representing a "substantial group" of well-heeled businessmen who could come up with the money to create a tanker fleet, but he did not mention Onassis. The Alirezas immediately expressed great interest and suggested that the discussions be moved from the gossipy Riviera to Paris to preserve secrecy. Once the conversation got to that point, it was clear that a deal could be done; the remaining discussions were about details, and especially about who would get how much money.

For Onassis and Catapodis, money was in fact the only issue; they had no political motivations. Mohammed Alireza was also seeking a big payoff, but for him there was an additional important consideration. Catapodis came to believe that Alireza "was strongly anti-American, since he constantly assailed the activities of Aramco and its 'monopolistic strangle' it held over Saudi Arabia. Mohamed Alireza told me on several occasions that his aim is to break up the Aramco combine and to bring into Saudi Arabia other foreign interests to whom oil concessions, or any other concessions, will be awarded," he said in an affidavit. If Alireza was able to bring that off, he certainly would expect a piece of the action for himself.

Negotiations continued through September and October of 1953, mostly indirectly: Catapodis represented Onassis, and Mohammed Alireza conveyed the various offers to the Saudi finance minister, Abdullah Sulaiman, who represented the king. Alireza told Catapodis that he wanted to be paid £350,000 upon the signing of a contract, arguing that the money would not be just for himself because "there were other people for whom it would be necessary to provide." Catapodis said that amount was too high and made a counter-offer: £125,000 on signature and another £75,000 when the first tanker load of oil sailed, plus a fee for each ton of cargo. (At the time, one British pound was worth $2.78.)

Alireza agreed to the amounts, but insisted upon knowing whom Catapodis represented. Told that it was Onassis, he then demanded a "bank guarantee" to ensure that the payments would actually be made. Onassis was reluctant to solicit such a guarantee from his New York bankers because he feared that the information would leak to the oil companies. At Catapodis's suggestion, Onassis then obtained a payment guarantee from his bank in Monaco. But treachery was afoot: Alireza thought Catapodis had double-crossed him. When Catapodis asked to see Alireza in Paris to present this offer, Alireza said the deal was off and that he did not want anything further to do with the entire affair.

Catapodis begged for an explanation. Alireza said he had learned that Finance Minister Sulaiman had brought into this arena a controversial German banker named Hjalmar Schacht. Schacht had been Minister of Economy in the Nazi government of Adolf Hitler until he quit in a policy dispute; Sulaiman apparently wanted Schacht to find collateral to back the financing Onassis would need to build the proposed tanker fleet.

In his account of these negotiations, the American scholar Nathan Citino said that when American officials learned of the involvement of Schacht, it raised fears that Saudi Arabia would "pursue a policy of state-directed development inimical to American corporate investment" because "the sort of autarkic, state-driven economy he had helped build in Nazi Germany was widely admired among the leaders of post-colonial states in the Middle East," where he was offering his services as an economic consultant.[25]

Breaking this news to Catapodis, Alireza said he had been present at a meeting in which Schacht told Sulaiman that he wanted to negotiate a tanker agreement with the Saudi Arabian government himself, on behalf of "an unnamed principal." That would have left Alireza outside looking in.

By Catapodis's account, "The terms were identical with those which I had put forward on behalf of Onassis." Alireza and Sulaiman "had concluded that Schacht's unnamed principal was in fact Onassis who had, they thought, sent Schacht to the minister of finance in order to eliminate him [Alireza] from the deal and thus avoid the agreed upon payments as well." An angry Alireza said he believed Catapodis "was a party to this attempt to approach the minister of finance behind his back" and thereby cut Alireza out of the deal.

Intrigue on the Riviera

Pleading for a chance to prove he knew nothing about the Schacht maneuver, Catapodis persuaded Alireza to give him one hour.

Catapodis recounted that he went immediately to Onassis's apartment on the Avenue Foch, one of the toniest addresses in Paris.

"When he came down," Catapodis said, "I told him to dress at once and come with me" back to the Plaza Athénée hotel, where Alireza was staying. There, Onassis assured Alireza that Catapodis knew nothing of his dealings with Schacht, "and attempted to make some feeble excuses for his conduct in this respect," according to Catapodis's account. That meant that Onassis had tried to pull an end run around both Catapodis and Alireza.

This version of events, which Catapodis delivered under oath, is hardly flattering to Onassis, but that was to be expected because by the time Catapodis told this story some months afterward, he was furious with Onassis and was looking for a way to kill the deal he had proposed in the first place. He believed, or claimed to believe, that Onassis had reneged on all his promises to pay him for his work on obtaining the Saudi Arabia contract.

The Deal Is Done

In reality, Alireza had little choice but to work with Catapodis and attempt to clinch the deal they had been negotiating because that was the only way he would get paid himself—he would have been cut out if Onassis and Schacht put the agreement together without him and Catapodis. How Onassis would finance the proposed fleet was of no concern to Alireza; his share depended only on getting the tanker contract in place. He demanded that their arrangement be formalized in two letters signed by Onassis: one would state the terms to be offered to the Saudi Arabian government, with no mention of payment to Alireza; the other would specify the payments to him.

On November 6, 1953, Onassis's banker informed Alireza by letter that the bank held "at your disposal, the sum of two hundred thousand free and transferable Pounds Sterling," to be delivered according to the 125,000-75,000 split already negotiated. Five days later, Onassis wrote to Alireza to specify the terms of the agreement in detail and appointed him his official agent in selling the terms to Abdullah Sulaiman and King Abdul Aziz. The king died three days later, to be succeeded by his son Saud.

Onassis's letter to Alireza is worth quoting at some length because it became the basis of the contract that eventually emerged, including provisions that were unrealistic or unworkable. The wording is sometimes garbled or ungrammatical because English was not the first language of any of the participants.

The letter began thus:

Dear Shaikh Alireza,

Following your proposal and the various conferences between your goodselves and your associates with regard to the registration of some oil tankers under the Saudi Arabia flag, we hereby authorize you to negotiate on our behalf with the Saudi Arabia government for obtaining their permission to form a Saudi Arabia tanker company and to sail the said tankers under the Saudi Arabia flag.

Your negotiations with the Saudi Arabia government must be conducted on the following basis:

1. We shall be allowed to form a private limited company under the name of "The Saudi Arabia Tankers Company Limited" with a minimum ownership of 500,000 tons deadweight and to register the said company in Saudi Arabia.
2. To hoist the Saudi Arabia flag over these tankers and to register them under Saudi Arabia names.
3. The vessels are to be of any size we choose, maximum draft suitable for passing the Suez Canal.
4. You undertake to obtain at the same time as the signing of the contract a written order from the Saudi Arabia government addressed to all oil companies connected with the production and purchase and export of Saudi Arabia oil directing them to give priority of shipment to the tankers of the "Saudi Arabia Tankers Company Limited." It is part of this agreement and understood that said priority is to come immediately after the tankers owned and used by said oil companies for the export and transportation of Saudi Arabia oil. It is also understood that said tonnage is to be limited to the tonnage registered to the ownership of said companies and used in this trade prior to the date of the signing of the abovementioned agreement between the Saudi Arabia Government and ourselves. The rate of freight per ton of oil to apply for such transportation to be the international rate in accordance with the United States Maritime Commission rate.
5. The agreement will be valid for 50 years, renewable for similar periods if both parties are satisfied.
6. The Saudi Arabia Government will pass Maritime Laws (including laws on Maritime Mortgages) acceptable internationally and similar to maritime laws of other friendly Maritime Nations.
7. In case the Saudi Arabia Government requires more tonnage of oil tankers than indicated in their agreement with us, we shall be given first refusal. (By first refusal it is meant and understood that we shall be given first option good for 90 days to supply the required additional tonnage under the same terms and conditions as herein mentioned.)
8. We reserve the right to sell or transfer flag (to a nation friendly to the Saudi Arabia Government) at all times provided we

maintain under the Saudi Arabia flag the tonnage agreed upon between the Saudi Arabia government and ourselves. The sale and transfer of flag of any tonnage already registered under the Saudi Arabia flag over and above the tonnage provided in this agreement will require no formality and the Consular authorities of Saudi Arabia upon application are to grant immediately the release of the vessels from Saudi Arabia registry.

9. The Saudi Arabia government will at all times protect and defend the vessels we register under the Saudi Arabia flag.

In return for the abovementioned you are authorized to offer as maximum to the Saudi Arabia government the following:

10. We shall set up within one year at our expense a Maritime Academy at any port in Saudi Arabia for navigating officers and engineers for 50 students per year who, upon graduation, will join the vessels as Cadets at the salaries applicable to cadets of other nationalities on the said company's vessels. It is understood that the training of Saudi Arabia nationals will be free of charge and that their upkeep will be borne by us.

11. We undertake to give priority to Saudi Arabia personnel and labor if and when available with the proper skill, qualifications and any certificates required by international rules and regulations (Lloyd's underwriters, Board of Trade, etc.)

12. We agree to carry free of charge to the Saudi Arabia Government oil or its products from the Persian Gulf to any Red Sea port up to 50,000 tons a year.

13. We agree to pay royalty to the Saudi Arabia Government 1/s (one shilling) for every ton shipped out of Saudi Arabia to any part of the world on the said company's fleet under the abovementioned contract; settlement of such account to be made every 3 months. This royalty is understood to cover the income tax.

14. We shall also be prepared to pay port and harbor dues in Saudi Arabia ports similar to all other ships calling in Saudi Arabia ports.

We also hereby confirm to you that while you negotiate the subject of this letter with the Saudi Arabia Government, no other individual or group connected with us or associated with us will interfere or negotiate with the Saudi Arabia Government the subject matter of this letter.

Before ending, we should like to remind you in negotiating with the Saudi Arabia Government to bear in mind our friendly relations with all the Oil Companies and please do nothing which might turn to the detriment of their interests.

Very truly yours,
(signed) A. O. Onassis[26]

Abdullah Sulaiman, renowned for his shrewdness, must have known that any such arrangement would violate the terms of Aramco's original 1933 concession agreement because he himself had negotiated those terms. But whatever their accomplishments in other fields, he and Mohammed Alireza were largely ignorant of the intricacies of international maritime contracts. Had they known more, or consulted a wider circle of advisers, they would have recognized some of the pitfalls in the terms Onassis laid out.

Saudi Arabia had no maritime tradition, no ships other than small fishing vessels, and no code of maritime law. The provision in Item 4 regarding freight rates was certain to be unacceptable to oil purchasers who wanted to negotiate shipping rates on their own. An FBI report on the Onassis deal said that the oil shipping rate on the free market at the time was 86 cents per barrel lower than the Maritime Commission's rate, and therefore "it will be seen that while paying $.03 per barrel to Saudi Arabia, Onassis has a prospective take of $.83 per barrel over and above current operating profits."[27]

The provision on salaries in Item 10 was virtually unenforceable because such salaries varied widely from country to country. The provision on port usage in Item 14 was also unworkable because the only port in Saudi Arabia with facilities for loading tankers was controlled by Aramco, which was unlikely to cooperate. Insurers would be reluctant to cover ships registered in a country with which they were entirely unfamiliar and where they would have no legal recourse.

Nevertheless, most of the terms specified by Onassis were incorporated into the agreement that would be signed in January, including the Priority clause in Item 4. That was critical to Onassis; its convoluted language made clear that Aramco and its buyers could continue to transport oil only on ships that were in service before 1954, and that as those vessels were retired their replacements would be ships supplied by Onassis. Without that clause, Onassis feared that Aramco's parent companies—or the big charter fleet operators—would simply add new ships to their own tanker fleets, leaving little oil for him to transport. Alireza stipulated that the final agreement would limit Aramco to shipping an annual amount equal to 90 percent of the oil it moved in 1953—ensuring that Onassis's share would rise rapidly as exports rose.

Once information about this arrangement began to circulate in Washington, a CIA analyst flagged the priority clause as especially objectionable. His memo noted that tankers already serving the Saudi route "will have first priority in carrying Saudi oil provided ships were registered in name of companies and regularly transporting Saudi oil before end December 1953." Those conditions "look okay but are loaded" because only a small portion of the oil exported from the kingdom met those terms and "clause means eventual freezeout since [there is] no provision replacement obsolete tankers."[28]

Alireza did object to the provision in Item 13 stipulating that royalty payments would cover whatever income tax might be due. He said income tax would have to be paid in addition to the royalty. When Catapodis told him Onassis would not agree to that, Alireza said he would delete the proposed income tax language if royalty payments were increased by six pence per ton and a separate payment of £100,000 was made to the government's negotiator, Sulaiman.

They were close to a deal, which Alireza believed would be easier to sell to the new king than to his father, but at this critical point the negotiations came to an unexpected detour: Onassis was in legal trouble with federal prosecutors in the United States, who had obtained a warrant for his arrest.

CHAPTER FOUR

Onassis in the Dock

Onassis had been indicted secretly by a federal grand jury in Washington in October 1953, while he was negotiating the Saudi deal. He and several business associates, along with shipping companies that they owned, were accused of violating the Merchant Ship Sales Act of 1946. That law had authorized the sale of surplus U.S. Navy ships from World War II. When enacted, the law allowed some ships to be sold to foreign citizens or corporations, and Greek shipowners snapped up several of the bargain vessels. But the law was amended in 1948 to specify that the purchasers must be U.S. citizens or corporations registered in the United States. The indictment accused Onassis of "conspiracy to defraud" the federal maritime agency that handled the sales and of conspiracy to file false statements to make it appear that the buyers were actually American.

As a citizen of Argentina, Onassis could not legally have purchased ships under his own name after the law was changed nor could any company he controlled. The indictment charged that when two of the shipping companies, United States Petroleum Carriers Inc. and Victory Carriers Inc., applied to buy the ships, they submitted "statements and representations" that they were U.S. corporate citizens and met the financial requirements specified by the government. "In fact," the indictment said, "as defendants then and there well knew," the purchasers were dummy corporations set up and controlled by Onassis, but ostensibly run by Americans who claimed to be the owners. The indictment alleged an elaborate scheme to file false records, hide identities, conceal transactions, and deceive regulators, all to the benefit of Onassis's operations in Panama.[1]

The Justice Department made similar allegations in a civil suit in New York over the same transactions.

A separate indictment alleging the same sort of fraud had been filed in April 1953 against another group of defendants, including Stavros Niarchos, Onassis's brother-in-law and greatest rival. Among the defendants in that case were Julian C. Holmes, who was on the staff of Secretary of State Dulles as a special assistant for Trieste affairs, and Joseph E. Casey, a former congressman from Massachusetts.[2] Overall, prosecutors obtained thirteen indictments against 91 defendants.

The purchasers had paid about $485,000 per ship, approximately one-third of the vessels' original cost. Most of the price was financed through long-term loans backed by the U.S. government.[3]

The indictments followed more than two years of investigation of the sales by Congress and by the Department of Justice. Some analysts at the time suggested that the Department of Justice could have filed the indictments earlier but held off so long as Truman remained in office, rather than embarrass the administration of which it was a part. After the change of administrations, the new Justice Department under Attorney General Herbert Brownell moved quickly to take the cases before a grand jury but said nothing publicly, even after the indictments were handed up by a grand jury: they were kept secret for months because many of the defendants were outside the United States and the government hoped to arrest them whenever they returned to U.S. jurisdiction.

Once the indictments were returned, the cases were under the supervision of Assistant Attorney General Warren E. Burger, later chief justice of the United States.

It was clear at the time, Gelina Harlaftis wrote, that the United States considered Onassis "to be part of the larger Greek shipping family that needed chastising because they were trading behind the Iron Curtain" using bargain vessels purchased from the United States.[4]

In a separate paper, Harlaftis described a complicated network of dummy companies set up to operate other dummy companies, using international networks of people who created no connections to each other on paper. Harlaftis wrote,

> What was at stake here was a group of Greek shipowners that had become extremely wealthy 1) by buying illegally war-built American ships under cover by American companies, 2) by operating these ships under the American flag, 3) by acquiring and/or building ships financed by American banks, 4) by carrying oil for the American oil companies, offending the interests of American shipowners, 5) by allying to high-placed American Democrats to proceed in [these] actions, 6) offending American policy by carrying cargoes for whoever paid them to, like the "red" trade of China and North Korea, disregarding foreign policy of the United States at the

peak of the Cold War. . . . Foreigners had acquired US vessels and were using them to undermine US security by trading with the Reds.[5]

Onassis was aware he was under suspicion because the U.S. government had seized 17 vessels owned by his companies when they sailed into American ports. U.S. Navy intelligence teams were tracking the movement of the ships as they sailed from port to port and knew when they were due to dock in the United States. The first to be taken under a court-issued "article of forfeiture" was the tanker *Lake George*, seized at Wilmington, Delaware, on March 24, 1953.[6]

Onassis tried to head off the indictment he feared was coming, not knowing it had already been handed up by the grand jury. On January 5, 1954, while his Saudi agent, Mohammed Alireza, was finalizing the Saudi tanker contract, Onassis met in Paris with a former FBI agent named Leon Turrou, who had also worked as a security operative for J. Paul Getty.

Turrou's life had been as colorful as that of any of the other characters in this drama. Born in Poland, orphaned as a child, adopted by a rich merchant, he had lived in half a dozen countries and spoke seven languages. He fought in World War I, started and failed at a dehydrated-mushroom business, worked as a translator for the *New York Times* and as a postal inspector, and spent several years as an FBI agent. During World War II, he was an intelligence officer on General Eisenhower's staff. He worked for Getty in the early 1950s.[7] By 1953, he was living in Paris and making a living as a writer. He had turned out several books and magazine articles about his experiences, including *The Nazi Conspiracy in America*, based on his FBI work investigating German spying in the United States. In Paris, he was one of those people who gave the impression of knowing everyone worth knowing.

Turrou recounted his conversation with Onassis to a former oil executive, who relayed it to Aramco. According to an internal Aramco memorandum, Onassis told Turrou that "he had received some indications which led him to believe that he might be indicted in the United States in connection with his acquisition" of the surplus ships. "He told Turrou that these purchases had been perfectly in order and handled in the same way as everyone else buying vessels." He offered Turrou "a substantial fee to go to New York and attempt to learn Onassis's status, vis-à-vis the indictment." Turrou said that he had no way of finding out because grand jury proceedings are secret and that an indictment, if any, would be revealed only when prosecutors chose to go public. In response to that, "Onassis stated that he was in the midst of one of the biggest deals of his career and could not afford the unfavorable publicity which would arise from such an indictment."[8] Even while Onassis was contemplating his strategy for dealing with the U.S. authorities, Mohammed Alireza and Finance Minister Abdullah Sulaiman resumed work on final details of the tanker contract. On January 20, 1954, Alireza as Onassis's agent and

Sulaiman signed the agreement at the minister's residence in Jeddah. Onassis, who with his wife had sailed into Jeddah harbor two days before aboard the tanker *Tina Onassis*, handed over two checks drawn on a bank in Zurich, both payable to Mohammed Alireza: £125,000 as the first installment of his commission and £100,000 for Abdullah Sulaiman. "The latter," according to Spyridon Catapodis, "was intended for the Minister of Finance in compensation for the exemption of the tax clause from the agreement."

That was still not enough for Alireza. Catapodis said later in an affidavit that after the agreement was signed but before King Saud ratified it, Alireza demanded a further $200,000 to obtain the king's approval. Catapodis's account is substantially confirmed by telegrams, hotel receipts, letters, and other documents that he submitted with the affidavit.[9]

Onassis was furious, but he paid because he had no alternative if he wanted to go ahead with the deal.

Facing the Music

When Turrou declined to get involved in his legal troubles, Onassis decided to go to the United States himself to confront his fate. On February 2, 1954, he was arrested as he ate lunch at a New York restaurant.[10] Onassis had notified Attorney General Brownell of his arrival, a development rich in irony because Brownell, as a lawyer in private practice, had been a partner in the firm that advised Onassis about setting up the companies that bought the ships from the navy in the first place. Onassis later accused Brownell of prosecuting him for following legal advice he himself had given, and he was not alone in that sentiment.

Brownell's role was still being debated in Washington even four years later. Representative Herbert Zelenko, a New York Democrat, demanded that Brownell appear before the House Merchant Marine and Fisheries Committee, which was scrutinizing the Justice Department's handling of the case. When Brownell appeared, Zelenko charged that under Brownell the Justice Department had indicted the Onassis companies "for the very thing you advised them to do." Brownell, out of office by that time, testified that he was not a party to the advice his law firm had given Onassis and in fact had never met Onassis.[11]

After his arrest, Onassis—against the advice of his lawyers—issued a lugubrious statement depicting himself as a longtime friend of the United States who valued what he said was his good reputation among Americans. He said he was proud of his role in keeping the struggling Bethlehem Shipyard in Baltimore alive by placing a large order for tankers. "At the outbreak of the Korean War," his statement said, "I offered unconditionally, my entire foreign fleet, together with my whaling fleet, and also my personal services and resources, to the United States Navy for the duration of the emergency—an offer which I believe was made by no other shipowner, and for which I was officially thanked by the Navy."[12] This theme of Onassis's ostensible esteem for all things American would recur throughout his legal entanglements.

Onassis later testified, before the same U.S. House subcommittee that heard from Brownell, that he and his lawyers had met to discuss the indictment with Assistant Attorney General Burger. Onassis said he began that meeting by saying, "Well, here I am. What is the ransom?"

"Twenty million dollars," Burger replied.

"I wanted to be a free man," Onassis testified. "I told them that if they would drop the criminal action, I would fight the civil suit in the courts, even if it took all my life, and that I would win it."[13]

In his biography of the lawyer Edward Bennett Williams, the writer Evan Thomas gives a different version of this "ransom" story. He said Williams represented Onassis during a discussion of the case with Brownell. "Williams could see that Onassis, who had come to the meeting wearing sunglasses and blue suede shoes, was getting impatient. Finally Onassis broke in: 'General,' he said to Brownell, 'let's cut the bullshit! What's the ransom for my ships?'"[14] According to Thomas, "It took about a year, but the answer finally came back: $7 million in fines," the amount Onassis eventually paid to settle the case.[15]

The FBI, alerted by congressional investigators, had carried out an exhaustive inquiry into the ship transactions, involving other purchasers as well as Onassis, and had already seized some vessels of several owners when they called at ports in the United States. The investigation did not represent the first time Onassis had appeared on the FBI's screen. The agency had been tracking him for more than a decade.

In July 1942, FBI director J. Edgar Hoover wrote to Rear Admiral Emory Land, administrator of the War Shipping Administration, to alert him that Onassis was planning to travel to the United States to try to sell two of his tankers to the U.S. government for use during the war. Hoover said that a "confidential source" had reported that Onassis "has expressed sentiments inimical to the United States war effort, and that his activities and movements while in the United States should be carefully scrutinized."[16]

Years later, in response to a press inquiry, an FBI official named W. R. Wannall wrote in an internal memo that "we did not initiate investigation of Onassis in 1942. However, in 1943 we initiated investigation of him because of information received that a captain of one of Onassis's ships was alleged to have been approached by German agents to act for them in the North Atlantic." In that instance, the memo said, "Investigation did not reveal Onassis to be engaged in any activities inimical to the United States," and he was not put under surveillance.[17] He may not have been under full-time surveillance, but his prominence was such that he was never entirely off the law-enforcement radar.

The First Court Appearance

After his arrest, Onassis was arraigned in federal court in Washington on February 8, 1954. He entered a plea of not guilty and was released on $10,000 bond. The conditions of his release did not permit him to leave the United States, which was, of course, quite inconvenient because his business affairs—including his new arrangement with the Saudis—were concentrated overseas and his family was in Paris. After a few weeks, he returned to court to ask Chief Judge Bolitha J. Laws to allow him to leave the country until his trial.[18]

He told the court that he had urgent business in Europe: he had 18 ships under construction in West Germany and 3 in France. He said problems had arisen "which require my personal attention," including "credit arrangements for many millions of dollars"—that is, the financing he would need to build the new fleet for Saudi Arabia.

There was no reason to doubt that he would return for trial, he said, because he had many reasons to do so.

"My wife and two children are American citizens. Along with them, I cherish my good reputation," he said in his written petition. Besides, he said, there was no place in Europe where he could hide from law enforcement authorities. "I am a well-known figure in every country in Europe, and am recognized everywhere I go," he said, truthfully. "In the face of these facts it makes no sense at all that I should attempt to hide out abroad and thus subject myself and my family to the ridicule and contempt of the entire world."

In a separate filing, he evoked the plight of his 25-year-old wife, Tina, and their children, ages 6 and 3, who were in Paris. "On the afternoon of February 15, 1954," he told the court, "I received a cable advising my wife had broken her leg in two places." She would be incapacitated for some time and needed his help. (His solicitousness did not save his marriage: Tina later divorced him after discovering his affair with Maria Callas, and, in lovely payback, married his hated rival Stavros Niarchos—at one time the husband of her own sister.)

Onassis added a statement of his devotion and gratitude to the United States, which he said had been inspired by an incident in his boyhood. In the dying days of the Ottoman Empire, the Turks regained control of Smyrna (today's Izmir) from Greece and turned savagely on the Christian population, mostly Armenians and Greeks, including Onassis's family. A flotilla of Western warships, including three U.S. destroyers, stood offshore but did not intervene.

"The victims of the massacre—Greeks and Armenians—were estimated at 150,000," according to George Horton, who was U.S. Consul in the city until the Turks arrived. "What was left of Smyrna was only its Turkish suburb. This very old and extremely beautiful Greek city had been founded in 3000 B.C. and restored by Alexander the Great. It used to be one of the most important economic centers of the Mediterranean. It used to be full of life and activity. It used to be prosperous. And now from one moment to the next it was turned into a dead city. To a huge pile of ruins which emitted smoke. Those of its inhabitants who escaped the massacre fled, ousted and miserable, to Greece."[19] Onassis was one of the survivors.

"I feel that I owe my life to the American spirit of justice," he told Judge Laws. "As a youth in Greece, in October 1922, I was imprisoned with my father by the Turks, it being their expressed intention to hang both me and my father merely because we had been born Greeks. A few days before my scheduled execution, and after other members of my family had been slaughtered, I was saved by the action of a Mr. Parker, then American vice-consul in Smyrna. I was clothed in a United States naval uniform, placed on a United States destroyer, and carried to safety. For this humane act I shall forever be indebted to the United States."[20]

Onassis said he repaid the United States by refusing to carry any cargoes to the Soviet Union, China, or North Korea during the Korean War, an assertion contradicted by evidence showing otherwise that had been unearthed by the CIA. According to Gelina Harlaftis, the agency obtained "photographic evidence" that Onassis not only transported cargo to China and North Korea, he did so on some of the ships he had purchased from the United States.[21]

Harlaftis wrote in another paper that "during the Korean War, freight rates rocketed high as demand for supplies reached extraordinary heights too. Greek shipowners made available their tonnage to whomever gave the best freight rate," communist or not. "The Cold War was not their war. After all, for a Greek citizen with ships under Greek, Panamanian, Honduran, or Liberian flags to trade with China, North Korea or other communist countries was not illegal. The ban on trading with communist countries applied only to U.S. ships. But in the high time of McCarthyism, of extreme communist fear and philology [sic] this was not to be tolerated. Foreigners had acquired U.S. vessels and were using them to undermine national security by trading with the Reds."[22] That was true, but Onassis was not accused of trading with the enemy; he was accused of fraud.

On March 31, Judge Laws gave Onassis permission to travel outside the United States, provided that he return 30 days before his scheduled trial date.

In the end, there never was a trial: the case was whittled down through legal arguments and plea-bargaining over the next year and a half. But during that time, the criminal case hovered like some noxious cloud over the entire Saudi Arabia tanker episode, which unfolded during the period between indictment and resolution. For the navy and the FBI, the criminal charges represented one more reason to find Onassis objectionable. State Department officials and diplomats used the case to try to discredit Onassis

Onassis in the Dock

in the eyes of the Saudis. On the other side, Onassis sought to use the indictment as a bargaining tool, suggesting that he might modify the Saudi Arabia contract in exchange for favorable treatment in the criminal case.

Duplicity and Disappearing Ink

The January 20 signing of the contract calling for creation of a Saudi-registered tanker company, known as SATCO, marked an end to the negotiations between Onassis and the Saudis over terms, at least for the time being, but it did not put an end to Onassis's duplicity.

He asked Finance Minister Sulaiman to refrain from informing Aramco of the contract. When Catapodis asked Onassis to explain the reason for this request, he replied that "he expected to enter into an agreement with Aramco whereby he would either get a large amount of money or some other valuable concessions, in return for cancelling his agreement" with the Saudi government. When Catapodis, by his own self-serving account, objected that "this amounted almost to blackmail," Onassis replied that "he did not care very much to do business with the Arabs anyway, and that was the reason why he intended that no penalty clause for non-performance of the agreement be incorporated in his agreement with the Saudi Arabia Government." What he really wanted, it appeared, was to be paid handsomely by Aramco to go away.[23]

Whether Catapodis actually had moral scruples about such an attempt at extortion is open to question, but that was hardly the cause of his falling out with Onassis. The real issue was that Onassis did not pay him the substantial finder's fee he had been led to expect. Catapodis later claimed in court that the total amount Onassis owed him was $14,210,000.[24]

According to Leon Turrou's account, which refers to Catapodis by the given name Spiros, after King Saud issued a decree ratifying the contract in April 1954, "Spiros again demanded his money and again met nothing but procrastination on Onassis's part. About this time Spiros discovered that the agreement between himself and Onassis, and prepared by the latter, had apparently been written with vanishing ink and was at that time only about 25% legible. He promptly had it photocopied and demanded that Onassis rewrite the agreement with a pen to be furnished by Spiros, which Onassis refused to do."[25]

Children play games with disappearing ink, but these were not children and this was no game. The matter of the invisible signature would arise time and again in the many months of argument and litigation that would follow the signing of the Onassis tanker contract. Catapodis's claim about the ink was validated much later by an FBI laboratory, but he would never be able to prove in court that Onassis had actually signed any agreement with him.

CHAPTER FIVE

The Shot Heard 'Round the World of Oil

Bill Owen earned his stripes as a lawyer for big oil companies when he was a junior member of their legal defense team in a major federal antitrust case during World War II. Owen had graduated from a small college in Missouri and then from Harvard Law School, where at the time he was the youngest person to receive a law degree. He was just 21.

He was recruited to the oil industry's legal team by the renowned New York lawyer William J. "Wild Bill" Donovan, who was soon to become director of the Office of Strategic Services, the wartime precursor of the CIA—just one of the many links that would later form between the intelligence community and the oil industry.

Donovan was the lead defense counsel in the antitrust case, a landmark prosecution known as the Madison Case because the government filed its indictment in Madison, Wisconsin. Owen recalled it as an "exciting trial."[1]

The case was filed by the U.S. attorney general at the time, Robert H. Jackson, later a justice of the Supreme Court.

No oil company was based in Madison, and it was inconvenient for everyone, so Jackson was asked why he picked that venue. According to Owen, he responded, "Well, it's hard enough for the government to win an antitrust case, so we thought we were entitled to a favorable judge and a favorable jury," which, in populist Wisconsin, he got. The jury convicted 12 corporations and 5 individuals.[2]

One of Owen's colleagues in that case was George W. Ray Jr., then assistant general counsel of Texaco, which was soon to become one of Chevron's partners in the Aramco consortium. After the war, Ray was appointed general counsel of Aramco and recruited Owen to join the company's legal staff in Dhahran.

In January 1954, Owen was working on price negotiations in his office there when Fred Davies, the company's chairman and chief executive, burst in and slammed a document on his desk.

Davies was a son of the American Midwest, born in South Dakota, trained as a mining engineer at the University of Minnesota. If it had been up to Davies, oil would have been discovered in Saudi Arabia several years earlier than it actually was; in 1930 he had spent weeks in Bahrain and Iraq, looking at oil domes similar to the terrain in Saudi Arabia and waiting in vain for an invitation to the kingdom that never came.[3] By now, in 1954, he had been working in the Saudi oil fields for nearly two decades and thought he knew the state of play in the kingdom. A company biography described him as "a tall, trim and jaunty man in khakis and sun helmet, sporting a Clark Gable mustache."[4] When he arrived at Owen's office, he was more flustered than jaunty.

"What do you think of this, Bill?" Davies sputtered.

It was a letter from Finance Minister Abdullah Sulaiman, who was all too well known to Aramco: he had been the government's chief negotiator in every deal with the oil company, beginning with the original concession agreement in 1933, and had become increasingly critical of the way the company conducted its business. This latest missive, written in Arabic and hastily translated by Aramco's staff, dropped on Aramco like a bolt from the blue.

The letter informed the company that the Saudis had signed a contract with Aristotle Onassis to create a fleet of oil tankers that would fly the Saudi flag, and to train Saudi crews to operate them. The contract reflected the provisions Onassis had negotiated with Mohammed Alireza, about which Aramco had previously had no clue. The ships would nominally be operated by a separate Saudi company called Saudi Arabian Tankers Company Limited, or SATCO, which Onassis would create and finance. Abdullah Sulaiman signed the contract on behalf of the government; the ceremony had taken place at his residence in Jeddah on January 20. Jeddah was a small community, and its circle of diplomats and business people was smaller still, but no word about the signing had reached any Americans.

When Is a Bribe Not a Bribe?

Onassis did not sign the contract himself. His well-paid Saudi agent, Alireza, had signed on his behalf. In the months to come, the amount of money that Onassis paid Alireza to promote the deal and represent Onassis—and whether that money represented a bribe or simply a commission of the sort common in the Arab world—would become a major issue.

In news accounts and court documents, these payments would be described as bribes, which they were by today's standards of international commerce. In the Arabian culture of the time, however, they were part of the normal course of business. Any man who took up arms on behalf of a ruler or leader, or who served in an administrative capacity, or conducted contract negotiations, was expected to benefit from his service. This was often the only form of payment he would receive, just as raiders who looted desert caravans drew no salaries but were paid out of the spoils.

King Abdul Aziz "believes that those who serve him well should be suitably rewarded with the result that those who remain high in his counsels for any length of time become very wealthy men through the King's own benefactions and the benefactions he permits them to confer upon themselves," U.S. Ambassador J. Rives Childs observed in a 1949 memo. "One must never forget that the tradition here is Oriental and that what might give moral offense to a Westerner, particularly in the capitalization of one's job, is an accepted perquisite of an official position in Arabia."[5]

As David Holden and Richard Johns wrote, "The concept [of corruption], as understood in the West, is hardly relevant to Saudi Arabia. Most of its inhabitants, from the humblest bedouin to the most urbane and worldly-wise merchant, consider anyone who does not profit from his status or ability to peddle influence foolish or incompetent."[6] If the tribal leader, military commander, wealthy trader, or national ruler whom a man served happened to be generous, so much the better.

In truth, what would be seen in Europe or the United States as corruption was the only way to do business with Saudi Arabia in those days. The king's word was law; there was no parliament, and thus no public oversight and no legislation. No one had subpoena power. Other than Abdullah Sulaiman, there was no cadre of public servants empowered to negotiate on behalf of the state. There were no big commercial banks. Personal connections and cash were the lubricants of commerce.

The long-standing prevalence of this casual attitude about self-enrichment in dealing with the Saudi government was the reason experienced analysts of Saudi affairs were shocked when, in the autumn of 2017, the government rounded up dozens of princes and prominent business tycoons in what was billed as an overdue campaign against corruption.

That would not have happened in the era of King Saud. At the time of the Onassis contract, the king knew perfectly well that Sulaiman had enriched himself through land deals and commercial arrangements during his years of royal service, and he would have taken for granted that Mohammed Alireza profited from his role in negotiating the agreement. The king showed his trust in Alireza by appointing him minister of commerce in March 1954, the month before he issued a royal decree ratifying the Onassis contract.

Welcome to Jeddah, Mr. Ambassador

The principal representative of the U.S. government in Saudi Arabia at the time the contract was signed was Ambassador George Wadsworth. He was appointed in 1953 but had presented his credentials only in January 1954 and had not had much time to meet the power players and understand the intrigues of the royal court. Like all foreign diplomats in that era, he was handicapped by the fact that the embassy was in Jeddah, the commercial capital and port on the Red Sea coast, while the king and princes spent most of the year in Riyadh, the royal capital, hundreds of miles of bad road into the interior, and there was no regular commercial air service. The American oil community was still farther away, on the Gulf coast. But Wadsworth knew the language and was well-versed in Arab affairs, having previously been a teacher in Beirut and ambassador to Lebanon, Syria, and Iraq. In Saudi Arabia, he proved to be a quick study and gained the trust of King Saud and his principal advisers. He and Aramco's Bill Eddy had been among the U.S. diplomats posted to Arab capitals who met with President Truman in 1945 to argue against acceding to Zionist aspirations in Palestine, and therefore he was regarded by the Arabs as a friend.[7]

Several weeks after the signing of the Onassis contract, Wadsworth reported on sentiment about the deal within king's inner circle. Two cabinet ministers supported it—Mohammed Alireza and Abdullah Sulaiman, who were being paid by Onassis, although Wadsworth did not yet know that—while the Royal Councilors Khalid Bey Gorgoni, Jamal Hussein, and Mohammed Surur wanted to scrap it.[8] Surur would succeed Sulaiman when the king dismissed him from the government at the end of August.

This division among his closest confidants, all smarter than he, contributed to the king's vacillation about formally ratifying the contract and ordering it into effect.

Sulaiman's letter notifying Aramco of the Onassis agreement was dated January 23, but Aramco did not see the entire contract document until months later. In his letter, the finance minister described only Article IV, by which "the Government undertakes to oblige all oil companies which now hold concessions, or which may come into existence in future in Saudi Arabia, to ship and transport oil and other products exported from Saudi Arabia to foreign countries, whether such shipment is being made by the concession companies themselves or by their parent companies or by the off-taking companies, in the tankers of Saudi Arabia Maritime Tankers Company Ltd." That requirement was to be phased in as existing tankers aged out of service and Onassis built or acquired new ones to replace them.[9]

That was unacceptable to Aramco, but in the absence of the full text the oil company did not know what other provisions it contained or what

Onassis was giving the government in return for the tanker arrangement. Aramco officials still knew nothing about the negotiations that led up to the agreement. The oil company and the U.S. government were obliged to shadow box with the king and Sulaiman until June, when the text of the contract was published.

The terms of the contract followed those laid out in Onassis's letter to Alireza the previous November. In exchange for creating SATCO and supplying the ships, Onassis would have the right to transport an ever-increasing share of Saudi Arabia's oil as this new fleet entered service and the current tankers were phased out. Onassis would have first option to transport Saudi oil from the Persian Gulf port of Ras Tanura, near the oil fields—which Aramco built and operated—and from the Mediterranean terminus of the Trans-Arabian Pipeline, or Tapline. Tapline carried crude oil overland from the Saudi fields to Sidon, Lebanon, three countries and 1,069 miles away. That pipeline had also been created by Aramco, which financed the project and set up a subsidiary to build it.

SATCO would eventually gain a virtual monopoly on transporting the Saudi output and would charge higher prices than the tanker fleets then under charter by Aramco's customers. The agreement would last for 30 years and was renewable. The Saudi government would receive a royalty of about 20 cents for every ton of oil carried by SATCO's fleet to any country. (Oil companies measured output by the number of 42-gallon barrels produced, but commercial fleet operators who carried bulk liquid measured by tons of cargo.)

The contract said nothing about oil produced in the Saudi sector of the Neutral Zone between Saudi Arabia and Kuwait, but the government took the position that its transportation provisions applied there as well, to oil shipped by J. Paul Getty's Pacific Western Company.

Sulaiman's letter describing the Saudi government's commitment to enforce Article IV—but omitting any details of the remainder of the contract—was the document that Davies carried into Owen's office. It left little room for interpretation or negotiation: "We hereby notify you to take the steps necessary to give preference in shipping Saudi oil to the tankers to be registered by Saudi Arabian Tankers Company Limited," it said. "His Majesty's government expects to hear from you about the steps you take to carry out this obligation."[10]

What Was in It for Saudi Arabia?

On the face of it, it appeared that the SATCO deal made sense for Saudi Arabia. It was hardly an outlandish idea; as early as 1946, State Department officials had raised the idea of breaking Aramco's "monopolistic transit rights" in order to increase Saudi Arabia's revenue stream, reducing the need for financial assistance from the U.S. government; Karl Twitchell had also proposed creation of a national merchant fleet when he was promoting the SAADCO deal.[11]

Under the Onassis plan, the kingdom would gain a commercial tanker fleet and the expertise to run it, much as the country was building a national airline with the help of Trans World Airlines, then known as Transcontinental and Western Air Co. (Development of a national airline with U.S. help had been part of the price King Abdul Aziz had extracted from the U.S. military for permission to build and operate the air base at Dhahran.) Onassis would finance construction of a fleet of 30 to 35 ships, and 50 Saudis would be trained every year in navigation and naval mechanics.

The contract would also enhance the political credentials of King Saud. He would demonstrate that he was his own man and did not take orders from the United States, enabling him to project a nationalist image that was politically useful in seeking accommodation with Egypt's fiery new antimonarchist leader, Gamal Abdel Nasser, who was not yet the outright enemy of Saudi Arabia he would become.

Those political considerations meant little to Onassis; for him it was a business deal and a bold power play, the kind of transaction that he relished, and it would give him a huge and lucrative new market.

Aramco, on the other hand, had nothing to gain and much to lose. Its executives were first stunned, then outraged because the Onassis contract appeared to be an obvious violation of the 1933 concession agreement that had allowed Chevron to enter Saudi Arabia in the first place. Under that agreement, Aramco had the exclusive right for 60 years to "explore, prospect, drill for, extract, treat, manufacture, transport, deal with, carry away, and export petroleum" and any other hydrocarbons it might find, by whatever means it wished to use.[12] In the drama that followed delivery of the minister's letter, Aramco never deviated from its position that the language was clear and indisputable: once the oil came out of the ground, it was at all times and at every point of the distribution chain under the company's control until loaded aboard whatever tankers the purchasers of the oil might wish to employ. Aramco did not transport oil for export in its own ships: it sold to buyers, including its parent companies, who made their own shipping arrangements. Aramco argued that in a competitive market, purchasers of oil were free to use whatever tankers they wished, chartering them from whatever fleet owner gave them the best rate. If Saudi Arabia took away their freedom to negotiate rates, they would buy their oil elsewhere.

In fact, the company argued, the issue should never have arisen because any such contract as the Onassis deal had been precluded by the income tax agreement of 1950. "It was the purpose of both parties in effectuating this settlement," the company's lawyers wrote in a legal document, "to dispose of every kind of objection that the Government had made or intended to make respecting any part of Aramco's operations or activities. No objection of any kind, either then or thereafter, was made concerning the arrangements for the transporting, dealing with, carrying away and exporting the oil Aramco produced or the products it manufactured." The tax settlement specified that "Aramco may continue to conduct its operations in accordance with the Aramco Concession agreements as in the past."[13]

All those arguments came later. In the immediate moment of receiving the finance minister's letter, Owen recognized that its meaning was unequivocal. He told Davies it meant that "Aristotle Socrates Onassis has the exclusive rights to ship all Aramco oil that is extracted by Aramco or any other company from Saudi Arabia to any place in the world."

When the finance minister's letter arrived, George Ray, the general counsel, was thousands of miles away, on a cruise ship in the Pacific. Before leaving, he had told Owen, "Bill, it's all up to you," but neither Ray nor Owen had anticipated any development of this magnitude. Years later, Owen recalled that upon reading the finance minister's letter, "I gulped a little bit [because] I thought it was a little beyond my capability to do much about it." He knew that Saudi Arabia was an absolute monarchy in which the king could do whatever he wanted, no matter what it said on any printed page other than the Quran itself. The concession agreement stipulated that any dispute between the kingdom and the oil company that could not be resolved through negotiation would be referred to arbitration in Europe, but Owen, Davies, and every other American at Aramco understood that the king held the ultimate weapon: he could revoke the entire concession and give it to some other company.

"Can they do this?" Davies asked Owen.

"You mean legally? No, they can't do this legally," Owen replied. "We've got this right in our Concession. It's one of the implied rights in all of this tabulation of rights we have, it leaves nothing out. We have the right to do this." Davies instructed Owen to write a "polite letter" telling Abdullah Sulaiman that the government did not control the shipping rights, Aramco did, and "therefore we would continue to operate as we had in the past." Saudi Arabia was free to create a tanker fleet and deploy as many ships as it wanted, the company said, but Aramco and its customers could not be compelled to use them.

The three-paragraph letter that Owen drafted, sent to Sulaiman over Davies's signature on February 8, stated the company's position in uncompromising language:

The arrangement set forth in your letter raises questions of the most serious and far reaching nature. . . . Its implementation would (1) be contrary to and violate both the letter and the spirit of the existing agreements between the Saudi Arab government and the Company; (2) be contrary to long established business arrangements and procedures developed in reliance on these agreements; (3) be contrary to established world-wide custom and practice in the international oil business; (4) have a disastrous effect upon the presently established sales outlets for Saudi oil and the possible future development thereof; and (5) be wholly impractical.

In view of these considerations, the Company has no alternative but to advise Your Excellency that it cannot accept the proposed arrangement.[14]

The wording of that letter was strikingly similar to language that appeared in the CIA's Current Intelligence Bulletin on April 28, 1954: "The agreement violates the oil concession in which Saudi Arabia granted Aramco the exclusive right to market Saudi oil, and is considered likely to have a disastrous effect on established sale outlets for Saudi Arabian oil."[15]

The company's legal position might have been unassailable, but it was soon evident that this was much more than a legal dispute about some business contract. It involved questions of Saudi sovereignty, the global flow of oil, freedom of maritime traffic, and even U.S. national security because Saudi Arabia was a major source of fuel for the U.S. Navy. Almost immediately, Aramco and its parent companies began to round up allies in the U.S. government.

Seeking Support in Washington

Aramco's first step was to share Sulaiman's original letter of notification with Ambassador Wadsworth. The next was to notify the parent companies back in the United States so they could begin making a case for assistance from the government.

In its dealing with officials in Washington, Aramco had a valuable lobbying asset: William A. Eddy, he of the intemperate letter accusing Sulaiman of telling the king "a pack of lies," was on the company's payroll.[16] Eddy was a Marine Corps war hero from World War I and a fluent speaker of Arabic who had been an intelligence agent in Morocco during World War II and then the senior U.S. diplomatic officer in Saudi Arabia in the 1940s. After leaving his post in Jeddah, he had served as the State Department's chief intelligence officer, a position in which he was part of the group of senior officials who created the Central Intelligence Agency in 1947. Now in 1954 he was Aramco's representative in Beirut, keeping track of oil politics throughout the region. In Beirut, besides working for Aramco, Eddy reported regularly to his former colleagues at the CIA and was probably on the agency's payroll as well as Aramco's. He knew all the principal officials of the Saudi government from his time in the kingdom, was well-liked in Riyadh, and was well-connected in Washington.[17]

Useful as Eddy's contacts were, the chiefs of Aramco's parent companies did not leave this vital matter entirely to him. They saw the Onassis contract as a threat to their business that required action at a high level. They quickly weighed in individually on behalf of their corporations, expecting that strong arguments from big business would be persuasive to a Republican administration.

On February 19, Monroe J. Rathbone, president of Standard Oil Company of New Jersey (Exxon) wrote to Henry Byroade, assistant secretary of state for Near East Affairs and the department's point man on this matter. "The arrangement would apparently attempt to obligate Aramco and its stockholder companies to use certain tanker transportation exclusively for shipments of oil from Saudi Arabia," his letter said. "This would be in conflict with Aramco's concession rights. If the Saudi government were, nevertheless, to say as an act of sovereignty that oil can only be exported from Saudi Arabia in certain tankers, the result would not be the large increase in revenue that Onassis is apparently leading the government to expect. The result would be that a great many buyers would go elsewhere for their oil, and that Aramco, its stockholders, and the Saudi Arab government would all suffer together."

He said that the "basic fallacy" of the contract "is that neither Aramco nor its stockholder companies control the choice of tankers used. . . . The buyer comes and gets the oil and takes it away, and is free to arrange his own transportation in whatever way he chooses." Oil buyers from any country wanted to be able to bargain over freight charges, he said, and if they could not bargain over shipments from Saudi Arabia they would take their business to a different producing country.[18] In his view, widely shared by his industry colleagues and, soon, by the State Department, the tanker contract would therefore be detrimental to Saudi Arabia, rather than beneficial, and would potentially lead to instability in a country that had become indispensable. They were arguing in their own interests, but they were also probably right.

R. Gwin Follis, board chairman of Standard Oil of California, wrote a similar letter to Byroade, enclosing a copy of Minister Sulaiman's original notification letter to Aramco.

"It is our belief," he said, "that the proposal outlined in the attached letter would not only be very detrimental to the interests of the companies directly concerned, but would be extremely detrimental to the interests of the United States. It would set a precedent of wide scope capable of burdening international commerce in a most serious degree. The proposal would tend to increase the price of petroleum in world markets [because shipping it would cost more], including the vital supplies to our own Military and Naval forces." In addition, he said, the contract would violate Aramco's concession agreement and negate the price structure the company had laboriously negotiated with Saudi Arabia. The proposed arrangement could not be improved nor its defects rectified by minor changes, he wrote.[19]

Two weeks later, the chief executive of Texaco, Augustus C. Long, wrote directly to Secretary of State John Foster Dulles. He raised arguments similar to those of Rathbone and noted that Aramco had advised Abdullah Sulaiman that it could not accept the Onassis agreement. He said that it "would have a disastrous effect upon the development and sale of Saudi Arabian oil and would be wholly impractical. The Texas Company concurs with Aramco's position and must likewise decline to submit to the conditions of the agreement. As a result of the above factors, the Aramco Concession itself may be in serious danger. The refusal of the companies to submit to the demands of the minister of Finance may lead to repercussions which would affect the concession rights of Aramco" and "could seriously disrupt relations between the Government and the company" once the Saudi government found out how much revenue it would lose as customers bailed out. Aramco sold most of its output to its parent companies, but it also sold to other buyers on what was known as the spot market. If those sales declined, so would the kingdom's revenue.[20]

This line of argument would be presented to King Saud through many channels over the next nine months: Your Majesty, you will not get what you are hoping for out of the Onassis deal. On the contrary, it will be detrimental to your country because there is plenty of oil in the world and buyers will go elsewhere, as they had done in the Iran crisis.

The oil companies' complaints could have been dismissed as the self-interested whining of a challenged monopoly, except that the governments of most of the world's maritime countries, including the United States, agreed with them.

Officials in Washington didn't need much convincing to join forces with Aramco to try to quash the tanker deal. They had learned about it on February 3 from Ambassador Wadsworth. It was immediately apparent, as the historian Nathan J. Citino wrote, that "Saud's deal with Onassis raised serious questions about whether the new king would continue his late father's intimate relations with Aramco and the United States or pursue a policy of state-directed development inimical to American corporate investment."[21]

In U.S. foreign policy, the Onassis contract took on a life of its own. In April, after King Saud had issued a decree formally ratifying the contract, Wadsworth discussed it with Owen and other Aramco officials. The next day, April 30, 1954, he went to see the king and delivered this message:

> I am directed by my government to inform Your Majesty that, on the basis of what it has learned about the so-called Onassis tanker agreement, which was confirmed by Your Majesty's decree of sixth Shabat [the date on the Muslim lunar calendar], my government is concerned over its effects on American interests, both those of private companies and those of America national defense.

He also told King Saud that "my government shares the opinion of Aramco, as already communicated to Your Majesty's government, and of other interested private companies that this agreement is not in keeping with the Aramco concession agreement with Saudi Arabia."[22]

Alarm at the Pentagon

The reference to "American national defense" meant the supply of fuel for the U.S. Navy, a matter of critical importance to the Defense Department that Wadsworth had been instructed to raise with the king.

On March 18, Robert B. Anderson, secretary of the navy, had sounded an alarm in a memo to Defense Secretary Charles E. Wilson.

"At the present time," Anderson wrote, "the Military Sea Transportation Service (MSTS) each month lifts from 27 to 30 tanker loads of Saudi Arabian produced oil products from the Persian Gulf ports of Bahrein and Ras Tanura. The tankers employed in this lift are MSTS owned and contract-operated. All but one are of the T-2 type (capacity 118,000 barrels), built in World War II." If the Saudis exempted military shipments, fine, but if they attempted to apply the reported agreement to these shipments, it would prohibit the navy from transporting its own fuel or at the least, because of Article IV, prevent the NSTS from introducing newer, more modern vessels. Such a development, Anderson said, "could result in the placing of virtual control of this source of armed services oil at the will of a foreign shipping enterprise."[23]

Wilson forwarded Anderson's memo to Secretary of State Dulles, noting that "I share fully the concern of the Secretary of the Navy and the Joint Chiefs of Staff as to the unacceptability of such limitation placed upon transportation of Saudi Arabian oil in U.S. government vessels, and I therefore request that you approach the Saudi Arabian government with a view to obtaining binding assurances" that there would be no restrictions on "present or future lifting of oil for the U.S. Armed Forces in ships controlled or owned by the U.S. government."

On April 24, Deputy Under Secretary of State Robert Murphy—who had been Bill Eddy's superior during his wartime spy operations in Morocco, when they both reported to Bill Donovan—wrote back to Wilson: "I fully appreciate and share your concern, and that of the Secretary of the Navy and the Joint Chiefs of Staff, over implications of the reported agreement as they affect United States interests. The Department has therefore authorized our Ambassador at Jidda to represent our interest in this matter to the king of Saudi Arabia" and seek the assurances the navy sought.[24]

That was the delicate message that Ambassador Wadsworth was now delivering to King Saud. He said he had been instructed to "refer in particular to the apparent stopping of United States Government tankers (specifically those operated by or under the control of the Maritime Sea Transport Service of the American navy) from lifting at Ras Tanura oil from Saudi Arabian fields; and I am to request Your Majesty's assurance that the transportation of such oil by these tankers will not be affected by this agreement."

Testifying before a Senate committee a few years later, Wadsworth said he had told the king that "we have the largest and most powerful fleet that has ever sailed the seas of the world in the Pacific. Our Navy buys a large proportion of the oil that that fleet uses from Aramco. Our Navy tankers and tankers chartered by our Navy carry off the largest single lot of oil which is bought from your country." He asked that navy fuel supply ships be allowed to continue to fill up at Ras Tanura.

Hearing this, the king told his advisers, "The Ambassador is quite right in bringing this to my attention." To Wadsworth, he said, "Mr. Ambassador, I thank you. Tell your government that your Navy tankers may come as in the past, irrespective of this agreement, and carry oil to your fleet in the Pacific."[25]

That was the only point on which the king gave any ground to Washington during the long dispute that ensued. Otherwise, he was unyielding. "In exercise of its sovereign rights," he said testily, Saudi Arabia would "act as it deemed best in [its] national interest." Wadsworth observed in his report to Washington that Saud "spoke with some heat and, I thought, irritation, not with me but rather, I surmise, because [the] whole matter was distasteful to him."

Wadsworth urged the king to give Aramco a "full hearing to present its views, those of other interested American companies, and broader considerations which had occasioned concern in high circles [of the] world oil industry." The king responded that "the door was always open to Aramco" but that he would "not hesitate" to do anything that was to his country's advantage.[26]

CHAPTER SIX

Oil and the Cold War

When President Eisenhower's National Security Council assembled at the White House on July 22, 1954, the president was at the table. It was time for decisions that only he could make. The agenda was both routine and momentous: to evaluate events unfolding around the world, such as the deteriorating French position in Indochina and the apparent defection to the Soviets of the security chief of West Germany, and to review the strategic picture across the entire Middle East, adopt a comprehensive set of policies and objectives for the region, and order specific actions to achieve those goals. According to the minutes of that meeting, much of Middle East conversation concerned Aristotle Onassis's tanker contract with Saudi Arabia.

The National Security Council, created by Congress in 1947, is "the president's principal forum for considering national security and policy matters with his senior national security advisers and cabinet officials."[1] By law, the membership includes the vice president, the secretaries of state, treasury, and defense, the chairman of the Joint Chiefs of Staff and the director of central intelligence. The president's national security advisor coordinates the group's activities and has his or her own staff at the White House.

Except in sudden emergencies, an official meeting of the NSC's members with the president that culminates in policy directives is not a spontaneous event. It follows weeks or months of review and discussion among the agencies involved and the NSC staff. In the case of the Onassis contract, the subject of those discussions in the months before the White House meeting was not whether to oppose it—opinion on that was unanimous—but how to prevent it from going into effect without alienating King Saud and blowing up relations with Saudi Arabia.

Six days before the meeting, Secretary of State Dulles had stressed his views in a telegram to Ambassador Wadsworth that was almost panicky in tone. He said the matter had been "discussed highest levels" of the State Department and the armed forces, where it had been "agreed USG [the U.S. government] should back companies," as they were beseeching the administration to do. The oil companies, Dulles said, vowed to refuse to service any Onassis-owned ships under the terms of the agreement even though they realized that "shut-down and possible eventual nationalization could result."

"Companies surrender to agreement likely create serious repercussion throughout oil and shipping world from point of view private and public commercial interests," Dulles said. He instructed Wadsworth to "express in manner you deem most effective very serious view we take of whole question and widespread ramifications which may result." One point Wadsworth should make, he said, was that "implementation would result in wide and serious public resentment," not just in the United States but in other countries that did business with Saudi Arabia.

Wadsworth was to make clear that implementation of the agreement would be an "act of bad faith," would be "inconsistent with established practice world commerce," and would violate "principle freedom of seas," damaging commerce worldwide. The government of the United States, Dulles said, "cannot passively acquiesce in establishment such pernicious precedent."[2] Dulles instructed Wadsworth to deliver this message in whatever way he deemed best, but the secretary did not say what actions the Eisenhower administration would take if the king refused to capitulate. That would be up to the president to decide at the upcoming White House meeting.

Despite the assurances that King Saud had given to Wadsworth about the fuel supply for the navy, Admiral Arthur W. Radford, chairman of the Joint Chiefs of Staff, was one of the most vocal officials lined up in opposition to the contract because of its wider implications. At the July 22 meeting, he argued that the contract "represented one of the most unusual steps ever taken in connection with world shipping." If it were implemented, he said, "We could expect all other oil-producing countries, including Venezuela, to follow the lead. In effect, each of these countries would say that everything that is exported out of them must be carried in the flag vessels of one particular country. Such a procedure would change the whole picture of world shipping, greatly to the disadvantage of the United States."[3]

A week earlier, Radford had written in a memo to Defense Secretary Charles E. Wilson that "the adverse implications of this agreement, as it would affect the operations of United States oil companies in the Middle East and the development of the oil resources of that area, appear to require more comprehensive measures than those proposed" in a draft policy paper circulated by the NSC staff.[4] By the time of the July 22 meeting, the NSC staff had accordingly toughened the draft policy statement to include a specific commitment to somehow undo the Onassis contract. That new version was the paper now under discussion with the president.

Eisenhower wanted to know if the United States could muster its economic and diplomatic power to "break" Onassis. "Let the rascal sign his contract and then proceed to break him," he said. His question indicated that he had not been personally briefed about the deal up to that point, or he would have known that the contract had been signed six months earlier.

To that, CIA director Allen Dulles and Treasury Secretary George M. Humphrey "pointed out to the president that Onassis was a dangerous and slippery character, and Secretary Humphrey in particular agreed that the activities of Onassis and other shady characters of his type in the Middle East presented the United States with a very dangerous problem," the official minutes say.

Radford told the president that "Aramco had come to the conclusion it would have to close up its operations in Saudi Arabia if the Onassis contract went through," which was clearly an overstatement, and went beyond the position the Joint Chiefs had taken in inter-agency discussions before this meeting. Radford "also pointed out that our own reserve of U.S. tankers would in this contingency have to go out of business. There would simply be no oil for them to carry if the pattern established in Saudi Arabia established itself in other oil-producing countries."

Eisenhower asked whether the United States could put pressure on the Saudis by purchasing oil from Iran instead. Some of that part of the conversation remains redacted, but this key paragraph is included in the declassified version of the minutes:

Secretary Humphrey "said he didn't know the answer to the problem, but that the United States had to do something or else all the oil in the Middle East will have to be shipped in this Greek's vessels. The President agreed with Secretary Humphrey, and said in any case we could not afford to sit around and get blackmailed. He then inquired where the Saudi Arabian oil was sold" and "why the United States did not do everything in its power to promote the sale of Middle East oil in Europe," another question that revealed how poorly briefed he was on the global oil trade. "Admiral Radford pointed out that 90% of Middle Eastern oil was already going to Europe and that the amount was increasing rapidly, an estimate confirmed by Mr. Allen Dulles." Eisenhower then asked why "friendly nations in Europe could not be induced to close their ports to 'this guy's' ships,'" as Britain had persuaded its allies to do in the Iran episode. "Secretary Humphrey pointed out that this would be very hard to do, as the Greeks were notoriously mobile." Onassis had deliberately made the true ownership of much of his fleet hard to decipher.

After this discussion, the council, with Eisenhower's approval, adopted a slightly modified version of the toughened draft policy statement that the staff had submitted, which specifically called for action to oppose the Onassis contract.

An Official "Statement of Policy"

The next day, James S. Lay Jr., executive secretary of the council, distributed to the members a "Statement of Policy" that embodied everything that they had decided and the president had approved. That document, including the Onassis statement, was designated NSC 5428. The president's signature formalized it.

The assessment of the Middle East that 5428 presented was not encouraging. The president and his advisers saw threats to American strategic, economic, and even religious interests all across the region, most of them attributable to emerging anti-Western sentiment among newly independent people and to the expanding reach of international communism.

"The Near East is of great strategic, political and economic importance to the free world," it began. "The area contains the greatest petroleum resources in the world; essential locations for strategic military bases in any world conflict against Communism; the Suez Canal; and natural defensive barriers. It also contains Holy Places of the Christian, Jewish and Moslem worlds, and cultural influences affecting people everywhere."[5]

Unfortunately, the policy assessment found that "current conditions and trends in the Near East are inimical to Western interests. During recent years the prestige and position of the West have declined. The nations of the Near East are determined to assert their independence and are suspicious of outside interest in their affairs." France and Britain were in disrepute because of their histories as colonizers, it said.

"The security interests of the United States would be critically endangered if the Near East should fall under Soviet influence or control," 5428 asserted. "In the Near East the current danger to the security of the free world arises not so much from the direct threat of Soviet military attack as from a continuation of the present unfavorable trends. Unless these trends are reversed, the Near East may well be lost to the West in the next few years."

The notion that the "Near East"—or any other region of the developing world—could be "lost to the West" seems risible now, six decades later, but at the time the fear of "losing" the region to communism was the overriding motivation driving Washington policy makers. They had watched with growing alarm as threatening events unfolded across the world in the short time since World War II had ended: the Berlin blockade, the communist takeovers of China and Czechoslovakia, the Korean War, the Viet Minh insurgency in Indochina, and the fall of the Egyptian monarchy. In Iraq, a critical oil-producing country at the northern end of the Persian Gulf, the Communist Party was growing rapidly and was believed to be responsible for stirring up popular demonstrations against the monarchy.[6] In neighboring Iran, fear of the rising influence of the communist Tudeh Party had motivated U.S. intervention in the coup of 1953, described by one scholar as "a calculated defense of Western oil assets against nationalist expropriation."[7] The Eisenhower administration suffered from what Senator Frank Church of Idaho would call "the Mossadegh syndrome," after the quirky prime minister who orchestrated the nationalization of Iran's oil industry.

Faced with this alarming scoreboard, the administration laid out in NSC 5428 a long list of "General Objectives," including the "availability to the United States and its allies of the resources, the strategic positions, and the passage rights of the area, and the denial of such resources and strategic positions to the Soviet bloc," the same goal that had given rise to the Denial Plan in the Truman administration.

To achieve those objectives, the policy document set out "General Courses of Action," saying that the United States should, among other things, "assume an increased share of responsibility for the area" and "seek to guide the revolutionary and nationalistic pressures throughout the area into orderly channels not antagonistic to the West, rather than attempt merely to preserve the *status quo*." Another of these "General Courses of Action" was to "win the Arab states to a belief that we sympathize with their legitimate aspirations and respect their interests."

That guidance was consistent with Eisenhower's personal views. The president understood that the era of European colonial empires was ending, and he sympathized with the aspirations for independence among those ruled by Britain, France, and Portugal.

"This Administration has never been antagonistic to Arab nationalism," he wrote to his Washington pastor. "Our own history as well as our sense of justice impels us to support peoples to achieve their own legitimate nationalistic aspirations."[8]

As the historian Roby Barrett wrote, "the new administration intended to chart its own course, and clearly viewed British opposition to emerging national movements and association with London's colonial past as a liability." In Eisenhower's view, U.S. efforts to shore up eroding empires would only damage Washington's standing among the peoples of what came to be known as the Third World and make them receptive to communist blandishments.[9]

The "Eisenhower Doctrine"

These two policies—keep communism out of the Middle East, but recognize and encourage the people's quest for independence and freedom from colonial domination—would coalesce after the Suez crisis of 1956 in the famous "Eisenhower Doctrine" speech to Congress.

"Our country supports without reservation the full sovereignty and independence of each and every nation of the Middle East," the president said, while the greatest threat to their sovereignty and independence was international communism, directed by Moscow. "In the situation now existing, the greatest risk, as is often the case, is that ambitious despots may miscalculate," he said. "If power-hungry Communists should either falsely or correctly estimate that the Middle East is inadequately defended, they might be tempted to use open measures of armed attack. If so, that would start a chain of circumstances which would almost surely involve the United States in military action. I am convinced that the best insurance against this dangerous contingency is to make clear now our readiness to cooperate fully and freely with our friends of the Middle East in ways consonant with the purposes and principles of the United Nations. I intend promptly to send a special mission to the Middle East to explain the cooperation we are prepared to give." He asked Congress for new economic assistance funds for Middle East countries, and for authorization to use force to protect those countries if necessary.[10]

His views were already well in evidence at the time of the Onassis affair. The president rebuffed appeals by British Prime Minister Winston Churchill for joint action to preserve the status quo in the Middle East, where Nasser was demanding the departure of all British troops from Egypt. He considered responding to a French appeal for help in relieving the besieged garrison at Dien Bien Phu, in Indochina, because the Viet Minh were perceived to be communists rather than noncommunist nationalists, but in the end decided it was not worth the risk of drawing China into the fight, as had happened in Korea.[11] The French surrendered on May 7, 1954, raising the anxiety level just as Washington was coming to grips with the full significance of the Onassis contract. In the spring, King Saud went to Cairo for a cordial visit with the troublesome Nasser, and then joined Nasser in denouncing the regional defense agreement known as the Baghdad Pact. At that same time, the CIA was busy organizing the coup that in July would overthrow the leftist Arbenz government in Guatemala, another manifestation of Washington's willingness to interfere abroad where it perceived a threat of communist expansion.

The heartland of the Arabian Peninsula had never been colonized by any country and Saudi Arabia was fully independent from the day it was created, but economically and strategically it was a de facto protectorate of the United States. Eisenhower's acceptance of nationalist sentiment in countries ruled, or formerly ruled, by European powers did not extend to the sole U.S. outpost in Arabia.

In addition to "General Courses of Action" for the region, NSC 5428 laid out "Specific Courses of Action" aimed at individual countries and activities. Among these was item 14b: "The United States should take all appropriate measures to bring about the cancellation of the agreement between the Saudi Arabian government and Onassis for the transport of Saudi Arabian-produced oil and, in any case, to make the agreement ineffective." It would be up to the State and Defense Departments and the CIA to determine what were "appropriate measures."

In the entire nine-page document, Onassis is the only individual mentioned by name.

If any member of Eisenhower's team argued that 14b was incompatible with the "general objectives" of winning the Arabs' friendship by supporting their "legitimate aspirations" and not just supporting the status quo, it is not reflected in the text of 5428 or in the minutes of the White House meeting the day before.

The Soviet Union itself, of course, had nothing to do with the Onassis affair. Moscow may not even have known about it until it was reported in the press because the USSR had no diplomatic relations with Saudi Arabia and no representatives in the kingdom. The USSR had been the first nation to officially recognize the Kingdom of Saudi Arabia when King Abdul Aziz created it in 1932, but the king's loathing of communism, an atheistic doctrine, put an end to bilateral relations in 1938. By 1954, Saudi Arabia's rigid opposition to communism and the Saudis' presumption that it was affiliated with Zionism precluded diplomatic commercial exchanges of any kind with the Soviet Union and its satellites. Moreover, the Soviet Union was more than self-sufficient in oil and had no need for supplies from the Gulf. Yevgeny Primakov, one the Soviet Union's leading Arabists and later intelligence director and foreign minister of post-communist Russia, mentions Saudi Arabia only in passing and Aramco not at all in his book, *Russia and the Arabs*.[12]

After the death of Joseph Stalin in 1953, his Politburo successors abandoned his narrow, inward-looking policy of establishing friendly relations only with, and giving aid only to, countries sympathetic to Soviet ideology. Instead, Moscow decided to offer a hand of friendship and assistance to all the newly independent and developing countries of the postcolonial era, regardless of political orientation, in the hope of eventually winning them over. An official statement from the Soviet Foreign Ministry said that "the Soviet Government will take a positive attitude toward any steps by the governments of the Near and Middle Eastern countries to apply these principles in their relations with the Soviet Union. The Soviet government, supporting the cause of peace, will defend the freedom and independence of the Near and Middle Eastern states and oppose interference in their internal affairs."[13] This new approach would have led to an effort to build ties with Saudi Arabia if the Saudis were receptive, but at the time of the Onassis contract the policy shift had not yet been announced publicly, let alone fully implemented. In any case, Washington's fear of Soviet expansionism predated that shift, as adoption of the Denial Plan under Truman had made clear.

America's Great Red Scare

More than half a century later, it may be difficult for new generations of Americans to grasp the deep conviction of Americans in the Eisenhower and Kennedy eras that the country was locked in an existential struggle against a ruthless Soviet Union bent on world domination that threatened U.S. interests at home and abroad. The United States feared not just Moscow's military power and nuclear weapons, but the communist ideology itself.

Fear of communism extended far beyond the offices of strategic planners in Washington. It penetrated politics, as seen in Senator Joseph McCarthy's inquisitions, and popular culture, as seen in the blacklisting of Hollywood film personalities suspected of communist sympathies. In 1953, the Cincinnati Reds baseball team changed its name to the "Redlegs" so fans would not associate the organization with communists. When a comedian named Vaughn Meader released a hugely popular record album lampooning President John F. Kennedy, Eisenhower's successor, Eisenhower's longtime press secretary, James Hagerty, complained that "every Communist country in the world would love this record," as if satire itself lent encouragement to the Red Menace.[14]

President Truman's administration published, and his successors maintained, a document known as the Attorney General's List of Subversive Organizations, which named dozens of groups and clubs suspected of communist sympathies or disloyalty to the United States. Membership present or past in any of them was grounds for rejecting a job application, not only in the government but in private business. Among the names on the list were the Protestant War Veterans of the United States and the North Philadelphia Forum, along with organizations of people with ethnic affinities such as the Japanese Association of America. Some of the groups were indeed thinly disguised fronts for communist or fascist regimes, and some had been penetrated by communists or communist sympathizers, but none presented any serious threat to the security of the country.[15]

That all-encompassing suspicion and fear of Soviet influence asserted itself within a year after the end of World War II, as the Soviet Union occupied much of Eastern Europe. It was reflected in a statement labeled "Fundamentals of U.S. Policy" written on November 29, 1946, by Gordon Merriam, chief of the State Department's Near East division at the time.

"The fundamentals of our Near Eastern policy," it said, "should be based on the realization that (a) the Near East is a strategic key area of vital importance to this nation, (b) that Russia must be regarded as a potential aggressor and thus it is evident that it is bent on dominating the Near East, (c) that the Near east is too weak in its present state to withstand Russian penetration and gradual absorption."[16] Those sentiments intensified over the following decade as the Soviet Union tightened its grip on Eastern Europe.

In January 1953, a few days before Eisenhower was to assume the presidency, the government's civilian and military intelligence agencies delivered a collective assessment—known as a National Intelligence Estimate—on the subject of "Conditions and Trends in the Middle East Affecting US Security."

The United States and its allies, the report said, had "a specific and basic concern with the extensive oil resources and strategic location of the area." Because the region's governments were generally weak and ineffective, it said, "The USSR will continue to encourage disorder and anti-Westernism and to exploit the substantial opportunities for creating friction among states of the area, between them and the West, and among the Western Powers." Throughout the region, the intelligence assessment said, "There is a general disposition to eliminate the powers that be, with little thought for what comes after." That sentiment derived from "a desire to eliminate foreign influence. The Middle Eastern governments and people are basically suspicious of Western motives and tend to become increasingly nationalist and neutralist."[17]

Saudi Arabia, dependent as it was on the United States, was not entirely immune to those sentiments.

Eisenhower did not need much convincing about the threat of Soviet expansionism; he essentially agreed with the intelligence analysts. In his first two years as president, the notorious Senator McCarthy was in full cry in his witch hunt about communists in the U.S. government. The president found McCarthy personally odious and disapproved of his bullying methods, but he shared the senator's view about the menace of global communism.

"American freedom is threatened so long as the world Communist conspiracy exists in its present scope, power and hostility," he said in his State of the Union Address on January 7, 1954. "More closely than ever before, American freedom is interlocked with the freedom of other people. In the unity of the free world lies our best chance to reduce the Communist threat without war. In the task of maintaining this unity and strengthening all its parts, the greatest responsibility falls naturally on those who, like ourselves, retain the most freedom and strength. We shall, therefore, continue to advance the cause of freedom on foreign fronts."[18] That was three years before he promulgated what came to be known as the Eisenhower Doctrine.

Secretary of State Dulles was fully on board with the president's views.

"The Soviet Communists are planning for what they call 'an entire historical era,' and we should do the same," he said at a meeting of the Council on Foreign Relations a few days after Eisenhower's speech. "They seek, through many types of maneuvers, gradually to divide and weaken the free nations by overextending them in efforts which, as Lenin put it, are 'beyond their strength, so that they come to practical bankruptcy.' Then, said Lenin, 'our victory is assured.' Then, said Stalin, will be 'the moment for the decisive blow.' In the face of this strategy, measures cannot be judged adequate merely because they ward off an immediate danger." He espoused a policy of "massive retaliation" in the event of a Soviet attack.[19]

The Arabs as Targets

Even as the National Security Council was putting together NSC 5428, the government's intelligence organizations were at work on another assessment that would be distributed on September 7, after they had all signed off on it. That document, National Intelligence Estimate 36-54, "Probable Developments in the Arab States," presented the collective assessment of the CIA, the State Department's intelligence unit, and the intelligence commands of the armed forces.

"Communist activity in the Arab states has increased noticeably over the past year," it said. "Continued instability in the area will favor a further increase in Communist activity and strength," although an outright communist takeover of any Arab state was "not likely."

These concerns were not abstractions. According to Peter Hahn, a historian of U.S. Middle East policy, U.S. analysts "interpreted Soviet broadcasts in Middle East media in 1953 about the arrests of prominent Jews in Prague and Moscow as a bid to impress Arab audiences." They were "especially sensitive about apparent Soviet support of a labor strike among oil workers in Dhahran."[20] In truth, there never was any serious communist penetration of Saudi Arabia, before or after the Onassis contract, but officials in Washington worried that there might be.

That was the context in which NSC 5428 was developed. Issued in July of 1954, NSC 5428 did not initiate the U.S. government's campaign against the Onassis contract. It merely gave the president's formal authorization to an effort that had begun in Washington almost as soon as the State Department learned about the deal. From the beginning, the question was not whether to torpedo the Onassis deal; it was how to go about it without embarrassing King Saud or further jeopardizing a bilateral relationship that was already under considerable strain over the Buraimi Oasis dispute, Israel, and the Point Four aid program. The objective was not just to get rid of the SATCO contract but to do it without leaving fingerprints.

CHAPTER SEVEN

The CIA Is on the Case

The Central Intelligence Agency in 1954 was a relatively new organization within the executive branch of the U.S. government. It had been created only seven years earlier, and its role in international affairs was not yet fully defined.

A month after the surrender of Japan ended World War II, President Truman had ordered the dissolution of the Office of Strategic Services (OSS), the global spy agency that had been created when the United States was preparing to enter the conflict. That organization was headed by William "Wild Bill" Donovan, a founding partner of the prominent New York law firm that represented the major oil companies in the Madison antitrust case. Donovan returned to his private law practice after the war.

The United States had no tradition of peacetime intelligence gathering. Truman, like many Americans, believed that in peacetime the United States should not have a full-time civilian intelligence agency. Many of the OSS's 13,000 operatives were not career employees of the government and, like Donovan, soon returned to their professional lives. Those who remained were relocated either to military intelligence units or to the State Department's Bureau of Intelligence and Research, which had no operational component.

As historians at the Central Intelligence Agency later wrote in a history of their organization, "Emerging from World War II as the world's strongest power, the United States was hardly equipped institutionally or temperamentally for world leadership. In the autumn of 1945, many Americans, in and out of government, were not at all eager to wield their nation's power to bring about some new global order. Indeed, many, perhaps most, Americans thought that victory over the Axis powers would in itself ensure peace and stability. In any event, Americans remained confident that the United States would always have enough time and resources to beat back any foreign threat before it could imperil our shores."[1]

The onset of the Cold War soon changed Truman's thinking and that of many members of Congress. It became clear that the United States, willingly or otherwise, had assumed worldwide strategic and economic responsibilities, that a large standing military force would be necessary to keep the peace, and that civilian departments in Washington would require information from all over the world in order to formulate and carry out effective foreign policy.

In January 1946, Truman directed the secretaries of state, war, and the navy to carry out whatever intelligence-gathering activities they deemed necessary to "assure the most effective accomplishment of the intelligence mission related to the national security" and to coordinate those activities through a Director of National Intelligence and a National Intelligence Authority. Military intelligence was to be directed by the army and navy; civilian spy activities were assigned to the Intelligence and Research unit of the State Department, where most of the remaining OSS civilians worked.[2] The assistant secretary in charge of that State Department unit was William A. Eddy, formerly Donovan's OSS agent in North Africa during the Allied landings and after that the senior U.S. diplomat in Saudi Arabia, who by the end of the Truman administration would be working for Aramco. He had been a military intelligence officer in World War I.

During the year after Truman's directives, this cumbersome arrangement became the subject of intense debate in Washington, mostly over the question of whether foreign intelligence activities would be controlled by the military or by civilians and whether it would be desirable to create an independent civilian agency that would deliver intelligence and analysis without political interference. The result was the National Security Act of 1947, which created the Central Intelligence Agency (CIA), formalized the National Security Council as an institution, and united all war planning and management under a new Department of Defense.

The intelligence components of the military services were excluded from the new civilian agency. Most of the new agency's initial personnel were obtained by transfer from Eddy's unit at the State Department.

One of the first products of the new CIA was a classified "Review of the World Situation As It Relates to the Security of the United States." It put into unequivocal language what became the foundation of U.S. foreign policy for the next several decades: the Soviet Union presented the greatest threat to international security and U.S. interests, and must be confronted.

The opening lines said, "Among foreign powers, only the U.S.S.R. is capable of threatening the security of the United States. The U.S.S.R. is presently incapable of military aggression outside of Europe and Asia, but is capable of overrunning most of continental Europe, the Near East, northern China, and

Korea." War had "obliterated" the power of Japan and Germany, this assessment said, and curtailed the power of Britain. China was in disarray. Therefore, "the balance of power which restrained the U.S.S.R. from 1921 to 1941 has ceased to exist. The only effective counterpoise to the power of the Soviet Union is that of the United States, which is both latent and remote."[3] This was, in effect, a declaration of war—not a shooting war, which the Soviet Union was then incapable of undertaking, but a war of economics and ideology. The Cold War had begun.

The New Spy Agency

The primary functions of the new CIA were to gather, analyze, and disseminate intelligence. As described in an agency history, the director of this civilian organization was authorized to deploy personnel for "operational" purposes, but those were not described or defined. With the arrival of the Eisenhower administration, the agency's "operational" profile was swiftly elevated.

"After January 1953," the agency historian wrote, "the CIA served a president who clearly understood the agency, a man who had become accustomed to the use of intelligence in tactical and strategic roles during a military career dating back to 1915." In Allen W. Dulles, whom Eisenhower appointed as CIA director, the agency had "a strong and charismatic leader with experience in diplomacy and policymaking," who fully agreed with the early agency assessment of the Soviet threat.[4]

A special U.S. Senate committee created after the Watergate and domestic spying scandals of the 1970s to review the CIA's history and actions found that "by the close of the Korean war, a broad consensus had developed about the nature of Soviet ambitions and the need for the United States to respond. Gradually, the Soviet Union was perceived as posing a worldwide political threat. In the minds of government officials, members of the press, and the informed public, the Soviets would try to achieve their purposes by the penetration and subversion of governments all over the world. The accepted role of the United States was to prevent that expansion."

The committee concluded that "Dulles's marked orientation toward clandestine activities, his brother's position as Secretary of State, and cold war tensions combined to maximize the Agency's operational capability. In terms of policymakers' reliance on the CIA, allocation of resources, and the attention of the Agency's leadership, clandestine activities had overtaken intelligence analysis as the CIA's primary mission."

Moreover, Allen Dulles's role as director of Central Intelligence "was rooted in his wartime experience with OSS," the Senate report said. "His interests and expertise lay with the operational aspects of intelligence, and his fascination with the details of operations continued." He knew all about, and admired, the brilliantly terrifying spy and sabotage missions that OSS agents, including Bill Eddy, had carried out during the war. In essence, the agency's mission under Dulles was not just to obtain information but to act on it.[5]

"Project Twixt"

Some of the clandestine ventures that the CIA undertook in this operational role were by their nature controversial, and possibly illegal in the countries where they were carried out. If discovered, they might have ignited congressional fury, provoked foreign policy crises, and exposed individuals to punishment, even death. "While our citizens may take pride in the solid front of high morality which our nation presents, they can also sleep more easily at night knowing that behind this front, we are in fact capable of matching the Soviets perfidy for perfidy," Miles Copeland observed in his classic, cynical book, *The Game of Nations*.[6]

To carry out these missions, the CIA deployed three groups of people: its own full-time operatives; citizens of other countries who were recruited to provide information; and a network of part-time contractors for whom the agency could deny responsibility if their work was exposed.

Of this last group, the most controversial was a private investigator named Robert A. Maheu, to whom the CIA would assign the task of undoing the Onassis contract.

As Washington's strategy developed, the State Department's job would be to use conventional diplomatic channels to try to persuade King Saud to abandon the agreement. From the beginning, the department coordinated this work with the oil companies. The CIA's mission was to undercut and embarrass Onassis, to expose his payments to Saudi government officials, and to squeeze him financially by sabotaging his worldwide business ventures. Maheu's assignment, he testified years later, was "to make sure that no oil was ever shipped under the contract, and ultimately scuttle the contract."[7]

The operation was code-named Project Twixt. To expedite it, the CIA arranged for Maheu to have what it called "Operational Security Clearance" because he would be deployed in a "highly sensitive manner" and the agency would need to be able to contact him.[8]

Robert A. Maheu (1919–2008) was one of the most shadowy and controversial figures of his time. A Google search of his name in 2017 produced 232,000 results. He is probably best remembered today as the manager of Howard Hughes's Las Vegas casino business, which he ran from 1955 to 1970 without ever meeting the eccentric billionaire—they communicated only by telephone and memorandum. But many of those Google hits are references to Maheu's involvement, or alleged involvement, in one shady undertaking after another, especially his role as go-between in the CIA's attempt to enlist Las Vegas mobsters in a plot to assassinate Cuban president Fidel Castro.[9] A 1973 internal CIA memo about that assassination plot said that "Robert A. Maheu, a cleared source of the Office of Security, was contacted, briefed generally on the project, and requested to ascertain if he could develop an entrée into the gangster elements as the first step toward accomplishing the desired goal."[10]

It has long been established from reams of declassified documents and congressional hearings that it was Maheu who recruited a mobster named Johnny Roselli to organize the Castro assassination plot. The CIA gave Maheu that assignment because he knew Roselli, to whom he had been introduced by his old friend Edward Bennett Williams, the renowned Washington lawyer. The agency authorized Maheu to offer Roselli $100,000 (or, by some accounts, $150,000) to take on the mission.[11] Maheu died in 2008, but even today he is a favorite topic of Kennedy assassination buffs, often linked to the infamous investigation by Jim Garrison, the New Orleans district attorney. A day spent tracking down references to Maheu in online archives turns up links, genuine or not, to every conspiracy and scandal of his time, including the Alger Hiss case and Watergate.

Over 20 years, the CIA entrusted Maheu with dubious covert missions on which it did not wish to leave its own fingerprints.

When public and congressional outrage over the scandals of the Watergate era forced the CIA in the 1970s to evaluate itself and its operations, its internal security division assembled memos the agency had produced about Maheu over the preceding two decades. Now mostly declassified, they recount Maheu's involvement in everything from the Castro plot to a public-opinion assessment of Jimmy Hoffa, president of the Teamsters Union. Maheu, one of the CIA memos said, is "a reputable private investigator" who "is known to and has been utilized by the Agency on several occasions."[12] The Onassis affair was the first of those "occasions."

A CIA biography, written for internal use in response to those congressional inquiries, gives an apparently straightforward account of how Maheu came to be associated with the agency and to be its partner in the Onassis affair.

Maheu was born in a small town in Maine, went to college at Holy Cross, and then studied law at Georgetown. His debate partner at Holy Cross and later classmate at Georgetown Law was Edward Bennett Williams. They would remain friends throughout Williams's career as the most powerful lawyer in Washington, representing famous clients in high-profile cases, including Senator McCarthy. Maheu once joined Williams on a clandestine expedition to Italy, where they secretly dug up evidence in a murder case that resulted in an astonishing acquittal for a Williams client.[13]

Maheu began his professional life as an FBI agent during World War II. According to the CIA biography, "He was employed as a Special Agent from 1940 to 1947, and upon resigning from the Bureau, formed a private enterprise doing business as 'Dairy Dream Products.' This venture culminated in bankruptcy in 1952. He then re-entered government service with the Small Business Administration in Washington, D.C. and was appointed Special Assistant to the Administrator with the specific duty of director of security. In February of 1954 he was forced to resign from the SBA because of political reasons," namely that he had supported Democrat Adlai Stevenson against Eisenhower in the 1952 presidential election. "He then set up his own investigative organization known as Robert A. Maheu Associates." February 1954 happened to be the same month in which Onassis was arrested and a few weeks after the signing of his Saudi tanker contract.[14]

As head of his own firm, Maheu began a long and lucrative career in which the interests of his private clients and the interests of the CIA frequently overlapped; sometimes his client was the agency itself, when it wanted some assignment done that would have caused a scandal if the CIA's role became known. The CIA, in fact, was one of his first clients.

The in-house CIA biography, prepared in 1976, said that Maheu "was recruited by the Office of Security in March of 1954. He was previously known to Mr. Robert H. Cunningham (deceased) who was, at that time, Chief, Special Security Division, through their mutual employment by the FBI. Cunningham saw in Maheu a covert asset who could be utilized by the Office in extremely sensitive cases. With the approval of the Director of Security, Subject [Maheu] was offered a proposition wherein he was to receive $500 per month, with the stipulation that he move into his own office and that he be on call for any assignments by the Office of Security. He agreed to this" and rented his own desk space in the office of another former FBI agent.[15]

Maheu later testified that after he rented his own office in Washington, the CIA sometimes used it as cover for operations. Maheu said he did not know what those operations were; his role was to disguise the agents as employees of Robert A. Maheu Associates and pay their salaries, for which he was reimbursed by the agency.[16]

In 1966, when a separate U.S. Senate subcommittee was planning to subpoena Maheu on another matter, the agency's assistant deputy director of security, James P. O'Connell, was asked to assess the possible impact Maheu's testimony might have on the agency.

"Mr. Maheu has been utilized by the Office of Security on many sensitive assignments since the early 1950s," O'Connell wrote. "We were wholly responsible for the relationship. It was on our initiative that Maheu was originally contacted in 1953. At that time he was just starting out as a private investigator with little capital and rented desk space in lieu of an office. Bob Cunningham, realizing our need for a covert assist, suggested to Colonel [Sheffield] Edwards that we subsidize Maheu to assist him to get on his feet. In turn, we expected services as required." Edwards was the CIA's director of security.[17]

When his role in the Onassis case was reported publicly, Maheu denied that he was on the CIA payroll, as did the agency. He was not on the payroll in the sense that he was not a full-time employee of the U.S. government, but the truth was that he was on retainer from the beginning. O'Connell's memo described the campaign against Onassis as a "joint venture" with him.

According to Jim Hougan's book *Spooks*, a study of the CIA's use of private citizens as covert agents, Maheu's firm was the prototype of the television series "Mission Impossible," about covert operations carried out by agents who know their affiliation with the agency will be denied if they are exposed.

Hougan said many of Maheu's clients were legitimate businesses, but many of the assignments his agency undertook were "dirty work, involving prostitution, pornography, illegal wiretaps, assassination, and a lot more."[18]

When President Sukarno of Indonesia was planning a visit to the United States in 1958, for example, the CIA decided to capitalize on his "weakness for women" to extract information from him. According to an internal CIA memo, Soviet agents had been successful with Sukarno in this manner and the agency "believed he may let down [his] guard and become expansive in discussion of plans with a female and accept advice that he would not ordinarily accept from a man."

Maheu was assigned to "Locate [an] intelligent, attractive, emotionally stable, and trustworthy female who would accept assignment that would involve eventual intimate relationship with Sukarno." He produced a "well to do widow, approximately 35 years old, resident of [redacted], considered highly intelligent and extremely attractive." He also arranged to have her paid by the producer of the movie "Journey to the Center of Earth" to scout locations for filming. The agency sent a female agent to New York with her, ostensibly as her secretary.[19]

A former associate of Maheu's who had fallen out with him said the Sukarno episode represented a violation of the Mann Act, the law that makes it a crime to transport a woman across a state line for prostitution or other "immoral purposes," but even if that was correct the government had no desire to make such a case because Maheu had acted at the CIA's request.[20]

It is not clear that Maheu himself ever did anything actually illegal, though he certainly tried to induce others to commit crimes. At one point Sam Giancana, a mobster who believed that his girlfriend—Phyllis McGuire, of the popular singing trio the McGuire Sisters—was having an affair with the

The CIA Is on the Case

comedian Dan Rowan, asked Maheu to tap the phone in Rowan's Las Vegas hotel room. The technician hired by Maheu to install the equipment was caught in the act. The Department of Justice announced its intent to prosecute Maheu along with the technician, but Robert F. Kennedy, then U.S. Attorney General, quashed the case at the request of the CIA. (Among Giancana's lawyers was Maheu's longtime friend Edward Bennett Williams.)[21]

"The wiretap was stupid anyway," Maheu said later, "because Rowan wasn't going to be talking on the phone while making love."[22]

Thus Maheu was never convicted of any crime, but he developed an unsavory reputation, except among his admirers in the CIA. A British scholar who studied his record observed that "by any stretch of the imagination, Maheu is a rather sinister fellow."[23] FBI Director J. Edgar Hoover said he was "astonished" when he learned of the Castro plot "in view of the bad reputation of Maheu."[24] Howard Hughes himself said in telephone conversation with reporters in 1972 that he fired Maheu because he was "a no-good, dishonest son-of-a-bitch, and he stole me blind."

For that, Maheu sued Hughes for defamation and won a judgment at trial, but the damage award was later thrown out by a federal appeals court. The judge who wrote the opinion called Maheu a liar.[25]

The appeals court ruled that the trial judge erred in his instructions to the jury when he offered these observations about Maheu's testimony:

> Now, ladies and gentlemen, the credibility of a witness is important. The most important live witness that we have heard from in this case is Mr. Maheu. To me Robert A. Maheu is an enigma, a puzzlement. On one hand he can be described as affable, intelligent, imaginative, articulate. He is a friendly man with important friends in high places. He has enormous energy and drive and the ability to get things done. Apparently, it was because of these assets that Robert Maheu served as Howard Hughes' ambassador-at-large. Looked at from another angle, Mr. Maheu appears to be talkative, somewhat naive, artless, careless, imprecise. An overly-trusting man whose personal affairs were in a state of disarray. Although Mr. Butler, the tax lawyer, described his client Maheu as a walking calamity, I would describe him as a walking paradox. Undoubtedly he is possessed of some unusual talents, but like all men he has his share of foibles.

The appellate court, in an opinion written by Judge Ben G. Duniway, ruled that the trial judge had prejudiced the jury in Maheu's favor because his instructions directed the jury's attention to Maheu's "assets" and "unusual talents." What the trial record really showed, Judge Duniway wrote, was that Maheu had been a "lying, prevaricating, equivocating, mendacious, dishonest, deceitful, untruthful, tergiversating witness."

Maheu's Other Client

Maheu's retainer arrangement with the CIA was newly in place when his fledgling agency signed up a lucrative client from the world of private business: Stavros Niarchos. According to the CIA biography, "Maheu was engaged by 'British shipping interests' to check on Aristotle Onassis' activities while in the United States. This included technical coverage of Onassis' New York office"—that is, tapping the telephone. "It was later learned that the principal 'British interest' was Stavros Niarchos and that the ultimate goal of this task was to scrap the Onassis/Saudi oil deal. Maheu took the job but conditioned his acceptance [on] the fact that he would do nothing inimical to the U.S. Government. Any information developed of interest to the United States was to be passed by Maheu to the appropriate government agency. During this operation Maheu had his staff prepare a paper citing dangers to the U.S. economy and trade resulting from the Onassis deal."

Maheu, the CIA narrative said, had unspecified "contacts" in the government's Foreign Operations Administration, a short-lived agency established by Eisenhower to coordinate U.S. operations overseas. At the time, the director of this agency was Harold Stassen, a well-connected Republican politician who unsuccessfully sought his party's presidential nomination nine times. According to the CIA biography, which was written years later, at Maheu's behest "Stassen read his paper about dangers of the Onassis contract at a White House National Security Council meeting on 22 June 1954."

That NSC meeting actually took place on July 22, not June 22. In the minutes, one paragraph in the discussion of the Onassis contract begins with the words, "Governor Stassen suggested" but the rest of the passage remains redacted.[26] It is clear, however, that the Maheu document figured in the White House discussions that led to the adoption of NSC 5428 because the NSC's findings adopted many of the points Maheu later said the paper contained.

Maheu described the paper's contents in his testimony before the "Senate Select Committee to Study Government Operations With Respect to Intelligence Activities," created in the 1970s to examine the CIA's past misconduct. It was known as the Church Committee after its chairman, Senator Frank Church, an Idaho Democrat. Maheu testified that

> Our statistics, after having studied the contract and making what we considered proper projections, indicated that at the completion of approximately five and a half years, Mr. Onassis would control more deadweight tonnage than the United States controlled in its entirety, that he would control on the high seas annually more oil by tens of thousands of gallons than were used by all of the Allied nations during the most severe year of the Korean War, that in the first year his profit would be approximately

$17 million, [and] that after five and a half years his annual profit would be in the area of $200 million. While this analysis was going on, we also found that a million-dollar payoff to one of the top ministers in Saudi Arabia had been made and we had the evidence [rest of sentence redacted.] We then prepared our inputs and presented them to the National Security Council.[27]

Archivists and researchers at the Eisenhower Presidential Library in Kansas, at the National Archives, and at the Minnesota Historical Society, repository of Stassen's papers, have been unable to find the actual paper Stassen read, but there is little doubt that Maheu's summary of its contents was accurate because its arguments were reflected in the NSC's deliberations.

"There were also other inputs about the background of Mr. Onassis that I would just as soon not make a matter of record, but they were none too favorable," Maheu testified. This information was provided to the NSC in oral briefings, not in writing, he said.

The CIA biography adds that "During this same period Maheu briefed Scott McLeod, Assistant Secretary of State for Security and Consular Affairs, on the project." McLeod, with the approval of Secretary of State Dulles, agreed to give Maheu access to State Department communications facilities and diplomatic pouches.

The Stassen paper was not Maheu's only channel to the highest levels of the administration. The CIA biography notes, without elaboration, that "additionally, Maheu briefed J. Edgar Hoover and Vice President [Richard M.] Nixon." Nixon evidently knew a great deal about Onassis because he had been a member of the Senate Permanent Subcommittee on Investigations, which had looked into the surplus ship deals. Some conspiracy theorists—including *Spooks* author Jim Hougan—have written that Nixon orchestrated Maheu's entire campaign against Onassis and went so far as to authorize Maheu to kill him. No records at the National Archives and no documents declassified by the CIA support that claim. A report compiled by researchers at the University of Essex, England, for the family of Abdullah Sulaiman said that "Maheu instituted wiretaps on Onassis telephone calls in an operation involving some of the figures who were later to feature in the Watergate scandal, with the tacit endorsement of Richard Nixon."[28] The British writer Peter Evans, who interviewed Maheu, went considerably further. He wrote that Maheu told him that he met with Nixon, who said, "If it turns out we have to kill the bastard, just don't do it on American soil."[29]

Niarchos's London solicitor and his New York office put him together with Maheu. According to Maheu, these representatives told him that Niarchos was seeking only to protect Western interests in the Middle East and maintain the current commercial arrangements there, but that was not the real motivation. "You didn't have to be Einstein to know that this was about two guys who loathed each other's guts, and would cut each other's throats for a dollar," he said.[30]

It is not entirely clear how Niarchos chose Maheu, but the probable conduit was Alfred C. Ulmer, a veteran U.S. intelligence operative who during this period was the CIA station chief in Athens. At the time, Niarchos was "regarded as one of the CIA's best assets in Greece [and] had gone out of his way to be helpful to Ulmer," according to Peter Evans.[31]

Jim Hougan wrote that "some of Maheu's supposedly private clients—Greek shipping magnate Stavros Niarchos may be a case in point—were themselves fronting for the Agency in their relations with the Maheu firm." That suspicion was confirmed at least in part by sworn testimony in 1975 from CIA general counsel Lawrence R. Houston, who said he had not been involved personally in the Onassis case but "we had some contacts, direct or indirect, with both of them. Both were sources of useful information, that is, Niarchos and Onassis."[32]

When Houston at one point reviewed the relationship with Maheu for an internal CIA inquiry, he reported to the agency's deputy director that "Maheu was at no time employed or directed by the agency in connection with this episode." That may have been technically true, but it was misleading. Maheu developed his own tactics in the campaign against Onassis, and his specific actions were not directed by the CIA, but he was on retainer and was carrying out a mission that the agency gave him.

When an excerpt from Jim Hougan's book was published in 1978, Maheu acknowledged that he had been on retainer to the CIA; he said he would not have taken the assignment from Niarchos without the agency's consent, and that he informed the CIA regularly about the progress of his anti-Onassis campaign.[33] But according to CIA records, it was not until August 1954, several months after taking on the CIA assignment, that he informed the agency that his client, the "British shipping interests," was Stavros Niarchos. The section of the CIA biography that recounted what Maheu said about that relationship was redacted and remains classified.[34]

Maheu himself testified that the initial contact was with a lawyer from London whom he knew only as "Tim Tyler," a popular comic strip character. The lawyer did not identify his client, who he learned later was Niarchos. "Tyler" told Maheu that he had come to the United States looking for an agent to take on the assignment to undo the Onassis contract, and that Maheu had been recommended to him by another former FBI agent named Robert C. Gresham, a well-connected Washington Republican.[35]

According to the O'Connell memo of 1966, Onassis's Saudi "achievement caused much consternation among the British, German, and American interests." That internal report also said that "Niarchos also realized as a result of this, the balance of power and influence weighed heavily in favor of Onassis in their own private battle. It was this mutual concern of the United States and Niarchos that set the stage for a joint venture. Niarchos supplied the money, personnel, and documents; the Agency furnished the communications, courier facilities, and direction in the form of our Commo channel [and] pouch system, and NEA Division's expertise and guidance."[36] NEA was the State Department's division of Near East Affairs.

Maheu told the CIA about his arrangement with Niarchos, but it is not clear from the declassified documents that Maheu ever informed Niarchos about his relationship with the CIA. It is probable that Niarchos knew. The Onassis biographer Peter Evans, who interviewed Maheu, wrote that Niarchos selected Maheu "under orders from the CIA."[37]

CHAPTER EIGHT

A Two-Tier Strategy

President Eisenhower's July 1954 endorsement of NSC 5428, the National Security Council's strategy document and plan of action for the Middle East, gave the full weight of the president's authority to his administration's campaign to undo the contract between Onassis and Saudi Arabia. That effort had been developing ever since Ambassador Wadsworth alerted the State Department in February.

When he first learned of the Onassis contract, in early February 1954, the ambassador told Washington that he had asked King Saud for permission to "obtain further information" about the contract from Finance Minister Abdullah Sulaiman because Aramco knew only the content of Article IV. The king agreed to that, but he balked when Wadsworth offered to set up an oil company briefing for "appropriate Saudi officials" and the king himself about the "implications [of the] agreement and its effect on Saudi Arabian interests." The king said they should take it up with Finance Minister Sulaiman, who had negotiated the terms of the agreement.[1]

In testimony before two U.S. Senate committees three years later, Wadsworth was less diplomatic about U.S. reaction to the Onassis contract. "Our government [and] every maritime government in the world . . . rose in horror at such a thought," he said. "The right of the buyer to choose his carrier, and the concessionary rights of Aramco, which included the exclusive right to export the oil, seemed violated."[2]

The State Department's first response to Wadsworth's cable was a brief message dated February 9, 1954, informing him of "press reports" that Onassis had been indicted in the surplus ship fraud case. In the truncated language of diplomatic cables, the department suggested that "You might wish bring this attention Saudi Arabia government."[3] That was the first sign of a two-front administration strategy that quickly emerged: (1) attack the

A Two-Tier Strategy

contract on its legal merits and its economic implications and (2) depict Onassis as an unworthy partner for the Saudis.

State Department archives indicate that the first official meeting in Washington on the subject of the Onassis contract was conducted on March 16, 1954, by John D. Jernegan, deputy assistant secretary for Near East Affairs. Deputy assistant secretary, or DAS, may not sound like an important title, but in the State Department system such a position is usually held by a well-regarded career diplomat who is sufficiently senior to do much of the actual work on any issue. Jernegan reported to assistant secretary Henry Byroade.

Jernegan's guest at the March 16 meeting was Robert L. L. McCormick, who was a partner with Charles B. Coates in a public relations firm, Coates and McCormick Inc. Both partners had held senior positions in the Hoover Commission, formally known as the Commission on Organization of the Executive Branch of Government, a group appointed by President Truman to recommend administrative revisions in the federal bureaucracy. It was named for its chairman, former president Herbert Hoover. McCormick was later director of research for the Republican National Committee. His résumé was that of a fully qualified member of the Washington establishment, those people who move easily in and out from government to politics to the law to the influence business and have access to the officials who make decisions.

McCormick told Jernegan that he represented Stavros Niarchos, and that Niarchos and Onassis, though related by marriage, were "violent competitors." He said that Niarchos, although under indictment himself in the surplus-ship cases, wanted to help the U.S. government undo the Onassis contract because, if ratified by King Saud, it would be "most unfortunate not only for American oil companies but for the United States government, from a strategic point of view."[4]

McCormick was hardly overstating the intensity of Niarchos's loathing of Onassis. "Everything between my father and Ari was personal," Niarchos's son Constantine told one of Onassis's biographers. "They goaded each other endlessly. I don't think the Jidda deal in itself bothered my father too much, but it was a great coup for Ari and he was determined to stop it, just as Ari would have been if the shoe had been on the other foot."[5]

At the time of that meeting, the text of the Onassis contract with the Saudis had not been made public; the oil company and the State Department had seen only Article IV. Niarchos, however, knew the details of the rest of it because his sister-in-law, Onassis's wife Tina, seeking revenge for her husband's many affairs, had slipped him a copy.[6]

McCormick reported that Onassis had "signed a loan agreement with the National City Bank and the Metropolitan Life Insurance Company to finance the necessary tankers that were to be built for the shipment of Saudi oil." The financing contract, he said, would allow the ships to fly the flags of any of four countries, the United States, Honduras, Liberia, or Panama, but that provision conflicted with a clause in Onassis's contract with the Saudis stipulating that they be registered in and fly the flag of Saudi Arabia. Niarchos recommended that the State Department approach the lenders and "suggest to them that it would not displease the department if they were to refuse to change their present registry requirements and that it would be preferable if they were to cancel" the loan agreement.

Jernegan said the department would be reluctant to do that because it wanted to avoid direct intervention. He said it would be preferable that "the Saudis themselves realize the unfortunate effects" of the Onassis contract—that is, that the king would come to see the wisdom of dropping it and not feel that he had been bullied by the United States.[7] His answer reflected the State Department's concern that it not be seen to take the lead on undoing the contract because relations with Saudi Arabia were already strained over other issues. Nevertheless, the question of the tankers' registry was now on the table.

McCormick did not tell Jernegan, and probably did not know, that at about the time of this meeting, his client, Niarchos, had already hired Robert Maheu to go after Onassis, or that Maheu at the same time had signed on with the CIA to make himself useful in clandestine operations.

More Money for Alireza

At this early point in the drama, Aramco and its friends in Washington faced two handicaps as they planned their strategy. First, they had not yet seen any of the terms of the Onassis contract except for Article IV, of which they had been informed by Finance Minister Sulaiman, and thus did not know what other potential for damage it contained. Second, it was not clear whether King Saud had formally ratified the contract, or would do so, and therefore they did not know how much firepower to unleash on him. If he had decided not to ratify it, the oil companies did not wish to criticize him, or the contract, so strongly that he became angry and changed his mind. If the king was still on the fence, they did not wish to push him so that he came down on the wrong side.

Voice of America and the BBC reported in February that Onassis himself had met with King Saud to obtain his formal approval. But a government newspaper in Mecca, *Al Bilad al-Saudiyah*, quoted "an official spokesman of the Saudi foreign office" as saying no such thing had happened, adding that "it would have been better if certain broadcasting stations did not transmit information on such important matters before being certain of fact." U.S. diplomats in Jeddah said Aramco officials were pleased by the news reports but skeptical—they did not believe it was really over.[8] Their skepticism was justified.

A Two-Tier Strategy

The cause of the delay in royal ratification was not reluctance on the part of King Saud. On the contrary, the king told Aramco's Floyd Ohliger he welcomed the deal because it "did not contravene" the original concession agreement, would not harm the oil company or his country financially, and would benefit the kingdom through the training of Saudi seamen.[9]

What held up ratification was first, a demand by Abdullah Alireza for yet more money, and second, a demand by Saudi officials that a clause be added to the contract that would exclude Israel or Israelis from participating or benefiting in any way. In addition, some of the king's advisers were also beginning to have, if not second thoughts, at least a sobering understanding of the seriousness of the arguments they were hearing from Aramco and U.S. officials that the shipping rate provision of Article IV was unenforceable because no oil purchasers chartering tankers would accept it. That article might require renegotiation.

According to Spyridon Catapodis, the original broker of the tanker contract, when Onassis returned to Paris in March 1954 after his court proceedings in Washington, the two met to discuss the status. Catapodis, in a sign of the complete rupture to come, complained that Onassis had not "paid me the monies which he had promised to pay to me when the agreement was signed."[10] The contract had indeed been signed, but Onassis was still not sure of any return on the payouts he had already made to Alireza because the king had not ratified it. Obtaining that royal seal of approval was the next urgent step. Onassis and his New York–based business manager, Nicolas Cokkinis, flew to Jeddah to seek to expedite issuance of the required royal decree. Once again, Mohammed Alireza was the conduit to the king.

Alireza—who by this time was minister of commerce in King Saud's government, as well as Onassis's agent—delivered bad news. According to Catapodis, he "informed [Onassis and Cokkinis] that in order to expedite the royal decree, it would be necessary for Onassis to pay Mohammed Alireza a further 200,000 dollars to bribe a number of palace officials who are close to the king." Alireza "further informed Onassis that the royal decree would be issued as soon as this sum of money had been deposited to his account in Zurich."

Back in France, Onassis told Catapodis that he was "extremely furious with this further unreasonable demand" because he had already paid Alireza £325,000. He said he had reluctantly agreed to pay what Alireza asked because that was the only way to ensure that the decree would be issued, but now he was having second thoughts and had decided to pay only $100,000, half the amount demanded.

Catapodis, in his self-serving but mostly verifiable account of these events, said he told Onassis that if he had agreed to pay $200,000 he should do so. Onassis consented grudgingly, and on April 7 deposited the requested sum in Alireza's account, asking that the Zurich bankers inform their client by cable that the money had been paid.

On that same day, the contract was amended to deal with the shipping rate issue and the Israel question. For some reason, Onassis insisted that the text also be amended to specify that this was not just any Mr. Onassis but "Mr. Aristotle Socrates Onassis, of Greek birth and Argentine nationality, a resident of Montevideo and domiciled in Paris at 88 Rue Foch."[11] Two days later, on April 9, the king issued the decree that gave it the force of law.[12]

In the version of this tale given to Aramco by Leon Turrou—the former FBI agent whom Onassis had consulted about his indictment, who was also a friend of Catapodis—the king's council of ministers voted nine to four in favor of ratifying the revised contract. "It was Abdullah Sulaiman's strong endorsement and support which produced the affirmative vote," over the objections of Crown Prince Faisal, Turrou said.

Turrou said that in addition to the payments to the Saudis, Onassis had delivered a substantial contribution "to arrange to have a letter sent by the Greek Patriarch to the King of Saudi Arabia extolling the virtues of Onassis and pointing out how firmly the ties would be cemented between Greece and Arabia if the deal were concluded."[13]

Once the king had issued his ratifying decree, Onassis wrote to Abdullah Sulaiman to lay out his understanding of what exactly was to happen to ensure implementation.

"Upon receipt of this letter," he wrote, the Saudi government "will take the necessary measures to issue and publish the decree," and "within a month" will order the oil companies to "make the necessary arrangements" to carry it out. If the oil companies balked, Onassis wrote, he and the Saudi government would work together to persuade them to submit. If consultations failed, "the Government will consult with me for the purpose of considering the possibility of suing the concession company or companies" that would not go along. "If it is decided to sue such concession company or companies individually, the Government will agree with me upon the method by which this suit will be undertaken, so as to safeguard the interests of both parties"—that is, the interests of Onassis and the royal government, not those of the oil companies.[14]

According to Aramco's lawyers, "This letter strikingly reveals Onassis' true intent to seize *control* of Aramco's business by stretching himself across Aramco's lifeline, from the producing areas in Saudi Arabia to the outside markets where he would permit movement only on *his* terms. Is it any wonder that Aramco would have none of it?"[15]

The Saudi government did not give the royal ratification document directly to Aramco or to the U.S. embassy. It had the text published, in Arabic, in its official gazette, *Umm al Qura*, on June 7.[16] The decree ordered that the agreement go into effect immediately.

Ambassador Wadsworth sent an English version to the State Department, attaching this cautionary advisory from James Terry Duce, Aramco's vice president for government relations: "I believe this matter is of critical importance not only to us but to the whole industry . . . I believe that if [the] contract says what we have reason to believe it says, we should consider notifying SAG [the Saudi Arabian government] we may be forced to cut back production to [the] amount which can be lifted by parent company tankers." Those tankers would be permitted to continue transporting oil until they were retired from the fleet if they had been engaged in that traffic before December 31, 1953. Duce's message presaged an argument that Aramco and U.S. diplomats would make often in the weeks to come: Saudi Arabia's revenue would go down, not up, because Aramco would cut production and buyers would go elsewhere.[17]

The King Wants a Yacht

According to Turrou, royal ratification still did not end Alireza's demands on Onassis. Alireza told Catapodis that "it was important that Onassis give the King a yacht and asked if he knew where one was available." Catapodis said he knew of one that had been built recently for the king of Cambodia for £500,000, had been little used, and was now on the market for £175,000.

Alireza said it was "very important that the yacht be presented to the King because, if the King ever found out that Mohamed [Alireza] and others had received something personally from this deal, he wanted to be in a position to point out to the King that the latter would have difficulty in convincing anyone he had been given a yacht because Onassis liked the color of his eyes." That is to say, if the king himself was complicit in what would look like corruption, presumably he would not blame Alireza if the story became public.

In June 1954, when Turrou told this tale, the yacht had not yet been purchased, "presumably because Onassis is becoming progressively less sure of the strength of the deal." Turrou did not say why he thought so.[18]

It is equally possible that Onassis did not purchase the yacht because he did not have as much money as everyone thought he did. Catapodis told Turrou that, despite published reports setting Onassis's wealth at $300 million, "if Onassis sold every asset he owns, including Monte Carlo, he might have as much as $20 million."

A yacht—possibly a different one from that of the king of Cambodia—did eventually make its way to Saudi Arabia. A British embassy official reported in November that it had been "somehow obtained from Onassis in the summer. It was formerly on Italian register and belonged to one Eugenides, who is said to be connected, by marriage, I think, with Onassis and Niarchos. It was commonly assumed here that Onassis had given this to the king as a present. It now turns out, however, that it was actually given or sold to Mohammed Alireza, who undertook to have the king accept it." Whoever was the actual owner, this official noted, "The very existence of the yacht certainly strengthens the allegations that someone has been taking favours. It all seems a much shadier deal than was even suspected at the beginning."[19]

According to Robert I. Brougham, the senior Aramco executive who reported this conversation with Turrou to company chairman Fred Davies, "With the story thus concluded, I asked Turrou what Spiros wanted of the company. Turrou replied that we would never persuade the King or Faisal of the truth of the matter without documentary evidence; that Spiros has documentary evidence—originals and photostat copies of all the documents, including side agreements [and] cancelled checks. Spiros is prepared to furnish a sworn statement outlining all the above information. He said Spiros has expended about £35.000 of his personal funds in connection with his trips to Arabia in order to negotiate the deal; that Spiros would expect to negotiate some figure with the company in return for making available the foregoing documentary evidence."

Those expenses should have been reimbursed by Onassis, but Catapodis said he was revealing this information because he had not been paid.

Brougham responded that Aramco "had never paid 'baksheesh'" and was unlikely to start doing so now. The company had a strong case on its own, he told Catapodis. "Furthermore," Brougham reported, "I stated that we had been scrupulous in abiding by our agreements, that we hoped to be in Arabia many years, and that personally I did not see how this would be possible were we to embark on a practice of attempting to buy off anyone and everyone who undertook to harass us."

He told Turrou that he was speaking only for himself, but a few days later called Turrou's office and left a message: he had spoken to Davies, and what he had said was "the official position taken by the company:" Aramco would not make any under-the-table payoffs.[20]

The Amended Article IV

As translated by Aramco when it obtained the full text in June, the amended contract—the version that was to go into effect with the issuance of the royal decree—specified that Onassis "shall have the right to combine the [tanker] company with one or more of the [other] companies whose shares are directly or indirectly owned by himself or (by himself jointly) with other members of his family of Greek origin, provided that Israelis have no direct or indirect interest in any of these companies."[21] That clause ensured that Saudi Arabia would remain compliant with the economic boycott of Israel and Israelis that had been decreed by the League of Arab States after Israel's creation in 1948.

Article IV had also been amended to say that ships owned by Aramco or its parent companies, and those owned by the purchasing companies would be allowed to continue transporting the oil if they had been doing so before December 31, 1953. That was an important concession by Onassis. It still meant, however, that as tankers were phased out of those fleets, their replacements would be excluded, and it left out tankers chartered by purchasers from third parties, rather than owned.

On the issue of freight rates, Article IV now specified that the fee charged by the new company's tankers for transporting oil would be "the rate announced monthly by the London Tanker Brokers Panel," paid in dollars if the oil went to the United States, in British pounds if it went to Europe. That rate-setting panel, established in 1953 by five prominent tanker-brokerage firms, describes itself as "an independent and impartial authority which provides a variety of rate assessments on a fee-paying basis for individual oil companies, traders, tanker operators and other interests worldwide."[22]

This amendment to the original contract thus tied the shipping rates to the actual prices charged in the rest of the world, rather than to those set by a regulatory commission in Washington. A rate chart of the time showed that the rate set by the U.S. Maritime Commission for transporting a barrel of oil from Ras Tanura to New York was 67 cents, whereas the London rate was $1.28, which obviously would be far more lucrative to Onassis.[23] It was not, however, acceptable to Aramco.[24]

The company's CEO, Davies, said in an affidavit that Aramco "owns no tankers," although its parent companies operated some under their own names. Customers who buy Aramco's oil "are highly competitive marketing organizations, which, in turn, cater to the needs and requirements of the ultimate consumer," Davies said. "No foreign consumer is compelled to buy oil from Saudi Arabia. He must be attracted by price or by such other considerations as may serve his wants," including the right to negotiate a shipping rate with tanker operators.

Aramco's position, he said, was that Saudi Arabia was, of course, free to create whatever sort of merchant fleet it desired, but it was not free to demand that Aramco and its buyers use that fleet to the exclusion of others.[25]

CHAPTER NINE

The World vs. Onassis

By the end of April 1954, the forces that would put pressure on King Saud throughout that year and organize a campaign against Onassis were hard at work. President Eisenhower's directive instructing his national security team to undo the Onassis contract with Saudi Arabia was still weeks away, but the State Department, the CIA, the Defense Department and their clandestine allies, Stavros Niarchos and Robert Maheu, were already busy. They were soon joined by influential allies: the governments of the major maritime nations of the noncommunist world, and many big foreign oil refiners and retailers.

As word of the Onassis agreement spread, so did alarm among the seafaring powers—among their governments, their shipowners, and their oil companies. They were not primarily concerned about Soviet influence or Arab nationalism. They were alarmed by the economic implications: if the Saudi Arabian contract with Onassis went into effect, other producing countries might follow the Saudi example, to the detriment of existing tanker operators, and of petroleum consumers, around the world.

The transportation of oil was big business. In 1954, the year the SATCO contract was signed, there were 2,602 ocean-going tankers in the world's fleets, of which 898 were owned by oil companies, 1,372 by other private corporations, and 332 by governments, including the U.S. Navy.[1] The total deadweight tonnage of those vessels was 39.1 million; Onassis's contract required that the SATCO fleet have a total deadweight tonnage of at least 500,000, a fraction of the world total but a major part of Saudi traffic—enough that as it grew to that capacity SATCO would carry almost all of Saudi Arabia's exports aside from shipments by the U.S. Navy.[2] Saudi Arabia's exports at the time amounted to about 6 percent of world supply but were growing rapidly.[3]

The largest fleets flew the flags of the United States, Norway, and Great Britain. Hundreds of vessels sailed under "flags of convenience," such as Liberia and Panama. (Only 16 were registered in Greece.) Oil from Saudi Arabia, Iraq, Iran, Kuwait, Libya, and Abu Dhabi represented a great part of these tankers' cargoes. In 1952, 1,496 tankers took on oil at Aramco's port at Ras Tanura, near Dhahran.[4]

Most of those ships filling up at Ras Tanura were owned by private operators such as Onassis and Stavros Niarchos, who competed for the business of the purchasers of oil. The purchasers would usually charter these ships for two or three years and then, as the charters expired, go back to the market to see if a different operator would offer a lower rate. Thus, the purchasers of oil and the tanker operators were dependent on each other, conducting their business by a well-understood set of rules.

At the time, in 1954, 80.3 percent of all crude oil and refined petroleum products exported by Aramco were shipped out of the country by tanker.[5] The rest went via Tapline, the pipeline to a port in Lebanon operated by an Aramco subsidiary. There, most of that portion of exports also was loaded onto tankers. Norway and Britain, which had the largest commercial tanker fleets outside the United States, did not produce any of their own oil. (The rich fields of the North Sea would not be developed until two decades later.) Thus, their fleets were dependent for their business upon oil produced in other countries, including the big Arab producers in the Gulf. The Onassis arrangement would disrupt those long-established patterns of maritime commerce.

Opposition from London

The British were the first to make their opposition known officially to the State Department.

The government in London was already upset because of a seemingly unrelated development in the Middle East: Egypt had struck a deal with the Soviet Union to barter cotton for oil. Egypt's British-owned refineries would process oil from Russia instead of oil from British-controlled fields in other Arab countries. The British Government, its embassy in Washington told the State Department in April, "has decided to protest to the Egyptian Government not against the origin of the oil but against a British company being compelled against its wishes and contrary to its commercial interests to handle foreign oil that displaces its own production."[6]

Onassis's SATCO contract contained the same sort of compulsory arrangement: oil destined for British refineries would have to be transported in SATCO tankers.

In late April, a British embassy official alerted the State Department to a "rumor that Onassis was hoping to conclude similar agreements with Iraq and possibly Iran," and that such arrangements "if applied on a considerable scale, would have damaging effects on UK maritime interests."[7] The CIA's "Current Intelligence Bulletin" of April 28 said the British were sounding the alarm about the possibility that Onassis would "be given the right to transport all or part of the crude oil produced by those countries."[8]

Two weeks later, a delegation from the British Embassy met at the State Department with a team that included Robert H. S. Eakens, chief of the department's Fuels division. A diplomat named John H. Brook, speaking for the Foreign Office in London, told the Americans that "the British Government was most unhappy over the [Onassis] agreement as it was understood from reports and rumors received. He mentioned in this connection that the British shipping interests had made strong representations to the [Saudi] Government." He said it was not entirely clear that any British interest was directly involved, but nevertheless, the British "had strong objections to this type of agreement based on: (1) The establishment of an undesirable precedent which could be used by other oil-producing countries; (2) The agreement as reported was believed to be a breach of unwritten law to the extent that it denied a generally accepted fact that title to oil following production passes to the company concerned which should then be free to dispose of it; and (3) The important maritime issue, i.e., flag discrimination is involved and this is of special interest to the U.K."

The State Department officials who were present agreed in principle and said they would renew efforts to obtain a complete copy of the contract, which they still had not seen.[9] But they did not promise to do anything other than convey concerns to the Saudi government nor could they have been expected to do so, given the administration's overall policy of not interfering with, or trying to dictate to, newly independent or developing countries.

No such ambivalence prevailed in Britain. The British government, unequivocally opposed to the deal, had the full support of, and gave its full support to, the British Chamber of Shipping, the industry trade association, which said the agreement would force their carriers out of the Saudi trade. That brought a furious response from the Jeddah Chamber of Commerce and Industry, then as now the most influential business group in the kingdom, which published its comments in a newspaper supplement.

It said in part:

> This Chamber of Shipping has referred to the consequences of this agreement (which we consider to be imaginary), the most important of which is that the transport companies which customarily participate in carrying Saudi oil will be eliminated from the field.
>
> The most effective refutation against this artificial opposition is the reliance of the government on the obvious reasonableness of the project. Thus, it calls for no answer or campaign of defense, because the allegations

put forward are, generally, efforts to create disturbances—disturbing the water of good relations in the hope of gaining strength behind the murk—which should not be given importance as it will be a waste of time to destroy false economic propaganda.

The refutation of this ridiculous propaganda gains force when we draw the attention of the British Chamber of Shipping to a British statute of 1871, the Cornwall Act, setting a similar restriction on ships transporting freight to Britain—they had to be British or from the exporting country whose products were on board, and that the US also had such laws.

We are proud that the new Saudi agreement was dictated by a pure spirit derived from deep sensibility, from the generosity of Islam and Arab justice, and from the awakening of the Saudi Arabian nation, revived by its far-sighted King and represented by the Council of Ministers.

The statement hailed the "brilliant" crown prince, Faisal, the "vigilant" minister of finance, Abdullah Sulaiman, and the "conscientious minister of commerce, Shaikh Mohmmad Alireza."

The U.S. diplomat in Jeddah who sent this translation to the State Department, J. Jefferson Jones, noted dryly that the conscientious Mohammed Alireza was the president of the Jeddah Chamber, the group that issued the statement, as well as of the national group, and that he and his company "will be the agents for the Saudi Arabia Maritime Tankers Company."[10]

Good Guys or Bad Guys?

If the Eisenhower administration was ambivalent about how much pressure to put on King Saud, it was even more so in its attitude about the oil companies. The State Department officials who dealt with the Onassis contract confronted a conundrum that had bedeviled the government for many years: in U.S. policy, were the giant companies that jointly owned Aramco good guys or bad guys? It was difficult to reconcile foreign policy and antitrust policy, which by definition discouraged cooperation among competitors. For the purposes of the Onassis case, the president would answer the question when he approved NSC directive 5428, instructing his team specifically to block the SATCO contract, but that would not happen until July. Before that, opinion within his administration was divided.

Throughout the months when the Onassis contract was on the table in Washington, conversations between the government and the oil companies, and among the oil companies themselves, were constrained by antitrust considerations. Supporting Aramco and its parent companies would make the United States government an ally of oil companies whose business practices it had long opposed as monopolistic, and the government would be defending Aramco's monopoly in Saudi Arabia. This issue was especially sensitive to Aramco, which was an operating consortium of four of the biggest companies. To what extent were international oil companies permitted to cooperate among themselves and share information? To what extent should the U.S. government permit or encourage them to act in concert? The Justice Department, which had filed the Madison antitrust case against the oil companies a decade earlier, and the State Department, which was concerned about what the oil-producing countries would think if American oil companies were branded as outlaws by the U.S. government, were on opposite sides of the argument.

The U.S. Federal Trade Commission, in a far-reaching and controversial 1952 report, had labeled the international oil giants a "cartel" and said their operations were detrimental to the interests of consumers and of the producing countries.

A chapter titled "Joint Control Through Purchase and Sale of Oil in the Middle East" said:

> Throughout the world the Big Seven oil companies transfer large quantities of crude oil and refined products among themselves, through contracts to purchase and sell. When these purchase agreements are discussed publicly by representatives of the petroleum companies, emphasis is usually placed on the ordinary commercial purchase and sale aspect which they share with all other sales contracts. However, since the companies participating in them often are already bound together through joint-ownership arrangements and participate in various production and marketing agreements, purchase and sale contracts among them often lack many of the arm's-length features that characterize ordinary commercial agreements among mutually independent buyers and sellers. Under these circumstances, the sales of oil covered by the contracts can often be utilized as an instrument to divide production, restrain competition in marketing, and protect the market positions both of the buyer and the seller. They determine who may or may not buy crude oil from particular producing properties. They tend to funnel the production from more or less diversified ownerships into the centralized marketing organizations of the large companies. They tend to keep surplus supplies of crude oil out of the hands of independent oil companies. The existence of these contracts in an atmosphere of joint ownership of production and marketing, the long periods for which they run, the manner in which prices are determined under them, and the marketing restrictions often written into them indicate that they are something more than ordinary commercial purchase and sale contracts.[11]

The extensive FTC report drew no conclusions and made no recommendations, but largely on the basis of the FTC's findings, President Truman's Justice Department sought to begin a new criminal antitrust prosecution of the oil companies. The State Department objected, largely because at that time the government was trying to persuade a group of international oil companies to take over oil operations in Iran, which had been disrupted by the political upheaval there. Iran had nationalized its fields, but the country lacked the technical ability to operate them, and Washington was trying to persuade oil companies, working together, to fill that gap in order to bolster the Shah. If it was acceptable for oil companies to work in concert to support U.S. policy in Iran, why would it not be acceptable in Saudi Arabia?

"It was a very complicated problem," the State Department's Henry Byroade recalled. "We couldn't even get our own oil companies together on the problem because of our anti-trust laws. They couldn't meet together except in the presence of [Truman's Secretary of State] Dean Acheson or myself. Then we would go and try to sell the proposition to the Justice Department. What we were trying to do really [in Iran] is to set up a big cartel which is contrary to American domestic economic policies, but that's what we thought the foreign affairs of the United States required. So it was very cumbersome."[12]

This question of how to balance or reconcile the vital position of the oil companies in ensuring adequate supplies with the government's long-standing objections to business arrangements between ostensible competitors divided the Truman administration throughout the spring and summer of 1952. The State Department and the CIA regarded the FTC's findings as so sensitive, and so potentially damaging to U.S. interests overseas, that Truman classified the report. But the Small Business Committee of the U.S. Senate, at whose behest the report had been prepared, was pressing to release it.

In May, the CIA sent to the White House a paper titled "Consequences of the Future Revelation of the Contents of Certain Government Documents." It did not dispute or even analyze the FTC's findings and conclusions, only "the effect of their revelation, individually or collectively, as allegations made under the sponsorship of an arm of the US Government." What would happen if one branch of the government depicted these international giants as potentially criminal conspirators while other branches were promoting them and their interests in Iran and Saudi Arabia?

"We estimate," the CIA said, "that official publication of this report would greatly assist Soviet propaganda, would further the achievement of Soviet objectives throughout the world and hinder the achievement of US foreign policy objectives, particularly in the Near and Middle East."

Publication would "assist the world-wide Soviet campaign to represent the US and other Western Powers as 'imperialist' and 'colonialist' powers." It would "further prejudice prospects for a settlement of the Iranian oil controversy, in particular by damaging, perhaps irreparably, the status of the US as a mediator between the UK and Iran," and thereby "contribute to the present economic deterioration and political instability in Iran, and increase opportunities for communist subversion." And the agency projected that beyond Iran—that is, in Saudi Arabia—publication would "assist forces in other oil-producing countries in the area which desire to alter present contractual arrangements with the international oil companies and thus jeopardize the flow of oil, which is of great strategic importance to the US and its allies."[13]

As word of the report began to circulate, Truman authorized publication of a redacted version. As the oil historian Daniel Yergin noted, "It found careful readers from Riyadh to Caracas and, not surprisingly, it became a subject of commentary even on Radio Baku's broadcasts to the Middle East." Baku is the capital of Azerbaijan, then the major oil-producing region of the Soviet Union, where the Bolsheviks had nationalized the oil fields in 1920.[14]

Harold F. Linder, the deputy assistant secretary of state for economic affairs, wrote in a December 16 memo to the White House that "the consequences of the premature publication of the FTC oil cartel report," coupled with news of a grand jury investigation by the Justice Department in preparation for criminal charges, "have been catastrophic and could lead to the expulsion of United States and United Kingdom oil companies from Venezuela and the Middle East and the loss of oil from those sources to the free world."[15] Why would the producing countries want to tie their economic futures to corporations that the United States government was branding as outlaws?

As the Truman administration contemplated how to proceed on the antitrust question, if at all, State Department officials met with James R. Withrow, a lawyer representing Mobil Oil, to consider the potential impact on the oil-producing countries of U.S. government action against the oil companies. He told them that one faction of Aramco's leadership believed the company was already in such disfavor with the Saudis that its concession was in jeopardy. "This group feels that if any new company came along and made a better offer to Saudi Arabia and Saudi Arabia was convinced that the new group could operate the properties, that would be the end of Aramco," he said. That conversation took place on January 27, 1954, a week after the Saudis signed the contract with Onassis, a development of which Washington at that point was not yet aware.[16]

Rebuffing the French

Two weeks before the end of his term, Truman decided against criminal antitrust prosecution of any oil companies, authorizing a civil suit only. That suit was duly filed by President Eisenhower's Justice Department in April 1953, accusing the five American companies among the Seven Sisters of "an unlawful combination and conspiracy to restrain interstate and foreign commerce of the United States in petroleum and products."

That case was still active at the time of the Onassis contract. In fact, it dragged on for a decade. The government had given the companies a specific exemption from antitrust law to allow them to operate jointly in Iran, but that did not cover Aramco or their united opposition to the SATCO deal.[17] On the contrary, one of the arguments the Eisenhower administration would use in trying to persuade King Saud to abandon the Onassis contract was that it was monopolistic.

By and large, the atmosphere in Washington was not supportive of collective action in any industry. In December 1952, just a few months before the Brook-Eakens meeting, the State Department, mindful of the Federal Trade Commission report, had rebuffed a French proposal for a multinational arrangement to help oil companies resist the growing demands of oil-producing countries.

At a meeting in Washington with French officials, the department's Parker T. Hart, who had previously served at the consulate in Dhahran and worked closely with Aramco executives, "noted that Aramco has, from the beginning of its operations in 1933, dealt with the Saudi Arabian Government on its problems." Hart was referring to the years from 1933 to 1943 when the United States had no resident diplomats in Saudi Arabia and Aramco was on its own. During that time and since, Hart said, according to the State Department record, that "the U.S. Government has not found it necessary to intervene on behalf of Aramco, although there have been frequent discussions between Aramco and the U.S. Government concerning those cases where U.S. interests are involved. Mr. Hart concluded by stating that he believed this has proved to be a particularly healthy situation."[18]

What Hart said was not exactly true, considering the conversations that Ambassador Raymond Hare had conducted with Abdullah Sulaiman and Yusuf Yassin that summer.[19] But Hart was reflecting the overall policy of his department, which was to maintain the fiction that the government was not carrying the ball for the oil companies. In fact, the administration coordinated closely with Aramco and its parent companies throughout the Onassis episode because the interests of the government and those of the oil companies were inseparable. Ambassador Wadsworth raised the issue with the king less than two weeks after Aramco received its first notice of the Onassis contract, and the issue would dominate his agenda for many months. But that coordination was largely concealed from the public because the partnership was uncomfortable for both sides. When the *New York Times* discovered in June that Hart and his boss, Assistant Secretary Henry Byroade, had met with Onassis to discuss his Saudi contract, the story merited a bold two-column headline.[20]

The French may not have known about the Brook-Eakens meeting, but it was hardly a secret that U.S. diplomats in the kingdom had worked closely with Aramco since the mid-1940s.

The head of the French delegation

agreed that the companies should be given as much latitude as possible in their negotiations with the local governments. However, he noted that the companies, in view of their specific responsibilities, are mainly guided in their negotiations by mercantile considerations. Yet negotiations between the local governments and the oil companies usually involve problems that transcend purely mercantile interests and should not properly be left entirely up to the companies. M. [Ghislain] Clauzel suggested that current problems should be discussed on a governmental level from time to time. The individual governments concerned could then make their viewpoints known to the companies, who in turn would negotiate within the framework of their governments over-all objectives. M. Clauzel then questioned whether the U.S. would agree to meet with England, France and Holland to discuss current petroleum problems.

That was not a good idea, Hart said. "Such a meeting would have the danger of appearing to the Middle Eastern countries as though we were ganging up against them."

U.S. officials and the oil companies were wary of public opinion in the Middle East and especially of the widespread Arab assumption that everything Americans did, whether they worked for the government or not, reflected the policy of whoever occupied the White House at the moment. As Daniel Yergin wrote, the government was not only concerned about the effect on competition of interlocking relationships between oil companies. It "worried even more about the perception both of the dominating role of such a small group of companies and of U.S. government support for them. The whole thing might look too much like a cartel, perfect grist for nationalist and communist mills in and around the region."[21]

Lawyers for the companies, including some from the same law firm that had represented many of them in the Madison Case, stressed that point in a State Department meeting on January 23, 1954—the same day that Aramco was first informed of Saudi Arabia's agreement with Onassis.

The lawyers were trying—unsuccessfully, it turned out—to persuade the Eisenhower administration to drop the civil antitrust suit it had filed the year before against the major companies, including the Aramco partners, the suit originally authorized by Truman.[22]

W. L. King, counsel to Socony-Vacuum (later renamed Mobil), argued that "it would be completely incomprehensible to the Arab mind that the United States Government, in the interests of destroying what they think of as at the most cooperation between companies naturally interested in the area, would undermine their whole position." What the Arabs would see, he said, is U.S. officials who had cited Aramco as "a shining example of what American free enterprise can offer" suddenly calling its partners "conspirators, price fixers, scoundrels." If the case proceeded, he said, "you have a search for what the underlying motive may be: 'Is it American imperialism? It can't be true that it is this minor aspect, which we don't understand. What else is it? And in what other direction is Arab animosity directed? There must be some other conspiracy than this.'"

James R. Withrow, also representing Mobil, said he had gone to the Middle East to gauge Arab leaders' sentiments about antitrust cases against the oil companies. Withrow said that the Saudis had obtained a copy of the FTC report, with the result that all through the second half of 1953, the oil company had been "berated with the use of this report on the occasion of absolutely every meeting between the Saudi Arab Government representatives and representatives of the Oil Company. The Saudi Arabs have made it quite clear on some occasions that they think that maybe Aramco has been repudiated by the United States. The new King, in some of his first remarks, said that 'I will deal fairly with anybody that deals fairly with me, and if my present friends are false, I will find friends elsewhere.'"

In response to a question, Withrow said that "there is no question in my mind that if that case went on, that the Saudi Arabia Government would eventually get to the point of this sort of analysis: that if the U.S. Government can examine into contracts and say they are no good because they are against the public interest, let's look at the concession and examine it and decide there is no concession because it is against the Saudi Arab's public interest."[23]

That conversation by itself was an illustration of the close ties that linked the government and the big oil companies. Withrow, the Mobil lawyer, was a partner in Donovan, Leisure, Newton and Irvine, the same law firm for which Aramco's Bill Owen had worked, founded by Wild Bill Donovan, the wartime chief of the OSS. Withrow's interpreter on his Middle East trip was Bill Eddy, who had been recruited into the OSS by Donovan and had been the OSS chief in North Africa during World War II. In that role, he had reported to Robert Murphy, Eisenhower's wartime coordinator for that region; Murphy, now deputy undersecretary of state, was one of the department officials in the meeting with the oil company lawyers. A five-member team from the CIA Agency, of which Eddy had been one of the founders, participated in that discussion, reflecting the strategic sensitivity of any matter having to do with the oil industry.

Murphy and his colleagues were sympathetic to the oil companies' arguments, but the State Department was still trying to answer the question raised by the Federal Trade Commission: in U.S. policy, were the Aramco parent companies good guys or bad guys? While that question was still open, it was difficult to formulate a response to the Onassis contract that all departments of the administration would accept and would be a sound basis for responding to the British and other maritime nations.

Other Countries Weigh In

The governments of countries friendly to the United States did not necessarily share Washington's view on the antitrust issue, and oil companies based in those countries were under not under the same legal restraints as the American companies. The Europeans in particular were much more open about the confluence of government and corporate interests. Even before the terms of the Onassis contract were finally made public in June, governments began to proclaim their opposition to it. After Britain had weighed in, the Norwegians were heard from on June 1.

The U.S. embassy in Oslo reported on Norwegian sentiment: "Now that the details have been closely studied, the awful possibilities of this arrangement become evident and the enormity of the proposition disconcerting. The Saudi Arabian royal decree gives Onassis the right to carry all the petroleum not lifted by the associated tanker fleet of Aramco as well as the possibility of establishing a monopoly to carry dry cargo and passengers to that country," the Norwegians complained—although nothing in the contract referred to dry cargo or passengers.

Norway believed that

> The traffic of the monopoly may amount to hundreds of thousands of tons of cargo per annum. The pilgrimage traffic to Mecca is also an important factor. In short, Onassis has been granted the concession to build a national merchant marine for a country which heretofore has never possessed vessels more important than dhows. Of course to obtain this concession he, Onassis, is offering an investment of between 25 and 30 of his ships, the promise to establish a merchant marine training school for natives so as to prepare them for the eventual manning of the ships under the Saudi Arabian flag, the building of a drydock and repair facilities, and the cash payment of a certain royalty per barrel on the petroleum lifted. It is undoubtedly the greatest single shipping deal ever formulated in maritime history.

The Norwegians felt that "something drastic must be done," the U.S. embassy reported, but didn't know what that might be. "The truth of the matter is that there is very little which can be done to thwart the development," the embassy said.[24]

France's Ministry of Industry and Trade warned refiners that the government, to protect its limited stocks of hard currency, would cut off their access to the U.S. dollars and British pounds they would need to pay for oil shipped under the Onassis contract.[25] The president of Esso Standard, the company's French operating division, said that because of French government restrictions on foreign-flagged ships, "one result which appears absolutely certain is that our purchases of Aramco crude will be sharply curtailed."

Another French refiner, Pétroles d'Atlantique, said that the French government would never authorize it to charter SATCO tankers "for the double reason of French flag protection and the saving of strong currency." As a result, the company would "avoid loading at Ras Tanura since we could, without any difficulty, obtain replacement crudes."

An Italian refiner that was buying more than 3.5 million tons of oil a year from Standard of New York, or Exxon, all shipped on chartered tankers, said that Italy's "ministry of Marine is active in defense of the interests of the Italian fleet. The Ministry of Commerce is unwilling to grant foreign exchange for any but the most necessary purposes." As a result, enforcement of the Onassis contract would "oblige the refiner to reduce or eliminate its purchases of oil originating in Saudi Arabia." Similar protests came from Denmark, Sweden, Spain, and the Netherlands. One Dutch company said that the Onassis agreement "is discriminatory in the highest degree. . . . [It] is completely contrary to the internationally established practice that the shipper should be free in his choice of the ship."

The Spanish division of Caltex, a Chevron-Texaco refining and retail partnership, said the Onassis agreement "would have the definite result of stopping the purchases of Arabian oil by Spain. The large investments in existing Spanish-operated tankers, the substantial program of new tanker shipbuilding, [and] the important savings in foreign exchange, are all of such vital interest to the Spanish state that it is inconceivable that the Spanish state would allow such interests to be destroyed by a scheme such as the Onassis Agreement." Caltex's French unit said it would be illegal under French law to acquire oil shipped under the terms of the Onassis contract.

Those warnings validated the argument that the Americans were making to King Saud: the Onassis contract would reduce the kingdom's revenue, not augment it, because buyers would go elsewhere.

Caltex Japan said it would face the same foreign currency restrictions as the European companies, and added the argument that the national interests of a Japan struggling to rebuild after World War II were incompatible with the restrictive terms of the Onassis contract.

"Japan, as an insular nation, is one of the great maritime nations of the world and is presently looking to the healthy development of its merchant marine for its national survival," Caltex director J. M. Voss wrote. "Historically, Japan has provided fleets to transport its imported materials and thus has created within its own economy employment for its ships and seamen. Also, a substantial portion of Japan's heavy industry is geared to the construction and repair of ships of all sizes. Any displacement of Japanese tankers will adversely affect commercial Japanese shipping companies and will also dislocate the business of shipyards, steel mills and associated industries." Given the effort the United States was making to rebuild Japan as a peaceful ally after the war, that was not a trivial consideration in Washington.

It is true that Chevron, Texaco, and Aramco's other two parent companies were defending their own interests here, more than they were defending those of independent tanker operators. Saudi Arabia was a major investment and profit center for them, and they derived additional benefits because Aramco was selling its oil to them at a discount to market price—much to the annoyance of the Saudis because that reduced the kingdom's revenue as well. But that did not invalidate their arguments or those of the foreign purchasers and shippers, who had many options about where to buy their oil and could walk away from Saudi Arabia, which would be the loser.

On July 30, Secretary of State Dulles asked Ambassador Wadsworth whether he thought it advisable to discuss the situation directly with the governments of the Netherlands, Sweden, France, Japan, Britain, and "possibly others." Wadsworth replied in the affirmative, recommending that the list be expanded to Norway, Denmark, Italy, and Greece, given the strong opposition to the Onassis contract in "Greek shipping circles."[26] Yet there is little evidence that the government in Athens ever took a strong position, probably because most of the tankers that would have been adversely affected, even those owned by Greek citizens, were not registered in Greece.

Splitting Hairs

British diplomats and Foreign Office officials spent weeks in the summer of 1954 in tedious hair-splitting arguments over whether their protests to Saudi Arabia about the contract were "official" or not.

One Foreign Office official, J. E. Coulsen, reported that when the Norwegian and Danish ambassadors in London went to the Saudi Arabian embassy to object to the contract, the first secretary there "asked why they wished to protest when the British had not done so. The Norwegian ambassador told me that he was surprised at the statement that we had not protested. I told him this was not so." Coulsen said that the Foreign Office's parliamentary under-secretary had made the British government's position clear in response to a question in Parliament.[27] That was not enough for the Saudis, who continued to insist that they had not received a formal, written protest delivered by the British government directly to them and therefore they could disregard whatever they had heard.

The British finally put an end to this fruitless back-and-forth by sending a formal diplomatic official message to the Saudi Ministry of Foreign Affairs saying that the government statement of the parliamentary under-secretary was in fact an official statement of the government's position. The British government, it said, "wished to record their strong disapproval of the features of this agreement to which the parliamentary under-secretary referred in his statement. They consider that the provisions of this agreement constitute flag discrimination and interference with the freedom of shippers to choose the vessel in which to ship his cargo." The message asked the Saudis "to reconsider this matter with a view to removing from the agreement those features to which not only the U.S. but many other Maritime Powers strongly object."[28]

In September, the Saudi Foreign Ministry delivered to the British embassy a formal response rejecting all of Britain's protests. It said that the Onassis contract was in Saudi Arabia's national interest and did not violate any international agreements. "His Majesty's government therefore regret," it said, "that they are unable to accept a protest by the British or any other government in a matter purely within the domestic jurisdiction of His Majesty's government."[29]

For all their legal and economic arguments, the objecting governments did not specify exactly what they wanted the United States to do about the Onassis contract—just as the Eisenhower administration itself did not know exactly what to do. By the end of the year, oil shippers had taken the matter into their own hands: without any public announcements, and without putting anything in writing, they simply stopped renewing their charters with Onassis-owned vessels as those charters expired. Even after the Saudi Arabia dispute was later submitted to arbitration, they continued the boycott to teach Onassis a lesson. By the end of 1955, almost half of Onassis's fleet would be idle, the boycott would have cost him more than $20 million, and he would be facing the prospect of bankruptcy.[30]

CHAPTER TEN

Too Many Moving Parts

On April 30, following instructions from Washington, Ambassador Wadsworth met with King Saud to make clear the unequivocal opposition of the U.S. government and the oil companies to the Onassis contract. His message was in writing, and he asked Crown Prince Faisal to read aloud the Arabic-language version. In a parenthetical note to his report to the home office, Wadsworth said he asked Faisal to read it because "the King's weak eyesight does not permit him [to] read ordinary type."

The words "antitrust" and "monopoly" did not appear in the message. "My government," it said, "shares the opinion of Aramco, as already communicated to Your Majesty's government, and of other interested private American companies that this agreement is not in keeping with the Aramco concession agreement with Saudi Arabia." He told the king that the "offtakers," the oil companies, wanted to inform the Saudi government "most emphatically that under no circumstances can they accept nor will they submit to any arrangement which infringes in any way the complete freedom of action of the offtakers, their affiliates, and customers in the employment of tankers."

The king replied that his government "would fulfill obligations it had assumed [but] where no obligations lay, it would, in exercise of its sovereign rights, act as it deemed best in [its] national interest." He said he would "not hesitate to do anything advantageous" to the kingdom. "This, any country would do."

As the meeting ended, the ambassador asked the king's advisers to provide a full text of the SATCO contract, of which he and Aramco had still seen only Article IV. They said they would take the request to the king and respond the next day, but neither Aramco nor the U.S. embassy saw the full text of the agreement they were trying to break until mid-June.[1]

A few days later, an official newspaper posted the royal decree ratifying the revised contract but not the text of the contract itself. Fred Davies wrote directly to the king to object—not just to the ratification decree but also to the idea of any contract along the lines of what Abdullah Sulaiman had conveyed to them in January, which he said would violate the concession agreement and therefore be unacceptable.

There is no way to know if the king himself actually read that letter, or had it read to him. The response came from Sulaiman, and it was not cordial.

Apparently Aramco's leaders had "not completely grasped the meaning" of his January letter, the minister wrote. Moreover, Davies's letter to the king was "inconsistent with the company's duty to maintain good relations with the government and to comply promptly with the laws of the state and its rightful (i.e. legitimate, lawful) decisions."

Nevertheless, Sulaiman said sarcastically, out of respect for the "common interest" of the company and the government, "we have decided not to record in an official letter that the considerations contained in the company's reply were improvised (i.e. unconsidered, impromptu, immature) as well as incorrect." The king and the finance minister had decided instead to authorize Onassis "to contact you directly for discussion and agreement with your company in regard to the necessary arrangements that will realize the carrying out of the said agreement."

These arrangements were to be made in "the shortest possible time," Sulaiman's letter said. If not, the government "will regretfully be obliged to take the steps that will insure the carrying out of its decisions."[2]

That was a not-so-veiled threat to revoke the consortium's concession outright and give it to some more cooperative company. If driven to it, the king would deploy this ultimate weapon. Leaders of other Arab countries had urged King Abdul Aziz to do just that when the United States recognized Israel in 1948. He had declined to take that step, but it was beyond dispute that his successor had the sovereign right to do so, for any reason, if he wished.

Going Public

Up to this point, Onassis's agreement with Saudi Arabia had attracted little attention among the public in the United States or Europe beyond a few scattered reports in the press. Then on May 18, Representative Emanuel Celler of New York, one of the most influential Democrats in Congress and no friend of Saudi Arabia, made a public issue of it.

At a meeting of the House Merchant Marine and Fisheries committee, he denounced the agreement as "pernicious" and as "unpalatable and monopolistic." He predicted that Onassis would try to use it as leverage to negotiate a way out of criminal prosecution.

"I hardly think it is necessary to warn the American oil companies against entering into any such agreement with a man whose conspiracies are adverse to the freedom of international trade and to the foreign policy of the United States," Celler said. He was aiming at the wrong target: it was the Saudi government, not the oil companies, that had made the deal with Onassis. The oil companies had made no deal with Onassis and had made clear their refusal to do so. But Celler had more to say.

He issued a press release saying that the contract "is detrimental to American oil distributing companies [and] to the American consumer and militates against American interests generally." He said the tanker phaseout provision of Article IV "will create an absolute monopoly in the transportation of all Saudi Arabian oil within a few years," and that the cost of shipping oil "will be approximately double what the independent operators now charge in a free competitive market." Celler also wrote directly to Secretary of State Dulles saying the reported agreement "might seriously damage American interests." He wanted to know if the "monopolistic concessions granted under this Agreements should in any way affect the Administration's request for funds" for military assistance to the kingdom.

At the same hearing, a State Department official named Harvey Klemmer warned that "if this sort of thing should spread, there is no reason why other countries with a major export—bananas, iron ore, manganese and so on—shouldn't do the same sort of thing."[3]

A few weeks later, the State Department replied to Celler that the amount of aid money designated for Saudi Arabia was modest, and said funding should continue "in view of our close relationship with Saudi Arabia."[4]

Celler, like everyone else in Washington and the executives of Aramco, was at that point still talking about a contract that none of them had seen. That would continue until the second week of June, when the text published in the Saudi government's official newspaper was translated and distributed by the U.S. embassy.[5]

For Secretary of State Dulles, who was dealing with fast-moving developments in many parts of the world, the Onassis matter was a time-consuming complication.

Part of Dulles's problem was that he was trying to maintain the close bilateral relationship with Saudi Arabia and protect American oil interests while simultaneously incurring Saudi displeasure by trying to undo the Onassis contract and refusing to back the kingdom in the Buraimi Oasis dispute.

The strains in the relationship were all too apparent to Ambassador Wadsworth in a long conversation with Crown Prince Faisal on June 1. The prince was cordial and polite until the end of their talk, Wadsworth said, when he interjected an unaccustomed note of sarcasm: "He had reluctantly concluded that its problems were too small be of real interest to the United States and that Saudi Arabia would no longer 'bother' us." That same day, King Saud cancelled his country's participation in the Point Four technical assistance program.[6]

This bilateral tension was highlighted in the July 16 edition of the CIA's "Current Intelligence Bulletin," a weekly report on developments worldwide that circulated only within the agency. Noting the Aramco dispute and the Point Four cancellation, the report said that "American relations with Saudi Arabia have been on a sharp decline since King Saud came to power in November 1953. Surrounded largely by anti-western advisers, he voices strong anti-Israeli sentiments and repeatedly decries alleged American support of Britain over the Buraimi area on the eastern coast." This deterioration of U.S.-Saudi relations was part of a "basically gloomy picture" for U.S. interests in the region, the bulletin said.[7]

Alireza Wants More

On May 20, Aramco's Fred Davies wrote a strongly worded letter to Finance Minister Sulaiman restating the unequivocal opposition to the agreement among the purchasers of Saudi oil, as if there had been any doubt: "Under no circumstances can they accept nor will they submit to any arrangement which restricts in any way their complete freedom of action in the selection of tankships for the carriage of oil they may buy."[8]

Two days later, a man named Said Alatas, described in an internal Aramco memo as "the number two man in the Netherlands Trading Society bank in Jeddah," met in Amsterdam with Mohammed Alireza. Alatas, a regular source of information for Aramco, later recounted the outcome of this meeting to a New York-based Aramco executive, Roy Lebkicher.

He said he and his wife had lunch with Alireza in Amsterdam, after which "Alireza suggested that they all go to Copenhagen the next day for a few days' visit. This was agreed to." Why Alireza wanted to move the conversation to Copenhagen is unexplained.

In the Danish capital, "Alireza suggested that he would be able to kill the Onassis deal if Aramco wished. Alireza pointed out that he had been put to considerable expense in the matter, and the implication was that he would expect to get something from Aramco." This greedy duplicity was on the same moral plane as Onassis's suggestion to Catapodis that what he really wanted from the Saudis was not an actual business deal but money to go away.

According to Lebkicher's memo, "When Alatas asked how this would be possible since the deal had gone as far as it had, Alireza explained that he himself had been responsible for promoting the deal in Saudi Arabia and that he would be able to revise it or kill it. As he described the situation, he had planted the tree and would be able to kill the tree; but it would be necessary to do so before the tree got too big or, in other words, before the deal had developed too far." When Lebkicher and another Aramco official, Garry Owen, talked to Alatas about Alireza's proposition, he said he did not know what was motivating Alireza but "said he thought that Alireza merely hoped to make some better deal for himself personally than he had made with Onassis."

Alatas said he doubted that Alireza could kill the deal even if Aramco paid him to do so "because of its great appeal to the King's vanity."[9] In any case, Aramco had previously made clear its "no *baksheesh*" policy.

A Film Mogul Enters the Picture

As the Americans were picking up support from Britain, Norway, and other maritime powers, another prominent Greek tycoon entered the arena—Spyros Skouras. With his son and daughter-in-law, Skouras held a controlling interest in Grace Lines, a major shipping company, and its parent ship holding company, Admiralty Enterprises Inc., but he was best known for another line of endeavor entirely. He was the president of 20th Century Fox, the Hollywood film studio.

Born in Greece, Skouras emigrated to the United States as a boy, learning English while working as a busboy in St. Louis. He and two brothers broke into the movie business by purchasing a failing theater in silent-film days. Over time, they built a nationwide cinema chain that they sold to Warner Brothers. Rising in the ranks of Hollywood power brokers, Spyros Skouras became president of 20th Century Fox in 1942, maintaining that position until he was forced out in a 1963 financial crisis for the company, exacerbated by the vastly over-budget extravaganza "Cleopatra."[10]

As a Greek in the shipping business, Skouras had naturally known Onassis and his father-in-law, "Stormy Weather" Livanos, for years. Now he tried to make himself useful in the Saudi Arabia affair. He arranged for Onassis to make his case in a meeting at the State Department. On May 26, 1954, Onassis met with Henry Byroade, the assistant secretary of state for Near East and South Asian Affairs, and Parker Hart, at that time director of the office of Near Eastern Affairs. Skouras was not present; he was represented by another business executive of Greek origin, Thomas Pappas.

The official State Department record of this conversation says that the meeting was prompted by a communication from Skouras suggesting that Onassis was "concerned" about the reaction to his agreement and wished to be heard by the department. It was, to say the least, unusual for an official of Byroade's rank to participate in a meeting with an accused felon, but in this case the matters at stake justified the breach of protocol.

"Throughout the conversation," the record said, "Mr. Onassis gave the impression of a man who is in a tight spot who wishes to make an accommodation to save himself further ill-will. He made brief reference to the indictment against him."

Onassis began the conversation by recounting "the background of shipping developments since World War II which had culminated in his agreement with the SAG [Saudi Arabian government.] The war years had brought home to many countries their vulnerability in the face of the monopoly of commercial shipping enjoyed by the few great maritime nations, especially as these nations suffered heavy shipping casualties."

In a time of independence from colonialism and rising nationalism, Onassis said, "Numerous states which had hitherto relied upon such shipping for their necessary trade were driven to the conclusion that they must henceforth have fleets of their own. Other states which did not require merchant fleets but which were emerging as new members of the world community felt the nationalistic urge to have vessels operating under their own flags. Such was the case of Saudi Arabia, following the example of other states such as Egypt." Here he was correct: the idea of a national merchant fleet had been on the table in Saudi Arabia since Karl Twitchell first proposed it in 1945, and Onassis knew well that the previous government in Iraq had taken it up with Spyridon Catapodis. Iran was already making such arrangements.

Onassis told Byroade and Hart that he had "recognized immediately the threat which such a movement posed to his own and to the oil companies' shipping interests. He had warned the oil companies that they could not expect to enjoy indefinitely a monopoly of offtakings from the producer companies where they enjoyed concessions. As the big companies ignored these warnings, Onassis felt obliged to move to protect himself as the tanker market became depressed. He had been approached at Monte Carlo by Saudi Arab leaders to conclude an agreement with the Saudi government which would provide Saudi Arabia with a tanker fleet." That was mostly true, although the Alireza brothers were not officially representing their government at the time of those conversations. But this argument was irrelevant: Aramco stipulated again and again that it did not object to the creation of a Saudi national fleet, only to the requirement that its buyers employ ships from that fleet.

The rest of the tale Onassis told appears to be completely unsupported by any evidence. He said he had "attempted for some time to argue the government out of the idea, but finally gave in and agreed to negotiate when he realized that should he not do so, Saudi Arabia would move to conclude an agreement with one of his competitors."

During the negotiations, Onassis said, he "recognized that the type of contract which the Saudi government desired was one which would give rise to considerable resentment by the oil companies and by other shipping interests. He therefore attempted to have a provision inserted in the text that the Saudi Arabian Tanker Company Ltd. enjoy only a specified share of the total offtake of oil from Saudi Arabia. This was rejected by the Saudi negotiators, who insisted on the provisions of Article IV." In the end, he told Byroade and Hart, he "lost his attempts to create a more flexible agreement" and signed in order not to lose the contract entirely.

Byroade then said that the agreement, or what the Americans knew of it, appeared to give Onassis's proposed company a monopoly.

"Mr. Onassis responded," the State Department record says "that the agreement provided for no monopoly whatsoever. Despite the terms of Article IV, sub paragraph a, off-taking oil companies or their buyers could replace obsolete ships in the oil movement from Saudi Arabia," and therefore the fears of oil companies and tanker fleet operators were unjustified.

At this point, the State Department note-taker departed from his stenographic function to note that Onassis's interpretation "does not appear justified by the text of Article IV of the agreement."

The official account continued:

> Mr. Onassis asserted categorically that the terms of his agreement with the SAG were not to be taken too literally and that he was prepared to use considerable latitude in their interpretation. Furthermore, he was prepared to re-negotiate the terms of this agreement to satisfy the USG [United States government] and the major oil companies, subject to the limitation that he would not 'double cross' the SAG. He personally owed his start in life to the oil companies and was not unmindful of his debt. He intimated that he would be prepared to again urge upon the Saudi government the acceptance of a provision limiting off-taking by the Saudi Arabian Tanker Company limited to a percentage of the total off-take from the country. Presumably this would be proportionate to the foreseen size of the Saudi tanker fleet, 500,000 tons, and would insure that this amount of shipping was kept fully occupied. With respect to tanker rates, he indicated a willingness to be flexible in the absence of any true U.S. Maritime Commission rate and the fact that market rates were well below the last published commission rate.

There is no way to tell how Mohammed Alireza and Abdullah Sulaiman would have reacted if they had heard that, but it was not the last time in the discussions of the Saudi contract that Onassis would tell his interlocutors whatever he thought they wanted to hear.

Byroade said, in effect, thanks for coming in, we'll get back to you—he would have to consult other people.[11]

The next day, May 27, the State Department learned from Aramco's Terry Duce that Onassis was in New York, talking to Aramco president Robert L. Keyes. General Counsel George Ray, who sat through that meeting and took notes, reported to CEO Davies that Onassis said he was not sure what he was supposed to say but had asked for the meeting because the Saudi government had instructed him to "clarify his position" to the oil company.

Keyes told him that it did not matter what he said: if the contract contained the shipping restrictions described by Abdullah Sulaiman, there was nothing to talk about.

According to Ray's note to Davies, "Mr. Onassis did not deny that the contract contained such provisions. He stated, on the contrary, that the contract on its face seemed to create a shipping monopoly of Saudi Arabian oil." Onassis said he had told the Saudis that such a provision might violate Aramco's legal rights but that the royal government "insisted on the inclusion of the provisions." The real purpose, he said, was to guarantee the proposed tanker company a "small share," about 20 percent, of Saudi shipments.

Onassis again said he had entered into the arrangement because the Saudis were going to establish their own fleet one way or another, if not with him then with one of his competitors, who were already seeking a similar deal.

Throughout the conversation, Ray reported, "Mr. Onassis' attitude was extremely conciliatory" and he said that he wished no harm to Aramco or its parent companies. Keyes and Ray were unmoved. They said, once again, that they had no objection to any Saudi plan to establish a national fleet, only to an arrangement that would give that fleet preferential treatment.[12]

Two days later, the U.S. embassy in Kuwait reported that "associates" of Onassis had approached a Kuwaiti merchant and asked him "to act for them to obtain from Kuwait [an] agreement similar to that with Saudi Arabia."[13]

The Teams Take the Field

By this time, a month or so before President Eisenhower signed off on the National Security Council directive to nullify the Onassis contract, all the players in the game were fully engaged. King Saud had ratified the agreement, and his government was pressing Aramco to implement it. Aramco was digging in against it, as the tone of correspondence between the oil company and Saudi government officials deteriorated sharply. The State Department was urging the king to cancel the deal while simultaneously trying to hold together the fraying bilateral relationship and working around the antitrust issue. Mohammed Alireza was playing a double or triple game, looking for ways to extract more money from the deal for himself. Spyridon

Catapodis was trying to get Onassis to pay him the fee he said he had earned through his role in brokering the agreement.

All these negotiations were clouded by the fact that no one individual or group had full knowledge of what the others were doing, and everyone seemed to have multiple agendas. Moreover, most of the parties did not see the full text of the contract until mid-June. After it was finally published, Secretary of State Dulles sent a terse note to the U.S. embassy in Jeddah and the consulate in Dhahran: "In the wake of publication this week of Onassis agreement text, there is a vacuum in news concerning its operation. Can the embassy or consulate general report any developments?"[14] The staffs there were, of course, regularly passing along whatever they learned, but it was fragmentary information because neither the Saudi government nor Aramco told the diplomats everything.

Onassis was beginning to realize the gravity of the situation for himself, but he was also currying favor with the king in the hope of implementing the contract. In a brazen gesture of flattery, he christened his newest tanker, the world's biggest, the *Al-Malik Saud Al-Awal* (*King Saud I*) when it was launched in Hamburg on June 4—although it was not suitable for the Saudi trade because it was too big to navigate the Suez Canal with a full load. At 1,104 feet in length and 47,000 tons in capacity, this new vessel took the "world's largest" title from the previous record holder, the *World Glory*, launched just four months earlier by Stavros Niarchos.[15]

A report in the CIA's Current Intelligence Bulletin a few weeks later said that "the forthcoming goodwill tour by the 47,000-ton Onassis tanker *King Saud I* is probably calculated to stir up so much publicity in the Arab world that Aramco will be compelled to load the vessel when it reaches Saudi Arabia in early September" despite the oil company's vow not to allow any Onassis-owned vessels into the oil port at Ras Tanura. [The writer either did not know that the ship was unsuited to the Saudi route or assumed that Onassis would let it sail carrying less than a full load so that it could transit the Suez Canal.] The tanker will probably leave Europe in mid-August and will call at important ports, particularly Beirut, Alexandria, and Suez. At each port, ceremonies will be held, government officials will be invited aboard, and the press will be alerted to give the maximum publicity.

"Comment: The tanker's arrival may mark the showdown in the struggle between Aramco and the Saudi government over the Onassis tanker agreement. [passage redacted] Onassis' reported negotiations with the Bonn government for the purchase of the Howaldtswerke shipyard in Hamburg—the yard where the *King Saud I* was built and one of the largest in Europe—*suggests that he is even more determined than previously indicated to carry out his agreement* with Saudi Arabia."[16]

All this time, Robert Maheu, working for the CIA and for Stavros Niarchos, was trying to dig up damaging information about Onassis that would discredit him with the Saudis and undermine his standing with the king. With the CIA's approval, he arranged to have a wiretap placed in Onassis's New York residence.

"On behalf of or with the complete knowledge of the United States government," he testified later, "that tap was on the phone I believe maybe eighteen or nineteen days." He said it turned out to be "entirely unproductive" and was not the source of any of the damaging information he later uncovered.[17]

The FBI Sounds an Alarm

A few weeks earlier, Gen. Arthur Trudeau, chief intelligence officer of the U.S. Army, had made a reconnaissance visit to Dhahran. One member of his delegation was an FBI official named Alan H. Belmont, who on June 16 delivered an alarming report to headquarters about what they had learned. The FBI's responsibilities were primarily domestic, not international, but Belmont's report added a new organization to the coalition of agencies within the Eisenhower administration opposed to the Onassis contract. The tenor of the report was not surprising, given that Belmont had obtained his information from Aramco, but nobody in the administration disagreed with it.

It said that "King Saud, unsuccessfully attempting to emulate his father, is believed controlled by some of his unscrupulous advisers, one of whom negotiated the Onassis agreement," a reference that could apply equally to the finance minister, Abdullah Sulaiman, or to Mohammed Alireza, now minister of commerce. "The King is trying to form an Arab League within the Arab League, with himself as a leader, meanwhile failing to properly administer his own country. Security of Aramco will be dependent on the U.S. Army in the event of imminent hostilities," Belmont wrote. "Despite the very serious import of this agreement from an economic, and possibly from a political, standpoint, the military aspects may be even more vital, although they cannot be estimated at the present time."

In Belmont's view, "The diversion of such oil to Soviet bloc interests, either for their use or for resale with the ruble as the monetary unit, would completely offset world trade, as well as increase the possibility of precipitating a conflict."[18] Those were the same concerns that had prompted the development of the Denial Plan in the Truman administration.

As often happened that summer, none of the people involved in these developments knew what all the others were up to at the same time. On the day after Belmont submitted his report in Washington, Onassis's friend Leon Turrou convened the meeting with Aramco officials in Paris in which he told them the whole story of how Spyridon Catapodis had put Onassis together with Mohammed Alireza and Onassis agreed to pay him to arrange the contract with Saudi Arabia. Also that same day, Aramco chairman Fred Davies composed a brief but unequivocal letter to Onassis restating Aramco's non-negotiable opposition to the tanker contract.

"Aramco cannot submit to or accept the agreement," Davies wrote, for two basic reasons. First, "the organizations which buy oil from the company have already notified the Company that they cannot accept nor will they submit to any arrangement which restricts in any way their complete freedom of action in the selection of tank ships for the carriage of oil they may buy." Second, he said, "Any restriction imposed by the Saudi Arabian government on the Company's freedom to select the means and manner of export is not only contrary to and a violation of the Company's rights as owners of the oil, but is also contrary to and a violation of the Company's exclusive right granted in Articles 1 and 22 [of the original 1933 concession agreement] to deal with, carry away, and export the petroleum it may produce, and to use all means and facilities it may deem necessary in the exercise of this right."[19]

That letter bears the handwritten notation "Not delivered" because a new ploy by Onassis changed the picture. Onassis had no way of knowing about the Belmont report, but he was well aware that the forces arrayed against him were powerful, determined, and growing, and that his position was increasingly tenuous. Through an emissary, he asked to meet face-to-face with Davies. Because of Abdullah Sulaiman's letter saying that the king wanted Aramco to work out an agreement with Onassis "in the shortest possible time," Davies had little choice but to agree, even though Aramco had previously told Onassis there was nothing to talk about.

CHAPTER ELEVEN

Onassis "in the Doghouse"

That emissary was Nicolas Cokkinis, a young man who represented Onassis in New York. When Davies was at Aramco's corporate headquarters in New York in mid-June, Cokkinis asked to see him. Cokkinis had been indicted along with Onassis in the navy ship sales case, but that was not what he wanted to talk to Davies about. He was sounding out the Aramco chief about having a face-to-face meeting with his boss.

Davies knew that King Saud wanted him to have such a meeting and he would have to comply, but he was not happy about it. George Ray, Aramco's general counsel, who was present during the conversation, wrote in a memorandum for his files that Davies was initially skeptical about talking directly to Onassis. Still not having seen the full text of the tanker contract, Davies told Cokkinis that if it contained "any restriction imposed by the SAG on the company's freedom to select the means and manner of export, it was contrary to and a violation of the company's exclusive rights granted in Articles 1 and 22 of the Aramco Concession. This being the case, Mr. Davies said no benefit probably would come from any talk with Mr. Onassis, but that he, Mr. Davies would be glad to talk with Mr. Onassis, if Mr. Onassis, with full knowledge of Aramco's position," still wished to meet. Ray interjected that "Mr. Davies wanted it fully understood that Aramco could not accept any restrictions upon Aramco's rights to deal with, carry away and export oil it produced in Arabia." Davies restated the position that Aramco had no problem with tankers flying the Saudi flag, but Aramco would charter them only if they were "willing to compete for business in the usual, normal way."[1]

When Cokkinis said Onassis was very eager to meet Davies and had often expressed a desire to do so, Davies gave him the address of the company's office in The Hague, where he would stop on his way back to Saudi Arabia.[2]

Onassis went there to see him.

According to Davies's extensive account of that conversation, he and Onassis talked for an hour and twenty minutes in the early evening of June 17. By coincidence, that was the same day Leon Turrou revealed the story of the Onassis contract's origin to Aramco's Robert Brougham. That information had not yet reached Davies.

Onassis began his conversation with Davies with a straightforward presentation of the revised tanker contract as it had been published earlier that month and of two letters about it, which for some reason were in French. "He read me portions of these letters which had to do with ratification, rate computation etc. I commented that the agreement as we had been advised in [the minister of finance's] first letter had not been modified in its fundamental concept. He agreed," Davies wrote.

Then Onassis the self-serving fabulist took over the narrative, presenting himself as a hapless victim: he

> went into a reiteration of his having been forced into this particular deal against his wishes by the peremptory attitude of SAG. He arrived in Jiddah and found that front men for two of his strongest competitors had been there for a year before his arrival, and prompt action on his part was necessary. He pleaded with SAG for permission to call on Mr. Davies and obtain Aramco's views on the matter. SAG refused to let him do this, and told him to sign, or else. He might have come to Mr. Davies anyway, but since he was actually living with SAG officials [at the time of the contract signing in January] he just didn't see how he could do it. Perhaps it was his fate to be forced into it—it might well have been better if he had let his competitors have it, but on reflection, of course, if he had, the odds would then have been against his getting any of the similar arrangements which will undoubtedly be made all over the world.

Davies had not achieved his position in the oil industry by being a pushover. He did not believe a word of this, but at this point in the conversation did not interject his opinion. He had already made clear to Onassis and his associates that the narrative made no difference—the contract that resulted, however it came about, was not acceptable. By his account, he simply let Onassis go on.

"Most of the conversation," Davies wrote, "was pitched on the plane [of] 'I made a mistake, I am in the doghouse, my former relations with the companies were excellent, they are now out to get me, they won't even talk to me, any man is entitled to one mistake; for God's sake Mr. Davies, how can I get out of this doghouse?'"

Onassis then volunteered the information that he had been in Houston discussing the contract with Torkild "Cap" Rieber, a controversial former chairman of Texaco. Rieber had been running Texaco when it bought its share of the Saudi Arabia concession, and he knew the territory. Rieber, Onassis said, "gave him hell, said he had done a terrible, inexcusable thing and he didn't know what to tell him to do, but if there was any way he, Cap, could help him, let him know."

Onassis said he "offered the agreement to the [Aramco parent] companies as if it were their own and he their employee when he signed it, the agreement to be modified or torn up as they saw fit," which was transparently untrue. The companies had talked to him, he said, but "now they wouldn't see him or even speak to him. The companies were being very foolish—individually and separately, several people had called at his bank to investigate his standing."

Davies, of course, was not inclined to offer Onassis any comfort or encouragement.

"I replied that it was certainly his problem, and that if his old friends couldn't think of a way to help him, he could hardly expect me to be smart enough to come up with an answer," Davies wrote. "He knew Aramco's position—the [tanker] agreement violates our concession agreement, and he knew that the purchasers of our oil had stated they would not submit to any agreement which restricted their freedom to make any arrangement they chose for the transport of the oil."

Davies told him that if he was admitting he had made a mistake, and if he had in fact told the Saudis before signing the agreement that it probably violated the concession agreement, he should

> go to SAG, refer to his former statement, [and] to the protests which had been lodged by the U.S. and other governments (which he had alluded to earlier in our conversation), and tell them the agreement was unworkable. His reply was that he would then be in two doghouses; the companies still wouldn't do business with him. He told Davies that because he had begun to fulfill his part of the contract by launching his new tanker, the Al Malik Saud al-Awal, it was now up to SAG to deliver on their part. He had them over a barrel, whereas they would have him in the same position if he were to go to them and say that the agreement was inoperable.

Davies then "pointed out that I knew nothing of his former relations with the companies and was certainly in no position to conjecture what they might be in the future, but if Saudi Arabia wanted a tanker fleet, the only way they could hope to have it was in a normal, strictly commercial manner—strictly competitive, and with no priority, restriction or monopoly in whole or part."

Finding Davies unyielding, Onassis put aside his supplications and became pugnacious. "Onassis mentioned 'fight' several times," Davies wrote. "He would fight before being crucified, he would carry the fight to every country in the world, be it producing or consuming." He asked if Aramco had a clause in its concession contract providing for international arbitration in the event of an irreconcilable dispute and if so whether Aramco was prepared to invoke it. Davies said yes.

At the end of this unpleasant conversation, Davies wrote, "I came away with the impression that, to put it mildly, Onassis had been something less than truthful in most of his statements to me and that he is prepared to fight for his position in any manner possible, ethical or otherwise."[3]

The Onassis who pledged to "fight" for his contract hardly seemed like the same person about whom a few weeks earlier Aramco general counsel George Ray had reported that his "attitude was extremely conciliatory. He referred again and again to the fact that he had been placed where he was in the shipping business by Aramco's owners, and that he was very grateful to them for what they had done; that it was not his wish to do them any harm whatsoever," Ray reported in an account of that conversation.[4]

Mood Swings, Real or Fake

This was a pattern of behavior with which Aramco officials, and U.S. diplomats, would become all too familiar as the summer wore on. Onassis was able to turn his emotional thermometer up or down at will—alternately abject and pugnacious, craven and brazen, even bursting into tears when he thought doing so would show his sincerity, all the while defending an agreement he said he wished to get rid of. It was not long before all his interlocutors saw through him. They knew that if the Saudi contract had put him in such dire straits as he was telling people it did, he could simply have walked away from it, at little loss except perhaps the money he had paid to Mohammed Alireza; he could have recouped whatever he had spent on creating the nascent Saudi tanker fleet by selling the ships. Saudi Arabia had little if any leverage over him. The fact that he did not walk away indicated that what he really wanted was to put the arrangement into effect and start collecting big money while somehow dodging the consequences.

One of the subjects about which Onassis had been "something less than truthful" in talking to Davies was his conversation with Torkild Rieber.

Rieber was a famous, or perhaps infamous, figure in the oil industry whose colorful life rivaled that of any other character in this drama for drama and controversy. Born in Norway, he ran away to sea at the age of 15, rose to become captain of an oil tanker—hence the nickname "Cap"—and parlayed ownership of a few Texaco gas stations into a rise to the executive suite. He was Texaco's leader when the company bought a half-interest in Chevron's Saudi Arabia operations in 1936. He wore a tuxedo to lunch at fancy restaurants in New York but remained a rough-hewn seaman who often behaved accordingly.

In the 1930s, under his leadership, Texaco made huge profits by providing oil and fuel to the fascist rebels led by Francisco Franco in the Spanish Civil War, supplies that were just as essential to the fascist victory as were the planes and guns supplied by Hitler and Mussolini. Sending the fuel to Franco's forces was illegal under U.S. neutrality laws, but to Rieber that was merely an inconvenience. To him, there was no moral issue—it was just business. In that sense, he and Onassis were cast from the same mould.

"Beneath his broad shoulders, iron handshake, sailors' oaths, and up-from-the-lower-decks persona, however, lay something far darker," the author Adam Hochschild wrote. "Although not particularly anti-Semitic by the standards of the time—'Why,' he would say, 'some of my best friends are goddam Jews, like Bernie Gimbel and Solomon Guggenheim'—he was an admirer of Adolf Hitler."[5]

Onassis was trying to apply to his Saudi contract the same politics-neutral framework that Rieber had embraced in Spain, but if he believed that Rieber was sympathetic to his position, he was mistaken.

A week after his conversation with Onassis, Rieber met in New York with two Aramco officials, Terry Duce and George Ray, and with John Noble, who represented Aramco's subsidiary, the Trans-Arabian Pipeline Co., or Tapline. Nicolas Cokkinis, Onassis's U.S. agent, was present at the meeting, listening as Rieber told the oil officials about his discussion with Onassis. Rieber said that Cokkinis had asked him to arrange for Onassis to have "personal contact" with executives of Aramco's parent companies so that he could make his case to them—in effect, going over the head of Aramco's management to the parent companies.

Rieber said it appeared that "Onassis is now seeking an opportunity to use charm and personality to accomplish what he realizes he cannot do by arm's length negotiating." Rieber said he had told Cokkinis at a previous meeting that the Saudi Arabia contract was a "flagrant violation" of Aramco's concessionary rights.

The deal was more than a contract violation, Rieber told the oil executives. He said it was a "blunder of equal magnitude with that of former Premier Mossadegh and the Iranian Government in the latter's attempt to nationalize Iranian oil. Drawing on his own experience as advisor to the Iranian Government, he pointed out the blind stupidity of the Iranians in precipitating a nationalization issue at a time when the World War II crude oil shortage was a thing of the past" so that oil consumers could buy elsewhere, as in fact they did. Rieber said that "blunder" had cost the Iranians more than $1 billion and had forced the U.S. government to "support the Iranian economy by means of foreign aid at the rate of approximately one million dollars per day." The Onassis contract, he said, was "no less ill-timed" because there was an ample worldwide supply of oil and of tankers. No one needed to buy oil from Saudi Arabia.

Aramco officials knew all that: they had made similar arguments to the Saudis. More revealing was Rieber's account of his conversation with Onassis.

He said he talked to Onassis "like a 'Dutch uncle,'" and Onassis wept." Rieber told Onassis that his "lust for wealth and power had led him into a tremendous blunder; that he had started from nothing and had been able to amass his fortune by reason of the private enterprise system and the principles which have made America great; that his present activities constitute a direct attack on the system and institutions that have enabled him to succeed; [and] that because of what he has done he deserves to be destroyed financially and as a power in maritime affairs."

Rieber said he advised Onassis to cancel all dealings with the Saudi government and to "avoid making any such error again." Onassis asked for assurance that if he did so there would be no reprisals. Rieber said he would "never get anything in writing," but it was possible that "Onassis might be allowed this one mistake provided he mends his ways forthwith."

Rieber then left the room, leaving Cokkinis to discuss his remarks with the oil executives. He told them that the Saudis had led Onassis and his associates to believe that the tanker contract would not violate the Aramco concession agreement, which he admitted he had not read. He "tried to give them impression that they had been taken advantage of by the Saudis—that they had entered into negotiations with a view to seeking only a small percentage of the Saudi export business, and only on a competitive basis. The Saudis, he said, had insisted on the objectionable features that are contained in the final agreement," according to a memorandum Noble wrote afterward.

The oilmen dismissed that argument out of hand. Noble "pointed out that Onassis had been free to accept or reject the Saudis' terms and had freely entered into the agreement. He must therefore be judged by the terms of the actual contract and not by what he may have originally offered to do." They said they had nothing further to discuss with Onassis.

Rieber then went back into the meeting room to make one final point. He said he was "sure that bribery had been committed in order to obtain the tanker agreement, and that Onassis deserved to be destroyed for the tactics which he had employed."[6] Cokkinis denied it, but Rieber knew how the system worked in places like Saudi Arabia.

The Lawyers Weigh In

Beginning with the first notification of the Onassis contract from Finance Minister Sulaiman in January, Aramco's lawyers had believed that the whole concept, and in particular the terms of Article IV, represented a de facto violation of the company's 1933 concession agreement. The company's white-shoe New York law firm, White & Case, agreed. The firm delivered its analysis to general counsel George Ray on June 11, noting that none of its lawyers had yet seen the full text. It was signed by Lowell Wadmond, a partner in the firm, who was Aramco's principal outside counsel.

"In our opinion," the document said, "this action on the part of the Saudi Arabian government is in clear and definite violation and breach of the basic agreements between the Saudi Arabian government and your company." In Wadmond's opinion, the only matter open to argument was: at what point does the oil pass out of the control of the producing company? Under Article I of the concession agreement, Wadmond's memo noted, "Your company has the exclusive right to carry away and send abroad the oil produced in the concession area." But the memo added a cautionary note, citing a 1946 U.S. Supreme Court case addressing the question of when oil actually passed out of the control of the producer.[7]

"The foreign purchaser furnished the ship to carry the oil abroad," the high court's opinion said. "Delivery was made into the hold of the vessel from the vendor's tanks located at the dock. That delivery marked the commencement of the movement of the oil abroad. It is true, as the Supreme Court of California observed, that at the time of the delivery the vessel was in California waters and was not bound for its destination until it started to move from the port. But when the oil was pumped into the hold of the vessel it passed into the control of a foreign purchaser. . . . " From this reasoning, it could be argued that under U.S. law, Aramco's exclusivity ended at the water's edge.[8]

Stanley D. Metzger, the State Department legal counsel, said after reading Wadmond's paper that overall it presented a strong argument in favor of Aramco, but because of that Supreme Court precedent "I am not convinced that this position would necessarily prevail" in court or in arbitration because of the lack of "clarity" about the meaning of the word "export." He noted that Wadmond had cited a dictionary definition, "to carry or send abroad," but said those do not mean the same thing. "If it means to carry abroad, the right might encompass the exclusive right to carry by whatever means the Company chooses. If, on the other hand, it means 'to send abroad,' this right does not necessarily carry with it the exclusive determination of choosing the particular means by which the oil is physically carried."[9]

That sounds like tedious legal hairsplitting, but it would be a crucial argument in the resolution of the Onassis affair. At what point did the oil pass out of Aramco's control—when it was loaded onto a tanker, when that tanker set sail, or when the oil was delivered to its purchaser? The question could not be answered by any Saudi statute because Saudi Arabia had no written code of maritime or commercial law.

A New Ploy by Niarchos

During this same period of intense activity, late June to mid-July 1954, Stavros Niarchos reinserted himself into the discussion with a new idea for foiling Onassis.

One of the charter contracts that Onassis had for his existing fleet was with Royal Dutch Shell, which was not part of the Aramco consortium and did not operate in Saudi Arabia. Though based in Britain, the company was paying Onassis in U.S. dollars to transport its oil to buyers. Niarchos suggested that the British government deny Onassis permission to transfer to the United States the dollars that Royal Dutch Shell was paying him. Without that stream of U.S. currency, Onassis would be unable to pay back the American lenders that had agreed to finance the Saudi fleet. According to Nathan J. Citino, the British Foreign Office favored the idea but the Treasury rejected it as "dangerous to public confidence in Sterling and unlikely to achieve the desired goal."[10] It was unlikely to achieve the goal because Onassis lived primarily in Europe and did most of his business there. His global network of bank accounts, shell companies, and subsidiaries made it prohibitively difficult to thwart any particular transaction. Undisclosed movements of money, often through shell companies, were everyday business to Onassis, as they were to Niarchos.

Not long after that, one of Aramco's parent companies, Socony-Vacuum (Mobil), proposed another unlikely ploy. The company's president, Brewster Jennings, and two other executives met with the State Department's John Jernegan. After repeating the oil companies' assertion that they would refuse to load any oil onto Onassis tankers at the port of Ras Tanura, which they controlled, Jennings said the companies "were increasingly taken with the idea of sending a special emissary to discuss our position with King Saud." Their "first choice" was Vice President Richard Nixon.[11]

That was a remarkably unsophisticated idea that showed little understanding of the Eisenhower administration's delicate position. The administration did not want to put overt pressure on King Saud that would further alienate him from Washington and would anger Crown Prince Faisal. Sending the vice president on such a mission—even if the king had been willing to receive him—would have advertised the administration's intervention to the world.

Besides, the State Department was dealing with a more urgent issue on this front. J. Paul Getty's Pacific Western Oil Co. (PacWest), which held the oil concession in Saudi Arabia's part of the Neutral Zone, was nearing a transportation agreement with Onassis. Getty, who spent summers in the south of France, and Onassis had been acquaintances for years—long enough for Onassis to become envious of Getty's much greater wealth. "Mr. Getty is in a rich man's business," he once remarked. "He produces oil and carries it. I am in a poor man's business. All I do is carry it."[12]

On July 12, a PacWest representative identified only as "Mr. Hadfield" went to the State Department to "ask the Department's position concerning Pacific Western reaching an agreement with Onassis to transport oil produced in the Saudi portion of the Saudi-Kuwaiti Neutral Zone," according to the official memorandum of this conversation.

Hadfield said PacWest had a "preliminary oral agreement" to deploy Onassis's new tanker, known in English as the *King Saud I*, in this service. Beginning in October, the ship would make three voyages to transport oil, two to California and one to the East Coast. (The memorandum does not mention that the vessel was too large to transit the Suez Canal when fully loaded and would therefore have to sail all the way around Africa to reach the United States.) He said the agreement would be "binding on Pacific Western unless Onassis reached an agreement with Aramco before the first shipment or at any time prior to the completion of the third shipment."[13]

It was not clear during this discussion about the Neutral Zone oil how PacWest would have loaded it onto the *King Saud I* because Aramco had made it clear that no Onassis vessel would be permitted to take on cargo at Ras Tanura, its Persian Gulf port. Ras Tanura was the only port in Saudi Arabia capable of loading oil cargoes onto seagoing vessels. It is possible that PacWest's oil could have been exported by way of Kuwait through facilities built in the Kuwaiti half of the Neutral Zone by another American consortium known as Aminoil, but Getty and Aminoil chairman Ralph Davies despised each other. In addition, as Daniel Yergin put it, "Pacific Western was a one-man band; Aminoil, an awkward consortium that required approvals from its many members."[14]

Any such arrangement would also have drawn opposition from the Foreign Office in London, which feared that Onassis would use it to break into the British-controlled oil trade in Kuwait.[15] Later on it became apparent that Onassis and Getty were operating on the theory that if PacWest chartered Onassis's ships, the vessels would be operating outside Onassis's agreement with the Saudi government and thus not subject to the Ras Tanura ban. In that case, Onassis would be able to draw revenue from his new tanker fleet because he could load his ships with oil that had not been produced by Aramco. Such an arrangement might offer a graceful way out of his increasingly untenable position, if Aramco had any reason to let him off the hook.

The Long Hot Summer

July can be oppressively hot in Washington, and in Saudi Arabia it is unbearably so. In this July of 1954, the temperature of the conversations was rising along with the temperature of the air. Part of the problem was that multiple meetings and conversations were taking place simultaneously in Riyadh, New York, Washington, and Europe, and that none of the major actors—Aramco, the U.S. government, the Saudi government, and Onassis himself—was fully aware of what the others were doing or saying. Efforts by well-intentioned outsiders to broker a solution only added to the confusion. This information gap stoked frustration on all sides, as Aramco's Bill Owen discovered on July 15, when King Saud summoned him for a dressing-down—not about the Onassis contract, but about other grievances, real or imagined.

The king and his extensive entourage had just returned from a tour of the "southern districts," meaning Buraimi—a tour that Aramco had organized on the king's behalf, at an estimated cost of $2 million. Saud complained that the company had "just stayed away," whatever that meant. He also groused about what he said was Aramco's refusal to guarantee bank loans that the kingdom was seeking—loans it needed to cover the cash shortage caused by extravagance and mismanagement.

Owen said it was a misunderstanding—the company had received no such loan guarantee request. The king said Finance Minister Sulaiman had told him a request was made and turned down.

"We have noticed a changed attitude on the part of the company toward the Saudi government," the king said. "If you have had instructions from your government to cause this change, we say it is not in your interest. Your government is pressing us politically and you press us financially." Owen replied that there had been no change and that Aramco did not take orders from Washington. But he also offered to arrange the loan guarantees, and later told a colleague that "the king appeared somewhat more friendly when I left than when I arrived."[16]

Meanwhile, the conversations with Pacific Western's Hadfield created a new sense of urgency at the top levels of the State Department to deal decisively with the Onassis matter. Any arrangement such as PacWest contemplated could undermine Aramco's position. Henry Byroade, the assistant secretary of state for Near East Affairs, sent a note to Under Secretary Robert Murphy pleading for firm policy decisions.

"It is not entirely clear at the moment what the next approach of [the] Department to SAG should be," he wrote. "A further strong démarche might heighten the King's antagonism and work damage to the interests of the oil companies and others concerned. The proposed action of Pacific Western, however, has made it essential that the Department make an early decision on its future course of action." He recommended that Ambassador Wadsworth be instructed to see King Saud again and make the case "more fully and firmly than has been done to date."[17]

The temperature rose again the next morning when PacWest's Hadfield was back at the State Department to meet with Murphy and Merrill Gay, the economic officer in the Near East department. Hadfield said that "time is 'of the essence' to Pacific Western, that Onassis representatives had been pressing him all week, that Mr. Getty has been under the same pressures in Paris and that Pacific Western hopes to finalize its position in a week or so." The State Department record of this conversation says Hadfield asked whether it would "hamper U.S. government plans" if PacWest went ahead with this deal. Murphy said it would, "to some extent," and asked Hadfield to get a decision deferred, which he agreed to try to do.[18]

One result of this new urgency was acceleration of the National Security Council process of preparing the Policy Directive labeled NSC 5428 for Eisenhower to approve, which he did the following week.[19]

Another result was a long, detailed note from the State Department to Ambassador Wadsworth on July 16 giving him new instructions for dealing with the king and the Saudi government. The note was signed by the secretary of state, but outgoing messages of that type almost always bear the secretary's signature. This one was probably drafted by Byroade and edited by Dulles before it was sent. In any case, it amounted to a directive to Wadsworth from the boss.

Written in the peculiar truncated language used in diplomatic dispatches to save money on cable fees, it began with a summary of the situation:

> Aramco and parent company officials have approached Department at various levels indicating emergency in relation Onassis shipping agreement may arise any time during next 30 days either through Davies talks with SAG or Onassis requests for cargo. Present position is that parent companies will refuse cargo under terms Agreement although realize shut-down and possible eventual nationalization could result. Officials fully realize seriousness of step but agree must stand ground and have sought assurances that U.S. Government agrees and will support them. They request prompt diplomatic action. Pacific Western on other hand confidentially informed Department (a) they have replied to Saudis' letter of notification that although Agreement contravenes concession rights they will do business Onassis if competitive rates offered and b) they about make deal Onassis covering three trips by *Saud I* to Western hemisphere at rates lower than Agreement level but slightly above present competitive rates. Department has requested Pacific Western hold off on finalizing deal pending reply this telegram.

Dulles said the matter had been discussed at the "highest levels" in the State Department and the Joint Chiefs of Staff. They agreed that the United States should stand with the oil companies because the Onassis agreement was "not in keeping Aramco concession" and because "Companies surrender to agreement likely create serious repercussion throughout shipping and oil world from point of view private and public commercial interests and general international trade policy."

The contract would prove damaging to Saudi Arabia, the secretary's cable said, because the "financial benefits to Saudi Government from Onassis deal bound to be infinitesimal compared potential loss oil royalties" if customers stopped buying Saudi oil. "From dollars and cents viewpoint Saudi government appears to have been seriously misled," and the United States was only trying to be helpful.

The U.S. government's position, like that of the oil companies, was that Saudi Arabia was free to establish a tanker fleet if it wished to do so, so long as it operated "in free competitive markets at going commercial rates," the cable said. Noting that Onassis was "probably anxious squirm out" of what he now realized was a bad deal, Dulles suggested Wadsworth tell the Saudis that the agreement could be modified "without fanfare or loss face and only Onassis who already seeking perpetrate similar pernicious deals in other countries would be loser."

Wadsworth was "authorized," which meant instructed, to proceed "immediately" to deliver these arguments to the king.[20]

CHAPTER TWELVE

Power Struggle in the Kingdom

Part of Aramco's problem that summer was that Finance Minister Abdullah Sulaiman, whose power was eroding rapidly under King Saud, became increasingly truculent as he sought to save his job by carrying through on the Onassis contract.

Once Saud became king even he, slow-witted though he was, understood that his country was entering a new era in which personalized administration by one man was no longer viable. An increasingly complex Saudi Arabia required institutions of government and delegation of authority.

At the end of his long reign, King Abdul Aziz had recognized this need. In one of his final acts, he decreed the establishment of an official Council of Ministers, or cabinet, which would be the closest thing the country had ever had to a formal government organization in the modern sense. King Saud duly created the council in March 1954. In announcing it, the king said that "the days during which the Ministry of Finance was responsible for all construction, economic, agricultural, industrial, and even military projects, have passed. Therefore, we have taken the responsibility to reduce the burden laid on this ministry and make it a Ministry of Finance in the true meaning of the words."[1] There would be no more GOVENCOs.

The new cabinet consisted of seven members, six of whom were brothers or cousins of the king: Faisal bin Abdul Aziz, minister of foreign affairs; Mishal bin Abdul Aziz, minister of defense and aviation; Fahd bin Abdul Aziz, minister of education; Sultan bin Abdul Aziz, minister of agriculture; Talal bin Abdul Aziz, minister of transport; and Abdullah al-Faisal, minister of interior and health. The only non-royal member was Abdullah Sulaiman, minister of finance. Thus he still held his title, but his power was considerably less than before.

He had already been relieved of responsibility for the extended, difficult negotiations with Aramco over the price it was paying for oil. When those negotiations resumed in May 1954, the government delegation was headed by Crown Prince Faisal and included Yusuf Yassin, listed as deputy foreign minister; Khalid Gorgoni, an adviser to the king; and Abdullah Tariki, director of the Petroleum Supervisory Office in the Ministry of Finance. Tariki's most important duty was to keep track of the amount of oil Aramco exported to ensure that the company paid all royalties and taxes that were due. Tariki was just the sort of nationalist agitator Aramco feared; he was an advocate of nationalizing the region's oil concessions, and later was one of the founders of the Organization of Petroleum Exporting Countries. When the Saudis finally forced Aramco to add two Arabs to its board of directors in 1959, Tariki was one of them.[2]

The new Council of Ministers formed an economic committee, which was led by Prince Faisal; it included Muhammad Surur, the deputy finance minister, but not Sulaiman himself. The king said that henceforth the ministry's duties would be to collect revenue and to spend it in accordance with a budget discussed and approved by the Council of Ministers, not just by the Finance Ministry. A five-year capital budget was to be established, also with cabinet approval. Those steps hardly sound revolutionary, but in Saudi Arabia they were. The kingdom had no central bank until the early 1950s, when the Saudi Arabian Monetary Agency was set up, with U.S. assistance under Point Four, and at the time of the Onassis contract still had no paper currency. Abdullah Sulaiman had been a one-man treasury.[3]

Shortly thereafter, the king added a Ministry of Commerce to the cabinet and gave that position to Mohammed Alireza, further eroding the responsibility of the economy minister. The irony of that was that Sulaiman had inadvertently brought it about. At one of the first sessions of the new cabinet, he had been shocked when one of the other ministers objected to the presence of Alireza, whom Sulaiman had brought along as an advisor. Requesting a short break, he wrote a quick letter asking the king to give cabinet status to Alireza, and the king complied. It clearly made no difference to King Saud that Alireza had enriched himself in the Onassis affair.

It soon became apparent that other powers in addition to the budget were to be transferred to the Council of Ministers, including negotiations over monopoly contracts and concessions, the establishment of corporate entities, and the licensing of foreign firms to operate in the kingdom. The council would have a subunit known as Control of State Accounts, its purpose being to "ascertain the accuracy of receipts and expenditure in all ministries, departments and administrations."

In the short term, all this meant little because King Saud was not serious about controlling royal expenditures, and the money continued to go out as fast as it came in. For Abdullah Sulaiman as an individual, however, it was clear that his days in power were numbered. As a sympathetic Arab biographer put it, "Abdullah Sulaiman spent unpleasant months with King Saud. Things were in a state of confusion. Under Abdul Aziz he used to discharge his duties with complete, absolute authority. Now things were totally different."[4]

Sulaiman faced the same problem as did the U.S. government and other actors in this tale: lack of information about what all the others were up to. He had no way of knowing, for example, that the White House National Security Council was preparing NSC resolution 5428, with its directive to undo the Onassis contract, for President Eisenhower's approval. He knew the oil companies were looking for ways to undo or circumvent the agreement with Onassis, but he did not know how they were going about it. The minister's anxiety was compounded by insecurity about his job.

Taking It Out on Aramco

As his power slipped away, Sulaiman took out his frustration on Aramco in increasingly intemperate language. The most striking example was a letter he sent to Davies on July 10, which he began by saying brusquely that "His Majesty the King is not pleased over the method of approach which you have followed" in refusing to comply with the Onassis agreement.

He complained that Davies, in his letter of May 5, had rejected the terms of the agreement without yet having read it, basing his objections on "conjecture." Davies had made his objections clear well before May 5, the minister said, "and yet you feel it is your duty to repeat" them.

"You will no doubt recognize that such statement and conjecture are indeed strange," Sulaiman wrote. "And what is yet stranger is that such should come from a company, and from a responsible Chairman of the Board of Directors, in whom are taken for granted sound judgment and good management." He said the Saudi government was "vigilant and eager in execution of the laws and decisions of the country, and shall not countenance taking recourse to grounds or excuses made of a claim of an ambiguity or a difference in the interpretation or execution of any contractual rights, for the purpose of suspending the execution of those laws and decisions."

Beyond the unpleasant tone, the minister's letter raised a critical argument that would inspire reams of legal analysis in the months ahead. As if he had somehow read the response of the State Department's Stanley Metzger to the legal analysis submitted by Aramco's outside counsel, Sulaiman said that the word "export" in the original concession agreement did not apply to transportation of the oil by sea.

"As a matter of fact," he said, "transportation is an independent business, having its own special character. It is an economic activity standing on its own, subject, like various kinds of national economic activities, to such policy as the State may prescribe and to such regulations as it may impose. The Government has the right to leave it to a special competition, or to monopolize it for itself, or to grant it a concession."[5]

That was the very argument that Metzger had flagged in his comments on Aramco's legal position. Aramco never accepted it. The company's lawyers wrote that Saudi Arabia itself had stipulated in a 1951 law that "To 'export' means take or send an imported or domestic article destined for a foreign country beyond the territorial jurisdiction" of the kingdom, and the word for "export" in the Arabic text of that law was the same as the word in the Arabic text of the Concession Agreement.[6]

Davies responded to Sulaiman with a letter of his own, saying the company was "disappointed" with the minister's letter and complaining that it was "unfair" that some phrases in his previous correspondence had been "plucked out" and used out of context.

Touching a sensitive Arab nerve, Davies reminded Sulaiman that "there was no established market for Saudi Arab oil when the Concession Agreement was made" in 1933—that is, he told Sulaiman to remember that before Aramco his country had nothing, and without Aramco it had nothing, an indisputable fact of which the Saudis did not like to be reminded. "That is why the company was given the right to connect the oil with a market; and so that this Company would always be sure of getting oil to the market on terms satisfactory to the Company, Aramco was given the exclusive right" to arrange its transportation. The agreement left "no room for an effort to make the contract say what it does not," Davies wrote.[7]

Sulaiman was unmoved. He said Onassis had notified him by cable that he had been unable to come to any agreement with Aramco. "This compels us," the minister wrote, "to address this letter to you requesting you to let us know at the earliest opportunity the true position you took in the direct contacts made by Mr. A. S. Onassis with you, and what steps you have taken" to carry out the royal decree and implement the contract. Once the Saudi government received that information, the minister said, it would "determine what the situation is and make whatever arrangements may be required in this respect," an implied threat to revoke the Aramco concession.[8]

Sulaiman could stonewall Aramco, but he could not entirely fend off pressure from the oil company's most powerful ally, the U.S. Government. In the midst of Sulaiman's testy exchanges with Davies, Ambassador Wadsworth, on the instructions of Secretary of State Dulles, laid down the law in a letter to Crown Prince Faisal.

Wadsworth reminded the prince that he had first expressed reservations about the Onassis contract in a letter dated April 30.

"At that time," he said, "the full text of the Onassis Agreement was not known either to the US Government or to private American interests. Since its publication their concern has increased. Consequently and because of its long friendship for Saudi Arabia the US Government feels it would be wanting in due frankness were it not to set forth the very serious view it takes of this question and of the widespread ramifications which will result if appropriate solution is not found."

What were those "ramifications"? To begin with, "implementation of the Onassis Agreement would result in wide and serious public resentment not only in the US but also in other countries having commercial relations with Saudi Arabia. There is already evidence of this. At minimum Saudi Arabia would be thought to have committed an act of bad faith. One important result would be the discouragement of foreign capital investment. Some investors currently displaying interest in Saudi Arabian possibilities may be deterred. Another likely result is the imposition of retaliatory measures by other countries."

The agreement, Wadsworth said, was "inconsistent with established world practice in the field of international commerce. An essential element of international ocean commerce long standard international practice is that buyer and seller by mutual agreement have the right to designate the carrier of the cargo. In accordance with this practice it is traditional in much of the petroleum industry, including Aramco, for the buyer to make choice of the carrier. Consequently the US Government could not acquiesce in the establishment of any such unfortunate precedent."

In addition, Wadsworth wrote:

> the US Government is persuaded that from the practical business point of view both Aramco and Saudi Arabia would suffer substantial loss of revenue were The Royal Saudi Arabian Government to attempt to implement the Onassis Agreement. There is today, and probably will be for some years to come, a world surplus of oil particularly in the Persian Gulf; it is a buyers market. This situation is today aggravated by a world surplus of tankers available at rates substantially lower than those described by the Onassis Agreement. Buyers of oil will not put up with restrictions or compulsions; they will shift their purchases elsewhere.

As a final point, the ambassador said that the United States believed that the interests of Saudi Arabia would be best served "by encouraging export of oil to the widest possible markets of the Free World. This can only be done by continuing to permit the buyers the greatest freedom to transport and handle this oil through means of their own choice. The market for oil from Saudi Arabia can thus be extended and the revenue of the Government of Saudi Arabia increased."[9] Wadsworth did not specify what actions Washington might take if Saudi Arabia went ahead anyway, nor could he have done so because no one had yet made any decisions about that other than the CIA's deployment of Robert Maheu.

The ambassador had good reason to address his message to Crown Prince Faisal rather than to the king. Faisal was as smart and canny as his brother was obtuse, had more experience in international affairs than anyone else in the ruling family, and had been his father's point man on relations with the United States. His name was not on the decree ratifying the Onassis contract, so he had no personal stake in it.

The ambassador's points were valid, but it could be argued that the Saudis had as much leverage as the United States did. The king could revoke the Aramco concession entirely, or order an end to fuel sales to the U.S. Navy. Moreover, Saudi Arabia had already pulled out of the Point Four aid program, and so did not fear being cut off from that. The U.S. Air Force's lease on its strategic military base in Dhahran was due to expire in 1956, and the king was under no obligation to extend it. Washington did not want to lose that asset.

In addition, during the same week as Wadsworth's letter to Faisal, Onassis's position, and that of the Saudis, was strengthened when Metropolitan Life, which was financing the construction of the tanker fleet, dropped a provision of the loan agreement requiring the ships to be registered in the United States, Honduras, Liberia, or Panama. That freed Onassis to register the ships in Saudi Arabia, as his contract required. This decision, the State Department's Henry Byroade noted, "followed payment of $540,000 in cash by Mr. Onassis" on the loan.[10]

King Saud was neither shrewd enough nor courageous enough to defy the United States or take decisive action against Aramco, but Faisal might have done so. On August 3, he sounded off at what Ambassador Wadsworth described as a "small farewell dinner" given by Ali Alireza, the commerce minister's brother, for a departing American diplomat named Fred H. Awalt. According to Wadsworth, Faisal expressed "great frustration" at the U.S. position on the Onassis matter and said that the contract was "an internal matter of no concern to the U.S. government."

A few days later, in Beirut on his way home, Awalt told Fred Davies and Bill Eddy that he had concluded that Faisal was "more bitterly and aggressively anti-American than is His Majesty."

Wadsworth waited two weeks before reporting these tidbits to Washington because they changed nothing. He sent a cable about this "collateral information," as he called it, only because Secretary of State Dulles on August 16 had asked for "the ambassador's estimate current SAG thinking."[11]

That request from Dulles reflected a lull in the action during much of August. That was the month in which diplomats from several countries engaged the Saudis in the absurd argument about whether their protests were "official," but those discussions did not move the ball. Despite the State Department's opposition, Pacific Western sent word in August that it intended to go ahead with its plan to charter Onassis's new tanker, the *Malik al Saud al Awal*, to haul its Neutral Zone oil, at shipping rates lower than those Onassis was proposing for SATCO; otherwise, the situation remained mostly static till the end of the month as the king, the Eisenhower administration, and Aramco held their positions.[12] Robert Maheu, on behalf of the CIA and Stavros Niarchos, was looking for a weapon that could strike a decisive blow against Onassis but had not yet found one.

This hiatus lasted until August 26, when Aramco proposed to the Saudis an amendment of Article IV, the source of their greatest concern about the Onassis contract, that it said "would be acceptable to the Company and to the buyers of oil and oil products produced and manufactured by the Company."

The proposed language said: "Nothing in this agreement shall be taken to establish any preference in Saudi Arabian Maritime Tanker Company Ltd. for the transport of oil and products from Saudi Arabia to foreign countries. Arabian American Oil Company and Pacific Western Oil Company, their affiliates and the customers of any of them shall be free to export oil and products produced by them pursuant to outstanding agreements by any means or under any conditions they may deem advisable."[13]

Aramco submitted the proposal to comply with the king's instructions to seek some accommodation with Onassis, but the wording would have nullified the most important clause in the contract—the one that would have guaranteed SATCO enough cargo to make Onassis's investment profitable. It did not take long for the Saudi government to reject it.

On the 29th, Abdullah Sulaiman told Bill Owen that he had shown the draft to the King and his advisers, who were "all surprised" because they had expected a "reasonable" proposal, not one that would in effect nullify Article IV. Owen said he was surprised at their surprise because Aramco had made clear that it would not accept any tanker preference or restrictions on shipping. The finance minister responded by saying his country "would know how to protect itself" and was satisfied with its legal position.[14]

The End of an Era

That was Sulaiman's last verbal joust with the oil company. Two days later, King Saud dismissed him from the government, though technically allowing him to resign, ostensibly for health reasons. His son, who had been working with him at the ministry, was also removed. Mohammed Alireza was still minister of commerce, but there was no longer anyone in the king's inner circle who was personally vested in fulfillment of the Onassis contract.

Sulaiman was replaced by Mohammed Surur, who had been his deputy but had no part in the Onassis negotiations. The king told a senior Aramco official that "his brothers had long urged him to dismiss Shaikh Abdullah, but he had taken his time. It was better when cutting down the tree to pull out its roots as well." In a note to Washington reporting these developments, Wadsworth said Surur was "generally considered wise choice," and had a "good reputation in royal family and 'merchant circles.'" Among other benefits, the ambassador said, the change would facilitate Saudi Arabia's effort to join the International Bank for Reconstruction and Development, or World Bank, which it did in 1957.[15]

Sulaiman had been indispensable to King Abdul Aziz during all the events of the kingdom's creation and the development of its oil industry, but King Saud was not the admirer of the minister that his father had been. He had no personal commitment to Sulaiman and had been at odds with him over several issues for the past few years. The minister's standing at the royal court had been damaged the by GOVENCO affair, and Saud was facing growing pressure from the United States over the SATCO tanker contract. In both cases, Sulaiman was closely involved in the contractual arrangements with, and supervision of, the companies in his official capacity as minister of finance.

As the British ambassador noted:

> Abdullah Sulaiman was for many years [Abdul Aziz] Ibn Saud's minister of finance and chief adviser, and the power he wielded was second only to the king's. Somewhat irrationally, he came to symbolise in the eyes of the younger men who now fill the ministerial posts all that was unsatisfactory in the old regime. With much face-saving he was gently removed from power and his placed filled by Sheikh Mohammed Surur, a competent man, but one who depends on Faisal for major decisions. Thus the reins of government passed to one who, though no more experienced than Abdullah Sulaiman, yet realises more clearly that Saudi Arabia can no longer be ruled in the arbitrary manner of the good old days.[16]

Ambassador Wadsworth's optimism about Surur was at best premature. Surur may have been "competent," as the British ambassador described him, and he was certainly easier to get along with than Sulaiman had been, but according to the historian Alexei Vassiliev, he was an "utterly servile figure who meekly complied with every demand by Saud and his court."[17] He was unlikely to defy the king on the matter of the Onassis contract. Moreover, the transition gave additional responsibilities for dealing with oil matters to the young Abdullah Tariki, who was even more confrontational toward Aramco that Sulaiman had been.

The minister's departure removed the final vestige of the Abdul Aziz era of Arabian history, the era in which the kingdom had been created and unified out of a vast, desolate land occupied by warring tribes and rival clans and set on the path to modernization and integration with the wider world. All subsequent kings have been sons of Abdul Aziz, but the people who run the country on a day-to-day basis are educated technocrats.

Power Struggle in the Kingdom

With the king's assent, Sulaiman's letter of resignation attributed his decision to declining health. He had gone to Germany the year before to seek treatment for an increasingly painful and debilitating gastric ailment that made it difficult for him to eat, an affliction that some who knew him attributed to excessive consumption of alcohol. And he had had a stroke during a visit to Egypt several years earlier, although after three months he recovered fully.[18]

It was true that Sulaiman's health was declining, but he would have stayed on if Saud and Faisal had wanted him to do so. Instead, the king pushed him out in a manner that maintained his dignity, accepting health as the reason and allowing him to remain on the payroll, but he no longer had any part to play in the royal government or in negotiations with Aramco or Onassis.

One Last Payoff?

He had served his country well, and he had more than enough money for a comfortable retirement. But according to Ray Close, a career CIA agent in the Arab world, it is possible that he got one last big payment from the Onassis affair.

Close at the time was a relatively junior CIA operative based in Beirut. He also happened to be a nephew of Bill Eddy, who was Aramco's representative there and maintained his ties with the CIA. Close said that on orders from CIA director Allen Dulles, he went to Eddy's apartment and picked up an Aramco check for $2 million, which he gave to Robert Maheu for distribution to Saudi officials.

"I can remember going to Uncle Bill's apartment and picking up the check, which I handed over in one of those restaurants in Pigeon Rocks," a Beirut neighborhood, Close said. "The person to whom I delivered the check was Robert Maheu," whom he described as "a courier for the Saudi minister of finance." Close said that "the instructions on what to do came right from Allen Dulles. I guess he picked me because he knew I was related to Bill Eddy."

He said that after so many years he could not remember to whom the check had been made out, but he described the money as "a payoff" and "a bribe to the Saudis,"[19] presumably to someone who could persuade the king to abandon the Onassis contract or at least accept Aramco's proposed modification. It might have been intended to ease the way to Sulaiman's retirement, removing the Onassis contract's strongest supporter from the royal entourage. Was this the company that insisted it never paid *baksheesh*?

Not a word about this transaction or its purpose can be found in Eddy's papers because he was rigorously discreet about his interactions with the CIA while he was on the Aramco payroll, but his daughter Mary, who also worked for the CIA, confirmed that he reported regularly to the agency during those years.[20]

CHAPTER THIRTEEN

Don't Embarrass the King

By September 1954, with Abdullah Sulaiman out of the Saudi government, it was clear that many officials in Washington, in Saudi Arabia, and at Aramco wanted an end to the stalemate over the SATCO contract. Few of them had much sympathy for the only remaining actor whose personal interests were at stake in implementation of the contract, namely Onassis himself. Abdullah Sulaiman and Mohammed Alireza had their money regardless of the outcome, though Alireza expected to make more as Onassis's agent when the tanker fleet went into operation; as for Spyridon Catapodis, Onassis had used him and then cast him aside, so there was nothing left in the deal for him.

Even before the dismissal of Sulaiman, U.S. officials perceived that the dynamics in the kingdom were shifting. In late August 1954, the CIA's Current Intelligence Weekly reported that Ambassador Wadsworth "believes the recent unfavorable trend in relations between the United States and Saudi Arabia has been reversed."[1] That assessment was based on Wadsworth's account of a long conversation he had with King Saud on August 24, an overall review of the bilateral relationship. "The King was extremely cordial," a State Department report said, "and agreed to discuss the [Onassis] agreement with Aramco representatives. In these discussions he expressed the desire to arrive at a formula acceptable to all sides and instructed that a joint SAG-Aramco committee be appointed to study the matter."[2] The outcome of that committee's deliberations, or rather the lack of outcome, would be central to the developments that followed.

As the number of people who talked to participants in the Onassis discussions expanded during that summer, so did the roster of well-connected individuals who sought a way out. In fact, their quest for a resolution in some ways complicated the situation. The parties involved now included well-intentioned freelancers as well as self-promoters, and while there was close communication between Aramco and the Eisenhower administration, there were too many channels of communication rather than too few, and they were not coordinated. Stavros Niarchos and Robert Maheu had their own agendas, as did some of the senior people in King Saud's entourage. The documentary record shows that on some days, there were conversations between different people in different countries that might affect the outcome, but the import of these discussions was not necessarily conveyed to the other participants. To chronicle these events in strict chronological order would be to write a chaotic narrative.

One of those who joined the fray was John McCone, another of those quintessentially Washington insiders who spend their careers moving in and out of government. For several years, he had been the business partner of Stephen Bechtel, the founder of Bechtel Corp., a giant international construction company that dominated big building projects in Saudi Arabia until it was supplanted by the ill-fated Michael Baker International.[3] McCone had been undersecretary of the Air Force in President Truman's administration and would later become head of the Atomic Energy Commission and director of the CIA. He and Bechtel had been members of the same board of directors of Pacific Carriers Inc., a shipping company, as Texaco's Cap Rieber.[4] These were men who understood each other and knew how the game was played.

McCone's point of contact at the State Department was deputy undersecretary Robert Murphy, the wartime OSS boss of Aramco's Bill Eddy. On September 1, the State Department's John Jernegan noted that McCone "had been in touch with Mr. [Robert] Murphy two or three times in recent weeks to report that Onassis has been seeking his (McCone's) intervention to help him out of the jam he has gotten into as a result of his Saudi Arabian deal." This was the supplicant Onassis who had whined to Aramco's Fred Davies in June that he was "in the doghouse" and needed a way out, not the pugnacious Onassis who had promised to fight.

"According to McCone, Onassis made a special trip to London a while back to see him," Jernegan reported. "He has telephoned at least a couple of times since then. The last time, McCone advised Onassis that the best thing he could do would be to cancel the Saudi agreement and make his peace with the oil companies." That was the same advice Onassis had received, and ignored, back in June when he sought the counsel of Cap Rieber.

McCone also told Murphy that Onassis had said he would be "willing to sell his entire tanker holdings at a loss," though it is not clear from the record why he would offer to do something that would be contrary to every business move he had made in his career.[5] McCone told Murphy he "would like to be helpful" and would be willing to be a conduit for messages to Onassis. Murphy was noncommittal: he said the department "should keep this offer in mind."[6]

Shifting Sands

By September 2, the day after Jernegan wrote his memo about McCone, it was becoming apparent that with the departure of Sulaiman from the government, the sand was beginning to shift in Saudi Arabia; Onassis was not the only one looking for a face-saving way out.

Ambassador Wadsworth had a long conversation with Khaled Gorgoni, a senior adviser to King Saud who was known as Khaled Bey, an honorific that recognized his high standing. Gorgoni had his own colorful history. Like many senior men in the entourage of King Abdul Aziz in the era when Saudi Arabia had few educated citizens, Gorgoni was of foreign birth, in his case Libya. In 1939, when Saudi Arabia established diplomatic relations with Nazi Germany, Gorgoni had been King Abdul Aziz's personal emissary to Hitler, with whom he met at the Berghof.[7]

Gorgoni, who had a long-standing interest in petroleum issues, told the ambassador that the king had asked him to study the Onassis matter closely. He said he wanted credible economic data that would "prove to the king with simple figures" that Saudi Arabia would actually lose money because of it, as Aramco and the State Department said it would. But he also said there was another issue that had to be taken into account: "The king's prestige must be protected and maintained in this country as well as abroad. We should not forget that it was the king himself who signed [the] decree confirming Onassis arrangement."[8]

That question of protecting the king's "prestige" hung over the maneuvering for months afterward.

Robert Maheu later said that "the biggest problem that we ended up having was not the fact that the contract had been signed or ratified, it was the fact that it had been published" and the king had celebrated it. King Saud, he said, "had lavishly published that for the first time in history the Saudi Arabian government would have its flag flying the high seas. . . . It turned out that the biggest problem that we had was to find a save-face gimmick."[9] At one point Muhammad Surur, the successor to Sulaiman as finance minister, told Fred Davies that

> It is no longer a business of Mr. Onassis. Mr. Onassis may be a small, insignificant insect that has interfered in order to make the atmosphere poisonous and most uncomfortable for both of us, but unfortunately he was successful in giving to our discussions a turn which is no longer insignificant. What he has been able to convince the government of is that its honor and prestige are at stake. Therefore the question now has become a question as to whether the government has the power and the right to render a decree such as the one that was rendered, or whether it has not.

It has become a far more important question than the person of Mr. Onassis.[10]

If Gorgoni and Surur were aware that the Eisenhower's administration had sought all along to avoid embarrassing the king, this conversation did not reflect it.

Concluding his report on his conversation with Gorgoni, Wadsworth said there was a third point to be considered as well: "Elimination of monopolistic character [of] Onassis arrangement. He agreed; and [a] practical formula must of course meet this point. If this meant only that Onassis would have to be told he must carry oil at 'going market rates,' it could easily be arranged. . . . What he wanted most was that Aramco come up with practical formula which he could persuade king was reasonable. Then it would be Onassis who would have to say 'no' and not Aramco; [the] company's future relations with [the] king was [sic] also an important factor."

This opposition by the U.S. administration to the "monopolistic character" of the agreement was nicely ironic for a government that had spent years accusing the oil companies of their own monopolistic arrangements, unrelated to the Onassis affair—a government in which the State and Justice departments had never fully resolved their differences over this issue. The monopoly question had been raised publicly in early June when Niarchos had lunch in Paris with *New York Times* correspondent C. S. Sulzberger to fill him in on the story, or at least on Niarchos's version of it. The article Sulzberger wrote studiously avoided listing any sources and was filled with such passive-voice evasions as "It is understood" and "it is estimated," without saying by whom. Sulzberger knew about Byroade's meeting with Onassis in late May—the meeting in which Onassis said he "was in a tight spot"—and reported that Onassis had brushed off Byroade's concerns about a monopoly by saying he was prepared to interpret the agreement's terms "with considerable latitude."[11]

The day after that article appeared in the *New York Times*, Onassis telephoned the newspaper's Paris office from Antibes, on the Riviera, to dispute it. He had never discussed the monopoly issue with Byroade, he said, and in any case his agreement was in no way monopolistic. He esteemed the United States, he said, and therefore "he would do anything desired by the United States to alter existing arrangements if it could be proved they were monopolistic."[12] This was Onassis once again untethered from veracity, saying what he thought his audience wanted to hear

A few days after Wadsworth's conversation with Gorgoni, on September 6, Spyros Skouras was back at the State Department in Washington, discussing the state of play with Jernegan and with Walter Bedell Smith, the undersecretary, who was running the department in the temporary absence of

Secretary Dulles. In Washington's world of insiders, Smith was as inside as anyone. He was a retired general who had been Eisenhower's chief of staff in Europe during the war, a position in which he worked closely with Robert Murphy and Bill Eddy in the preparation for the Allied landings in North Africa. After the war, Truman appointed him ambassador to the Soviet Union and then named him director of the CIA. His deputy at the CIA was Allen Dulles, who now in 1954 was the director himself.

Smith began by telling Skouras about Onassis's discussion with McCone, including Onassis's purported willingness to sell his tankers at a loss. Skouras then asked what solution the State Department would propose.

Jernegan responded that "the simplest thing might be for Onassis to tell the Saudis he thought a mistake had been made, that they had failed to take into account all aspects, and to propose cancelling the agreement. Mr. Skouras thought this was not feasible because of the amount of money Onassis had already invested" in tankers for his proposed Saudi fleet. Skouras "fully agreed however that the agreement was a bad one and could not possibly be accepted by the oil companies. He had told Onassis himself that he had made a bad mistake."

Skouras, who was in the shipping business before he was in the movie business, said that "the only solution would be for the oil companies to buy the Onassis tankers on a basis satisfactory to them. This would provide a solution to the whole problem without financial loss to the companies, without their having to give way on the important principle involved. It would also save the companies the expense of a long fight. If Mr. McCone had correctly understood Mr. Onassis's statement that he would be willing to sell out at a loss, Mr. Skouras thought the two parties should be gotten together."

That would probably not have been acceptable to Aramco because its companies were not primarily in the tanker business and they supported the freedom of those who bought oil to select their own carriers. But Smith, who had no experience in the oil industry and may not have known that, said Skouras's idea was acceptable to him, and that he would run it by McCone. If McCone approved, and if Aramco was willing, Skouras would take the proposal to Onassis when he saw him next in Europe.[13]

The next day Jernegan, doubtless with Smith's approval, wrote a brief memo to Attorney General Herbert Brownell. He said the State Department had heard that the Justice Department was considering settlements in its legal cases against Onassis and urged him to hold off. "You will doubtless be interested," he wrote, in the president's policy directive urging the use of "all appropriate measures" to break Onassis's contract with Saudi Arabia.[14] Jernegan thought that Brownell, who had not been present during the discussions that led to NSC 5428, was unaware of it or needed to be reminded of it.

According to the scholar Nathan Citino, "bureaucratic tensions now emerged between Justice officials, who feared losing out on a generous settlement offer if forced to go to trial, and the State Department, which wanted to keep the pressure on Onassis. 'Justice is in the uncomfortable position,' Undersecretary of State Robert Murphy observed, 'of holding the bag on account of State's intervention.'"[15] State prevailed, and Justice rejected the defendants' offer to settle civil suit. In the parallel criminal case, on September 9 Judge Luther Youngdahl in Washington dismissed the indictments against five of Onassis's co-defendants but not the indictment of Onassis himself or of his companies. The indictment and the civil suit would hang over Onassis's head for months to come.[16]

Another Intermediary

Yet another potential intermediary who inserted himself into the multi-front discussions at about this time was a prominent British maritime consultant named H. P. Drewry, whose company even today describes itself as "a leading independent provider of research and consulting services to the maritime and shipping industry."[17] Drewry reported to the Foreign Office that one of Onassis's bankers in Paris had asked him to "discuss a possible settlement of this troublesome business." Drewry, perhaps surprisingly, feared that a campaign against Onassis might turn him into a sympathetic figure victimized by a monopolistic oil industry.

"I have advised my Standard Oil friends of the proposals," Drewry wrote, "and suggested that while Mr. Onassis is heading for a fall similar to the Kruger 'Match King' empire, this might not be politically expedient and [might] lead to an anti-Middle East Oil campaign against the big oil interests in the Middle East. And, as Mr. Onassis has some very strong press support, he might be featured as a 'Private Enterprise' victim of Oil Trusts." Onassis might be seen as more victim than perpetrator.

Drewry counseled persuasion rather than coercion. Onassis, he said, "is a very wily person, of semi-Oriental origin, and if he can be quietly persuaded to transfer his activities from the shipping world and the Middle East to the social life of his Monte Carlo enterprise it will I believe be the best solution." He cautioned that "the recent downfall of the Saudi Arabian Minister of Finance . . . will weaken Mr. Onassis's position, but he still has considerable support."[18]

On September 7, the CIA's Office of National Estimates—which Walter Bedell Smith had created when he was director—distributed "National Intelligence Estimate Number 36–54, Probable Developments in the Arab States," the consensus intelligence assessment that warned of the probability of increased "Communist activity" in the region. On the whole, it did not paint an encouraging picture about the Arab countries or the prospects for U.S. interests.

It said that the Arabs, unable to resolve the conflicts between Western culture and their own, "have found expression for their discontent and frustration in nationalist and other movements which will, at least in the short term, increase general instability. . . . The governments of the Arab states will continue to be unstable and subject to change." As for U.S. and other Western interests, it said, "current conditions and trends in the Arab world on the whole are adverse to the continuation of special military, political, and economic positions for the West."[19]

In that context, preservation of Saudi Arabia's strategic and economic dependence on the United States and on the American oil companies became all the more important.

The Onassis contract was the most immediate issue but not the only one. The removal of Abdullah Sulaiman from the government had opened the way to resolution of long-standing arguments about the price the company was paying and what taxes it owed. On a per-barrel basis, the amounts of money involved might have seemed small, but by late 1954 Aramco was producing 953,000 barrels a day.[20] (A barrel is 42 gallons).

On September 19, the U.S. Embassy reported that after arduous negotiations, Aramco and the government had reached a "definitive settlement" of the government's claim for back taxes under the 1950 tax law. They basically split the difference: the government, which had claimed $150 million, accepted an offer of $70 million. The embassy's cable said that the State Department "will recognize high importance this final achievement settlement this three year old dispute. It has long since been sine qua non for settlement so-called pricing dispute under fifty-fifty agreement." Aramco's Davies, this cable reported, was "hopeful early agreement pricing dispute now also possible," as it turned out to be.[21]

The Finance Ministry's agreements with Aramco on the tax and price issues, however, did not eliminate the objections of the Eisenhower administration and the British to the Onassis tanker deal, which were largely political rather than economic.

On September 24, Spyros Skouras made one last effort to bridge the gap between Onassis and his opponents.

At the State Department, he told Smith and Jernegan that he had recently seen Onassis, who "had expressed himself as ready, willing and anxious to arrive at an understanding with the oil company." Specifically, he had offered to sell his tankers at their cost price less depreciation.

Skouras produced a telegram Onassis had sent him, in which Onassis said he was "was willing to negotiate but felt he had a very strong legal position, supported by legal opinions from several countries to the effect that his agreement did not infringe either the Aramco concession or international law and that if Aramco remained intransigent arbitration under the concession terms would become inevitable." Onassis predicted that the company would lose in arbitration, creating "a precedent for similar shipping agreements in other oil producing countries which was just the thing Aramco most wanted to avoid."

Smith commented dryly that judging by that telegram Onassis did not seem to be in a "chastened mood" and expressed doubt that Aramco would want to negotiate further with him. Skouras said he hoped that Aramco would at least let company officials talk to him "so that he could determine for himself whether any basis for negotiation existed."[22] By that time, of course, Aramco was beyond any hope of reaching an agreement with Onassis.

A New Argument

On September 14, the British embassy in Jeddah received a written response from the Saudi Foreign Ministry to Britain's protests against the tanker arrangement. "They assert," an embassy diplomat notified London, "that the agreement is in the national interest of Saudi Arabia and does not conflict with any other international agreement entered into by the Saudi Arabian government. The latter therefore regret they cannot accept a protest by the Government of the United Kingdom or any other country in a matter entirely within Saudi domestic jurisdiction." He said the same message had been delivered to the U.S. embassy.[23]

By this time, the government of Saudi Arabia, hampered by the king's incompetence and by the rivalries and ambitions of his senior advisers, was no longer speaking with one voice. After the death of their protector, King Abdul Aziz, the foreigners such as Gorgoni and Yusuf Yassin, whom he had imported to take on bureaucratic assignments of which his subjects were then incapable, found themselves competing for influence with each other and with a rising generation of educated young Saudi citizens.

Yassin's official title was deputy foreign minister. According to one British account, Yassin "came as a teacher to the King's family and quickly rose to be political secretary and, especially in later years, a notorious thorn in the flesh of all Westerners in the Kingdom."[24] The Russian historian Alexei Vassiliev described him as the leader of a "clique of Syrians" who by the time Saud became king was "old, clever and cynical."[25]

In a long conversation with a British diplomat in mid-September, Yassin raised an entirely new argument in defense of the Onassis agreement.

Yassin said that "the real aim of the United Kingdom as well as the United States and the other great maritime powers was to monopolise the oil transport industry. Thus, if their policy demanded that oil should at any time be denied to a specific country, they wanted to be in a position to deny it. Saudi Arabia wanted to be able to carry oil to any of her Moslem friends at any time without outside help. That was the real reason for the Onassis agreement." Given Saudi Arabia's self-image as protector of all the world's Muslims, that argument might have made sense if it had been offered nine months earlier, but this was the first London or Washington had heard of it.

In his report to the Foreign Office, the British diplomat, Horace Phillips, said Yassin offered this example: "When recently the Imam [ruler] of the Yemen had asked King Saud to send a cargo of oil products to his country, the Arabian-American Oil Company, when approached, had said that they could not ship anything to [the Yemeni port of] Hodeida, nor deliver overland, nor by air. His Majesty had therefore been obliged to send a (very small) cargo to Hodeida with difficulty by tug and barge. It was not fitting that a sovereign of the King's stature should be so obviously at the mercy of foreign operators to that extent." The Onassis contract specified that SATCO would ship oil free to any Red Sea port, including Hodeida.

In reality, King Saud could have ordered Aramco to ship oil to Hodeida, just as his father had ordered the company to build a railroad it did not want to build. Aramco never openly defied a royal order, out of fear of losing its exclusive concession. Besides, Yassin's argument ignored the fact that Aramco did not object to creation of a Saudi tanker fleet that it could deploy as it wished, only to a requirement that oil buyers employ it, and therefore the religion issue was irrelevant. But Phillips chose to let it pass. Instead, he returned to the economic and legal arguments, and by his account made some progress in persuading the normally truculent Yassin.

The diplomat restated his government's official position, which was that Saudi Arabia was free to create whatever sort of merchant fleet it wanted, but not to impose "restrictive monopoly positions." He asked Yassin "whether he thought that potential buyers of oil from Saudi Arabia were likely to submit to being not only told how to carry their oil away but at the same time forced to pay a higher price than they pay if they bought oil elsewhere and had it shipped by a carrier of their own choice. The result of this could only be that the demand for Saudi oil would fall off, there would be a consequent drop in production, and Saudi revenue would fall."

Phillips noted in his report to London that Yassin, "despite the face-saving front which he put up to me, is worried about the affair." In addition, he said, he had heard from Aramco's Davies that the king and his brother, Crown Prince Faisal, "were slowly coming around to the view that the contract was misconceived." He noted a parallel to the ill-fated GOVENCO contract, which had also been negotiated by Abdullah Sulaiman, and suggested that Sulaiman's departure from government might make it easier for the king to repudiate the Onassis contract as he had the GOVENCO deal. The crucial difference was that the king had "publicly ratified the Onassis agreement but not the Govenco contract. He has therefore been able to repudiate the latter easily—but not the former." Even if sentiment in the king's entourage was shifting away from the Onassis deal, it remained difficult "to find a face-saving way out of an agreement which he had personally ratified."[26]

Neither the participants in this conversation nor anyone else in the Saudi or British governments, or at Aramco, knew that at that very moment the "face-saving way out" Onassis claimed he wanted was about to be delivered, by none other than the man who started the entire affair, Spyridon Catapodis.

The rupture between Catapodis and Onassis was by this time complete, and it was well known because it had burst into public view in a notorious incident. Encountering Onassis at the airport in Nice, Catapodis throttled him and yelled, "You're not even a true Greek! You're nothing but a goddam Turk!" As Peter Evans observed in his authorized biography of Onassis, "a crowded departure lounge is not a good place to have a private quarrel; within hours, it was the talk of the Riviera."[27] Catapodis was unpaid, but he was not without weapons to deploy against Onassis.

CHAPTER FOURTEEN

The Revenge of Spyridon Catapodis

By late summer 1954, Catapodis had reached a moment of decision. His breach with Onassis was irreversible. He had not been paid and had little hope of being paid. He had nothing to lose if the entire Onassis contract blew apart, and he believed he had the weapon to make that happen.

He asked Onassis's confidant Leon Turrou to convey an extensive message to Aramco explaining how his arrangement with Onassis had cratered and what he planned to do about it. After describing his futile attempts in the spring to persuade Onassis to pay what he thought was due him, he brought up the barely credible story of the disappearing ink.

According to Turrou's account, shortly after King Saud ratified the Onassis contract, "Catapodis discovered that the agreement between himself and Onassis, which had been written by the latter, had apparently been written with vanishing ink and was at that time only about 25% legible. He promptly had it photostated and demanded that Onassis rewrite the agreement with a pen furnished by Catapodis, which Onassis refused to do."

Then came this melodramatic scene:

> When it became clear to Catapodis that Onassis was trying to welch on his agreement, he promptly called Muhammed [Alireza] to come to Paris. A meeting was held at the Hotel Claridge in Muhammed's suite. Onassis was also present. Catapodis ignored Onassis and told Muhammed that Onassis had failed to meet his obligations with him. Onassis pleaded with Catapodis for more time, explaining that he was temporarily short of funds. At this point, Onassis fell on his knees and kissed Catapodis' feet and said that if the deal were exposed he would be forced to commit suicide. He

The Revenge of Spyridon Catapodis

added further that he (Onassis) had only a 15% equity in his tankers. Muhammed urged Catapodis to be patient, and assured him that he would get "his $1,000,000 per year" if he would only be patient.

Catapodis was unmoved. He said he had expended £35,000 of his own money to make the arrangements and would now take matters into his own hands. He said he was "prepared to furnish a sworn statement covering the foregoing together with photostat copies of all documents, including the side agreement, and cancelled checks," in the expectation that this material would become public. He said he also planned to sue Onassis in a French court to seek the money he believed was due.[1]

He soon carried through on both threats.

In the third week of September—probably on September 20, and no later than September 21, though records differ—he went to the British consulate in Nice. There, before vice consul P. R. Payne, he delivered under oath a lengthy account of the entire affair, or at least his version of it. It covered everything from his original discussions with the Iraqis to his commitments to Alireza to Onassis's alleged duplicity in his dealings with the Saudis. The 13-page affidavit gave a detailed account of whom Onassis paid to get the contract, and how much. Catapodis also delivered what he said were supporting documents, such as letters, hotel receipts, and telegrams, to back up his story. One document was a letter from Onassis to Alireza, dated the previous November 11, stipulating how much he was to be paid.[2] Catapodis's file included photographs of himself with Aristotle and Tina Onassis, Abdullah Sulaiman, and Mohammed Alireza taken during the signing celebration in Jeddah in January. He even included a statement from a handwriting and typography expert who said various letters in the file appeared to come from the same model typewriter that Onassis used in his Paris apartment.[3]

Catapodis, of course, knew that the British government was strongly opposed to the Onassis contract, but it is not clear from the documentary record why a Greek resident of France would give evidence about his dealings with a Greek-born citizen of Argentina who lived in Paris to a British official. The Foreign Office in London took the position that "the British Consular seal on an affidavit in no way involves Her Majesty's Government [and] that the officer before whom an affidavit is sworn is not responsible for the truth or otherwise of its content."[4]

Shrewd schemer that he was, Catapodis knew that career diplomats in the British Foreign Service would keep this dossier under wraps at least until it could be evaluated and verified in London, but he wanted the documents deployed promptly to damage Onassis. So he photocopied them and sold one set to Stavros Niarchos. Within a week, the State Department, the CIA, and Royal Dutch Shell Chairman Frank Hopwood had the file, and State and the CIA were already strategizing about how to use the material.

Hopwood went to see Harold Caccia, a senior diplomat at the Foreign Office in London, "about the possibility of making some use of them in order to frustrate the [Onassis] Agreement." The Foreign Office record of this conversation says that Hopwood "could not be sure, but his guess was that the documents were genuine. His idea was that the Saudis might be willing to modify or cancel the agreement rather than see the documents published and have the whole scandalous negotiation revealed." Hopwood was hardly the only person thinking along those lines.

Hopwood and Caccia agreed that "the most suitable Saudi to approach would be Yusuf Yassin, the deputy foreign minister. Not only did he not receive any of the bribes which were distributed during the negotiation of the agreement, but he was known to have been angry with Abdullah Suleiman, the ex-Minister of Finance, for having made the agreement without his, Yasin's, knowledge." Yassin, they agreed, was influential, untainted, and conveniently available because he was at that moment in Europe.

The two men recognized that "there could be no certainty whether the Saudis would give way when faced with these revelations; they might become more intransigent than ever." Still, Hopwood said it was worth the risk because otherwise similar oil transport arrangements might develop in Iran, Kuwait, and Iraq. Before contacting Yassin, however, Hopwood said it was important to coordinate with Aramco because "the oil companies must act in concert."[5]

Maheu Goes to Work

In August, Robert Maheu had spent a long day and night in London discussing the state of play with Niarchos; they had identified the malcontent Catapodis as a potential ally in their campaign against Onassis. Now, by happy accident, Catapodis had come through.[6] Armed with the damaging dossier, Maheu wasted little time.

In a memorandum of conversation in the State Department's files, dated September 24, the subject line is "Utilization of Papers Showing Bribery in Connection with Onassis Contract." The three participants in that conversation were John Jernegan, deputy assistant secretary of state for Near East and South Asian affairs; Scott McLeod, administrator of the department's Bureau of Security and Consular Affairs; and John F. Gerrity, a former *Washington Post* reporter who was working for Maheu. They met on the same day that Walter Bedell Smith had his conversation with Spyros Skouras. Jernegan was present at both meetings, but there is no indication in the record that either conversation was discussed during the other.

Catapodis or Niarchos had evidently reproduced his dossier several times: Gerrity brought with him a complete set of the papers, and he said Maheu had a set, as did the CIA.

Gerrity recommended that "these papers should be gotten into the hands of King Saud and that this should be done quickly before there was any publicity about bribery in connection with the Onassis agreement, since such publicity would embarrass the King and make future relations more difficult."

The idea that Onassis's payments to Mohammed Alireza and Abdullah Sulaiman constituted "bribery" misread the business history of Saudi Arabia. King Saud well knew that Mohammed Alireza at least, if not also Abdullah Sulaiman, had been handsomely paid for his part in negotiating the deal. It would have been an aberration if he had not; such payoffs, known as "commissions" rather than bribes, were a standard part of doing business in the kingdom. If King Saud had been displeased with Alireza or thought him corrupt, he would hardly have appointed him minister of commerce. The issue was not the payments in themselves but, as Gerrity correctly noted, the likelihood of publicity about the system that would be embarrassing to the king and to Crown Prince Faisal.

As to how to get the information to King Saud, Gerrity—speaking for Maheu—nominated a more reliable and trusted conduit than Yusuf Yassin, Hopwood's choice, who had his own agenda inside the royal court. "He thought the best channel would be Mr. Karl Twitchell," the State Department memorandum reported. That was the same Karl Twitchell who 20 years earlier had persuaded King Abdul Aziz to allow oil exploration in Saudi Arabia and later was a partner in the failed SAADCO development proposal of 1945. He was widely respected in Saudi Arabia and had access to the royal court. And better yet, he was already in Jeddah. Maheu had tracked him down in Connecticut, recruited him for this task, and dispatched him to Saudi Arabia in anticipation of this assignment.

Gerrity noted that using Twitchell to take the Catapodis dossier to the king "would avoid any involvement of the U.S. government or Aramco."

Jernegan was receptive but cautious. He "agreed it would be undesirable for either the US government or Aramco to be in any way involved, and he thought Mr. Twitchell might be the proper man to carry out the operation. However, he could not give an opinion offhand. He thought it necessary to consult [the] CIA and considered that organization should continue to be the channel for handling this matter. Mr. Gerrity agreed and observed that his firm had been working with CIA all along."[7]

Now Maheu and Gerrity, and their behind-the-scenes backers in Washington, had the material that could give King Saud a reason to do what they believed he wanted to do: cancel the Onassis contract. And they had a workable plan for delivering that material to the king. But there remained the same issue that Khalid Bey Gorgoni had raised with Ambassador Wadsworth three weeks before: shielding the king from embarrassment or from having to admit error.

According to the State Department memorandum, Gerrity said he and Niarchos "thought it essential that everything possible be done to save King Saud's face" if he could be persuaded to abrogate the Onassis agreement. Earning their money, Maheu and Gerrity had already developed a plan: the Saudi Arabian, British, and U.S. governments would issue "a joint factual statement" saying the deal was off. "This statement would merely include the fact of the abrogation and explain in general terms that it had been decided upon because the agreement had been found injurious to the interests of Saudi Arabia and of the other two countries involved." The British government had already approved this plan, Gerrity said, and he "was sure the king would likewise endorse it."

Jernegan said the whole plan—the proposed Twitchell mission, the trilateral statement—was acceptable if the CIA approved. When his contact at the intelligence agency endorsed it, Jernegan the next morning telephoned Gerrity to let him know—only to find out that Gerrity was well ahead of him. He already knew about the CIA's endorsement and had already turned over his copy of the Catapodis papers to the agency for transmission to Twitchell. And Twitchell, in Jeddah, already "had an appointment to see the Saudi Finance Minister on Wednesday, September 29," just a few days later. The CIA and Maheu expected that the minister, Mohammed Surur, would convey the file to King Saud and Crown Prince Faisal.[8]

As the conversation between Gerrity and Jernegan was ending, Gerrity offered a new proposal, which undoubtedly originated with Niarchos, for getting rid of Onassis while still giving the king some of what he had hoped to gain. He said that "both the Aramco parent companies and Niarchos would be willing to place some of their tankers under the Saudi flag, thus giving the King one of the advantages he had hoped to obtain from the Onassis agreement, namely a Saudi Arabian merchant marine. Niarchos would also be willing to assume the obligation of establishing a maritime academy in Saudi Arabia."[9]

The possibility of a deal involving the reflagging of existing tankers, or of oil company charters of some of the ships that Onassis was building but at commercial rates, came up again and again over the next several months.

A Nerve-Wracking Journey

Maheu then set out for Saudi Arabia to join up with Twitchell. That sounds simple, but for Maheu such a journey entailed considerable risk. He knew almost nothing about Saudi Arabia or the Arabs, although he had been reading about them, including a book by Twitchell, and he had no way to know how King Saud and his advisers would react to the Catapodis papers.

In those days, foreigners who were allowed into Saudi Arabia could not just leave when their business was done. They had to obtain an exit visa, which required royal assent. Foreigners who lost their passports while in the kingdom, or had them confiscated in a dispute with a Saudi employer or client, were in trouble: their embassies could give them new passports, but these would not have valid entry stamps, so the bearers could not prove they had entered the country legally, so the authorities would not issue exit visas. Some travelers were stranded in this limbo for months. In Maheu's case, if the king was angry about the message, he might take it out on the messenger. Twitchell had sufficient stature in the kingdom that he would probably be spared, but Maheu could find himself unable to leave Saudi Arabia.

Years later, Maheu described this adventure to the U.S. Senate's Church Committee.

Twitchell, he said, "was highly, highly loved by the Saudis and although the old king was then gone and King Saud, the son was in power, Karl Twitchell had the same respect and reverence from the present leaders as he did from the father and I convinced [him] that—he already had a clearance, a satisfactory clearance—and I convinced him precede me to Saudi Arabia to try to lay the groundwork." Twitchell accepted no payment other than reimbursement of his expenses, according to Maheu. "Anyway, I finally ended up going to Saudi Arabia, having a meeting with the King's confidential assistant, presenting all of this evidence, frankly at the time not knowing if the King himself had a piece of the action. . . ."

At that point, Senator Walter Huddleston of Kentucky broke in with a question: "Had some of this evidence come from the wiretap?" He was referring to the phone tap Maheu's agent had planted on Onassis in New York.

"That tap was entirely unproductive," Maheu responded.

By Maheu's account, he never saw King Saud himself and met only with the "confidential assistant," whom he did not identify in his public testimony. Some accounts have said it was Abdullah Sulaiman, but that is unlikely because by this time Sulaiman was out of favor and out of the government, retired to his farm in northern Saudi Arabia.

In any case, Maheu said, the day he had hoped to meet King Saud was the last day of the king's summer sojourn in Jeddah; he was due to return to Riyadh the next morning. To mark the occasion, "they were having a big parade for him," which Maheu watched from his hotel room while worrying about obtaining permission to leave the country.

"I frankly was not too comfortable," he told the senators, because of this uncertainty. He said he was in "constant contact" with Ambassador Wadsworth, who "made it very clear that the [U.S.] government approved of everything I was doing, but if something went wrong they could not come to my rescue. I would have to be the fall guy, and I was prepared to do it."

After a lengthy discussion with the "special assistant" and a few aides, Maheu was told to be in his hotel room at noon the following day and wait for a telephone call. "Sure enough," Maheu said, "the following morning at

12 sharp he called me and he said—well, first of all, here's your exit visa." He told Maheu he was welcome to see whatever he wanted in Saudi Arabia, but "frankly [His Excellency] would like for you to get out as soon as possible."

As for the material in the Catapodis file, the royal confidential assistant was "very appreciative of all the information that you have made available." He told Maheu that they wanted him to leak the material to the press in Europe and the Middle East, but not in the United States. It would not look good for U.S.-Saudi relations if the United States government were perceived to be the source of the file.

Making the material public was exactly what Catapodis had in mind when he gave his affidavit in Nice, and Maheu knew how to spread the dossier around. But getting the news out turned out to be much more difficult than he expected.

"We spent several weeks trying to break the story—Rome, France, Athens, and there's just no way," he said. "No one would touch it. It was too hot."[10]

CHAPTER FIFTEEN

The Power of the Press

The reason that "no one would touch it," as Maheu told the Church Committee, was that the Catapodis documents arrived in the mail unaccompanied by any background material or indication of who sent them. Lacking independent verification, recipients hesitated to publicize them. As the Saudis had suggested, and as he had planned since first learning of the Catapodis file, Maheu quickly sent copies all around Europe, not just to news outlets but also to corporate executives and to Onassis's rival shipowners, but the inflammatory content of the material inspired caution. No one wanted to be the first to publish or the first to be sued.

Among the news outlets that declined to publish the substance of the Catapodis file was the *Daily Telegraph* in London, where editors feared they would be sued under Britain's restrictive libel laws, a common reaction among editors and among news organizations' lawyers.[1] An Athens-based reporter for the United Press wrote an article, but the U.S.-based news agency's libel lawyers nixed it, so it was not distributed. The International News Service decided not to publish because, when its reporters in Washington inquired about the file, they were told that the State Department knew nothing about it—which at that point was true.[2]

Maheu knew just the solution, he later told senators on the Church Committee. "Finally," he said, in order to get the news out, "we bought a newspaper in Athens, and that was the way we broke the story."

Senator Huddleston interrupted again. "You said you bought a paper in Athens? You mean by that you actually bought the paper or just paid them to run the story?"

"We bought a newspaper," Maheu replied. He said that in some European cities in those days there were as many as 50 newspapers, most with circulations below 20,000. It was not expensive to acquire one.[3]

In London, the Foreign Office wrote a note to the British embassy in Jeddah reporting that the *Telegraph* had decided not to publish but noted that "reports are reaching the London press, however, that the text of the affidavit has been published in Athens."[4] The circle of people in governments and the maritime industry who knew about the Catapodis papers was growing fast, but the information had still not reached the public, nor had it reached King Saud or Crown Prince Faisal.

Once the first newspaper published the documents, it legitimized the story for everyone else to pursue.

"They started smuggling the papers into Saudi Arabia, which gave the king the reason to fire the minister who had been involved," Maheu said. "And if you don't think this guy had a racket going for him, my recollection is that he had both the Cadillac and Lincoln agencies at the same time" and received a percentage of the value of all cargo shipped into the port of Jeddah, which his family controlled.[5]

Maheu's memory was faulty at the time of his testimony, 20 years after these events. He mixed up the roles of Abdullah Sulaiman, who was "the minister who had been involved," and Abdullah Alireza, whose family ran the port. No cabinet minister was dismissed as a direct result of the Catapodis revelations. Abdullah Sulaiman was already gone, and Mohammed Alireza stayed at the Ministry of Commerce until 1958.

Using the News Media

When Maheu said "we bought a newspaper," the "we" was the CIA, which in that era routinely used the news media as a weapon. It took more than two decades for the scope of this CIA dissemination network to come into full public view. In late 1977, the *New York Times* published a series of articles labeled "C.I.A: Secret Shaper of World Opinion," detailing what it called the "C.I.A.'s Three-Decade Effort to Mold the World's Views."

The articles reported that "The C.I.A. has at various times owned or subsidized more than 50 newspapers, news services, radio stations, periodicals and other communications entities, sometimes in the United States but mostly overseas, that were used as vehicles for its extensive propaganda efforts, as 'cover' for its operatives, or both. Another dozen foreign-based news organizations, while not financed by the C.I.A., were infiltrated by paid C.I.A. agents."[6]

The use of news organizations overseas to spread the gospel according to Washington was only one aspect of the U.S. government's Cold War information campaign. Most of the work was not clandestine but was conducted openly through the United States Information Agency and Radio Free Europe. In an extensive report on this campaign, the National Security

Archive, a nonprofit research group in Washington, found that the tools used included financial assistance, pamphlets and posters, news manipulation, magazines, radio broadcasts, books, libraries, music, movies, cartoons, educational activities, person-to-person exchanges, and, of great significance for the Middle East, religion. Information could also be placed with American media outlets for playback in the region.[7] The U.S. Information Agency established reading rooms and libraries in many foreign capitals.

In the case of Onassis, success was virtually immediate. An account in one news outlet cleared the way for others to pursue the story. "The minute this story was broken," Maheu told the Senate committee, "it was picked up" by other news organs in Europe, Egypt, and the United States.

"Then it turned out that Onassis had signed with his agent in Saudi a contract that was in disappearing ink," just as Catapodis had claimed, Maheu said. "We were able to restore the signature through the services of Charlie Appel." This was a reference to the legendary Charles A. "Uncle Charlie" Appel Jr., creator of the FBI's Technical Services Laboratory, the country's premier forensic laboratory

The lab's forensic analysis was critical to the solution of some of the country's most notorious crimes, including the 1932 kidnapping of 20-month-old Charles A. Lindbergh Jr., son of the renowned aviator.

After he retired in 1948, according to an FBI in-house biography, Appel went into private practice as a document examiner in legal cases—including "the 1970 disputed firing of Robert Maheu, manager of Hughes' $300 million Las Vegas gambling operations, both involving forged signatures of Hughes."

By verifying Catapodis's claim, Appel's laboratory may have resolved the matter of the supposed disappearing signature, but it did so only after it had ceased to matter. In any case, that was an issue between Catapodis and Onassis. Settling it did nothing at the moment to resolve the larger issue of the Onassis contract with Saudi Arabia. More important in Riyadh were the allegations of payoffs to Saudi officials.

On October 2, less than a week after delivery of the Catapodis dossier to King Saud, Aramco's Garry Owen and Fred Davies met the king and found him "reasonably disposed to talk sense," a British diplomat reported. The company is "just afraid that his brother, Crown Prince Faisal, may take longer to come round." Owen said that Aramco was "still trying to convince the King that the agreement with Onassis would harm Saudi Arabia, not benefit her. It was on this basis that they hoped to make him change his mind about it. They did not want to press the legal issue at this stage, but in fact they were prepared to if necessary." Aramco had already "retained the foremost Moslem lawyer in Cairo, and he gave his view that the Onassis agreement was even in Moslem law an infringement of the terms of the company's concession."[8]

When in Doubt, Appoint a Committee

About two weeks after Catapodis's session with the British consul in Nice, Richard Dorsey of the State Department's Near East Bureau wrote a "story so far" memorandum to Deputy Undersecretary Robert Murphy, updating him on developments since August.

One bit of good news Dorsey reported was that J. Paul Getty's Pacific Western Company had decided not to charter any Onassis tankers, thus eliminating a possible avenue of relief for Onassis. A few weeks later, that would turn out not to be true.

As for the Onassis contract itself, Dorsey wrote, "Encouraged by our strong position in the matter, Aramco has continued its unyielding policy in opposition to the Onassis agreement, basing it primarily on the conflict between the Aramco concession agreement and the Onassis agreement," a position the State Department supported.

Dorsey noted that after the August 24 meeting at which Ambassador Wadsworth had found King Saud "extremely cordial," the king had directed officials in his government to form a joint committee with Aramco to seek a compromise. But on October 3, Garry Owen, Aramco's representative in Jeddah, told Horace Phillips of the British Embassy that the committee had "achieved nothing" because Mohammed Surur, a key member as the new finance minister, was still feeling his way.[9]

Dorsey took note of that in his memo to Murphy. "Little progress has been made in committee discussions," he wrote, "and the Saudis complain of Aramco's unwillingness to agree to any compromise which would give Onassis any degree of preference. It is clear that the matter is a question of how to devise a formula acceptable to Aramco and our own policies which will save face for the king."

The departure of Sulaiman from the Saudi government and his replacement by the "generally reasonable" Surur, coupled with agreement on the long-standing tax issue, had created a "good atmosphere for settlement of the Onassis matter," Dorsey said. "During an audience Ambassador Wadsworth had with the King on October 1, the King expressed keen satisfaction over the agreement with Aramco on taxes and stated he welcomed further meetings of SAG and Aramco representatives and expressed hope that the Onassis matter would be settled."

Without mentioning Catapodis or his role in the entire affair, Dorsey said that "evidence in certain hands clearly shows that several Saudi ministers have personally benefited to a very large extent through the conclusion of the agreement," and this "evidence" has been delivered to King Saud.

Nevertheless, the issue remained unresolved, prompting Maheu, through John Gerrity, to offer his own proposed way to "bring about abrogation of the Onassis agreement in a way acceptable to King Saud," a plan that had been sent to Wadsworth for comment.[10] Dorsey did not say what that proposal was, but Secretary Dulles described it in messages he sent that same morning to the U.S. embassies in London and Jeddah asking for their comment.

Dulles told them that Gerrity had brought to the State Department a plan for a statement to be issued jointly by the governments of Britain, the United States, and Saudi Arabia.[11] The proposed text:

> The Onassis agreement was concluded and promulgated by the Saudi Arabian government in the hope that it would contribute to rapid economic development in Saudi Arabia and nations of the free world. Since its promulgation King Saud has devoted much study to the agreement and especially to its effect upon relations with countries in close relationships with Saudi Arabia and, acting under the advice of loyal and patriotic US, UK and Saudi citizens, has decided to abrogate the agreement and undertakes to make no similar agreement which would tend to defeat free trade principles. The United States and the United Kingdom join the Saudi Arabian government in condemning such agreements and agree to direct their combined efforts toward eliminating such agreements.

Dulles's note said the State Department believed any effort to persuade King Saud to accept such a declaration "would be most inadvisable." Ambassador Wadsworth agreed. He said that the proposed statement "does not make good sense either to me or to [Fred] Davies of Aramco."[12] Their opposition was not difficult to understand: the proposed statement would in effect be an admission by King Saud that he had made a major mistake, exactly the kind of embarrassing gesture the State Department and the oil company wanted to avoid.

Welcome to Beirut

A few days later, Onassis and his wife, Tina, sailed into the harbor of Beirut, Lebanon, aboard his lavish yacht, the *Christina*. He was on his way to Jeddah, where he was to meet with the king.

Beirut was the information and financial center of the Arab world. The U.S. Embassy there reported to the State Department that Onassis took a serious beating from the press. Onassis dined with Prime Minister Sami el-Solh, but that is not what the newspapers were interested in. They wanted to know about reports that Onassis had secretly carried oil to Israel. He told the newspaper *Al-Hayat* that he had never done so "not because my oil agreement with Saudi Arabia prevents me from doing so but because I have never dealt with Israel, even before this agreement was concluded." To *Al-Jarida*, he complained that "there is a campaign in certain Arab newspapers which attempts to present me to the world as a Zionist," whereas in the United

States he was being denounced as "a notorious anti-Zionist" because of the clause in his Saudi agreement that excluded Israeli participation.[13]

The embassy's report about this press coverage did not say where the Lebanese papers had obtained their information about Onassis's alleged dealings with Israel, but it is easy to surmise who planted those stories: any American journalist who has worked in foreign capitals is familiar with the CIA's practice of leaking information it wants disseminated. The agency and Robert Maheu knew well that if the Arabs blackballed Onassis, his fleet would lose access to several of the most important oil-producing countries, including Iraq and Kuwait, as well as Saudi Arabia.

On November 13, the newspaper that the CIA had bought published a story about the Catapodis documents. Then, just as that article was beginning to receive attention, Catapodis stirred worldwide interest in his tale through another channel: he sued Onassis for fraud in a Paris court. Given Onassis's global fame, Catapodis's accusations were widely and prominently reported. The *New York Times* published its article about the lawsuit on the front page.

In the lawsuit, Catapodis alleged that he and Onassis had signed a contract in which Onassis authorized him to negotiate with the Saudis on his behalf. He had done so successfully, he said, but Onassis had refused to pay him £200,000 in commissions and benefits that were due. (At the time, that was about $560,000, equivalent to almost $14 million today.) He also claimed that Onassis had agreed to give him a 5 percent share of ownership in the Saudi shipping company he was to create.

According to the *New York Times*, Catapodis told the court that sometime after signing his contract with Onassis, he had discovered that Onassis's signature "had been written in disappearing ink and that it had begun to disappear. Mr. Catapodis said he had made photostatic copies of this agreement before the ink entirely disappeared. He added that when he called Mr. Onassis's attention to this, the latter promised" to fix it but, upon obtaining Catapodis's copy for re-signing, he refused to return it.

Catapodis filed the case in Paris because he and Onassis were both legal residents of France. Under French law, although this was a civil complaint filed by an individual, a magistrate could have sent Onassis to prison for as long as five years if the accusations were verified.

Catapodis told reporters that if he won a monetary judgment in the case, "I intend to give the money to charities in France and in Greece."

Onassis, who was in New York, told reporters there the next day that Catapodis's accusations were completely unfounded. "These accusations are a part of the propaganda that has been going on ever since the [tanker] agreement was signed," he said, and were filed "for the sole purpose of jeopardizing the agreement." After reviewing a set of the Catapodis documents that the *New York Times* had obtained, Onassis said that "the contents were a palpable fraud and that the signature at the bottom" of the purported contract with Catapodis "was not his. He also denied that Mr. Catapodis had ever been a negotiator for him." He said similar things to reporters from the *New York Herald Tribune*, *Newsweek*, and *Time*.[14]

Niarchos and Maheu had been right about the effect of spreading the news about the documents; the filing of the lawsuit in Paris was a one-day story, but the Catapodis dossier turned out to be the gift that kept on giving. On November 20, the *Journal of Commerce*, a New York newspaper widely regarded as authoritative on maritime matters, published an article detailing the bribery accusations. It was a straightforward account, couched in neutral language, saying that Onassis "is reported to have paid approximately $1 million to government officials through an intermediary to help close the deal." It described the arrangement between Onassis and the Saudi government as "somewhat similar to the Govenco case," which it recalled as "the scandal that led to the resignation of Abdullah Suleiman."[15]

That article contained no denial or other response from Onassis, but the next day Onassis gave an interview to the United Press news service to deny its allegations.

"No officials have ever received any money and there has never been any question of receiving any in this connection," he said. Asked about the *Journal of Commerce* report and the money for Alireza, he replied, "There is nothing true in all this. We have an arrangement with the Alireza Brothers, a shipping company founded in 1860 and one which is well known in shipping circles, whereby they will act as our agents."

He said the news articles describing the payments were inspired by a "former sea captain" whom he belittled as just "a dummy for one of my toughest competitors" who is "disgruntled" because he failed to obtain the Saudi contract for himself.[16]

Onassis was making it up. There is no record that Niarchos or any other tanker fleet owner ever sought any contract to conduct tanker operations in Saudi Arabia. But even if it had been true it would not have made much difference in Riyadh. "From the Saudi point of view," as Robert Lacey put it, "the deal was dead as soon as it hit the headlines, for certain subjects are considered very private in Arabia, and business commissions rank second only to family scandals in that respect."[17]

New Country, New Crisis

In mid-November, shortly after accounts of the Catapodis documents began to appear in the press, Onassis suffered a new blow from an unexpected development that had nothing to do with Saudi Arabia: the Peruvian Navy seized five vessels of his whaling fleet in the Pacific.

In those days the taking of whales was still considered a legitimate business, regulated by an international commission established in 1946 that allocated quotas for the annual catch. Onassis was not apologetic about being involved in it. On the contrary, he flaunted it; he went so far as to tell Greta Garbo when she was a guest aboard his yacht that the barstool on which she sat was upholstered with whale foreskin.[18] Hand railings were made of whale-tooth ivory.[19] As Peter Evans put it, "the slaughter meant nothing to Ari except in terms of profits and adventure."[20]

Onassis had jumped into the trade in 1949, to the chagrin of the Norwegians, who dominated the business and feared that quotas would be allotted to him at their expense. The Norwegians were looking for ways to get him out of the whaling trade, and now Peru had handed them a tool they would wield vigorously.

The government in Lima said the Onassis ships had been whaling without permission inside the offshore boundary of 200 nautical miles claimed by Peru, Ecuador, and Chile. As Peru's leading newspaper branded Onassis a "whaling pirate," the government said it acted in "defense of national sovereignty and of the country's marine wealth."[21] Two destroyers captured four of the ships without resistance from their crews and put them under the control of Peruvian sailors, who took them into port. When the fifth vessel ignored the Peruvians' orders and tried to escape, the Peruvian air force bombed it into surrender.

At a news conference in London, Onassis said the Peruvian seizure represented an outbreak of "tropical madness." He said the 200-mile limit was inherently ridiculous—why not make it 2,000, he asked sarcastically, or all the way to the opposite shore so Russia could take over Vancouver? And the issue was not just whaling, he said: "whaling, waterskiing, what's the difference?"[22]

The business had been bringing Onassis millions of dollars in profit every year. But now, as Jim Hougan put it in *Spooks*, "The war against Onassis was suddenly a literal one, and the pressure was almost crushing. His operations were being devastated, with a dozen tankers under seizure in the United States [in the navy fraud case], half his whaling fleet impounded in Peru, and his supertankers (including the recently launched *Al Malik Saud Al Awal*) boycotted at a cost of ten thousand dollars a day. In addition, his reputation was in ruins, he remained under indictment, and the word was out that doing business with Onassis meant trouble."[23]

The maritime historian Gelina Harlaftis, the scholar most knowledgeable about Onassis and his businesses, wrote that this development was part of an "orchestrated attack" against Onassis by the U.S. government, but the evidence for that is thin because Washington had refused to accept Peru's territorial waters claim and did not want to validate it by encouraging its enforcement.[24]

The issue had come to Washington's attention in August, when a retired U.S. diplomat named Reginald P. Mitchell had raised the subject in a meeting with a mid-level official at the State Department. Mitchell was working for the public relations firm Coates & McCormick Inc., which represented Stavros Niarchos and therefore, Mitchell said, maintained "constant surveillance over Onassis's activities." This was the same firm of which a name partner, Robert L. L. McCormick, had met with the State Department's John Jernegan on Niarchos's behalf back in March.

Mitchell said an Onassis-owned whaling fleet consisting of a "factory ship" and "about twenty tenders" was assembling off the coast of Peru. Onassis, he said, "is an outlaw whaler who does not abide by the international agreements concerning whaling. He bribes inspectors set on his ships to observe activities." He said Onassis might use two new tankers in his fleet, "the *King Saud I* and the *Tina Onassis*, each of 45,000 tons capacity, on their first voyages to take whale oil from the fleet to Germany where it could be bartered to pay off his debts."[25]

Secretary Dulles then instructed the U.S. consulate in Hamburg to watch the activities of those two tankers and to "telegraph departure and destination" back to Washington. There is no indication that the State Department notified the Peruvian government of this conversation.

In fact, the United States and all other major seafaring nations opposed the 200-mile limit adopted by the South Americans, and therefore the State Department was unlikely to encourage Peru to enforce it, even against Onassis. The Eisenhower administration had no love for Onassis, of course, but Peru's action had the paradoxical effect of making the administration and Onassis into temporary allies, at least on this issue.

The State Department had instructed the U.S. embassy in Lima to make clear that

> the position of Peru is not only contrary to the position of the United States as contained in Section 3 of the Outer Continental Shelf Lands Act, enacted on August 7, 1953, but is also inconsistent with the Articles on the continental shelf adopted by the International Law Commission of the United Nations at its Fifth Session, which articles the United States regards as generally expressive of international law. The Peruvian claims to jurisdiction over great areas of the high seas, which find little support elsewhere, cannot be recognized by the United States, which considers that under international law there is no obligation to recognize claims to territorial waters in excess of three miles from low-water mark on the shore.

The message warned the Peruvians that the United States reserved the right to do whatever was necessary to protect the rights of American vessels off the South American coast.[26]

The whalers of Onassis's fleet were not registered in the United States, so Washington did not intervene directly in the Peruvian seizure; the Peruvians held firm in the face of outcries from Britain and Norway, among other countries. The Lima government fined Onassis 57 million Peruvian soles, or about $2.8 million, and gave him five days to pay or the ships would be sold at auction.

Yet Onassis emerged financially unscathed. He had taken the precaution of having the ships and their cargoes insured by Lloyds of London, which covered his claim for the fine only reluctantly because doing so appeared to validate the Peruvian territorial claim. The vessels were allowed to proceed to the Antarctic in time for the start of whaling season there and reportedly had an excellent catch.

Moreover, the military action by the Peruvians turned out to be a public relations boon to Onassis. Indicted in the United States, damned in Paris as a swindler and corrupter of public officials, reviled by the world's maritime nations, he suddenly became a sympathetic victim, hailed by the *Times* of London for "involuntarily bringing to a head a situation against which most of the major maritime powers have already made vehement protest."[27]

That victory was transitory. The following year the Norwegians conducted an intense campaign, complete with photographs taken by whaling crew members in the government's pay, to show that the Onassis vessels violated rules of the hunt, took some whales from protected species, hunted with illegal weapons, and exceeded the permitted catch. The Norwegian Whaling Association produced documents and photographs proving that "at least half the whales killed by Onassis's fleet since 1951 were either caught out of season or were below minimum size." Within a year the Norwegians succeeded in hounding Onassis out of the lucrative whaling business, but according to a comprehensive Norwegian account, "He very conveniently received an offer from Japan" for his whaling ships "and he succeeded in forcing the price up to $8.5 million."[28]

CHAPTER SIXTEEN

Impasse

Desultory and fruitless meetings among Saudi and U.S. government officials, Onassis, and Aramco dragged on through the late summer of 1954. They were not really negotiations because there was no give and take. The contract with Onassis that King Saud had ratified in the spring remained in place, but none of his ships had carried any Saudi oil and Aramco's refusal to deal with him was unwavering.

In July, the *Journal of Commerce* reported that the Onassis contract was causing widespread concern among the operators of the world's tanker fleets, who stood to lose a substantial number of charters if the agreement went into effect. That was hardly surprising, given the initial reactions of international fleet owners, oil buyers, and their governments a month or so earlier.

The biggest tankers of that era could carry approximately 40,000 tons. The largest of all, Onassis's own *Al-Malik Saud Al-Awal*, still sitting in the port of Hamburg awaiting a charter, was 46,800 tons. The *Journal of Commerce* article said that Onassis could place 500,000 tons of tanker capacity, as specified in the SATCO contract, into the Saudi service "in a reasonably short time," and had another 250,000 tons under construction. "The Saudi deal," the article said, "is thus considered a perfect formula for Onassis to use an extraordinary amount of tonnage that might otherwise be left idle shortly in the present depressed shipping market."[1]

Onassis said nothing publicly at the time, but a few weeks later, he gave the *Journal of Commerce* the first full-length interview he had given to the press since the details of the contract had become public.

The newspaper had sent him written questions about the deal: Was it a monopoly? Was Onassis the sole owner of SATCO, or a majority or minority shareholder? How can the government of a producing country impose such a requirement upon buyers in other countries?

"Mr. Onassis refused to answer any of these questions directly, and stigmatized them initially as 'all lies,'" the newspaper said, but then he gave the newspaper an interview at his residence in Monte Carlo. It was vintage Onassis, long on bluster and short on facts.

He said Saudi Arabia had planned for some time to create a modest fleet of tankers under its own flag capable of handling 10 percent of its exports. If the kingdom failed to interest shipowners, it planned to create a state-owned fleet and engage competent operators to run it for a fee. "For two years I followed the evolution of this project and when convinced that an agreement would be concluded with one of my competitors I stepped in," Onassis said.

He complained that "what was meant to be an ordinary shipping contract on a modest scale has been blown up to appear a fantastic monopoly and discrimination of flag. The 500,000 tons of tankers, which will amount to about 20 to 25 ships out of several hundred employed at present in the transportation of Saudi Arabia oil, were boosted up to millions of tons and hundreds of ships. Furthermore, the opponents of this deal, disregarding the sovereign right of a government, are saying the Saudi Arabia government may extend this original modest 10 percent to 100 percent. Who is able or allowed to foretell what a government will or will not do in years to come?"

He also griped that "these far fetched and deliberately imaginary calculations" had led to questions from the U.S. Congress and Britain's House of Commons and had turned "a simple, ordinary, modest shipping matter into a problem worth the great concern of the Foreign Office and State Department." He said that "nothing could be more ridiculous" than reports that his rates would be higher than others' and would "secure fantastic profits for me." He objected that a high percentage of Saudi oil was being carried on ships registered in countries that had "nothing whatsoever to do" with either the production or consumption of oil, such as Panama, Liberia, and Honduras, as well as Greece and Norway. As he well knew, such arrangements were common throughout the shipping industry.[2]

If Onassis's comments had any impact on the discussions that summer in the United States or Saudi Arabia, it is not reflected in the documentary record. By this time all involved knew that nothing he said should be taken at face value. To the extent that his remarks were at variance with the facts, they further undermined his credibility.

Shortly afterward, Aramco submitted the proposed substitute language for Article IV that the king had asked for.[3]

"Nothing came of it," the company reported. That was hardly surprising because the proposed wording that "Nothing in this agreement shall be taken to establish any preference" for SATCO tankers would have essentially negated the Onassis contract.[4]

Impasse

According to Aramco's narrative, the impasse continued until October 23 when "the government appointed a commission to investigate and decide the Onassis matter." (In fact the king had directed in August that such a committee be appointed, though it did little because Mohammed Surur did not yet have enough information.) "The commission met with representatives of Aramco on several occasions. On one of these, held 24 October 1954, Onassis and his colleagues attended. At this meeting, His Excellency Khalid Abu Walid, the Chairman of the Committee, suggested that Onassis meet with Aramco representatives in the afternoon" without government representatives, to eliminate the need for translation. "The meeting was held as suggested. Onassis at the time stated that there would no use of further meetings unless a guaranteed employment or a preference for his ships was granted by Aramco. He was told that this could not be done. The Government was advised of the outcome of this meeting."[5]

Ambassador Wadsworth sent Washington an interim report that gave this sequence of events: On October 23, Onassis met with King Saud. The only other person in the room was Mohammed Alireza. The outcome was a royal order directing Onassis to meet the next morning with Surur and Davies.

Then the king saw Davies and Floyd Ohliger, another senior Aramco official. This conversation was "cordial throughout," Wadsworth said. "The King assured them he wished to clear up all remaining questions at issue with Aramco, including the Onassis agreement. He would approve any understanding they could reach with Onassis, in particular any modification of Article IV." But the king insisted that "the agreement itself should not be cancelled—his honor was at stake—and if no understanding could be reached he was not averse to 'letting the matter go to a higher court.'"

Davies said arbitration should be "a matter of last resort" because the oil company and the Saudi government had always been able to resolve their differences amicably. If arbitration proved necessary in this case, he said, he hoped that relations "would not be adversely affected." The king "gave ready assurance on this score," Wadsworth reported.

That afternoon, Davies met with Onassis, who was accompanied by Nicolas Cokkinis and Mohammed Alireza. According to Wadsworth, "Onassis repeated his version of events leading up to signature of the agreement, engaging in histrionics which only tended to confirm Aramco's thinking, that to make any concessions to his position would be to subject the company to continuing future pressures."

There was no need for any action by the U.S. government, Wadsworth told the State Department: "My feeling is we should let Davies carry the ball for the time being." He said he agreed with Davies that the issue appeared headed for arbitration. The ambassador said he was scheduled to meet the king again on November 28, should the State Department wish to send him any new talking points.[6]

Wadsworth may have felt that the issue no longer required the administration to intervene, but FBI Director J. Edgar Hoover had a different view. His agents were continuing to examine transactions by Onassis in Europe and South America. On October 19, he wrote to T. Coleman Andrews, commissioner of the Internal Revenue Service, that Onassis "may not report certain monies received by him as income." It is not clear from the heavily redacted FBI files what prompted this note from Hoover, or why Hoover thought that Onassis, an Argentine citizen living in Paris, was subject to taxation in the United States.[7] There is no record that the IRS took any action against Onassis.

The Last Talks Break Down

A few days later, Wadsworth reported to Washington that as he had predicted, the joint Aramco-Saudi committee that King Saud had ordered created to work out some agreement "has ended in failure." Onassis had gone back to Monte Carlo, Aramco's Fred Davies had left for New York, and the king and his entourage had moved back to the isolated royal capital of Riyadh, which in those days foreigners could not visit without royal permission.

Davies was going to New York to report on this final round of negotiations and relay to his Board of Directors a new proposal Onassis had offered. He was confident the board would reject it, and he had made that clear to Onassis. The British Embassy in Jeddah reported that several people, including Karl Twitchell, described Onassis as "a dejected man" when he left town.[8]

With the breakup of the committee, Wadsworth told the State Department, "Aramco has yielded nothing in substance or principle and has gained valuable Royal assurance" that if the matter went to arbitration, relations between the government and Aramco would continue "on the basis of full cooperation their joint venture" regardless of the outcome. "Onassis, when finally pinned down on rate issue, has weaseled and outsmarted himself."[9]

Onassis had tried to craft a compromise: he would give up the monopoly for his proposed tanker fleet if Aramco would guarantee that fleet a specified percentage of its export cargoes.[10] Alternatively, he proposed that Aramco itself charter his tanker *Al Malik Saud al-Awal*, which was sitting unused in Hamburg. He was wasting his breath; Davies was not amenable to any offer or proposal that would have involved doing business with Onassis, and he said so to Horace Phillips of the British Embassy.

Phillips reported to London that he met with Davies while these talks were underway. Davies told him that "the talks were not getting anywhere and he did not intend that they should. He had again made clear to the King his company's firm opposition to the Onassis agreement; and [Garry] Owen, the head of Aramco's Jedda office, told me afterwards that he was confident that Davies would not change his stand on this."

That evening, Phillips reported, he met Onassis and Cokkinis at a dinner given by Mohammed and Ali Alireza, "who had of course sponsored the tanker agreement in the first place." Phillips said he "found Onassis a small, swarthy, tough man, blasphemous and emphatic in his talk in several languages. He tried to tell me that he was not out to make money—he had enough millions already. What he wanted was to help the Saudis realise their natural aspirations and build up a merchant fleet. It was inevitable that someone should have come along and helped them towards this, and who better than himself?"

Onassis complained that Aramco "put all kinds of obstacles in his way," and that the U.S. government was supporting the oil company.

"I thought it as well to remind both the Greeks that the United Kingdom government is also firmly opposed to any such restrictive monopoly agreement," in response to which Onassis "tried to impress me with the good will which he said existed" between him and British tanker companies, Phillips wrote. Besides, Onassis said, if Aramco would "be reasonable, he could come to terms with them on certain 'minor' aspects of the deal to which the company objected," including his share of tanker operations. He said he never envisioned controlling more than 10 percent of the traffic.

Phillips did not find this persuasive. The account he sent to London oozed incredulity, and contempt for Onassis. He said, "Onassis went on blustering like this for some time, ably supported by the more urbane Cokkinis, but I was glad to see that they were quite depressed over the whole affair. The hypocritical talk about their interest in benefits for the Saudi government is of course laughable. Davies said Onassis had tried this line on Aramco as well."

Phillips's suspicions of Onassis's motives went beyond even those of Davies and his Aramco colleagues. In truth, Phillips wrote, "It is quite clear that what the Greeks want is ultimately to oust Aramco's parent companies completely from the Saudi oil transport trade. But to start on this, they need guaranteed minimum freight hauls for some years, and that is what the Saudi-Onassis agreement is intended to ensure. Onassis evidently thought that the Saudis would be able to force Aramco into line, and it infuriates him to find that they cannot, or have not been able to up to now, at any rate." He said he was confident that Aramco would stay "tough," but he said he could not predict what would happen if the Saudis actually did try to force Aramco into compliance by threatening to cancel its entire concession. That was Saudi Arabia's ultimate weapon, if the king chose to deploy it.[11]

According to another British diplomatic report, Onassis "had apparently given Aramco and the Saudi government different versions of the rates he intended to charge, and at Aramco's instigation was under instructions from the Saudi Government to clarify the position."[12]

Even without that anomaly, nothing that Onassis could offer would have mattered. Aramco, which had held all along to the position that all export shipping must be arranged through competitive bids on the open market—the mechanism stated explicitly in its proposed alternate language of Article IV—immediately refused Onassis's proposition.

The next day, October 26, Finance Minister Surur sent Davies a letter that had been approved by King Saud. "I have learnt with great regret," he wrote, "that the meeting which was held yesterday evening between you and Mr. A. S. Onassis has not resulted in an agreement. I have been charged to inform you that the government of His Majesty the King is not pleased at this conclusion. It wishes you to reconsider the matter in order to reach a prompt solution," which he said meant within 30 days. "Otherwise, the Government would be forced to submit the case to arbitration. I sincerely hope that your Company will be able to find a solution that would be satisfactory to both sides during that period."[13]

Davies wasted no time in responding to Surur's letter. "I, too, regret that the meetings with Mr. Onassis did not result in agreement," he wrote back the same day. "Mr. Onassis made it plain that any agreement must guarantee that a specified percentage of crude and [refined] products should be exported from Saudi Arabia in tankships he supplies to the Saudi Arab tanker company at rates substantially higher than the rates for tankships chartered in the open tanker market."

Aramco and its parent companies had, of course, refused from the beginning to consider such a plan or any other arrangement that gave one tanker operator an advantage over others. At this moment, however, Davies did not firmly slam the door. He said he found it "advisable to discuss your letter with my Board of Directors and I am planning to go to New York promptly for that purpose." Assuming that the board would adhere to the company's previous position, he said, Aramco would cooperate with the Saudi government in preparing "terms of reference" for an arbitration proceeding.[14] Wadsworth, upon learning of this exchange, said that in his judgment, Saudi Arabia had "opened the way to a face-saving solution through arbitration under Article 31" of its original 1933 concession agreement.[15]

Article 31 said that "if any doubt, difference, or dispute shall arise between the Government and the Company concerning the interpretation or execution of this contract, or anything herein contained or in connection herewith, or the rights and liabilities of the parties hereunder, it shall, failing any agreement to settle it in another way, be referred to two arbitrators, one of whom shall be chosen by each party, and a referee who shall be chosen by the arbitrators before proceeding to arbitration."[16]

According to Wadsworth's narrative, the day after that exchange of letters, before Davies left Jeddah, the Aramco chief met with Surur and then the king, to seek clarification on the freight rates question. He then had a third and final meeting with Onassis "which only confirmed impossibility compromise without sacrifice Aramco principles which Davies would not consider."

Surur then wrote to Onassis to ask if he concurred with the position on rates given by Davies. Onassis's reply was "the essence of weasel," Wadsworth wrote. "He offered four, partially contradictory, answers, none of which frankly answered Surur's question and all of which when analyzed meant rates higher than current market rates for spot or term charters. This turned tide in Aramco favor and led to final cordial Davies-Surur meeting."[17]

While the predictably unsuccessful negotiations were taking place in Jeddah, Stavros Niarchos, who evidently didn't have enough to do in his life, was back in Washington, where he met with Jernegan and other State Department officials. Niarchos predicted that the Onassis matter would go to arbitration. He suggested that "it might be a wise move on the part of Aramco to let it be known that it had no intention of doing business with Onassis regardless of the outcome of any arbitration proceedings."

The U.S. government, which favored the use of arbitration in international business disputes, was not about to endorse the idea of refusing to comply with an unfavorable arbitration ruling, Jernegan said. "Aramco could hardly defend a position to the effect that it would refuse to do business with any concessionary company appointed by the Saudi government to engage in tanker operations [if] such operations were determined to be in keeping with Aramco concession agreement" rather than a violation of it. Moreover, he said, such an approach would indicate that Aramco had judged "Saudis implicated in the Onassis deal" before the royal government itself had made a judgment about them. "This could be interpreted as an affront to the dignity of the King and his Government."[18]

The Saudis had limited experience with arbitration, and what experience they did have did not give them a favorable view of the process. A few months earlier, in July, Britain and Saudi Arabia had agreed to submit their dispute over the Buraimi Oasis to arbitration. That process would ultimately fail because the British torpedoed it, but in the meantime that agreement, along with the departure of Abdullah Sulaiman from the government and resolution of the Aramco price issue, had contributed to a relaxation of tension between Riyadh and Washington, a relaxation now advanced by the Saudis' apparently lessened commitment to the Onassis contract. On November 12, President Eisenhower sent King Saud a congratulatory letter on the first anniversary of his accession to the throne. "The people of the United States," it said, "join me in sending to your majesty and to the people of Saudi Arabia felicitations and warmest good wishes." On a draft of the statement prepared by the White House chief of protocol, the president had written "OK if Sec'y of State personally approves." Sending such a message was a routine courtesy, but the Saudis always appreciated such gestures.[19]

Such statements are usually released to the press, as was this one. Otherwise, these critical developments of late October and the first ten days of November attracted little public attention in the United States, where media attention had waned during the summer because—except for Onassis's interview with the *Journal of Commerce*—most of the discussions had been kept private, and mid-term congressional elections were dominating the news. Eisenhower held press conferences on November 3 and November 10, but no reporter asked a question about Saudi Arabia. This lull in coverage ended abruptly when, on the 13th, the Athens paper owned by the CIA published the Catapodis documents. Two days later, the Peruvians announced the seizure of Onassis's whaling ships. On the 19th, Catapodis filed his legal case against Onassis in Paris. Matters appeared to be moving swiftly, but in truth resolution of the Onassis contract issue was many months away.

Aramco as Br'er Rabbit

To most Aramco executives, Surur's threat to go to arbitration was the equivalent of Br'er Fox threatening to throw Br'er Rabbit into the briar patch. The language of Article 31 ensured that Onassis would have no part in any arbitration proceedings: the participants would be lawyers for Aramco and lawyers for a royal Saudi government less committed to the Onassis deal than it had been previously. The issue would be whether the Onassis contract violated the original 1933 concession agreement, and that, from the company's perspective, "was an open and shut case. The lawyers were very confident," said Mike Ameen, who was Aramco's representative in Riyadh. To them, the issue had been persuading the Saudis to go to arbitration in the first place, not which party would prevail.[20]

That degree of confidence was unwarranted. Ameen and Aramco's lawyers at the time were apparently not aware of the legal doubts that had been raised by the State Department's Stanley Metzger in June. But Terry Duce, the company's vice president for government relations, shared those doubts.

On the same day as the final meeting of the joint committee that Wadsworth described in his report to Washington, Duce was at the State Department for a review of the situation.

The State Department's memorandum of this conversation says that while the Department had not yet received a report from Wadsworth about the meetings in Jeddah, arbitration now seemed to be the likely outcome. But Duce "expressed some doubt as to the desirability of proceeding with arbitration proceedings, feeling apparently that Aramco's case in arbitration might not be as strong as company lawyers have described it." In any case, "it was generally agreed that arbitration per se would not necessarily settle the basic

Impasse

issue involved," which was whether King Saud could be persuaded to abandon an agreement that he had approved and ratified.[21]

Regardless of Duce's doubts, Aramco apparently never drafted a plan for what it would do if the case went to arbitration and the government prevailed. If the company considered taking the path recommended by Niarchos's advice—defying an unfavorable ruling—there is no record of it in Fred Davies's papers.

CHAPTER SEVENTEEN

Dark Days for Onassis

As John Jernegan had told Stavros Niarchos, the State Department was not at first receptive to the idea that Aramco take the position that it would refuse to do business with any Onassis company no matter what might be the outcome of an arbitration case. But after the failure and breakup of the joint committee, opinion in Foggy Bottom changed.

On November 26, an Aramco delegation, led by Fred Davies and including General Counsel George Ray, met at the department with Henry Byroade.

They told him that they had had another round of conversations with Onassis in which they indicated that if he cancelled the Saudi agreement or somehow modified it to remove all "preferential provisions," the company would "consider chartering from him again on a strictly competitive basis." The significance of this offer is not clear because it was usually not Aramco itself but its buyers who chartered tankers, but in any case it did not satisfy Onassis.

Onassis wanted the company at least to give him some inside track to the Saudi business, but "he was informed he would have to take his chances."

Onassis said he could not simply propose cancellation of the contract for "face-saving reasons," but indicated he might try again to devise some revision of Article IV that would satisfy the king and Aramco. Then he complained that the U.S. Justice Department was holding the indictment in the navy fraud case over his head to strengthen the position of the oil companies, and asked that the Aramco parent companies intervene to have the case dropped. They refused to do that. Thus, the matter of the Onassis contract was not much closer to resolution than it had been when the committee broke up in early November, although the prospects for implementation of the contract had diminished.

Dark Days for Onassis

Davies, who was about to return to Saudi Arabia, asked that the State Department instruct the embassy in Jeddah before his arrival to emphasize that if the matter went to arbitration, whatever the outcome, "neither the offtakers nor the U.S. government could recognize [a] preferential position for any carrier of oil." That message, Davies asked, should also say that Aramco was unable to "influence" oil buyers, including its parent companies, who were "prepared to purchase oil elsewhere rather than recognize so disruptive a precedent in oil trade."

Byroade was convinced. The next day the State Department sent Wadsworth new instructions: meet with the appropriate Saudi officials as soon as possible and "make clear United States government feels it must emphasize to SAG in friendliest possible spirit that arbitration might not advance an answer to present impasse since neither oil purchasers nor most maritime nations (including United States) could accept or do business under such preferential clauses regardless of outcome of this particular case." That was just what Niarchos had proposed and Jernegan had at first rejected. The reversal made sense, because even if an arbitration panel ruled against the oil companies and declared the Onassis contract valid, Aramco and its owners had no way to compel purchasers to buy from them.

If the Saudis raised the question of the Onassis indictment, Wadsworth was instructed to "remind them sealed indictment antedates their agreement with Onassis and is based on quite independent considerations."[1]

Wadsworth delivered those messages two days later in a long, unpleasant conversation over dinner with Deputy Foreign Minister Yusuf Yassin, who was again trying to reinforce his standing with the king by taking a hard line on Aramco. Before Wadsworth could bring up the subject of the Onassis contract, Yassin did so.

He said he understood from a previous conversation that he and the ambassador agreed that it would be "unfortunate" if the issue went to arbitration. He had hoped that Onassis and Aramco would come to some agreement that would include a commitment to give SATCO tankers at least "a small percentage of total Aramco oil shipments at a reasonable rate." Now that Aramco had refused and the talks had ended, he said, the Saudi government "had no recourse but to insist on arbitration."

Yassin blamed Aramco's negotiators for the failure of the talks. "He could not understand why, on so simple an issue, they had found no solution," Wadsworth reported to Washington. Even at this last moment, Yassin said, "a solution without arbitration was possible. Could not a guarantee be given that a small amount, say 5,000,000 tons, be carried by these Saudi tankers?"

"This gave me an opening," Wadsworth said, to lay out once again the position of the Eisenhower administration.[2]

"It had been over this very point of guaranteed preferential treatment, as well as on the question of rates, that the recent negotiations here had failed," he told Yassin. "It was a basic practice of the world-wide oil industry that tanker companies must compete in the oil carrying trade; it followed that oil companies would conclude charters only at competitive rates.

"This basic position had been reiterated in subsequent discussions held with Onassis in the United States. He was told that the oil companies could not do business with him so long as the preferential provisions of his Agreement with SAG were maintained. Mr. Davies had already, following these last discussions, left New York for Dhahran. And our information was that Onassis planned to return to Saudi Arabia soon; it seemed possible he might intend himself to propose to SAG elimination of those provisions."

That is, the State Department still hoped Onassis might yield on this fundamental point; Aramco would not, and the State Department would support Aramco's position.

"As for arbitration," the ambassador said, "this would at best settle only one of the three principal points made in my note of last August to Prince Faisal, i.e. whether the Onassis Agreement violated the Aramco Concession Agreement. Mr. Davies had left Jidda with the assurance that arbitration would be a friendly test as to which partner was right; he would return, I felt sure, still ready to cooperate fully with SAG in that same spirit."

Wadsworth then reminded Yassin of the two other points he had made to Crown Prince Faisal: "The preferential provisions of the Onassis Agreement were inconsistent with the international trade practices of all leading maritime nations and were, as well, contrary to the established practice of the worldwide petroleum industry."

Those views still prevailed in the United States and the other maritime nations, he said. "It was, therefore, in the friendliest possible spirit that my Government wished me to reiterate them at this time. Surely Shaikh Yusuf could see even more clearly now than last August how strongly all the leading maritime nations and the great oil companies felt, and this quite irrespective of how arbitration of the first point might go."

From his long experience in the Arab world, Wadsworth surely knew how irritating it would be for a prominent Arab official such as Yassin to be told what the "leading maritime nations" and "great oil companies"—that is, the imperialists—wanted an Arab regime to do. Wadsworth's job was to represent the interests of the United States government, not those of other countries or of corporations. But in this case the interests of the U.S. government and those of the others coincided. If laying them out made Wadsworth uncomfortable, his report to the State Department did not reflect it. When he finished, it was Yassin's turn.

He said he understood the positions of the oil companies and the maritime countries and how strongly they felt about defending them. "Then, with customary acid touch, he added, 'It was, of course, Aramco, which by its campaign against us made these two points more important,'" Wadsworth reported.

Relying on the notes he took during this conversation, the ambassador quoted Yassin: "When arbitration is ended and Aramco loses, the whole monopolistic oil industry will find out it has no proof [sic] because there will be no international agreement against which SAG has acted."

"As for Aramco," Yassin continued, "I say with great regret it has never understood this country or this people. Had it done so, it could have settled this case in one day with His Majesty. Instead, it has built up this international front against Saudi Arabia. To me it seems incredible the Company's managers can have its interests at heart and act as they do. In fact, they are acting against its interests. It is important that they know what I have said and that the Company's shareholders also know it. We had thought that, if others acted against Saudi Arabia, Aramco as our partner would support us."

Aramco was, of course, the principal reason the United States had forged its close relations with Saudi Arabia in the first place. Wadsworth felt obliged to defend the company.

"I answered that I must differ with his views on Aramco," he said. "In my view it was incorrect to say the company had worked to build up an international front against Saudi Arabia. I would say, however, only what I had said before, that the King and Mr. Davies had agreed as friends that this difference between partners would be settled amicably by arbitration. I felt sure that this was still true, and I was still more than ready to be of any possible help in seeking a mutually agreeable solution."

Yassin said it was "not pleasant for him to talk as he had done," but he found Wadsworth's information "helpful" and would relay his comments to Prince Faisal.

The Administration Stands Down

After that conversation, it was no longer necessary for the U.S. government to take any direct part in the resolution of the Onassis issue. The State Department had rallied other countries to the cause and had done everything in its power to convince the Saudis that the agreement violated international law and would do their country more harm than good. The embassy in Jeddah had secured a royal commitment that the shipping arrangements with Onassis would not affect fuel supplies for the U.S. Navy. The Central Intelligence Agency had done its part, deploying Robert Maheu and enabling him to publicize the Catapodis dossier and deliver it to King Saud; not long afterward the contents were described at length, with front-page treatment, in the Cairo newspaper *Akhbar al-Yom*. That Arabic-language paper also had a substantial circulation in Jeddah and was widely read in other Arab capitals, ensuring that everyone in the Arab world knew about the payoff allegations. Wadsworth and his diplomats, as well as Byroade and Jernegan at the State Department, would continue to evaluate developments and consult with Aramco, but the events to come would occur in other arenas, including the king's palace in Riyadh, courts in Europe and the United States, and an arbitration proceeding in Switzerland. On December 12, the Saudi government officially announced that it would refer the dispute to an arbitration panel if Aramco and Onassis did not come to agreement by January 15.[3] There was no possibility that they would.

Fred Davies met privately with King Saud four days after that announcement and told Wadsworth that he found the monarch "in excellent spirits, well pleased with agreement re arbitration, which he apparently felt would enable him to 'finish with Onassis.'"[4] The king could, of course, have "finished with" Onassis whenever he wished to do so, but for the inconvenient fact that doing so would be embarrassing because he had issued the decree ratifying the contract.

The king told Davies that Pacific Western had finally struck a deal with Onassis to charter the *Al Malik Saud al-Awal*, as Aramco had already learned from other sources. The State Department then notified Wadsworth that upon learning of that arrangement, Aramco's board of directors had "decided as a compromise measure to place some Aramco tankers under [the] Saudi flag," under two conditions: that the kingdom enact "suitable" shipping laws—which was unlikely, because in Saudi Arabia there was no body of commercial law; the only laws other than those in the Quran were those issued by royal decree—and that the shipping preferences accorded in Article IV of the Onassis contract be eliminated. Aramco's Terry Duce reported this decision to the State Department, emphasizing that it was "not final" and the "some directors still have considerable misgivings this undertaking."[5] No such arrangement was ever established, nor is it clear what message Duce actually conveyed because Aramco did not operate its own tankers.

The extensive summary of the case that Aramco eventually submitted to a panel of arbitrators said tersely that "In addition to discussions and correspondence with representatives of the [Saudi] Government, several of Aramco's officers discussed the Onassis Agreement with Onassis from time to time. Onassis would not give up his claimed preference and Aramco could not accept it, with the result that no solution for the difficulty was found."[6]

Catapodis Strikes Again

Meanwhile, Spyridon Catapodis once again grabbed the headlines. On December 3, 1954, in federal court in Washington, he sued Onassis for libel and defamation, based on what Onassis had said to reporters after the case in Paris was filed. Catapodis's lawyer was the redoubtable Edward Bennett

Williams, who—not coincidentally—was a longtime friend of Robert Maheu, his college debate partner. How Williams could represent Catapodis when he had earlier represented Onassis in his meeting with Attorney General Brownell about the shipping fraud case was the sort of ethical question that apparently never troubled him.

Onassis was inherently newsworthy, so the Associated Press distributed an article about the libel suit to its clients worldwide. It described Onassis as "the shipping magnate who owns Monte Carlo."[7]

The lawsuit alleged that comments Onassis had made to American reporters when he denied Catapodis's accusations of bribery and fraud in connection with the Saudi tanker contract were "intended to convey and did convey the impression that plaintiff [i.e., Catapodis] had committed the crime of forgery, or that plaintiff had fraudulently attested to the authenticity of documents which he well knew to be forgeries."

Onassis's remarks in his own defense were "untrue, false, and defamatory," the complaint said. Because of those remarks, the court filing asserted, Catapodis "has been gravely injured in his name, fame, and reputation, has been subjected to odium and contempt in the minds of right-thinking persons, and has suffered serious impairment of his business and social relations throughout the world, including his relations with persons engaged in the international maritime industry, which industry has long constituted plaintiff's business and profession."[8]

The suit asked for $1.6 million in compensatory and punitive damages.

Onassis was not in the United States at the time, and some months passed before court officers were able to serve him with papers requiring him to appear. During that interval, Catapodis filed a similar lawsuit in a state court in New York. In both cases, Catapodis's lawyers gave Onassis's address as 16 Sutton Place, in New York, but the responses filed by Onassis's lawyer gave his address as 88 Avenue Foch, Paris. The question of where Onassis was legally domiciled would become a decisive factor in the New York lawsuit.

In the Washington case, Onassis's lawyer, Edward J. Ross, did not file a formal response until the following September. When he finally did, the document he submitted to the court on Onassis's behalf was 33 pages long and, by legal standards, strongly worded.

In essence, it said Catapodis had filed his affidavit in Nice and the court case in Paris for the sole purpose of discrediting Onassis, and Onassis had every right to defend himself.

Ross's filing denied "each and every allegation" in Catapodis's case except that the publications in which Onassis had been quoted existed and had indeed published articles about him, and that "the matter in controversy exceeds the sum of $3000."

According to Ross's filing, Onassis did not admit having said what the newspapers and magazines quoted him as saying, but if he had said those things, they were true and therefore not actionable. The filing said that if anyone had been defamed, it was Onassis, because Catapodis had filed his affidavit in Nice "intending that the contents thereof should have widespread publicity in the press of this country and elsewhere, caused the same to have such publicity and to circulate as news stories throughout the world, with the objective of defaming and injuring the defendant and jeopardizing the Saudi Arabian agreement." Catapodis did not file his affidavit with the British consul in Nice as part of any legal proceeding, the filing said: it was "an irregular, extrajudicial and entirely gratuitous act and deed on the part of the plaintiff," done in the expectation that it would "be given widespread circulation and publicity, and he caused said affidavit and exhibits to be sent to newspapers and magazines throughout the world, and to authors of books and the like, to assure that the false claims and charges made in said affidavit would be given, and they were promptly given, widespread circulation and publicity and made the subject of public interest and discussion throughout the world." Onassis's opinion about Catapodis's motive, as reported by Ross, was certainly correct.

Ross's response to the lawsuit said Onassis "did not employ the plaintiff as a negotiator to act in his behalf in the negotiations for the Saudi Arabian agreement." It said Onassis "did not sign in disappearing ink, or any kind of ink whatsoever" any contract promising payment to Catapodis. And it said Catapodis had violated French law by publicizing his charges in the Paris case.

In subsequent notices to the court, Ross said he intended to take depositions from Catapodis and from Robert Maheu, and asked the court to order them to deliver all records, contracts, bills, letters, canceled checks, photographs, and any other documents they had given to or received from Leon Turrou, Stavros Niarchos, the Alireza brothers, Abdullah Sulaiman, and King Saud himself.

In the end, Catapodis did not prevail in any of the three cases, in Paris, Washington, or New York. Only in the Paris case was Onassis required to testify, facing Catapodis in a closed hearing at which he dismissed the allegations as "a joke" and denied knowledge of any document signed in disappearing ink.[9] Nevertheless, Catapodis achieved his real purpose, which was to discredit Onassis and make his life as difficult as possible.

A Global Boycott

By the winter of 1954–1955, Onassis's tanker fleet was hemorrhaging customers because oil buyers took their business elsewhere. With a worldwide surplus of tanker capacity, the buyers did not need Onassis. As his existing contracts with shippers expired, the shippers declined to renew them, and

Dark Days for Onassis

he was unable to obtain new charters. By the end of 1955, more than half his fleet was idle.[10]

Among the unused vessels was the *Al-Malik Saud al-Awal*, or *King Saud I*, still dockside in Hamburg, all dressed up with no place to go. It had cost $6 million to build, and Onassis was spending an estimated $5,000 a day to maintain it.[11] Pacific Western had not in fact chartered it: J. Paul Getty told the U.S. Embassy in London that the company did not charter any tankers and that "he had carefully examined his [Neutral Zone] concession from SAG, and had concluded there was nothing therein to require him to comply with Onassis tanker agreement with SAG."[12]

No one made any formal or official announcement of a boycott, and no government had ordered it, so there was no authority to which Onassis could appeal. The *New York Times*, in an unsigned story from Cairo that relied heavily on the passive voice and named no individual sources, reported that "the boycott is described by oil circles here . . . as the first phase of a worldwide strategy to destroy Mr. Onassis's tanker empire" unless the Saudi contract was modified to meet the objections of "major oil interests." The article said this "projected campaign against Mr. Onassis is reported to have the tacit endorsement of the United States Government."[13] It did not say who had made such a report, but the fact that the Eisenhower administration did not oppose the boycott could be considered a tacit endorsement.

Aramco, which had insisted that it would not allow ships controlled by Onassis to load oil at its port in Saudi Arabia, denied that it was participating in any boycott, saying that it would "load any tanker, regardless of ownership, designated by our offtakers."[14] That denial was virtually meaningless because Aramco knew its buyers would not charter any of Onassis's ships under the terms of Article IV, so Aramco's commitment to load them would never be tested.

Onassis was so deflated that "at one point he considered selling his entire tanker fleet," according to one biography. "At another he considered filing an antitrust suit against Aramco in the United States. The sale of his whaling fleet to the Japanese in the spring of 1956 helped ease his precarious cash position, but it was no more than a palliative."[15]

The combination of the whaling fleet episode, the U.S. criminal case against him, the U.S. government's seizure of some of his tankers, the international boycott of his ships, and the civil lawsuits in three courts in two countries, sent Onassis into the darkest two years of his business life. For the first time since his escape from the Turks as a youth, he was not in control of his own fate.

CHAPTER EIGHTEEN

New Issues Emerge

Terry Duce was not alone among the executives of Aramco and its parent companies in feeling uncertainty about the arbitration process. There were a few others who did not share Fred Davies's confidence that the oil company would prevail. John E. Case, vice president of Socony-Vacuum Company (Mobil), told the State Department that "he had never favored the arbitration idea because of strong likelihood Aramco losing." He predicted that if the Saudi government succeeded in having the question of its sovereign rights included among the issues a tribunal would be asked to decide, "The case would almost certainly go against Aramco."[1]

George Ray, Aramco's general counsel, was worried that the question of the king's honor or pride would somehow muddle the legal issues.

A newcomer to the case who read a memorandum Ray wrote about preparing for arbitration might gain the impression that Onassis himself would be a party to the arbitration proceedings, but he was not. It was up to Aramco and the government to set the "terms of reference," that is, to decide what matters the proposed arbitration panel would be asked to resolve. Onassis's role was limited to advising the Saudi government about whom to include on the legal team that would represent it.

"It is too bad that Onassis 'has been able to convince the Government' that the Government's honor and prestige are at stake," Ray wrote in a memo to Davies. "It is difficult to see why the Government has been convinced . . . that the Government's honor can be sustained only by fulfillment of the Onassis agreement. The Aramco Concession was signed long before the Onassis agreement was ever heard of."

He said there was "no need to raise the question of the Government's or the King's honor in this arbitration. Aramco will do all in its power to protect the Government's and the King's honor. It is apparently a tactic of Onassis to

New Issues Emerge

create false impressions that Aramco questions the Government's or the King's honor or prestige. When the facts are viewed, the precise contrary is the case."[2] Ray seemed oblivious to the fact that it was Yusuf Yassin and other Saudi officials, not Onassis, who had raised this question.

Mobil's John Case and some U.S. government officials feared that if Aramco prevailed before an arbitration tribunal, an angry and insulted King Saud would respond by nationalizing Aramco's assets, as the Iranians had done in 1951.

Onassis had not given up. He was again trying to find some compromise because Finance Minister Surur's deadline for reaching agreement or going to arbitration was imminent. In February 1955, even as Aramco and the Saudi government were selecting their arbitrators, Onassis went to Saudi Arabia for one last effort to reach an agreement that would stave off arbitration. He proposed to sell tankers to the Saudi government, which in turn would designate him to manage what would become its national fleet.

It was not clear if Saudi Arabia, chronically strapped for money despite its oil revenue, could muster enough cash to make such a purchase; in any case the proposed arrangement would not resolve the overall question of whether a deal between the government and Onassis violated the original Aramco concession. Nor was it clear whether this proposed national fleet would have any sort of preferential status.[3]

But such arguments no longer mattered; a lot had happened in 13 months, and yet nothing fundamental had changed. Now the Saudi government had made up its mind to go to arbitration and Davies had assented. On February 23, 1955, Surur and Davies signed an agreement to proceed.

The arbitration agreement specified that there would be two arbitrators, one appointed by the Saudi government, one by Aramco, and that those two would choose a "referee" who would "not be of the same nationality as either party nor be of the same nationality as either of the Arbitrators."

That was the easy part. Much harder was specifying what questions exactly the arbitration panel should be asked to address. The Davies-Surur agreement left it up to the arbitrators to decide which questions to arbitrate. That did not augur well for a speedy process.[4]

Aramco wanted to limit the questions to one: "Is Article IV of the agreement between the Government and Mr. A. S. Onassis as amended April 7, 1954 in conflict with the Aramco Concession Agreement?"

The Saudi government, however, wanted the tribunal to decide whether the concession agreement applied to transportation of oil and refined products by sea, and whether Aramco had "any right to refuse or deny a Government-requested preferential treatment to tankers flying the Saudi Arab flag," especially if "the cost of transportation of the oil it produces and sells is not going to be higher than the average cost of transportation of the

Company in using non-national tankers." That was the "sovereign rights" issue that made Mobil's John Case apprehensive.

The government also wanted the tribunal to rule on whether Aramco itself had violated the concession agreement by transferring the right to transport oil by sea to third parties, without consent of the government.[5]

Another question was, what law applied? The dispute was about a contract for transportation in international waters between a private corporation based in the United States and a foreign government operated according to Muslim law. The arbitration agreement stipulated that the Hanbali school of Muslim law would be applied in matters "within the jurisdiction of Saudi Arabia," but it was up to the Tribunal to decide which matters those were.[6]

On Aramco's behalf, a professor of religious law at Cairo University submitted to the arbitrators a statement concluding that "the sovereignty of the Saudi Arab state does not extend to transportation on the high seas, because it has neither possession thereof nor control thereon. The Saudi Arab state cannot therefore enforce its edicts or implement its decisions in connection with transportation or with any other matter on the high seas." This paper said that "the state has concluded an agreement in the name of sovereignty. It cannot, in the name of sovereignty, repudiate the agreement which it has concluded."[7] Even if the professor's analysis was correct, however, it did not address the Saudi side's argument that the maritime transportation issue was entirely beyond the scope of the 1933 concession agreement.

Aramco's position on the religious law question was that it was irrelevant: "Whether Muslim law, as applied locally in Saudi Arabia, or general principles of law recognized in common by Saudi Arabia and other civilized nations, or the principles of any legal system of which the writers of this Memorial have any knowledge, the result will be the same."[8]

The agreement to go to arbitration did not by itself resolve the dispute between Aramco and the government; a beleaguered Onassis still had a contract with the Saudi government, the king's order ratifying it was still in effect, and Aramco still refused to abide by it. The arbitration agreement merely transferred the dispute to a new forum in a new country, Switzerland, where more than two years of procedural and substantive arguments lay ahead. But going to arbitration removed the SATCO contract as the central focus of relations between the company and the government and between the Eisenhower administration and Saudi Arabia. In effect, the Onassis matter remained an irritant, and a potential threat to U.S. domination of Saudi oil, but it diminished in urgency as new issues emerged. It lingered, but as part of a more complicated picture. The bilateral relationship would soon grow more strained, rather than less. The tanker contract was on the periphery of the momentous Middle East events of the next two years; these events would drive Onassis's businesses to the brink of extinction, then enrich him beyond his dreams.

The Baghdad Pact

On February 25, 1955, Iraq and Turkey signed a mutual defense treaty known as the Baghdad Pact. By the end of October, Britain, Pakistan, and Iran had joined them. The Eisenhower administration had for some time been promoting such a "northern tier" strategy for confronting Soviet expansionism in Iran and the Arab world, but the United States did not join the Baghdad group for fear of provoking the Soviet Union, antagonizing Egypt's Nasser, or raising Israeli demands for a similar commitment.[9] The leaders of almost all Arab states other than Iraq, seeing the Baghdad Pact as a new manifestation of Western imperialism, believed the United States was behind it because of its "northern tier" strategy.

Among the Arabs angry about the treaty were the Saudis. King Saud, still hoping to establish credentials as a nationalist, went so far as to sign a mutual defense agreement with Nasser's Egypt.[10] The two countries were destined soon to become avowed enemies, but at this point Saud and Nasser both wanted accommodation.

George V. Allen, who succeeded Henry Byroade as assistant secretary of state for Near East affairs in January 1955, wrote to Undersecretary Robert Murphy on March 3 a long memo titled "U.S. Policy Toward Saudi Arabia with Special Reference to Our Oil Interests." Its tone was decidedly pessimistic, even alarmist.

The memo said that "Aramco's dispute with the Saudi Arabian Government over the Onassis agreement has recently taken a turn for the worse and this fact, together with violent Saudi objections to the Turk-Iraqi pact, bodes ill for US-SA relations. The whole complex of our relations with SAG is now under review."

In Allen's opinion, the arbitration agreement itself had become part of the problem:

> While it had originally been understood that arbitration between Aramco and the SAG would be confined to the question whether the Onassis agreement is in conflict with the rights granted to the SAG by Aramco under Aramco's concession agreement, the SAG has apparently succeeded in injecting the sovereignty issue as well, i.e. whether the concession agreement prevents the SAG from exercising the right to regulate transportation of oil exports and grant priority to Saudi flag vessels. The arbitration award may well go against Aramco, although off-takers may refuse to be bound by the results.
>
> This development suggests the possibility that the Saudis may become increasingly hostile toward Aramco and the USG and that they may have in their minds a threat or bluff of expropriation and nationalization of Aramco's properties.[11]

Allen was also apprehensive about the bilateral agreement that allowed the United States to operate its strategic air base at Dhahran, an agreement that the Saudis had an option to cancel. At the end of 1955, unless the lease was extended, they would have the right to serve notice that the United States had to leave the facility by the following June.

King Abdul Aziz had reluctantly granted permission for construction of that base during World War II, when the United States was fighting a two-front war. Now, Allen said in his memo to Murphy, "recent soundings at the Pentagon suggest that Defense no longer places the same degree of importance on Dhahran airfield as formerly;" he warned against paying too high a price to keep the base or "giving any indication that our interests in Saudi Arabia are of such a magnitude that we would be warranted in resorting to extreme measures to satisfy our demands."

Negotiations over the future of the air base grew increasingly contentious over the next year and a half as the Saudis sought to use their leverage to extract donations of far more weapons and military equipment than Washington was willing to provide. The king and his advisers were demanding that the United States supply Saudi Arabia with combat jets and other weaponry that the Saudis were not capable of operating, and they insisted that the United States cover the costs because, they said, the kingdom's abundant oil revenue was committed to civilian development.

In his March 3 memo, Allen recommended that the State Department send new instructions to Ambassador Wadsworth making clear exactly what the administration's position was on the issues between the countries. Deputy Secretary of State Herbert Hoover Jr. did so two days later.

"Department naturally concerned over recent but not unexpected unfavorable drift US-Saudi relations which we attribute in large part to conclusion Turk-Iraq pact and our well-known support development 'northern tier' defense arrangement," his message said. "Department is facing possibility USG may be reaching a cross-roads in its relations with SAG. Obvious remedies for Saudi bitterness [such as] radical change in our defense policy, one-sided support Saudi border claims and Arab attitudes toward Israel and North Africa out of question. Furthermore record our recent relations with Saudi Arabia does not encourage belief that sizeable economic or military assistance would give our position in country solid strength for any appreciable period of time. On contrary we question whether willingness our part give such assistance (which cannot be justified either from financial or military-potential point of view) would not be interpreted as degree of weakness and would pave way for future heavy demands. We therefore doubt real improvement in our relations possible without reorientation of King's policy."

He suggested that Wadsworth remind King Saud that the United States had spent a lot of money to build and operate the Dhahran air base and that

New Issues Emerge

the facility had greatly benefited the kingdom, and that he bring up other programs to which the United States was already providing assistance, such as construction of a railroad. If the Saudis nevertheless "insist on the impossible in exchange for continued base rights," Wadsworth was to say that "we have no intention of being blackmailed," and would pack up and leave Dhahran "without recrimination or hard feeling." In other words, the ambassador was to call the Saudis' bluff.[12]

The previous June, Crown Prince Faisal had informed Wadsworth that Saudi Arabia would no longer accept the technical assistance it had been receiving under the Truman-era Point Four program. He said the decision was not a reflection on the program itself, but resulted from a decision "not to bother the U.S. government," a cryptic statement that Wadsworth and State Department officials thought reflected growing Saudi dissatisfaction on a variety of issues. At that point, according to Parker Hart, "the United States began to worry that if the Saudis would cancel Point Four on short notice, might they not do the same with the Dhahran Airfield agreement, soon to be up for renewal or to lapse on June 18, 1956?"[13]

That was where matters stood in July 1955, with the airfield issue still in doubt, when Wadsworth was a guest at a royal dinner for President Sukarno of Indonesia, who was visiting Saudi Arabia.

At that event the king's private secretary took the ambassador aside to deliver "highly confidential news": Crown Prince Faisal had been invited to visit "Communist China." The king's closest counselors had advised acceptance, but the king had decided otherwise because he wanted nothing to do with any communists. A telegram of regrets had been sent to Beijing.

At the same dinner, Yusuf Yassin asked to see Wadsworth afterward to convey another alarming message: through its embassy in Iran, the Soviet Union expressed a desire to re-establish diplomatic relations with Saudi Arabia, which had been ruptured in 1938.[14]

This one-two punch was clearly intended to raise alarm in Washington about possible communist encroachment into the most anticommunist country in the Arab world. Wadsworth's report got the attention of Secretary of State Dulles, who replied the same day he received it.

Establishment of diplomatic missions from communist countries in Saudi Arabia has "particularly dangerous potential," the secretary's cable said, but such decisions were up to the king and it would be counter-productive for the United States to take a strong position that could be resented as bullying. If the king raised the subject himself, the secretary said Wadsworth should "remind him privately that we have substantial evidence indicating Soviet Embassies in other countries have assisted local Communist activity and that he may wish consider whether establishment relations with Soviet at this time might unduly aid disruptive forces threatening unrest in Arab world." Dulles also played the religion card, suggesting that Wadsworth emphasize that King Saud "should consider carefully before associating himself with regime where Moslems are under persecution and where Haj [the pilgrimage to Mecca] is utilized primarily as propaganda weapon to hide true facts."[15]

King Saud rebuffed that feeler from the Soviets, and the two countries did not establish formal relations again until 1990. The negative response from Saudi Arabia was a minor setback for the Kremlin, which two months later would score a major coup in an Arab country of far greater political significance than Saudi Arabia, Egypt.

Article IV, Clarified?

Even after signing the agreement to submit the Onassis case to arbitration, Finance Minister Surur made one last attempt to win Aramco's assent to a revised Article IV of the contract. In a letter to the oil company dated June 6, 1955, he offered what he called a "clarification." The language of this supposed "clarification" was murky and legalistic: "The concessionary companies or their parent companies or the buyers of oil and its products will have the right to renew or replace such tankers, provided that the total tonnage of tankers entitled to the right of priority under article (4) paragraph (a) shall not at any time exceed the total tonnage of the tankers, ownership of which was registered in the name of said concession companies or parent companies or buyers which had been actually engaged in the regular transportation of Saudi Arabian oil and its products prior to 31st December 1953." In plain English, when Saudi Arabia's oil exports rose, as they surely would, shippers could not expand their fleets to accommodate the increase. Only SATCO ships could handle the new traffic.[16]

Citing an understanding he said had been reached at a meeting the previous December 8, Surur's "clarification" also specified that shipping rates to be charged during the life of the Onassis contract would not be greater than the international average, calculated quarterly.

Fred Davies's response—six weeks later—was polite but unequivocal: no. Even if that language were adopted, he wrote, it would still violate the Aramco concession agreement, as Aramco expected the arbitrators to rule. As for the supposed agreement on rate language, he said that there had been no meeting on December 8 and that Aramco had never been consulted about the proposed new wording.[17]

A more formal response that Aramco's lawyers submitted to the arbitrators said that this "clarified" version of Article IV "*does not permit chartered tankships to stay in service nor does it permit renewal of such charter parties, nor the making of additional charters as the need exists. It does not permit* Aramco, or its owner companies, or their customers to put new tankships owned by them into the service over and above the total tonnage owned and regularly employed on 31 December 1953. It does not permit new buyers of Aramco oil to put the tonnage into service which they had owned or had under charter on 31 December 1953, or which they might thereafter own or charter." The legal paper said that the proposed clarification "is tantamount to the Government writing a new clause into the Aramco Concession Agreement, with the aid of a third party, an outsider, without consultation with, or the consent of Aramco, whereby the Government would take away something which the Government sold, bargained and granted to Aramco more than 20 years ago."[18]

The tensions and grievances that had arisen in the relationship between Saudi Arabia and the United States—over the Baghdad Pact, Buraimi, the Onassis contract, Point Four, armaments, and the Dhahran base—were nowhere to be seen when the kingdom's new ambassador to Washington, Abdullah Al-Khayal, presented his credentials to President Eisenhower in August.

"It is my earnest desire to work for strengthening and cultivating the friendly relations that have always bound our two countries together," he said. "Moreover, I pledge my cooperation with you and your officials toward such a goal, which is synonymous with the personal desire of His Majesty and his Government." He said King Saud had instructed him to "convey to you his wish that the United States of America will eventually come to understand genuine Arab interests and Arab aims," which included "repelling of aggression by the strong against the weak." That was an obvious reference to British claims to the Buraimi Oasis and to Israel, but the language was measured and polite.

The president responded in like terms. "You may be assured," he said, "that the officials of the United States government will cooperate fully in the furtherance of the good relations which have so long prevailed between our peoples."[19]

Presentation of ambassadorial credentials is usually a ceremonial event, not the occasion for serious discussion or disagreements. In this case, however, the remarks of the ambassador and the president reflected the fact that the two countries, however different they were and however much they might disagree, needed each other and genuinely did wish to maintain good relations. Those sentiments were about to be sorely tested by developments on several fronts. These events were not directly related to each other but all added tension to U.S.-Saudi relations in one way or another.

In late summer, the Saudi government demanded that the Socony-Vacuum Company, or Mobil, one of the Aramco partners, either stop doing business in Israel or get out of the kingdom. This was another long-standing issue between Washington and Riyadh: Saudi Arabia not only subscribed to the overall Arab boycott of Israel but refused almost entirely to allow Jews into the country, not even to transit through Dhahran on civilian airlines.[20]

Deputy Secretary of State Hoover told Wadsworth that the oil consortium had not asked the government for assistance on this matter, but said the State Department was nevertheless "much concerned over far-reaching implications SAG demand. If SAG can determine where Aramco members can do business, concession could be rendered inoperative. While present action is directed against Socony, next victim could be any present or future partners of Aramco and third country may not be Israel. Whole operation would rest on whim."[21] As was the U.S. government's standard practice in that era, its opposition to the ultimatum to Mobil was not based on any principled objection to Saudi Arabia's attitudes about Jews, but only on its potential implications for business.

Mobil's business in Israel was a tiny fraction of its worldwide operations, so the company complied with the Saudi demand rather than risk its share of Aramco.

The British Power Play in Buraimi

Britain and Saudi Arabia had agreed to submit their dispute over the Buraimi Oasis to arbitration. The arbitrators were to settle the boundary between Saudi Arabia and Abu Dhabi. But the panel had hardly begun its deliberations when, in October 1955, the British abandoned the proceedings, accusing Saudi Arabia of trying to bribe members of the panel and of trying to buy the loyalty of tribesmen in the area. Arab tribal forces under British control seized the oasis region and expelled the Saudi garrison. An Aramco drilling crew narrowly escaped the cross-fire. Once again the United States was caught in the middle of this intractable dispute.[22]

CIA Director Allen Dulles sent an alarmed memo to his brother, the secretary of state.

"In view of talks you are having about dangerous situation in Middle East," it said, "I wish to pass on to you the substance of a report given to me by Terry Duce," Aramco's vice president for governmental affairs. "It concerns disturbing developments with regard to Buraimi. Recent British forcible occupation of Buraimi negates five years U.S. Government effort to get Saudi Arabs and British to arbitrate their boundary controversies. It creates particularly bad impression, and undermines confidence in arbitration as a means of settlement, because of the manner in which the British appear to have sabotaged arbitration and resorted to force when arbitration appeared to be going somewhat against them." That point was especially sensitive to the Saudis because they had agreed to arbitration on the Onassis contract and now had reason to doubt its effectiveness.

Dulles's note said that "Aramco's name [had been] mentioned in extensive publicity on bribery charges in British press and Duce gives categorical assurances Aramco played no role in Buraimi goings-on and is convinced that bribery story submitted to the Tribunal and carried to the press is sheer invention."

Dulles said Crown Prince Faisal did not believe the British would have taken such a step without the concurrence of the United States. The British action could result in "complete nullification in Middle East of years of effort to establish arbitration as peaceful and workable method" of resolving disagreements, he warned. The State Department feared Saudi Arabia would refer the Buraimi case to the United Nations Security Council, where the Soviet Union would no doubt seize upon it to condemn Western imperialism, which in turn would make Moscow's offer of weapons more attractive to the Saudis.[23]

Part of Dulles's concern about "nullification" of efforts to persuade the Saudis to have faith in arbitration proceedings was the impact it could have on the Onassis case, which was before the tribunal in Switzerland. The Saudis had agreed to the arbitration clause in the 1933 agreement, but its actual use was new to them and they did not trust the entire concept. Britain's move to nullify the Buraimi proceedings only increased their suspicions.

A few days later, the U.S. Consul in Dhahran, John W. Carrigan, reported that Saudis who lived in that part of the country were shocked and bitter about Britain's power play in Buraimi. The local governor, Saud bin Jiluwi, told Carrigan that he would continue to ensure the safety of the American U.S. staff at Aramco and at the consulate unless it became "impossible." Carrigan said he was "afraid that 'impossible' phase may lie before us if we concur with the British action" or fail to oppose it vigorously. He said Saudi officials had adopted the attitude that those were not with them on the Buraimi issue were against them.[24]

His fears may have been well grounded, but by that time the Buraimi dispute and Aramco were not the State Department's first concerns in the region. On September 27, 1955, Egyptian President Gamal Abdel Nasser announced what came to be known as the Czech Arms Deal.

CHAPTER NINETEEN

New Crisis, Old Cases

In February 1955, Israeli troops raided an Egyptian military camp in the Gaza Strip and killed 37 Egyptian soldiers. That raid cemented Nasser's determination to acquire modern weapons in sufficient quantities to enable Egypt to stand up to the Israelis.

"When the Israelis struck at Gaza, Nasser came under great pressure," according to his longtime confidant and spokesman, Mohamed Heikal. "He had little support from the other Arab nations. He was threatened by the Baghdad Pact. He was disturbed by the CIA's machinations. He had to get arms from somewhere" to confront Israel.[1]

Subsequent scholarship, based on Soviet-era documents, has established that the negotiations leading to Cairo's purchase of weapons from a Warsaw Pact country began well before the Gaza raid and were conducted even as U.S. officials were trying to assemble an arms package that would have kept Egypt in the Western orbit.[2] Nasser would gladly have accepted weapons from the United States, but despite Eisenhower's early efforts to establish good relations with the Egyptian leader, opposition from pro-Israel forces in Washington cut off that avenue. Nasser "tried to buy obsolete arms from World War II dumps in Belgium," Heikal wrote. He tried Italy, Sweden, Switzerland, and Spain. He even tried Britain, which was predictably unreceptive because of his opposition to the Baghdad Pact. Meanwhile, Egypt learned that France had begun supplying modern weapons to Israel. What choice did Nasser have but to turn toward a very willing Soviet Union?

By this time, Joseph Stalin had died and his replacement as leader of the Soviet Union, Nikita Khrushchev, took a far more engaged and active approach to postcolonial countries in the developing world, whether or not these new regimes were sympathetic to communism. Engagement with, and aid to, them offered opportunities for the rapid expansion of Soviet influence. Egypt, resentful of Britain and rebuffed by the United States over weapons and over financing for construction of the Aswan High Dam, was a promising target.³

Under the arms agreement announced by Nasser, Egypt would acquire jet fighters, long-range bombers, tanks, and other equipment. Nominally the weaponry would be supplied by Czechoslovakia, which had a well-established record as an arms supplier and might be regarded in the West as more politically palatable than the Soviet Union because it had earlier provided weapons to Israel. But Czechoslovakia was a satellite of the Soviet Union and would not have entered into such an arrangement with Egypt without Moscow's approval. There was no real distinction between Soviet weapons and Czech weapons.

This Cold War coup by the Soviets set off a new bout of anxiety in Washington about communist inroads in the Arab world, but it was highly popular among the Arab masses.

"In Palestinian refugee camps, in growing city slums, in liberation movements, universities, and new Arab middle-class homes from Rabat to the Gulf, Nasser was suddenly the man to follow," as one British account put it.⁴

"The Arab world was thrilled by Nasser's boldness and the end to the Western monopoly of arms supplies," the Russian historian Alexei Vassiliev wrote. "The massive crowds of Arabs that took to the streets of Damascus, Baghdad, Amman and even the British protectorates in Arabia saw this deal as an Arab victory over 'imperialism' and its 'bastard offspring,' Israel." Even Crown Prince Faisal was "openly in favour," despite his opposition to communism in any form.⁵

The Saudis saw Egypt's arms purchase agreement as a new opportunity to seek their own weapons deal with the United States; they calculated that Washington would want to find some balance to the Soviets among the Arabs. In that, they were correct. The arms agreement between Czechoslovakia and Egypt touched off a long struggle between the Soviet Union and the United States over influence in the Arab world. Saudi Arabia would be the principal anchor for Washington's efforts for the next two decades.

Two weeks after Nasser's announcement of the weapons deal, the State Department gave guidance to Ambassador Wadsworth on what to say to the Saudis about weapons assistance. He was to say that the United States was aware that Moscow had made an offer to Riyadh similar to the agreement with Egypt. In accordance with U.S. policy of noninterference in the affairs of other countries, no ultimatums were to be issued to the king, no demands made. Any attempt to enlist King Saud or other Arab leaders to persuade Nasser to change his mind might be counterproductive. "We feel best approach is merely to inform King our position in view his importance in Arab and Islamic worlds" and try to persuade him not to follow Egypt's example.⁶

What Washington did not do was offer to increase its modest pipeline of weapons to Saudi Arabia. The Saudis predictably found Washington's response, or lack of it, wanting.

In Washington, Ambassador Khayyal told State Department officials that Saudi Arabia wanted to maintain its friendship with the United States, but was in urgent need of modern weapons to defend itself. Despite its oil wealth, Saudi Arabia was the "poorest armed of all countries" in the area, he said. If the State Department's message, as delivered by Wadsworth, was the final answer, the king would consider it a refusal and "wishes [to] be excused if he tries to find arms where no conditions are attached."[7]

The Nonaligned Movement

Some months earlier, in April, Saudi Arabia had participated in a landmark international gathering in Indonesia known as the Bandung Conference. At that meeting, 29 postcolonial and newly independent countries—led by India, Egypt, and Indonesia—asserted their collective neutrality in the Cold War and their resolve to align themselves with neither Washington and the West nor Moscow and its satellites.[8] The participants varied widely in history and ideology, but they were unanimous in their opposition to the Baghdad Pact, which they regarded as a reassertion of Western dominance in the Middle East. The Saudis opposed the pact primarily because of the al-Saud family's historic rivalry with the Hashemite clan, which Britain had installed on the throne of Iraq. For the Eisenhower administration, dominated by the "with us or against us" view of the Dulles brothers, it was more than disconcerting to see the Saudis in such company at Bandung, lining themselves up with the likes of Nasser, India's Jawaharlal Nehru, and Yugoslavia's Josip Broz Tito, who was independent of Moscow but nevertheless a communist. It was clear in Washington and London that the position of ostensible Cold War neutrality adopted by the Bandung participants would give those countries opportunities to play off the Soviets and the West against each other.

A new U.S. National Intelligence Assessment distributed in June forecast that Saudi Arabia would "continue to maintain close ties with Egypt and to favor a new anti-Iraqi alignment." In addition, the document said, "In negotiations with the US over the Dhahran air base agreement, due for renewal in 1956, the Saudis will probably cite US support of the Turkish-Iraqi pact as an instance of aiding Saudi enemies, and use this argument to seek a higher price for renewal."[9]

A few months later, in the wake of Egypt's Czech arms agreement, George V. Allen, the assistant secretary of state for Near East affairs, wrote a memo to Secretary Dulles titled "Current Problems of the Arabian Peninsula and

Persian Gulf." Its tone was gloomy, similar to that of the memo he had sent to Robert Murphy the previous summer.

His new memo warned that "the stability of this region and the continuance of the paramount position of the West are threatened" by recent developments. "The determination of land boundaries in previously undemarcated areas [i.e., Buraimi] has created serious disputes between Saudi Arabia and its neighbors on the Persian Gulf, represented by the United Kingdom." Saudi Arabia, Allen wrote, "is using its extensive resources to oppose the inclusion of Jordan, Syria, and Lebanon in Western-sponsored collective security arrangements. In so doing, Saudi Arabia is cooperating with anti-Western and, in some cases, leftist elements."[10] That was exactly the sort of drift in Saudi policy to which Washington had feared the Onassis tanker contract would open the door.

Britain was not willing to give ground in Buraimi to make the U.S. position in Saudi Arabia less difficult. In preparation for an upcoming trip to Washington by Prime Minister Anthony Eden, Foreign Secretary Selwyn Lloyd fired a preemptive strike: he served notice that Britain was not prepared to be flexible or to yield on Buraimi, even if Washington regarded its position on that controversy to be an indefensible vestige of a bygone era.

Britain understood American interests in resolving the dispute and assuaging Saudi feelings, Lloyd wrote to Secretary Dulles, but "I must tell you that the stakes for us are even more vital and that we cannot afford to lose. Our position in the Persian Gulf states depends upon the confidence of the rulers and people in our ability to protect their interests. Any sign that we were going to let the Saudis back into Buraimi would be fatal to that position." Britain's economy was "entirely" dependent on oil from the Arab sheikhdoms on the shores of the Persian Gulf, Lloyd wrote. "We must retain at all costs control of this oil."

He was concerned primarily about the oil in the undisputed territory of the sheikhdom of Abu Dhabi, today the largest of the United Arab Emirates. The contested area around the Buraimi Oasis itself has no oil deposits, Lloyd said, although Aramco had supported Saudi Arabia's claims to it in the belief that it might. "Its only value to Saudi Arabia is as a base from which to suborn and penetrate" the neighboring smaller sheikhdoms, he said. "The present position, therefore, though it may be wounding to King Saud's pride in that it marks the failure of his expansionist policy, represents no threat to Saudi Arabian security or to her interests."[11] In his view, the oasis region was vital to Britain but of no economic or strategic value to Saudi Arabia and therefore Riyadh should back off.

When Eisenhower and Eden met in January, Eden was equally resolute. The Saudis, he said, were corrupt and trying to corrupt their neighbors. If Britain gave up on Buraimi, he said, it would soon be pushed out of the

Middle East altogether. Eisenhower, who did not believe in shoring up outdated colonial claims, was uncomfortable, but the two leaders left the question unresolved, as it would remain for many years.[12]

Resolving the Court Cases

In light of these major international developments, the Onassis affair receded from the headlines but it did not recede in importance to Onassis himself, the world's tanker fleet operators, and the oil companies. The arbitration proceedings were still in their early stages. The Saudi tanker contract was still in place, and the various court cases involving Onassis were still open.

The most important of those cases were the criminal indictment in the United States and the U.S. government's parallel civil lawsuit on the same issue against Onassis and his affiliated companies. After many months of negotiations between Onassis's lawyer, Edward J. Ross, and a Justice Department legal team directed by Assistant Attorney General Warren E. Burger, the government announced settlements of these cases on December 21, 1955. Coincidentally or otherwise, the settlement was reached about six weeks after Ambassador Wadsworth advised Washington that no further U.S. government action against Onassis in the SATCO matter was required.

In the name of Attorney General Brownell, the Justice Department issued a statement about the resolution of the civil lawsuit, quoting Burger as saying, "This brings to a close an unusual chapter in the history of Maritime litigation, with the Government receiving not only the original payments on the agreed purchase price of the vessels but $7 million from the Onassis interests. Total government recoveries from other purchasers in the past two years aggregate an additional $15,000,000."

In exchange for the $7 million and a commitment by Onassis to reorganize his companies to make them corporate citizens of the United States and thus legal operators of the ships, the government agreed to return 17 vessels it had seized and to drop forfeiture proceedings against 6 more that had escaped seizure by staying out of American ports. If the United States had kept those ships, it would have had to lay them up in floating storage for activation in an emergency. Keeping them in operation, Brownell said, "carries out a basic national defense policy in that the vessels will be maintained in ready condition the event of any national emergency and the Government will thereby save the substantial costs" of maintaining them in reserve and readying them for use when necessary. The government estimated the costs of maintaining a ship in reserve at $30,000,000 per year per vessel, and the reactivation cost at $90 million per vessel. That was money the government would not have to spend if Onassis kept the ships in service and registered in the United States, which he agreed to do.[13]

The Justice Department's announcement did not address the question of what use Onassis would make of those ships in the face of the international boycott of his fleet, but that was not the U.S. government's problem.

The announcement said that settlement of the civil lawsuit "does not dispose of" the criminal case, but that was a technicality because the cases were in different federal courts. The criminal case ended the same day when Judge Luther Youngdahl in Washington accepted pleas of guilty from the six corporate defendants and agreed to the Justice Department's request to dismiss the indictments of the remaining individual defendants, including Onassis. The companies paid nominal fines.

For Onassis, Gelina Harlaftis wrote, "Although the result was intended as public humiliation, his business edifice remained untouched." She quoted Ross as declaring, "It was all dressed up to look like a government victory but even they knew we had won."[14] Indeed, some members of Congress regarded the settlement as so lenient that they later demanded that Brownell appear to explain why he agreed to it. At hearings in 1958, Brownell denied ever meeting Onassis face-to-face when his firm represented him, and Onassis denied that he had received any preferential treatment because of their previous connection.[15]

Those settlements left open the multiple complaints against Onassis filed by Catapodis. Within the next four months, all of them ended in victory for Onassis. In ruling against Catapodis, the courts did not find that Onassis had behaved honorably or that Catapodis had not been swindled; the question was whether Catapodis could find the legally appropriate forum for pursuing his case or, if so, could provide acceptable evidence.

On March 20, 1956, a Parisian magistrate threw out Catapodis's complaint because Catapodis was unable to produce the one crucial document the court wanted to see, a signed contract between himself and Onassis.[16] The disappearing ink stunt had worked; the FBI lab's confirmation of it was still in the future, and the French magistrate therefore had no way to confirm Catapodis's claim about the vanished signature.

A week after the ruling in France, with several of his planned witnesses outside the United States and out of reach, Catapodis dropped the defamation suit in Washington. The last document in the case file, dated May 8, 1956, is a request by the lawyers for Catapodis and Onassis to dismiss the case "with prejudice," meaning that the complaint could not be filed again.

In the New York case, there was a brief moment of drama when Onassis's lawyers were questioning Stavros Niarchos in a pretrial hearing. Niarchos confirmed that he had hired Robert Maheu in the Onassis matter, and that Maheu had shown him the Catapodis affidavit about bribes before taking it to Saudi Arabia. But then he refused to answer any further questions, saying that the matter involved U.S. national security.

According to an internal CIA document, "Niarchos claimed government privilege in answering certain questions. This tact [sic] was challenged by the attorney and pursued to the point that eventually it was recorded in the briefs filed by both the plaintiff and the defendant that the CIA was in fact the Government agency of interest. Close coordination was maintained during this period with [the] Justice and State [departments]. At our request, a representative of the U.S. Attorney's office in New York monitored all of the hearings."[17]

Not a word about any CIA involvement appeared in an order issued by Judge Samuel Gold of the New York State Supreme Court on April 4, 1956. The judge granted a motion filed by Onassis's lawyers to throw out the case on the grounds that a New York court was a "forum non conveniens"—that is, the wrong place for such a proceeding.

Catapodis's lawyer had argued that Onassis was in fact a resident of New York because his wife owned an apartment on the East Side of Manhattan and he had spent a lot of money renovating it, and the New York telephone directory listed a number for his wife at that address. In addition, Catapodis's lawyer argued, Tina Onassis was a naturalized citizen of the United States, she and Aristotle had been married in New York, and their two children were born there. He also said, without providing evidence, that Onassis owned two cars registered in New York, a claim that Onassis denied.

Judge Gold did not find any of that persuasive.

"Both parties to this action reside in France," he wrote. "The alleged contract was made in France. The alleged acts of performance by plaintiff [Catapodis] took place in France and, to a lesser extent, in Saudi Arabia. The alleged breach [of contract] occurred in France." In addition, the alleged acts of bribery took place in France and Saudi Arabia, and "all the possible witnesses on both sides reside in France, in Saudi Arabia, and elsewhere abroad. Not a single witness resides in this country . . . all the material and documentary evidence is in France and Saudi Arabia." Moreover, the judge noted, it was in France that "this very plaintiff is presently prosecuting an action against this very defendant on substantially the same facts as those upon which the instant action is based." Judge Gold noted that the magistrate in Paris had dismissed that complaint, but said that Catapodis was planning to appeal that decision and thus the case remained in French jurisdiction.

Judge Gold was not ruling on the merits of Catapodis's claim of fraud nor on the details of the Onassis contract itself, only on whether the case should be heard in New York. But he made clear his contempt for Catapodis: "The attempt of plaintiff's attorneys to condemn defendant's activities in his relations with Saudi Arabia overlooks the fact that the plaintiff himself, by his own admissions, sought to procure the contract for defendant and participated in the alleged bribes which he now criticizes."[18]

Defense motion granted: case dismissed.

Onassis was now free of legal entanglements involving the Saudi Arabia contract; there remained only the international arbitration proceeding. He was still dealing with the messy whaling fleet matter, and would be for the next several months, but his biggest problem now was the continuing worldwide boycott of his ships. That picture was about to be changed by dramatic events in the Middle East—events that would have massive impact on the transportation of oil and on Onassis himself, as well as on the political and strategic balance of the entire region.

CHAPTER TWENTY

The Suez Crisis

By the end of 1955, Saudi Arabia had not exercised its option to terminate the agreement that allowed the United States to operate the strategic air base at Dhahran, but neither had it agreed to a renewal. Therefore, the lease expired as scheduled in June 1956, but operations continued while the two countries haggled over terms for an extension.

The Saudis continued to demand more weapons as part of the price, while the Eisenhower administration dithered over how much to offer. On July 2, Robert Murphy, George Allen, and other State Department officials met with their Defense Department counterparts. If that meeting accomplished anything, it was to underscore the lack of coherence within the government.

The State Department representatives said that Ambassador Wadsworth was awaiting instructions, and that it was time to send King Saud a letter saying that unless an agreement on terms for renewal was reached, the United States was prepared to walk away.

E. Perkins McGuire, representing the Pentagon as deputy assistant secretary of defense for international security affairs, objected on the reasonable grounds that there was no point in delivering an ultimatum if the United States had not made up its mind what it was actually prepared to do.

"What if the King says, 'All right, get out'? We have not considered what our next move would be," McGuire said. "What if the King says, 'All right, we'll negotiate?' We have not determined the size of our 'package.'"[1]

The Joint Chiefs of Staff, the country's most senior military officers, took the position that the base was essential to U.S. regional defense commitments and worth paying a high price for. Besides, they said, there was no ready alternative: "There is no alternate base in the general area of Dhahran which is currently capable of satisfying all of the U.S. military requirements presently being accommodated at Dhahran. Any alternate base which would satisfy U.S. military requirements would necessitate base rights, funds, and construction to provide the needed facilities. Assuming that base rights for a fully satisfactory alternate could be obtained without delay and that funds were made available for the construction of additional facilities, the earliest date of beneficial occupancy is estimated to be late 1959."[2]

On July 7, Wadsworth informed the State Department that the administration had a few more weeks to debate the question because King Saud and his entourage had gone to Mecca for the annual pilgrimage; no government business would be conducted during that time. That was where matters stood when, on July 26, Egypt's President Nasser overturned the entire strategic and economic balance of the Middle East. He announced the nationalization of the Suez Canal.

An Ill Wind Blows

From the perspective of London, Paris, and Washington, the wind was blowing the wrong way all across the Middle East in the first half of 1956. In Algeria, the vicious war for independence from France intensified. The last British troops were leaving Egypt, in grudging compliance with Nasser's demands. Egypt fomented region-wide hostility to Iraq because of the Baghdad Pact. In May, Egypt recognized the communist government in China. Largely in response to that move, the United States withdrew a commitment to help finance construction of Egypt's planned High Dam on the Nile at Aswan, creating a gap Moscow would fill. With upheaval wracking Jordan, the young King Hussein dismissed General John Bagot Glubb, the British commander of Jordan's Arab Legion, a decision for which British Prime Minister Anthony Eden wrongly blamed Nasser.

Angrily rebuffing talk from a senior foreign affairs official about "isolating" Nasser, Eden said, "I want him destroyed, can't you understand? I want him removed, and if you and the Foreign Office don't agree, then you'd better come to the Cabinet and say why."[3]

In that atmosphere, nationalization of the Suez Canal was a logical step for Nasser. The canal, built in the 19th century, was owned by a private Anglo-French company, not by any government, and with the departure of British troops it was the Egyptians, not the British, who were responsible for the waterway's security. The entire length of the canal, from the Mediterranean to the Gulf of Suez, was indisputably on Egyptian territory. Nasser promised to keep the canal operating and to pay compensation to its ousted owners. He knew that other Arab leaders would support him.

None of that mattered to the French or British governments. The British in particular regarded the canal as an indispensable lifeline, even though India, the jewel in their colonial crown to which it had been the vital link, had been independent since 1947.

As Nasser's biographer, Robert Stephens, explained, "The British and French governments totally lacked confidence in Nasser's word and feared that he was implacably hostile to their interests. They were interested in the legal, technical, and financial arguments about the Canal only in so far as these provided a public justification for their political aim of destroying Nasser's influence in the Arab world or removing him from power altogether."[4]

Yet Nasser and his citizens could not be expected to accede to British and French sentiment on control of the canal, especially because Nasser's nationalization became an overnight symbol of the independence and freedom from imperialism that the postcolonial countries had embraced at Bandung. The only way for Britain and France to regain control of the canal was to take it by force.

The day after Nasser's announcement, Prime Minister Eden wrote a "Dear Friend" letter to Eisenhower: "The Canal is an international asset and facility, which is vital to the free world. The maritime powers cannot afford to allow Egypt to expropriate it and to exploit it by using the revenues for her own internal purposes irrespective of the interests of the Canal and of the Canal users," he said. "Apart from the Egyptians' complete lack of technical qualifications, their past behaviour gives no confidence that they can be trusted to manage it with any sense of international obligation. Nor are they capable of providing the capital which will soon be needed to widen and deepen it so that it may be capable of handling the increased volume of traffic which it must carry in the years to come. We should, I am convinced, take this opportunity to put its management on a firm and lasting basis as an international trust."

If all else failed, Eden said, "My colleagues and I are convinced that we must be ready, in the last resort, to use force to bring Nasser to his senses. For our part we are prepared to do so. I have this morning instructed our Chiefs of Staff to prepare a military plan accordingly."[5]

The United States' policy on the Suez Canal had been laid out in NSC 5428, the same document that called for breaking the Onassis tanker contract. The document said that the United States should "take such steps, and secure the necessary commitments, as to best insure that the Suez Canal remains open to international trade."[6] But Nasser was not threatening to close the canal, and Eisenhower was unwilling to commit the United States to participation in military action to retake the waterway unless there was an immediate threat to American citizens. A U.S. military planning committee, instructed by the Joint Chiefs of Staff to evaluate the possibilities, reported that direct participation in or support for such a campaign "would alienate the Arab states and involve the risk of limiting U.S. ability to meet commitments in other theaters." But that report was not well received by the Joint

Chiefs, who argued that the study "did not sufficiently emphasize how militarily unacceptable the Egyptian action was to the United States."[7]

At a 22-nation conference in London in August, in which the United States and the Soviet Union participated but Egypt did not, the United States joined Britain and France in proposing creation of "an international board for operating, maintaining and developing the Canal and enlarging it so as to increase the volume of traffic in the interest of the world trade and of Egypt as a participant in the benefits of the Canal. Egypt would grant this board all rights and facilities appropriate to its functioning," to ensure that the waterway was operated safely and maintained properly.[8] But the Soviet Union, along with India and several other nonaligned countries, objected, largely because Egypt was not represented, and the conference ended inconclusively.[9] British and French military planning continued.

Extensive but fruitless diplomatic meetings and conferences continued well into October, in London and Washington and at the United Nations. No one was able to devise a formula that would guarantee safe operation and maintenance of the canal, determine control of canal revenue, satisfy the British and French desire to establish some form of international control, comport with Egypt's nationalist aspirations, and win the endorsement of the U.N. Security Council. Eisenhower, who in July had been nominated by the Republican Party for a second term as president, was busy campaigning for re-election, but he kept a close eye on Suez Canal developments and never wavered in his opposition to military action.

In late October, representatives of Britain, France, and Israel met secretly at Sevres, France, to finalize plans for military action to take the canal. Israeli forces would invade the Sinai Peninsula from the East on October 29, aiming to reach the canal within 24 hours. Britain and France would then call on Israel to withdraw its troops—on the understanding that this was a sham gesture and the Israelis, by prearrangement, would not comply. That would give Britain and France a concocted threat to the canal to justify their intervention. Britain and France would also issue an ultimatum to Egypt to open the canal to all international shipping, including Israeli vessels. If Egypt declined to comply, which it certainly would, British and French forces would enter the conflict alongside Israel. The Israelis would also seize and occupy the western shore of the Gulf of Aqaba, ensuring free access to the port of Eilat.[10]

The Israelis attacked as planned and duly refused to comply with an ultimatum from London and Paris. British and French paratroopers landed in Egypt on November 5.

The United States was a longtime ally of Britain and France and a strong protector of Israel, but if those countries were expecting Washington to support the invasion, or even to remain neutral about it, they were quickly disabused. In an address to the nation after the Israelis invaded and Britain and France sent their ultimatum, Eisenhower said flatly that "there will be no United States involvement in these present hostilities."

The president said that "the United States was not consulted in any way about any phase of these actions. Nor were we informed of them in advance. As it is the manifest right of any of these nations to take such decisions and actions, it is likewise our right, if our judgment so dictates, to dissent. We believe these actions to have been taken in error, for we do not accept the use of force as a wise or proper instrument for the settlement of international disputes."[11]

By time British and French troops hit the ground, the Arab world was in an uproar and the Soviet Union was threatening to intervene to support the Egyptians. That threat should have been foreseen in London and Paris because it fit perfectly with Moscow's strategy of spreading influence by posing as the great defender of imperialism's victims.

The prospect of global war spurred Eisenhower to act. He demanded that all four parties in the conflict, including Egypt, accept a cease-fire ordered by the United Nations, and he expedited the deployment of an international peacekeeping force headed by Canada.

The conflict, still known to Arabs as the "Tripartite Aggression," was brief, but it had far-reaching and long-lasting consequences. It ended in humiliating failure as France and Britain were obliged to withdraw their troops. The era when colonial powers asserted their rule over the colonized by force of arms was drawing to a close, although Algeria and Angola still lay ahead. Prime Minister Eden was forced to resign. Nasser cemented his image as a nationalist hero. All across the Arab world, leaders and subjects alike were grateful to Eisenhower; the United States, scorned by many Arabs since it supported the partition of Palestine and then recognized Israel in 1948, rose sharply in Arab esteem. The United States was inevitably drawn into the vacuum of regional influence created by the decline of Britain and France to become, however reluctantly, the dominant Western power in the Middle East. Eisenhower and Secretary of State Dulles understood that if the United States did not fill that vacuum, the Soviet Union surely would attempt to do so.

A Windfall for Onassis

Other than Nasser, the person who benefited the most from the Suez crisis was one who had nothing to do with it: Aristotle Onassis. The war resulted in closure of the canal until the following March. Overnight, most of the oil shipped from Saudi Arabia, Kuwait, Iraq, Iran, Bahrain, and Abu Dhabi, the lifeblood of the economies of Western Europe, had to be transported all the way around the Cape of Good Hope at the tip of Africa, adding some 9,000 miles and many weeks to the journey. Because tankers would now be at sea for so much longer than when they transited the canal, demand for tanker tonnage soared. Twice as many ships as before were required to transport the 95 million tons of oil yearly destined for Europe. The only major fleet owner who had ships available to fill that demand was Onassis, most of whose vessels were idle because of the oil buyers' boycott. The boycott vaporized in the new reality.

"Demand for tankers rocketed, as did the freight rates," Gelina Harlaftis wrote. "Oil companies competed for free tanker tonnage. Onassis with so many tankers laid up had the most available tanker tonnage in the world. The Suez crisis made him an extremely rich man. On his own calculations, in the six months the canal was closed, he made $60 [million] to $70 million in the spot market,"[12] or nearly $600 million in 2019 dollars.

That tanker boom evaporated quickly after the canal reopened, but by that time Onassis's fleet manager had secured long-term contracts at favorable rates—some of them on the same tankers Onassis had purchased fraudulently from the U.S. government but had been allowed to keep after settlement of the court cases. Onassis banked so much money as a result of the Suez war that he no longer needed the money he expected to reap from SATCO. His arrangement with Saudi Arabia was now more trouble than it was worth.

A Grateful King Saud

No Arab leader was more effusive in his praise of Eisenhower's actions in the Suez crisis than King Saud.

The day after Israel struck, he sent the president a telegram saying he had "learned from the news the great concern shown by Your Excellency regarding the Jewish aggression on Egyptian territory and the efforts you have made in warning the aggressor that America will be on the side of the country encroached upon." In a reflection of the deep loathing of Israel that characterized the kingdom's leadership then and for decades afterward, he added that "Your Excellency and the whole world have seen that we were right when we considered the occupation of Arab territory by this Zionist group has been and still is the cause of trouble and disorder in the East."[13]

A few days later, while the conflict was still unfolding, Saud sent a message to the White House saying that "His Majesty greatly appreciates the efforts of President Eisenhower to bring to an end the aggression of Israel, France and Britain against Egypt. His Majesty sincerely wishes that President Eisenhower's efforts in repulsing the aggressors and effecting the withdrawal of the aggressive forces from Egyptian territory be crowned with success."[14]

In December, he sent the president a long "Dear Friend" letter—four single-spaced pages in the translated version. It began with lavish praise but included complaints about the fact that Israel had still refused to withdraw its troops from Egyptian territory. (They would not leave until March 1957.)

"I thank God, Your Excellency and the United States," the king wrote, "for the excellent results which we and the entire world have obtained in dealing with the aggression of Britain, France and Israel against Egypt—that unjustifiable aggression which was launched against an Arab country and which was dragging the world toward disaster. I, the Arab Nation, and the entire world will always remember the good efforts of Your Excellency and the United States government to bring about the present results."

The king asked that he be consulted before the United States proceeded with any United Nations resolution aimed at a long-term solution to "the Palestine question," and that U.S. officials tone down their "malicious campaign against Syria and its alleged communist tendencies." Syria bought Soviet weapons to confront "the Zionist menace" but would never become a communist country, the letter said. Demonization of Syria, the king said, would be counterproductive, forcing Syria to adopt "a policy which it neither seeks nor desires."

Then King Saud warned the United States not to join the Baghdad Pact. If it did so, he wrote, "Certain other countries in the Middle East might conclude a Pact with another bloc, thereby bringing about the very thing we all fear."

He concluded by expressing, "as a faithful friend," the desire "to cooperate with the United States in all matters which advance justice and equity to the interest of the world in general and our two countries in particular."[15]

The president then agreed to a suggestion from the State Department that he invite King Saud to the White House. On January 7, 1957, White House press secretary James C. Hagerty announced that "the King of Saudi Arabia, His Majesty Saud Ibn Abdul Aziz al-Saud, has accepted the President's invitation to visit the United States. The King and his party will visit Washington January 30, 31, and February 1. This is the first state visit of 1957, and marks the first time a reigning monarch of Saudi Arabia has visited the United States."[16]

The king crossed the Atlantic by sea, so his first stop was New York, where he was not well received. Mayor Robert F. Wagner refused to have anything to do with the ruler of a country that practiced slavery, excluded Jews, and forbade Christian worship.[17] When Saud arrived in Washington some days later, the president took the opposite approach, going to the airport to greet the king in person, ordering up military honors with a 21-gun salute, and making his own suite at Walter Reed Medical Center available to the king's three-year-old son, who was fitted with prosthetic devices to overcome the partial paralysis that had afflicted him from birth.[18]

Eisenhower also put on a formal state dinner in the king's honor. It may have been the only state dinner in modern White House history at which all the guests were men. Among them were Aramco's Fred Davies and the chief executives or presidents of all four of Aramco's parent companies. Both Dulles brothers were present, as was Ambassador Wadsworth, along with the ambassadors of Egypt and six other Arab countries. No one from any communist country was invited, nor were the ambassadors of Britain, France, or Israel.[19]

Secretary of State Dulles participated in the first meeting between Eisenhower and the king, and the president asked him to deliver an overview of how the United States assessed the situation in the Middle East.

Dulles said that the United States, once a colony itself, sympathized with the aspirations of colonized peoples. "However," he said, "the greatest danger at present was from international Communism, which started with a conspiracy of a small number of people who were able to take over all Russia and since then have seized control over approximately one third of the peoples of the world. The doctrine of Communism contradicted every religion in the world and aimed at the destruction of every form of free society. The Communists, once they gained control, were entirely ruthless." The policy of the United States, he said, was to "assist countries endangered by the ambitions of the Communists," not to expand U.S. influence for the sake of doing so.

That brought him to the subject of the Dhahran Airfield, which he said was "useful, but by no means indispensable." As for the Suez Canal, he said the United States accepted the Egyptian takeover, but wanted assurances that the waterway would be open to the ships of all nations, including Israel.

The king responded that he had brought with him a memorandum on the main topics he wished to discuss, including bilateral relations and the communist threat to the region. He said that Saudi Arabia wanted to extend the Dhahran Airfield agreement and that the proof of this sentiment was that he "had not raised the question of renewal of the agreement, although it expired some months ago."

King Saud spoke mostly in vague terms and generalizations about "the present situation in the Middle East," but there was no need for him to be specific. The Americans knew quite well, because he had said many times, that he believed the main threat to regional stability was the existence of Israel.[20]

In all, the president and the king met three times, once with no one else present except an interpreter. Neither side took notes at that one-on-one meeting; Eisenhower dictated from memory a memorandum of the conversation. This remarkable document, unusual in that is written in the first person, filled 11 legal-size pages. The president had apparently not fully understood beforehand the king's erratic thought processes and undisciplined approach.

"The King started off by saying that he wanted to talk to me mainly about very secret, confidential things, some of them really personal," Eisenhower wrote. "At the same time he said there were others that I could discuss with my advisers. However, I failed to get a clear understanding of which ones he considered absolutely secret (except for the last subject, which I shall mention later) and which ones were of greater sensitivity. Consequently, I write this paper only for my own use and the personal use of the Secretary of State." He said Secretary Dulles was authorized to share it with a maximum of three other State Department officials.

In Eisenhower's account, the king spoke bitterly about the British, who he said "had a deliberate policy of keeping the Arabs weak." Because of their collective weakness, Saud said, "the Arabs had suffered many indignities," including the seizure of Buraimi by the British and abuses by Israel that he did not specify. He said the Arabs in general and he in particular had to obtain modern weapons to defend themselves, and had no choice but to deal with whatever supplier was willing.

He said, the president wrote, that "about a year and a half ago, the Soviets approached him with what he said were wide open and very enticing offers. The Soviets told him that they would provide any amount of arms he desired, together with adequate training teams to bring his forces to a good state of readiness," at a lower cost than any other potential supplier. Saud told the president that he had so far declined the offer, but the time had come to respond to "the demands of his people and the strength of public opinion." In the face of rising anti-colonial sentiment among the Arabs, stoked by Nasser, it was a political liability for Saud to have a foreign military base in the kingdom. He wanted the Americans to take that into account.

The president was noncommittal. In general, he said, it was best for developing countries to use their resources for economic growth and public works, spending only so much on military forces as was necessary to keep order. It was the role of the United Nations, he said, "to preserve weak nations from unjustified and unprovoked aggression."

The king replied that his vast and underpopulated country had suffered border incursions by Britain, repeated raids by Israel, and even "aggression" by Iran, an apparent reference to Iran's claim to small islands in the Gulf. Then, the president wrote, the king "said that he had a program for armament which had been approved by training teams in his country. (It is possible I misunderstood this particular statement, but that is what I thought he said.)"

Saud said his country was indeed spending heavily on schools, hospitals, roads, and communications, but did not have the resources to pursue those programs, feed the kingdom's penniless Bedouin, and at the same time acquire the weapons it needed.

The president wrote,

> In reply to this, I repeated my assertion that technical help should probably come first. I pointed out that schools were no good without teachers; that irrigation systems were of little use except where there were people who knew how to make economic use of water and land. . . . I emphasized that money alone could not make a country prosperous or raise its level of industrialization. It took investment, brains, experience in organization and professional matters, and a provision for balance among various segments of the economy. I pointed out that purchasing power had to go along with the production of goods. Most of this was lost on him, but at least he did not express to me any thoughts of rushing into "big business" and he seemed to be responsive to the idea when I told him that small village and household industries were far more important to a country with very low living standards than were heavy goods industries.[21]

The president was saying these things to a ruler who had only recently withdrawn from the Point Four technical assistance program set up by Harry Truman. Two decades later, President Richard Nixon would create a vast program of technical assistance to Saudi Arabia along the very lines Eisenhower was talking about, but that was under a different and much more competent king.

After King Saud's plea for weapons, he and Eisenhower had an extensive but inconclusive discussion of Arab-Israeli relations, on some aspects of which the president found the king "completely misinformed."

That brought Saud to the private, personal matter he had said he wanted to discuss, which was, Eisenhower wrote, "the suggestion that I invite Nasser and the King of Syria to visit me." (There was no "King of Syria"; Syria was a republic, led by President Shukri al-Quwatli. It is not clear whether this was the king's mistake, or Eisenhower's.)

Saud's idea caught the president by surprise. "I had not expected this, so I stalled a little bit," he wrote. He said he would, of course, consider the idea, but added that if he invited two more Arab leaders to the White House shortly after meeting King Saud, it would upset the Israelis.

Although the entire session was inconclusive, Eisenhower wrote, the king "seemed very happy that I had given him an hour and three quarters to get all of these matters off his chest."[22]

The king did not leave Washington empty-handed. After further consultations with Dulles, Eisenhower agreed to provide modest amounts of military equipment to Saudi Arabia. When Dulles signaled this decision to Saud, the king asked him point-blank, "Did the U.S. really intend to arm Saudi Arabia? The Secretary replied in the affirmative but stated it was a matter of how much arms could be supplied."[23]

As is customary after a meeting between heads of state, the two countries issued a joint communiqué about what had been discussed and accomplished. This was the key paragraph:

> With respect to the military defense of Saudi Arabia, including the Dhahran Airfield, President Eisenhower assured his Majesty King Saud of the willingness of the United States to provide assistance for the strengthening of the Saudi Arabian armed forces, within the constitutional processes of the United States. To this end, plans are being made by representatives of both countries for the supply of military equipment, services and training, for the purpose of defense and the maintenance of internal security in the Kingdom. In the same spirit, His Majesty King Saud assured President Eisenhower of His Majesty's intention that the United States continue for another five years to use the facilities accorded to it at the Dhahran Airfield under conditions provided for in the Agreement concluded between the two countries [in 1951, the previous time the lease had come up for renewal].[24]

The king would get his weapons, in some package that the Saudis could afford and the White House and the Defense Department did not consider excessive. After the gracious welcome, the generous commitment of the president's time, and the weapons agreement, the king was gratified. As the State Department's Pete Hart put it, "Just as U.S.-Saudi relations had reached their lowest point in 1953–54, in 1957–58 they rode on a crest."[25]

Still, irritants remained. The king and the president in effect agreed to disagree about Israel. The king could not commit Nasser to allow Israeli ships to transit the Suez Canal, nor could Eisenhower commit the British to evacuate Buraimi. The Saudis had hoped that the United States would supply weapons without requiring payment, or would at least offer financial assistance for the purchases, and were irked when no such promise was forthcoming. The official records of the summit meeting contain no indication that the king or the president had brought up the Onassis contract, but others in the Saudi delegation made clear that it was still a very sore point.

Yusuf Yassin and Mohammed Surur, who had been in the king's entourage for the visit, stayed on in Washington for additional meetings after Saud's departure. In a conversation with Secretary Dulles, Yassin said the king "wanted to know why the U.S. was able to offer grant aid to some countries purchasing arms from the U.S. whereas it was apparently unable to do so in Saudi Arabia's case. Shaikh Yusuf [Yassin] said that the only difference he could see between the agreement offered to Saudi Arabia and the mutual security agreements that the U.S. had with some other countries was in Article IV. Was Article IV as important as all that?"[26] Was that shipping preference so important that because of it the United States would require Saudi Arabia to pay for weapons when it armed other countries free of charge?

Article IV was, of course, the major point of the entire dispute over the Onassis contract. The State Department's memorandum of this conversation does not record any response from Dulles, but the Eisenhower administration had ample reasons other than Article IV to treat Saudi Arabia differently from other countries to which the United States was providing military assistance. The Saudis had abundant resources and ample income, although the royal regime was squandering the money in mismanagement, corruption, and white elephant projects; a little fiscal discipline would make the weapons affordable. Besides, the Onassis contract was now out of the U.S. government's hands; its fate would be determined by the arbitrators in Switzerland.

CHAPTER TWENTY-ONE

The End of the Affair

Anyone at Aramco or in the Saudi Arabian government who thought that submitting their dispute over the Onassis contract to arbitration would bring a quick, clean end to the argument soon learned otherwise. It marked only the beginning of a messy, tedious process that consumed more than three years and incalculable amounts of money for legal fees and expenses.

For the Eisenhower administration, events elsewhere in the region and the overall improvement in relations with Saudi Arabia had moved the Onassis matter far down the agenda. For Aramco, the world's tanker fleets, the maritime countries, and the Saudi government, the issue remained critically important, but it was out of their hands. It was unclear what they would do in the event of an unfavorable arbitration ruling. The tanker deal mattered less than before to Onassis, now enjoying his ship charter money. The SATCO contract had brought him mostly grief.

Because of their limited experience in corporate and international law, officials in the Saudi government were largely unfamiliar with arbitration as a dispute-settling mechanism, and they were mistrustful of it after Britain scuttled the arbitration process in the Buraimi Oasis matter. They had agreed to it in the Onassis case because it was the only available way out of the impasse with Aramco other than the embarrassing repudiation they had tried to avoid.

The case became a landmark of international arbitration law. According to Stephen M. Schwebel, a junior member of Aramco's legal team in the case who later became president of the International Court of Justice, "The question to be decided was whether Aramco itself, or its parent companies and buyers, could be compelled to use for transportation on the high seas tankers which they had not freely chosen. The parties sought a declaratory award and the Tribunal was not empowered to do more than to issue such an award. In particular, the Tribunal was not empowered to effect reconciliation between the Onassis Agreement and the Aramco Concession Agreement; it was not competent to prescribe or suggest measures that would make it possible to harmonize the two. The Tribunal's mission was to give a decision on the legal position resulting from these agreements and to interpret them as they were. The Tribunal's duty was to state the law, not to modify it."[1]

In their own filings with the arbitration panel, Aramco's lawyers included a brief section on "Matters Not at Issue." They specified that the proceeding was not about the government's right to have a national fleet, which Aramco did not contest, nor about its right to put that fleet under the Saudi flag. The only issue, they said, was "whether Aramco and its buyers can be *compelled* to use tankers not freely chosen by them."[2]

However the arbitrators ruled, they had no enforcement power. The panel could not compel the government to abandon the contract, nor could the panel compel Aramco to acquiesce. In their agreement to go to arbitration, the government and the oil company specified that "the award of the arbitration panel shall be final and binding on the two parties," but compliance was up to them.[3]

Aramco and its parent companies had welcomed the agreement to submit the dispute to arbitration, but now they worried that if Aramco prevailed, the Saudis would simply nationalize the company. Among Fred Davies's papers is a handwritten note summarizing an assessment of this possibility by Mobil president B. Brewster Jennings:

> The concession agreements between Middle Eastern countries and international oil companies "were a pledge on the part of the governments to give up their rights of nationalization for the period of the contracts. For a government to tear up such a contract after the [word illegible] of other nations have been placed in their facilities can hardly be accepted as the normal expression of a government's right to nationalize. Have we reached the absurd point in world relations where a sovereign state like a minor child is incapable to giving investors the assurance that it will what it specifically promises to do, and will not do what it specifically promises not to do?"

Howard Page, Exxon's Middle East negotiator, sent a "Memorandum on Nationalization" to the State Department, warning that "If countries could unilaterally repudiate their freely undertaken, solemn engagements, international agreements among states would become a mockery and the broad economic development of the free world which is required to improve the living standards of all its people would cease." Nationalization, he wrote, while politically appealing to some audiences, was just a euphemism for expropriation.[4] Both letters misconstrued Saudi Arabia's position: the kingdom was not trying to breach or circumvent the concession agreement because that agreement did not apply to international transportation.

Both sides in the arbitration proceedings, Aramco and the Saudi government, assembled teams of high-powered lawyers. Aramco's group was led by General Counsel George Ray and by its principal outside counsel, Lowell Wadmond, a partner in the New York firm White and Case. The Saudi government's group, selected at least in part on recommendations from Onassis, was headed by Professor Myres McDougal of Yale Law School, whom Schwebel described as "a famous academic whose distinctive prose some saw as especially academic, but he was in fact a formidable, fully comprehensible advocate."[5]

The first procedural step was to select the members of the arbitration panel. Naturally, each side wanted a panelist who would be amenable to its arguments, rather than impartial.

"So we both appointed very partial arbitrators," Aramco's Bill Owen later said, ruefully recalling "how stupid a system it is where you have partial arbitrators. It just adds another layer of counsel, and you really end up with just one arbitrator to settle it," namely the "referee" chosen by the two members selected by the parties. "It just adds to the expense and delay, and it makes no sense," Owen said, "but at any rate that was the system in those days. These days, if you appoint an arbitrator, he's got to be impartial" and contact with panelists outside the formal proceedings is prohibited.[6]

The Saudi government chose as its member Dr. Helmy Baghat Badawi, a prominent Egyptian lawyer. Aramco chose Dr. Saba Habachy, described by Schwebel as "a brilliant Egyptian former Cabinet minister knighted by the British Government for his wartime services." He had previously represented Aramco on the Buraimi boundary issue. Those two then selected a Swiss judge and legal scholar, Georges Sauser-Hall, as referee. In effect, Sauser-Hall would be the deciding vote.

Once the panel had assembled in Switzerland, the case proceeded in a manner that would be familiar to anyone who has observed proceedings in an appellate court in the United States. The two sides submitted reams of documents giving the background of the dispute and their interpretations of the contracts, and citing what they said was relevant law.

Davies also submitted an affidavit recounting the history of the oil enterprise in Saudi Arabia and suggesting that the Saudis ought to be grateful for everything the oil company had done for them.

When the first oilmen arrived in 1933, he said,

> The country had little to sell. Over vast areas of rock and sandy waste, a nomadic society depended on the scant and uncertain provision of the desert. The culture—tribal, patriarchal, and Islamic—was ancient and little changed from the time of the Prophet Mohammed. Some foreign

The End of the Affair

trade took place in the vicinity of the holy cities and through the settlements adjacent to the Persian Gulf, but contact with the outside world was slight and the amenities and opportunities of the western world almost entirely lacking. Even the basic requirements of human life—food, clothing, and the simplest household and agrarian implements—were in short supply. . . . No one can gainsay that the success of the Arabian American Oil Company, in finding both oil and markets for the oil, has met these needs to a degree far exceeding the hopes and expectations entertained at the time the Concession was first granted.[7]

Floyd W. Ohliger, an Aramco vice president, submitted another affidavit relating how difficult it had been to achieve the advances narrated by Davies.[8]

Everything they said was true, but irrelevant to the issues before the tribunal. And Davies, a veteran of Saudi Arabia, ought to have known that the Saudis resented it when foreigners reminded them of how poor and backward they had been. They would be put off by such an argument, not persuaded.

An Arbitrator Dies

In the summer of 1956, the legal teams gathered in Switzerland for eight weeks of oral argument, after which the panel began its consideration of the issues.

In March 1957—while the panel was still deliberating, two years after the proceedings began—Helmy Badawi, the panelist appointed by the Saudi government, died. The Saudi government, in the person of a well-known legal scholar named Hamed Sultan, who had an ill-defined role as its "agent" in the case, took the position that because of Badawi's death, the entire proceeding would have to be scrapped and restarted from scratch. Sultan wanted a new start with new panelists because, he said, any replacement for Badawi, coming in cold to represent the Saudi side, would inevitably be at a disadvantage.

Aramco rejected that proposition because the arbitration agreement specified that "if the office of either of the arbitrators becomes vacant for any reason whatsoever the designation of his successor shall be made within fourteen days from the date the vacancy occurs." It made no provision for starting over; the arbitration agreement had created the position, not the individual who filled it, and that position still existed.[9]

Sultan, who had been selected as an agent of the Saudi government by Finance Minister Mohammed Surur, was in Cairo at the time because he was advising Nasser in the aftermath of the Suez conflict. George Ray met him there for two days of strained conversation on April 13 and 14.

According to Ray's memorandum of these talks, Sultan argued that "as a matter of law Badawi's death ended the Arbitration Panel's existence with the consequence that the only fair and just way that the objectives of the parties to settle the dispute by arbitration could be carried out would be to appoint a new board."

Ray rejected the argument that a new panelist would be at a disadvantage. "I said that in so far as equality was concerned, any lawyer of intelligence and integrity, or any layman for that matter, could take the record, study it, listen to the tape recordings and be in as strong a position to deliberate" as the other panelist and the referee. Besides, if a new panel were assembled, Aramco would simply reappoint its original choice, Habachy, who would still have all the knowledge he had already accumulated.

If the government persisted in its refusal to appoint a new representative to the existing panel, Ray said, Aramco would agree to let Referee Sauser-Hall decide the case himself.

Sultan "seemed displeased with this suggestion and somewhat embarrassed by it," Ray wrote. "He could not answer why Sauser-Hall, who admittedly was one of the greatest living authorities on international law, a man of integrity and honour and the Government's own choice for referee, could not do an effective job of deciding the case."

After a long but fruitless discussion, they broke off for the evening. The next morning, Sultan appeared at Ray's room in Cairo's Semiramis Hotel to ask if he had changed his mind after sleeping on it. When Ray said no, Sultan restated his position that "the Tribunal was dead and we could not revive it, that it was his way or nothing."

From that, Ray concluded that "it was obvious that he was determined to get rid not only of Saba [Habachy] but of Sauser-Hall."[10]

That was where matters stood until 10 days later, when Davies received a letter from Surur that not only agreed with Sultan's position that a new start was necessary but did so in language so similar that he and other Aramco officials concluded that Sultan had actually written it.

Davies, citing the "any reason whatsoever" clause of the arbitration agreement, rejected what he called the "fallacy" of the argument that a new panel must be convened. "It would neither be practical, nor compatible with principles of fairness and justice," he wrote, "to dismiss the remaining members of the Tribunal—men of outstanding character, integrity and fitness for the task assigned to them—who have already devoted so much time and effort to the work of the Tribunal, before completion of their task."

He urged Surur to take it up with the king. He politely refrained from pointing out that the king, a man of limited intellect accustomed to ruling as an absolute monarch, would be unable to fully grasp the complexity of the issue.

The End of the Affair

On the evening of May 7, 1957, Davies and his colleague Garry Owen met with Surur at the minister's home in Riyadh. Davies restated all the points George Ray had made to Sultan, and added one new argument: the arbitration agreement provided that both sides "shall respect all obligations they have undertaken and now undertake," and both sides had agreed to abide by the panel's ruling.

"These provisions of the arbitration agreement," Davies said, "have brought great acclaim in international legal circles to His Majesty. If the government were at this time to throw over the Arbitration Tribunal, the good faith of the King and his Government would be questioned and the reputation of the King and his Government would be severely damaged in international circles."

To use an American expression, Davies said, "people might well be inclined to say that 'Saudi Arabia had pulled a Buraimi,'" a reference to Britain's nullification of the arbitration proceedings in the border dispute, a move Saudi Arabia had strongly criticized.

According to a report on this conversation by Owen, Surur accepted these arguments. He said the government now had a better lawyer than Sultan. He asked for, and virtually dictated, a letter summarizing Davies's position, which the minister would take to "the appropriate authorities in the government." The letter should say nothing about the king; it should stress the legal arguments and the points Ray had made about Sauser-Hall and the integrity of the Tribunal.

He also said it was important to resolve the matter quickly because "Onassis is 'quiet' at this time. Perhaps this is because his tankers are busy. This situation, however, may change in the future, and he may then bring pressure to bear to employ his tankers."[11] Surur feared that when the post-Suez tanker market cooled off after the canal was reopened, Onassis would be back, demanding implementation of his contract.

Two days letter, an Aramco envoy delivered the requested letter. According to Bill Owen, the letter omitted any mention of the cost of the arbitration proceedings because the government might refuse to allow Aramco to deduct those costs on its tax returns, so "we prefer to avoid stimulating any further S.A.G. interest in this point at the present time."

When the letter arrived, Surur read it and said, "Tell Mr. Davies that this is the letter we wanted."[12]

Shortly thereafter, the government appointed Mahmoud Hassan to replace Badawi. After a pause to allow Hassan to familiarize himself with the record, the Tribunal at last proceeded to complete its deliberations and render a judgment.

The ruling, issued on August 23, 1958, was an unequivocal victory for Aramco. The Tribunal ruled that the Onassis contract violated the company's

1933 concession agreement. The government's argument about its sovereign rights was invalid because it had exercised its sovereign rights to grant the concession in the first place, and that concession was a binding contract, not a law that could be repealed. As for the transportation issue, the panel said that the right to transport the oil would be without value if it stopped at the water's edge.

"In an enterprise of world-wide importance whose success is entirely dependent on the flow of oil and oil products to foreign markets," the ruling said, "it is impossible to imagine that the Parties would have wanted to give the concessionaire an exclusive right of transport restricted to the territorial waters, while denying this right as regards transportation overseas, which is the only kind of transportation which is of real interest to the concessionaire."[13]

Therefore, the panel ruled, "the purpose of the Onassis Agreement cannot be achieved without the indisputable rights and interests of the company being infringed . . . the Government is not legally entitled to compel Aramco to implement the Onassis agreement."[14]

Mahmoud Hassan, the replacement panelist appointed by the Saudi government, dissented on one key point. "The word 'transport' which occurs in the nomenclature of Aramco's exclusive rights," he wrote, "can only cover transport which pertains to operations to be performed in the exclusive area of the concession." Had the parties wished it to cover international transportation, he wrote, they would have said so specifically.[15] He accepted the government's argument that maritime transport is a vast international enterprise "independent of and distinct from" oil operations on land and is therefore subject to separate contractual arrangements.[16] That was the argument the State Department's Stanley Metzger had flagged three years earlier and that Abdullah Sulaiman had put forward, but the other two arbitration panelists did not accept it.

Had the panel ruled otherwise, the redoubtable Wanda Jablonski observed, it would have meant that "a sovereign could grant a concession because it was sovereign—and then turn around and ungrant it because it was sovereign."[17]

The government's response was twofold: it abided by the ruling and made no further attempt to interfere with whatever transportation arrangements Aramco and its buyers set up. But because of their disappointment at the outcome, the king and the Council of Ministers declared a ban on arbitration clauses in any new contracts or agreements, a decision that made it legally risky for foreign companies to do business in Saudi Arabia for the next 30 years.[18]

By the time the ruling was issued, however, it was basically moot because Onassis had abandoned the field. As Surur had surmised, Onassis now had

The End of the Affair

more important and less troublesome contracts elsewhere, as his business had boomed with the closure of the Suez Canal. The Saudis, bowing to reality in the face of international unanimity, now offered him a way out, and he took it.

Welcome News

On June 21, 1957, Brewster Jennings of Mobil called Aramco headquarters in New York with interesting news. Nicholas Cokkinis had come to his office "pursuant to instructions" from his boss, Aristotle Onassis.

Cokkinis reported that Finance Minister Surur had sent an envoy to Geneva to inquire "whether Onassis would be willing to terminate all phases [of the] shipping arrangements previously entered into, including dissolution of the company without any financial payment or claim. Onassis advised [the envoy] he would be entirely willing to do this and agreed to write a confirming letter to Surur accordingly." His Saudi gambit unfulfilled, Onassis was moving on.

Nothing in the record indicates why Surur suddenly asked Onassis if he would be willing to abandon the contract even as the arbitration case was still going on; it seems likely that Surur acted to preclude the possibility he had raised a month earlier: that Onassis would eventually be back seeking to implement the agreement.

In a cable to Fred Davies reporting this development, an Aramco official named Harry J. McDonald said Onassis had asked for the company's advice about what to say in that letter he would write to Surur. Jennings recommended that Aramco not offer any opinion to the Saudi government but should tell Onassis that if the government wished to terminate the contract, he, Onassis, should say that was an "understandable decision" and accept it. General Counsel Ray agreed that "Aramco should have no part of any kind" in the matter.[19]

That brought the SATCO case to its anticlimactic end, even though the arbitration panel had yet to rule. But the issues raised in the case turned out to have wider and longer-term implications, in addition to the Saudi government's decision to exclude arbitration clauses from future contracts.

For the Eisenhower administration and its allies, nullification of the Onassis contract represented a substantial victory: preservation of full Western control of the global oil market outside the communist world and a rebuff, at least for some time, to nationalist agitation in the producing states. The concession system, repudiated by Iran and threatened by Onassis, was not seriously challenged again for nearly 20 years, by which time the development of major new oil fields in Alaska and the North Sea had made control of the Middle East's resources less critical to the United States and Europe.

When the concession system finally died, it did so in dramatic fashion. By the early 1970s, the producing countries had organized themselves into the Organization of Petroleum Exporting Countries (OPEC), and radical nationalist regimes among such members as Libya and Algeria led the group to seize control of pricing; then, some members simply expropriated entire concessions. The embargo imposed by Arab oil producers on the United States and some European countries during the 1973 Middle East war further strengthened the hand of the oil states.

The global oil order that the United States and its allies had struggled so hard to preserve blew apart forever in late 1973 when OPEC's members collectively raised the base price of a barrel of oil from $5.12 to $11.65. They did not negotiate the price with the international oil companies, which no longer had any bargaining power: they simply imposed it. By 1980 the price of oil was about 10 times as high as it had been in 1970. Saudi Arabia, as the biggest exporter in OPEC, benefited the most.

A New Concession Partner?

Even after the telephone call from Cokkinis appeared to put an end to the long SATCO dispute, Onassis did not vanish entirely from the picture.

One of the founders of OPEC was Abdullah Tariki, the nationalist firebrand who had risen through the ranks of Aramco and then the Saudi Finance Ministry to become the oil policy chief after Mohammed Surur became minister. In that post, eager to break Aramco's grip on Saudi oil, he went so far as to propose that Aramco share the concession with another partner—and he proposed that Aristotle Onassis be that partner.

In August 1957—two months after Cokkinis let it be known that Onassis was willing to give up the tanker contract—Fred Davies was in Washington to bring the State Department up to date on developments.

He said Onassis "had told Aramco recently that the King had asked him to bid on a concession. Onassis had asked Aramco if it wished to join with him," according to the department's memorandum of this conversation. "Mr. Davies replied that the company did not take this proposal seriously," but he added that "Aramco would welcome another company to 'shoulder the burden' of dealing with the Saudi Arabian government."[20]

Tariki fell out of favor with Crown Prince Faisal and was ousted when Faisal became king in 1964, but by then his ideas had taken root throughout the oil patch. One by one the producing states demanded greater control over prices and greater state "participation" in the oil business. Libya broke through to outright ownership in 1973 when it nationalized 51 percent of the assets of the foreign companies operating there.[21] Other OPEC states soon followed.[22]

The Saudis wanted to maintain good relations with the United States, so they did not unilaterally expropriate Aramco's assets. After the Arab oil

The End of the Affair

embargo ended in the spring of 1974, President Richard Nixon visited Riyadh and received a lavish welcome, even though his presidency was about to be terminated by the Watergate scandal. As a result of that visit, Riyadh and Washington established a new, formal organization called the U.S.-Saudi Arabian Joint Economic Commission, or JECOR.

Through JECOR, the United States provided training in virtually every aspect of government operations, from collecting customs duties to running a national park, along the lines of what Eisenhower had suggested to King Saud, but it was the opposite of a traditional foreign aid program such as Point Four because the Saudis paid for it with their surging oil wealth.[23] In this new relationship of ever-closer bilateral cooperation, the Aramco concession came to its inevitable end through phased negotiated purchases.

Instead of rejecting the ruling of the arbitration tribunal, two legal scholars wrote in a paper about the aftermath, "The Kingdom re-negotiated the concession with Aramco's shareholders. This resulted in an agreement by which the government began a staged purchase of the entire interest of the company's assets and operations. The Kingdom acquired a 25 % interest in Aramco in 1973, increasing to 60 % in 1974, with the final transfer of the company's assets and operations in 1980."[24] Over the next 20 years, almost all of the company's American officials and executives were replaced by Saudi Arabian citizens, many of them originally trained by Aramco.

That outcome fit squarely into the pattern of the Saudi-American bilateral relationship that has now prevailed for seven decades: close cooperation and mutual dependence that survives even the most severe tests. The pattern was established when King Abdul Aziz refused to revoke the Aramco concession after President Truman recognized the State of Israel in 1948. It has held ever since, through the Arab oil embargo, the terror attacks of September 11, 2001, the U.S. invasion of Iraq, and other disagreements, though it has been sorely tested since the royal government arranged the murder of a respected Washington-based Saudi journalist in 2018.

As Eisenhower and his advisers feared, the Soviet Union did expand its strategic and economic interests in the Arab world throughout the 1960s, becoming the dominant external power in Egypt, Iraq, Syria, and other major states. But it never penetrated Saudi Arabia, which remained close to the United States. If anything, the bilateral relationship became stronger than ever, at least for a while, because of President Donald Trump's courtship of the rulers.

Moving On

Robert Maheu, his work in Saudi Arabia done, resumed building his private investigation business and then took over operations of Howard Hughes's hotel and casino operations in Las Vegas. He maintained his ties to the CIA until 1971, when director Richard Helms accepted the recommendation of the agency's director of security that Maheu be cut loose because of "adverse publicity Maheu had received as a result of his court battles" with Hughes and his company. Maheu at the time owed the CIA $15,000 that it had advanced to cover the salaries of its agents working under Maheu and Associates cover, but the agency made no attempt to collect.[25]

Onassis tried to put the Saudi affair behind him, but he had not heard the last of it from powerful people in Washington.

In the settlement of the government's civil case against him, he was permitted to keep 14 of the smaller ships and transfer them to foreign registry. In exchange, he promised to build three very large tankers in American shipyards, which he eventually ordered from a Bethlehem Steel Company yard.

But the post-Suez tanker boom that had enriched Onassis to the point where he could walk away from the Saudi Arabia contract dissipated almost as fast as it had arisen, just as Mohammed Surur had anticipated. By 1958, Onassis no longer needed or wanted the three ships from Bethlehem and signaled his intention to cancel the order.

Facing pressure from Federal Maritime Commission chairman Clarence Morse to proceed with construction and a possible additional penalty of $8 million if he did not, he said, "Why don't you just take the money and we kiss each other goodbye?"[26]

The Merchant Marine and Fisheries Committee of the U.S. House of Representatives thought Onassis was hoodwinking the government again and scheduled hearings. A special subcommittee subpoenaed him and required him to testify in public.

The hearing was lively, even entertaining, as Onassis sparred verbally with Rep. Herbert Zelenko and other committee members, but it was inconclusive. Onassis said that because he paid for the surplus tankers in the first place and then paid the $7 million fine in the criminal case, "I paid the United States government twice for my ships." He said the trusts he had set up in the names of his children, Alexander and Christina, to operate the ships he kept had paid many millions to the U.S. government in taxes.

"If it was another country I would be knighted," he said. "Here I'm penalized."[27]

Zelenko, a Democrat from New York, suspected that Onassis himself secretly controlled the trusts.

Onassis acknowledged that he had 25 percent interest in the trusts, but insisted that his true interest was personal, not financial. He said he was bound by "the God-made interest and there is no law or constitution by manmade law that can interfere or change in any way whatsoever that God-made interest. By that I mean, Mr. Zelenko, the fact that I happen to be the father of those two children. No matter what laws you can put, that is made by

The End of the Affair

God. I belong to those children and they belong to me. Therefore I have a great, great, great interest."[28]

In the end nothing came of this confrontation, and the Eisenhower administration apparently did not hold any grudge against Onassis over the surplus ship fraud or the Saudi tanker affair. In 1960, Secretary of State Dulles sought his help in an unsuccessful attempt to organize an international shipping boycott against the new Cuban government of Fidel Castro.[29]

His mistake in Saudi Arabia, Onassis later said, "was that I woke up too early and disturbed those who were still asleep, and as a result I got into the biggest mess of my life." He said that he "continued to believe that his idea made general economic political sense" and that the opposition was misguided.[30]

In a way he was right: the oil-exporting countries were inevitably going to create their own tanker fleets. Even before the resolution of the SATCO issue, Iran announced that it had ordered two tankers from a Dutch shipyard to begin building its own fleet.[31] By 2016, the National Iranian Tanker Company, a subsidiary of the state oil company, operated the fourth-largest tanker fleet in the world, with 42 supertankers hauling oil to China and other customers.[32] In Saudi Arabia, Onassis's problem was that he was decades ahead of his time. Half a century later, in the summer of 2016, the kingdom, by then owner of a national merchant fleet that was one of the world's biggest operators of large tankers, announced a contract to acquire 15 more of the behemoths known as Very Large Crude Carriers. The new ships, flying the Saudi flag, would give the national fleet enough capacity to become the exclusive carrier of petroleum products exported by the state oil company now known as Saudi Aramco.[33] How much shipping is that? In 2017, 2,821 ships, or almost eight a day, sailed from Saudi ports with cargoes of crude oil and refined products. That figure actually represented a slight decrease from the four preceding years.[34]

Ever since Saudi Arabia bought out the Aramco concession holders nearly 40 years ago, the kingdom has been the sole owner of its oil company, and in an energy-hungry world it can enforce whatever arrangements it wants for tankers to carry its output. Its purchasers may object, as they did in 1954, but they have little choice because Saudi Arabia, by far the most powerful force in the global oil market and now a fully modernized, well-armed nation with very deep pockets, is no longer susceptible to the sort of pressure that the United States and other seafaring nations put on King Saud. Governments in many countries still use oil and, increasingly, natural gas as instruments of strategic policy, but no country today can dominate the international market as the United States did in the Eisenhower era.

As for Onassis, he recovered quickly from the Saudi Arabia affair and resumed his life as a rich, high-living wheeler-dealer. When he married John

F. Kennedy's glamorous widow Jacqueline in 1968, he rose to an exalted position in the stratosphere of fame. He had been chastened by the Saudi fiasco, but it left no permanent wounds.

Within the Saudi ruling family, the Onassis misadventure was a symptom of the erratic policy-making and ill-advised decisions that characterized the disastrous rule of King Saud and finally inspired Crown Prince Faisal to engineer his ouster. The Saudi-born historian Madawi al-Rasheed was not exaggerating when she wrote that "throughout the 1950s, the Saudi state came close to collapse on several occasions and the future of the country seemed uncertain as a result of the volatile internal political struggle between the two Saudi brothers."[35] The extended family of princes lined up in three opposing factions; one supporting Saud, one backing Faisal, and one, known as the Free Princes and headed by Prince Talal bin Abdul Aziz, advocating transition to a constitutional monarchy. The power struggle ended only when the princes united behind Faisal and sent Saud into ignominious exile in 1964. When the British writer Robert Lacey was conducting interviews for his massive history of the kingdom in 1980, he learned that Faisal, upon becoming king, asked how much cash was on and in the royal treasury. The answer was 317 riyals, less than $100.[36]

The long struggle known as the Cold War dragged on until the dissolution of the Soviet Union in 1991. At its peak, Soviet influence in the Arab world extended from Somalia to Algeria and from Sudan to Iraq. It began to decline when Anwar Sadat, Nasser's successor, repudiated Egypt's alliance with Moscow and turned to Washington. At no time did the Kremlin's long arm reach into Saudi Arabia.

Notes

Source Notes

These are the principal archives of documents cited in the book. Individual end notes are keyed to these archives.

1. The papers of Fred A. Davies, Minnesota Historical Society, St. Paul. Papers related to the Onassis case are in Box 2. (These files are not digitized), accessed September 23, 2018, http://www2.mnhs.org/library/findaids/01049.xml
Cited in the reference notes as Davies papers.

2. Federal Bureau of Investigation files on Aristotle Onassis.
These documents, in 11 parts, accessed September 9, 2018, https://vault.fbi.gov/Aristotle%20Onassis/Aristotle%20Onassis
Cited as FBI files.

3. National Archives of the United Kingdom, Kew, England.
Material related to the Onassis case, in chronological order, is in FO 371/110124. These are not digitized but the staff will photocopy and send them for a nominal fee.
Cited as NA/UK.

4. Foreign Relations of the United States.
These massive volumes are compilations of declassified documents annotated and edited by the office of the historian, U.S. Department of State, sorted by year and geographic region or topic, as in "Foreign Relations of the United States, 1952–1954, The Near and Middle East, Volume IX, Part 1."
Printed volumes available in most research libraries, accessed September 22, 2018, https://history.state.gov/historicaldocuments
Cited as FRUS, with volume number and document number.

5. National Archives of the United States, Washington, D.C., and College Park, MD.
Organized by records group, as in RG 59, General Records of the Department of State. Not digitized.
Cited as NA, with location information, as in NA RG 59, 890F/6363 box 7213.

6. Documentary archives of the Mary Ferrell Foundation, Ipswich, Mass. This nonprofit organization has a vast repository of declassified documents, including many internal files of the Central Intelligence Agency. Membership is required; the fee is nominal. Documents from this source are cited by their online links, as in https://www.maryferrell.org/showDoc.html?docId=103946&relPageId=5&search=Maheu. All documents from the Mary Ferrell archives cited in this book were accessed on September 14 and 15, 2018.

7. Central Intelligence Agency declassified documents.
Most of the material that is readily available consists of newspaper and magazine articles that were of interest to the agency at the time, https://www.cia.gov/library/readingroom/collection/general-cia-records.
The agency's internal documents related to the Onassis matter and Robert Maheu are more easily accessible at the Mary Ferrell Foundation.

8. Central Intelligence Agency, CREST FILES.
Until 2017, some of the CIA's declassified files were available only on agency-controlled computers called CREST servers at the National Archives. Many of the items are simply newspaper and magazine articles that should never have been classified in the first place, but some of the material is useful, such as the agency's Weekly Intelligence Bulletin. These files are now available on the agency's online reading room, accessed September 1, 2018, https://www.cia.gov/library/readingroom/collection/crest-25-year-program-archive
Cited as CIA CREST files.

9. Records, testimony and reports of the Church Committee.
These documents—including an interim report, "Alleged Assassination Plots Involving Foreign Leaders" and the "Final Report"—were generated by the U.S. Senate Select Committee to Study Governmental Operations with Respect to Intelligence Activities, known as the Church Committee, for its chairman, Sen. Frank Church. "Final Report," accessed September 23, 2018, https://archive.org/stream/finalreportofsel01unit/finalreportofsel01unit_djvu.txtInterim report on assassination plots, accessed September 23, 2018, https://history-matters.com/archive/church/reports/ir/contents.htm
Many of the documents and files that the committee used in preparing those reports, including Robert Maheu's testimony, are in the Mary Ferrell files. Cited as Church Committee papers.

10. Family Papers of Abdullah Sulaiman al-Hamdan, made available privately to the author. These files, including correspondence, biographies by Arab writers, and reports prepared for the family by scholars at the University of Essex, England, are cited as Sulaiman family papers, but they are not available to the public.

11. Arbitration Proceedings between the Government of Saudi Arabia and Arabian American Oil Company, "First Memorial" of Arabian American Oil Company. This is a massive bound collection of documents compiled by Aramco about the history of the oil concession; it includes the Onassis contract, legal

memorandums, and related correspondence, in sixteen "annexes." Few copies circulated; the author has one, and one is in the Hoover Institution Library, Stanford University. Cited as Aramco Memorial.

A companion volume containing the text of the arbitration ruling in English, French, and Arabic, is cited as Award volume.

12. White House Presidential Papers of Dwight D. Eisenhower, Eisenhower Presidential Library, Abilene, Kansas. The files include correspondence and memoranda of conversations from John Foster Dulles's tenure as secretary of state. Cited as Eisenhower Papers.

13. "Frontline Diplomacy," oral histories and interviews with U.S. diplomats compiled by the Association for Diplomatic Studies and Training, Arlington, VA. Library of Congress, accessed September 23, 2018, www.memory.loc.gov /ammem/collections/diplomacy

Cited as "Frontline Diplomacy."

14. Papers of William E. Mulligan, Georgetown University Library, Washington, D.C. This is an extensive collection of internal Aramco documents, compiled over many years by an Aramco public relations official. Not digitized. A finding aid is at https://findingaids.library.georgetown.edu/repositories/15/resources/10670.

Cited as Mulligan Papers.

Introduction

1. Sam Kashner, "A Delicate Balance," *Vanity Fair*, May 2016, 136.
2. Belmont to Boardman, June 16, 1954. FBI files, part 11.
3. Statement of Policy by the National Security Council, July 23, 1954, FRUS 1952–1954, vol. IX, part 1, document 219.
4. The corporate names were Standard Oil Co. of New Jersey (Exxon, or Esso as it is still branded in many countries); Standard Oil Co. of California (Chevron); the Texas Company (Texaco, later acquired by Chevron); and Socony-Vacuum Co. (Mobil).

Chapter 1

1. "The International Petroleum Cartel," Staff Report to the Federal Trade Commission, released through the Subcommittee on Monopoly of Select Committee on Small Business, U.S. Senate, 1952, chapter 2, accessed August 21, 2018, https://www.mtholyoke.edu/acad/intrel/Petroleum/ftc2.htm.
2. "Riding the Waves: BP Shipping 1915–2015," chapter 2, unpaginated, BP, 2015.
3. Aramco Memorial, annex 1, 1.
4. Wallace Stegner, *Discovery! The Search for Arabian Oil* (Vista, CA: Selwa Press, 2007), 26.

5. Arabian American Oil Company, *Aramco Handbook: Oil and the Middle East*, rev. ed. (Dhahran, Saudi Arabia: Aramco, 1968), 135.

6. Stegner, *Discovery!*, 23.

7. Michael Sheldon Cheney, *Big Oil Man from Arabia* (New York: Ballantine Books, 1958), 125.

8. Daniel Yergin, *The Prize: The Epic Quest for Oil, Money, and Power* (New York: Simon and Schuster, 1991), 421.

9. Yergin, *The Prize*, 410.

10. National Security Council, Removal and Demolition of Oil Facilities, transmission to president, January 6, 1949, accessed August 21, 2018, https://nsarchive2.gwu.edu//dc.html?doc=2869657-Document-02-National-Security-Council-NSC-26-2.

11. CIA/OPC Strategic War Plan, FRUS 1955, The Intelligence Community, 1950–1955, retrospective volume, document 61.

12. Record of Meeting Held in the State Department, May 1, 1953, accessed December 5, 2018, https://nsarchive2.gwu.edu//dc.html?doc=2869660-Document-05-Minutes-of-briefing-by-CIA-to.

13. Bruce to Lay, April 7, 1952, FRUS 1950–1955, retrospective volume, The Intelligence Community 1950–1955, document 105.

14. National Security Council, NSC 176 statement of policy, December 22, 1953, Eisenhower Presidential Library, NSC Series, Policy Papers Subseries, box 8.

15. Wilbur Crane Eveland, *Ropes of Sand: America's Failure in the Middle East* (New York: W. W. Norton, 1980), 84.

16. Memorandum for James S. Lay, March 9, 1953, Eisenhower Papers, NSC staff papers, Disaster file, box 65.

17. Originally designated NSC 176, Denial and Conservation of Middle East Oil Resources and Facilities in the Event of War, December 22, 1953, accessed August 21, 2018, https://nsarchive2.gwu.edu//dc.html?doc=2869667-Document-National-Security-Council-NSC-176.

18. Eveland, *Ropes of Sand*, 84.

19. Yergin, *The Prize*, 438.

20. Yergin, *The Prize*, 439–442.

21. Leonard Mosley, *Power Play: Oil in the Middle East* (New York: Random House, 1973), 194.

22. Pierre Terzian, *OPEC: The Inside Story* (London: Zed Books, 1985), 5–12.

23. This material is from an authorized but unpublished biography in the Sulaiman family papers.

24. Stegner, *Discovery!*, 237.

25. David Holden and Richard Johns, *The House of Saud: The Rise and Rule of the Most Powerful Dynasty in the Arab World* (New York: Holt, Rinehart and Winston, 1981), 154; Rachel Bronson, *Thicker Than Oil: America's Uneasy Partnership with Saudi Arabia* (New York: Oxford University Press, 2006), 55–56.

26. Joe Stork, *Middle East Oil and the Energy Crisis* (New York: Monthly Review Press, 1975), 47; Islam Yassin Qasem, *Oil and Security Policies: Saudi Arabia, 1950–2012* (Leiden: Brill, 2015), 48.

27. Testimony before the Subcommittee on Multinational Corporations, U.S. Senate Committee on Foreign Relations, February 20, 1974.

28. Testimony before the Subcommittee on Multinational Corporations, U.S. Senate Committee on Foreign Relations, January 28, 1974.

29. Byroade memorandum, FRUS 1952–1954, vol. IX, part 1, document 284.

30. Anthony Sampson, *The Seven Sisters: The Great Oil Companies and the World They Made* (New York: Viking Press, 1975), 112.

31. Memorandum of Conversation by Ambassador Hare, July 6, 1953, FRUS 1954, vol. IX, part 1, document 299.

32. Papers of William A. Eddy, Princeton University Library, box 6, folder 4. Eddy's title during his tenure in Jeddah was "minster plenipotentiary" because the U.S. diplomatic mission had not yet been elevated to embassy status. The first U.S. ambassador during the period of these events was J. Rives Childs, 1946–1950, followed by Raymond A. Hare, 1950–1953; and George Wadsworth, 1953–1957. Parker T. Hart, consul in Dhahran 1949–1952 and an official of the State Department's Near East Affairs Bureau during the time of the events in this book, became ambassador to Saudi Arabia in 1961.

33. Memorandum of Conversation by Ambassador Hare, July 6, 1953, FRUS 1952–1954, vol. IX, document 300.

Chapter 2

1. The text of the concession agreement is in Aramco Memorial, annex 1. For details on these labor issues, see Thomas W. Lippman, *Inside the Mirage: America's Fragile Partnership with Saudi Arabia* (Boulder, CO: Westview, 2004), 79; and Thomas A. Pledge, *Saudi Aramco and Its People* (Houston, TX: Aramco Services Co., 1998), chapters 1 and 2.

2. State Department internal memorandum, NA RG 59, 890f.6363, box 7213.

3. "Dear Folks" letter from an Aramco worker, accessed August 22, 2018, https://www.Aramcoexpats.com/articles/dear-folks-chapter-15.

4. Mulligan Papers, box 5, folder 25.

5. Cheney, *Big Oil Man from Arabia*, 125.

6. Gary Sick, *All Fall Down: America's Tragic Encounter with Iran* (New York: Random House, 1985), 6; Andrew Scott Cooper, *The Oil Kings: How the U.S., Iran, and Saudi Arabia Changed the Balance of Power in the Middle East* (New York: Simon & Schuster Paperbacks, 2011), 21–22; Yergin, *The Prize*, 459–470.

7. Parker T. Hart, "Frontline Diplomacy" interview.

8. Ambassador's Annual Report for 1954, in Robert L. Jarman, ed., *Foreign Office Reports from Arabia, 1930–1960* (London: Archive Editions, 1993), vol. 4, 71–82.

9. "History of King Saud," accessed August 22, 2018, https://thekingsaudlibrary.org/en/history/.

10. Hart, "Frontline Diplomacy" interview.

11. "Probable Developments in the Arab States," National Intelligence Estimate 36–54, September 7, 1954, accessed August 22, 2018, https://www.cia.gov/library/readingroom/docs/DOC_0000119699.pdf.

12. Holden and Johns, *The House of Saud*, 192.

13. Telephone interview with the author, May 1, 2016.

14. J. B. Kelly, *Arabia, the Gulf and the West* (New York: Basic Books, 1980), 239.

15. U.S. Embassy report, NA, RG59, 786A.2553/10-454.

16. National Intelligence Estimate 73, January 15, 1953, accessed August 22, 2018, https://www.cia.gov/library/readingroom/docs/DOC_0000119704.pdf.

17. Jarman, *Foreign Office Reports from Arabia*, vol. 4, 197.

18. Ali al-Naimi, *Out of the Desert: My Journey from Nomadic Bedouin to the Heart of Global Oil* (London: Portfolio Penguin, 2016), 42–44.

19. CIA, National Intelligence Estimate 36–54.

20. Cheney, *Big Oil Man from Arabia*, 240–241; Anthony Cave Brown, *Oil, God, and Gold: The Story of Aramco and the Saudi Kings* (New York: Houghton Mifflin, 1999), 229–236.

21. Holden and Johns, *The House of Saud*, 145–147; Eisenhower Library, NSC staff papers, box 23, folder 732; CIA, National Intelligence Estimate 36–54.

22. Bronson, *Thicker Than Oil*, 64.

23. Cable to the embassy in Saudi Arabia, March 27, 1953, FRUS 1954, vol. IX, part 2, document 1507.

24. Joseph A. Kéchichian, *Faysal: Saudi Arabia's Man for All Seasons* (Gainesville: University Press of Florida, 2008), 60.

25. Letter from King Abdul Aziz, July 27, 1953, Eisenhower Papers, International Series, box 46.

26. Letter of June 12, 1953, Eisenhower Papers, International Series, box 46.

27. See his obituary in the *New York Times*, March 19, 1989, 44.

28. Eveland, *Ropes of Sand*, 141–142.

29. See chapter 1.

30. Jarman, *Foreign Office Reports from Arabia*, annual report for 1954.

31. K. S. Twitchell, *Saudi Arabia, with an Account of the Development of Its Natural Resources* (Princeton, NJ: Princeton University Press, 1947), 140–142.

32. This account of the SAADCO, MBJI, and GOVENCO contracts is derived from privately funded British research reports, from an authorized but unpublished biography of Sulaiman, and from private documents and letters, all made available by Sulaiman's family. The text of Twitchell's letter, dated January 29, 1945, is in NA RG 59, 890F/6363, box 7213.

33. Merriam letter, February 21, 1945, in NA RG 59 890FD.63A, box 7213.

34. This history was deleted, apparently when the Web site was redesigned in 2017.

35. From a British researcher's authorized but unpublished biography, in the Sulaiman family papers, privately held in Jeddah.

Notes

Chapter 3

1. Holden and Johns, *The House of Saud*, 181.
2. Nicholas Fraser et al., *Aristotle Onassis* (Philadelphia: J. B. Lippincott, 1977), 134.
3. The account that follows is based largely on an affidavit and supporting documents that Catapodis gave to the British consul in Nice on September 18, 1954. The documents are in NA/UK. They are not digitized, but for a fee the archives staff will make photocopies. Additional information is from an account given by Leon Turrou on June 17, 1954, labeled "Very Confidential. Onassis Deal," in Davies papers; from a definitive article by the Greek maritime historian Gelina Harlaftis, "The Onassis Global Shipping Business, 1920s–1950s," *Business History Review* 88 (Summer 2014): 241–271; and from CIA documents and FBI files, cited separately.
4. Fraser et al., *Aristotle Onassis*, 74.
5. Peter Evans, *Ari: The Life and Times of Aristotle Onassis* (New York: Summit Books, 1986), 116.
6. See note 3 above.
7. Burger to Hoover, February 4, 1953, FBI files, part 1.
8. Tate Gallery, "The Niarchos Collection," accessed August 24, 2018, http://www.tate.org.uk/whats-on/tate-britain/exhibition/niarchos-collection.
9. See note 3 above.
10. This article, by Michael G. Crissan, was widely published. It appeared, for example, in the *Watertown (NY) Daily Times* on February 5, 1966.
11. Peter Evans, *Nemesis: The True Story of Aristotle Onassis, Jackie O, and the Love Triangle That Brought Down the Kennedys* (New York: HarperCollins, 2004), chapter 1. See also Fraser et al., *Aristotle Onassis*, 67–68.
12. Evans, *Ari*, 15.
13. Harlaftis, "The Onassis Global Shipping Business."
14. Fraser et al., *Aristotle Onassis*, 264.
15. Evans, *Ari*, 55.
16. Jarman, *Foreign Office Reports from Arabia*, vol. 4, Ambassador's Annual Report for 1954.
17. Undated "summary of information," FBI files, part 1.
18. J. Edgar Hoover memo, February 6, 1944, FBI files, part 1.
19. "The Man Who Bought the Bank," *TIME*, January 19, 1953.
20. This chart was compiled by Gelina Harlaftis from Lloyd's data. It is reproduced in "The Onassis Global Shipping Business," 259.
21. White House memorandum of conversation, March 23, 1953, Eisenhower Library files, International Series, box 46.
22. Mulligan Papers, box 2, folder 3.
23. Mulligan Papers, box 2, folder 3.
24. See "Adventure Sports, Risky or Extreme," Deportesrecreativos.com, accessed August 25, 2018, https://www.deportesrecreativos.com/deportes-aventura-riesgo-extremos/. See also Kevin Desmond, *The Golden Age of Water Skiing*,

p. 40, accessed August 25, 2018, https://www.amazon.com/Golden-Age-Water skiing-Kevin-Desmond/dp/0760311919/ref=sr_1_4?ie=UTF8&qid=1423442711 &sr=8-4&keywords=the+golden+age+of+water+skiing.

25. Nathan J. Citino, "Defending the 'Postwar Petroleum Order': The US, Britain, and the Onassis Tanker Deal," *Diplomacy and Statecraft* 11 (July 2000): 146.

26. This letter was included among documents Catapodis submitted to the British consulate in Nice, in NA/UK.

27. Belmont to Boardman, June 16, 1954, FBI files, part 4.

28. NSC Briefing Document, "The Onassis Agreement," July 21, 1954, accessed August 25, 2018, https://www.cia.gov/library/readingroom/document/cia-rdp80r01443r000200370002-9.

Chapter 4

1. The case is Criminal Action 1647-53, filed in the U.S. District Court for the District of Columbia. The records of the case, including the materials quoted in this chapter, are at the National Archives in Washington, D.C.

2. *New York Times*, February 24, 1954, 1.

3. Harlaftis, "The Onassis Global Shipping Business."

4. Harlaftis, "The Onassis Global Shipping Business."

5. Gelina Harlaftis, "Mr. Onassis and Game Theory," accessed August 25, 2018, http://aristotle-onassis.blogspot.com/2015/01/mr-onassis-business-structure-analysis.html.

6. The FBI's report on its investigation of the *Lake George* is in FBI files, part 11.

7. Biography of Turrou, accessed August 26, 2018, http://www.imdb.com/name/nm0878103/bio.

8. Undated memo labeled "Very Confidential. Onassis Deal," Davies Papers.

9. Catapodis affidavit and supporting documents, NA/UK.

10. Jones to Nichols, December 2, 1954, FBI files, part 4.

11. "Brownell Defends Ships Settlement," *Washington Post*, August 21, 1958.

12. Evans, *Ari*, 123.

13. *New York Times*, June 20, 1958.

14. It is common in the United States to address the attorney general as "general," although the word is just an adjective, not a military title.

15. Evan Thomas, *The Man to See* (New York: Simon & Schuster, 1991), 84 of Kindle edition.

16. Hoover to Land, FBI files, part 2.

17. Wannall to Sullivan, June 15, 1970, FBI files, part 2.

18. This material is in the records of U.S. District Court, Washington, D.C., criminal case number 1647-53. See note 2 above.

19. "Smyrna 1922: The Destruction of a City," accessed August 26, 2018, http://www.greecetravel.com/smyrna/.

20. Onassis's biographers give somewhat different versions of this story. See Fraser et al., *Aristotle Onassis*, 19–21, and Evans, *Ari*, 40.

21. Harlaftis, "The Onassis Global Shipping Business."

22. Harlaftis, "Mr. Onassis and Game Theory," see note 7 above.

23. Catapodis affidavit, NA/UK.

24. Opinion of Judge Gold in *Catapodis v. Onassis*, Supreme Court of New York, New York County, 1956 NY 41265.

25. Leon Turrou account, memo labeled "Very Confidential. Onassis Deal," June 17, 1954, Davies Papers.

Chapter 5

1. Owen's comments and observations are from his oral history interview in "American Perspectives of Aramco, the Saudi Arabian Oil-Producing Company," a compilation of interviews conducted by the Regional Oral History Office, Bancroft Library, University of California, Berkeley, 1995.

2. The verdict was later upheld by the U.S. Supreme Court: *United States v. Socony-Vacuum Oil Co*, 310 US 150.

3. Stegner, *Discovery!*, 11–12.

4. Mulligan Papers, box 1, folder 10.

5. Childs to State Department, June 6, 1949, NA, RG 59, 890F/001, box 7208.

6. Holden and Johns, *The House of Saud*, 535.

7. William A. Eddy, *F.D.R. Meets Ibn Saud* (New York: American Friends of the Middle East, 1954), 36.

8. Wadsworth to secretary of state, sent from Dhahran, May 1, 1954, NA, RG 59, 886A, Z553, box 5472.

9. Aramco Memorial, annex 2, 82.

10. Aramco Memorial, annex 3, 106.

11. Sulaiman family papers.

12. The full text of the original 1933 concession agreement is in Aramco Memorial, annex 1, 1–14.

13. Aramco Memorial, 27.

14. Aramco Memorial, annex 4, 107.

15. CIA CREST files.

16. See chapter 1.

17. Thomas W. Lippman, *Arabian Knight: Col. Bill Eddy USMC and the Rise of American Power in the Middle East* (Vista, CA: Selwa Press, 2008), chapters 8 and 9.

18. Rathbone to Byroade, February 17, 1954, NA RG 59, 886A Z553, box 5472.

19. Follis to Byroade, February 24, 1954, NA RG 59, 886A Z553, box 5472.

20. Long to Dulles, March 2, 1954, NA RG 59, 886A Z553, box 5472.

21. Citino, "Defending the 'Postwar Petroleum Order,'" 146.

22. Wadsworth to State Department, May 1, 1954, NA RG 59, 886A Z553, box 5472.

23. Anderson to Wilson, March 18, 1954, NA RG 59, 886A Z553, box 5472.

24. Wilson to Dulles and Murphy to Wilson, NA RG 59, 886A Z553, box 5472.

25. Wadsworth testimony at joint hearings of U.S. Senate committees on Armed Services and Foreign Relations, "The President's Proposal on the Middle East," January 14–February 4, 1957, 638–639.

26. Wadsworth to State Department, May 1, 1954, NA RG 59, 886A Z553, box 5472.

Chapter 6

1. From the NSC Web site, accessed August 27, 2018, https://www.whitehouse.gov/nsc/.

2. Dulles to Wadsworth, July 16, 1954, FRUS 1952–1954, vol. XI, document 351.

3. This account of the July 22 meeting is drawn from the official minutes, "Discussion at the 207th Meeting of the National Security Council," Eisenhower Library, Ann Whitman file, Papers as President, NSC Series, box 5, folder 207.

4. Radford to Wilson, July 13, 1954, Eisenhower Library, NSC staff papers, "Disaster File," box 64.

5. The text of NSC 5428 is in FRUS 1952–1954, vol. IX, part 1, document 219.

6. Phebe Marr, *The Modern History of Iraq*, 3rd ed. (Boulder, CO: Westview Press, 2012), 64.

7. Nathan J. Citino, *From Arab Nationalism to OPEC: Eisenhower, King Saud, and the Making of U.S.-Saudi Relations* (Bloomington: Indiana University Press, 2002), 53.

8. Eisenhower to Elson, July 31, 1958. Copy provided to author by Dr. Elson's daughter. The Eisenhower-Elson correspondence has since been donated to the Eisenhower Library.

9. Roby C. Barrett, *The Greater Middle East and the Cold War: US Foreign Policy Under Eisenhower and Kennedy* (London: I. B. Tauris, 2007), 11–12.

10. "Special Message to Congress on the Situation in the Middle East," January 5, 1957. Public Papers of the Presidents Series, accessed December 29, 2018, https://millercenter.org/the-presidency/presidential-speeches/january-5-1957-eisenhower-doctrine.

11. Stanley Karnow, *Vietnam: A History* (New York: Viking, 1983), 196–198.

12. Yevgeny Primakov, *Russia and the Arabs: Behind the Scenes in the Middle East from the Cold War to the Present* (New York: Basic Books, 2009).

13. English version published in *Current Digest of the Soviet Press*, vol. 7, no. 16, June 1, 1955.

14. Jennifer Finley Boylan, "Who Was Vaughn Meader?" *New York Times*, November 22, 2017.

15. List of Subversive Organizations, accessed December 29, 2018, https://en.wikipedia.org/wiki/Attorney_General%27s_List_of_Subversive_Organizations#List_as_of_1959.

16. Merriam to secretary of state, NA RG 59, 54D 403, NEA subject file 1920–1952, box 1.

17. National Intelligence Estimate 73, accessed August 27, 2018, https://www.cia.gov/library/readingroom/docs/DOC_0000119704.pdf.

18. State of the Union Address, January 7, 1954, accessed December 29, 2018, https://www.presidency.ucsb.edu/documents/annual-message-the-congress-the-state-the-union-13.

19. Address to the Council on Foreign Relations, January 22, 1954, text in *Department of State Bulletin*, January 25, 1954.

20. Peter L. Hahn, *Caught in the Middle East: U.S. Policy toward the Arab-Israeli Conflict, 1945–1961* (Chapel Hill: University of North Carolina Press, 2004), 151.

Chapter 7

1. "The CIA Under Harry Truman," accessed August 27, 2018, https://www.cia.gov/library/center-for-the-study-of-intelligence/csi-publications/books-and-monographs/the-cia-under-harry-truman.

2. Public Papers of the Presidents, "Directive on Coordination of Foreign Intelligence Activities," accessed August 17, 2018, http://www.presidency.ucsb.edu/ws/index.php?pid=12478.

3. Reproduced in "CIA Cold War Records: The CIA Under Harry Truman," part II, 139, accessed August 27, 2018, https://www.cia.gov/library/center-for-the-study-of-intelligence/csi-publications/books-and-monographs/the-cia-under-harry-truman.

4. Clayton D. Laurie, "A New President, a Better CIA, and an Old War: Eisenhower and Intelligence Reporting on Korea, 1953," *Studies in Intelligence* 54, no. 4 (December 2010): 16–17.

5. Final Report of the Select Committee to Study Governmental Organizations With Respect to Intelligence Activities, United States Senate (The "Church Committee"), April 23, 1976, accessed August 27, 2018, https://archive.org/details/finalreportofsel06unit.

6. Miles Copeland, *The Game of Nations: The Amorality of Power Politics* (London: Weidenfeld and Nicolson, 1969), 13.

7. Maheu testimony before Church Committee, July 30, 1975, available online from the Mary Ferrell Foundation, https://www.maryferrell.org/showDoc.html?docId=33943&search=Maheu#relPageId=28&tab=page. All documents from the Mary Ferrell archives cited in this chapter were accessed in August or December, 2018.

8. Memorandum from chief, Special Security Division, August 16, 1954, accessed December 24, 2018, https://www.maryferrell.org/showDoc.html?docId=48617&relPageId=2&search=Operation_TWIXT.

9. Details of this plan are in "Alleged Assassination Plots Against Foreign Leaders, an "Interim Report" of the Church Committee," November 20, 1975, 74–81.

10. Memo to the executive secretary, CIA management committee, May 16, 1973. Online document accessed 2017, since deleted from the archive where it had been posted.

11. See, for example, undated memo MM 92-517, accessed December 24, 2018, https://www.maryferrell.org/showDoc.html?docId=129581&relPageId=119&search=Maheu; and "Miscellaneous Records of the Church Committee, Part B, Cuba," accessed December 24, 2018, https://www.maryferrell.org/showDoc.html?docId=148886&relPageId=46&search=Maheu.

12. Undated "Memorandum for the Record," accessed December 24, 2018, https://www.maryferrell.org/showDoc.html?docId=55405&search=Onassis#relPageId=24&tab=page.

13. Thomas, *The Man to See*, 87.

14. Stembridge memo, March 16, 1976, accessed December 24, 2018, https://www.maryferrell.org/showDoc.html?docId=33943&search=Maheu#relPageId=28&tab=page.

15. Stembridge memo, note 14 above.

16. Testimony to Church Committee, accessed December 24, 2018, https://www.maryferrell.org/showDoc.html?docId=33943&search=Maheu#relPageId=28&tab=page.

17. O'Connell memo, May 31, 1966, accessed December 30, 2018, https://www.maryferrell.org/showDoc.html?docId=15210&search=James_P.+O%27Connell#relPageId=7&tab=page.

18. Jim Hougan, *Spooks: The Haunting of America—The Private Use of Secret Agents* (New York: William Morrow, 1978), 278.

19. The Sukarno escapade is recounted in a 1975 "Memo RE Relationship between CIA and Robert Maheu," accessed December 24, 2018, https://www.maryferrell.org/showDoc.html?docId=29953&search=Maheu_Sukarno#relPageId=1&tab=page.

20. The Mann Act accusation is in the 1975 memo cited in note 19 above and in a separate 1957 CIA memo with the names of the author and recipient redacted, accessed December 24, 2018, https://www.maryferrell.org/showDoc.html?docId=148719&relPageId=2&search=%22Mann_Act%22%20.

21. The most complete account of the CIA's recruitment of Roselli, Maheu's role, and the Las Vegas wiretap fiasco is in an "unsanitized" 1967 report by the CIA's inspector general, accessed December 24, 2018, https://www.maryferrell.org/showDoc.html?docId=55405&search=Onassis#relPageId=3&tab=page.

22. "2 Mafiosi Linked to CIA Treated Leniently by U.S.," *New York Times*, April 12, 1976.

23. Sulaiman family papers.

24. "Staff Report on the Evolution and Implications of the CIA-sponsored Assassination Conspiracies Against Fidel Castro," U.S. House of Representatives

Notes

Select Committee on Assassinations, 1979, accessed December 24, 2018, https://www.maryferrell.org/showDoc.html?docId=31501&relPageId=96&search=Hoover_astonished%20reputation%20Maheu.

25. The materials quoted here are from the appellate court opinion in *Robert A. Maheu v. Hughes Tool Company*, 569 F.2d 459, accessed August 29, 2018, https://openjurist.org/569/f2d/459/maheu-v-hughes-tool-company.

26. Minutes of NSC meeting, July 22, 1954, Eisenhower Library, Papers as President, box 5.

27. Testimony before Church Committee, accessed August 29, 2018, https://www.maryferrell.org/showDoc.html?docId=148816&search=Maheu_Onassis#relPageId=3&tab=page.

28. "Notes Concerning the SATCO Affair," Sulaiman family documents.

29. Evans, *Nemesis*, chapter 2 of Kindle edition, note 14; Evans, *Ari*, 126–127. A slightly different version of the comment attributed to Nixon appears in Chris Hutchins and Peter Thompson, *The Last Onassis* (London: Neville Ness, 2014), chapter 5 of Kindle edition, unpaginated.

30. Evans, *Nemesis*, chapter 2, note 7.

31. Evans, *Nemesis*, chapter 2. Ulmer's role in the CIA is well-documented in agency archives and several books.

32. Lawrence R. Houston, testimony before the Church Committee, August 12, 1975.

33. *Washington Post*, August 2, 1978.

34. CIA biography, see note 14 above.

35. Church Committee testimony, see note 27 above.

36. See note 17 above.

37. Evans, *Nemesis*, chapter 2.

Chapter 8

1. Wadsworth to secretary of state, February 6, 1954, NA RG 59, 886A Z553, box 5472.

2. Testimony before joint hearing, Senate committees on Armed Services and Foreign Relations, 85th Congress, 1st session, January 14–February 4, 1957, "The President's Proposal on the Middle East," 638–639.

3. State to Wadsworth, NA RG 59, 886A Z553, box 5472.

4. Jernegan memorandum of conversation, March 16, 1954, NA RG 59, 886A Z553, box 5472.

5. Evans, *Nemesis*, chapter 2.

6. Evans, *Nemesis*, chapter 1.

7. Jernegan memorandum of conversation, March 16, 1954, NA RG 59, 886A Z553, box 5472.

8. Embassy to Washington, February 16, 1954, NA RG 59, 886A Z553, box 5472.

9. Wadsworth to State Department, April 20, 1954, NA RG 59, 886A Z553, box 5472.
10. The comments attributed to Catapodis in this chapter are from the affidavit he gave to the British consul in Nice on September 18, 1954, NA/UK.
11. Aramco Memorial, annex 2, 91.
12. Aramco Memorial, 32.
13. Turrou's account is attached to a letter from General Counsel Ray to CEO Davies, June 16, 1954, Davies Papers.
14. Aramco Memorial, annex 2, 94–95.
15. Aramco Memorial, 8, italics in original.
16. The decree was translated the same day at the U.S. embassy and sent to the State Department, but because it went in the diplomatic pouch instead of by cable, it was not received until June 10. NA RG 59, 886A Z553, box 5472.
17. Wadsworth to State, FRUS 1952–1954, vol. IX, part 1, document 341.
18. Davies Papers, note 14 above.
19. Phillips to Foreign Office, November 21, 1954, NA/UK.
20. Brougham letter attached to Ray's letter to Davies, June 16, 1954, Davies Papers.
21. Aramco Memorial, annex 1, 97.
22. From the Panel's Web site, accessed September 14, 2018, http://www.ltbp.com.
23. Rate chart in Davies Papers.
24. The text of the amendment to Article IV is in Aramco Memorial, annex 2, 92; side-by-side texts of the original agreement and the April amendments are in Aramco Memorial, annex 2, 96–103.
25. Aramco Memorial, annex 2, 112.

Chapter 9

1. Aramco Memorial, annex 13, 241–242.
2. The text of the Onassis contract, as translated by Aramco staff, is in Aramco Memorial, annex 2, 81–85.
3. From an analysis done for Aramco by Sir Oliver Franks, chairman of Lloyd's Bank and former British ambassador to the United States, Aramco Memorial, annex 14, 256–257.
4. Aramco Memorial, annex 11, 204–205.
5. Aramco Memorial, chart 6.
6. State Department memorandum of conversation, April 8, 1954, FRUS 1954, vol. IX, part 1, document 338.
7. Memorandum of conversation, April 29, 1954, NA, RG 59, 886A Z553, box 5472.
8. CIA CREST files.
9. Memorandum of conversation, NA RG 59, 886A Z553, box 5472.

10. Jones to State Department, June 12, 1954, NA RG 59, 886A Z553, box 5472.

11. "The International Petroleum Cartel," Staff Report to the Federal Trade Commission, released through the Subcommittee on Monopoly of Select Committee on Small Business, U.S. Senate, 1952, accessed August 21, 2018, https://www.mtholyoke.edu/acad/intrel/Petroleum/ftc2.htm.

12. Truman Presidential Library, oral history interview with Henry Byroade, accessed August 31, 2018, https://www.trumanlibrary.org/oralhist/byroade.htm.

13. FRUS 1952–1954, vol. I, part 2, document 139.

14. Yergin, *The Prize*, 473.

15. FRUS 1952–1954, vol. IX, part 2, document 150.

16. FRUS 1952–2954, vol. IX, part 1, document 328.

17. Yergin, *The Prize*, 473–478.

18. This conversation is recorded in FRUS 1952–1954, vol. IX, part 1, document 323.

19. See chapter 1.

20. "U.S. Officials Met With Onassis on His Saudi Arabian Agreement," June 26, 1954.

21. Yergin, *The Prize*, 437.

22. For a thorough review of that case, see William H. McLenahan Jr. and William H. Becker, *Eisenhower and the Cold War Economy* (Baltimore: Johns Hopkins University Press, 2011), chapter 5.

23. Meeting with oil executives, FRUS 1952–1954, vol. IX, part 1, document 327.

24. Embassy in Oslo to State Department, June 1, 1954, NA RG 59, 886A Z553, box 5472.

25. The statements of the French and of other foreign governments and oil companies that follow in this chapter are in Aramco Memorial, annex 15, 297–334.

26. Wadsworth to Dulles, July 30, 1954, NA RG 59, 886A Z553, box 5472.

27. Coulsen to Eastern Department, July 27, 1954, NA/UK.

28. The files related to this argument are in NA/UK, beginning with an undated draft "note verbale" to the Saudi Ministry of Foreign Affairs.

29. Message of September 19, 1954, NA/UK. There is no explanation for the diplomat's use of the term "His Majesty's Government" when Queen Elizabeth II had taken the throne two years earlier.

30. Fraser et al., *Aristotle Onassis*, 154–156; "Onassis' Oil Tankers Boycotted; Saudi Arabian Contract Scored," *New York Times*, January 21, 1955.

Chapter 10

1. Wadsworth to State Department, May 1, 1954, NA RG 59, 886A Z553, box 5472.

2. Sulaiman to Davies, May 5, 1954, Aramco Memorial, annex 12, 208.

3. Celler and Klemmer remarks reported in "State Dept. and Celler Hit Onassis-Saudi Pact," *New York Herald Tribune*, May 19, 1954.

4. Morton to Celler, June 3, 1954, RG 59, 886A Z553, box 5472.

5. The texts of the original January 1954 contract between Onassis and the Saudi government and of the revised version ratified by the king are in Aramco Memorial, annex 2, 81–85.

6. Wadsworth to State Department, June 1, 1954, NA RG 59, 886A Z553, box 5472. On Point Four cancellation, see Parker T. Hart, *Saudi Arabia and the United States: Birth of a Security Partnership* (Bloomington: Indiana University Press, 1998), 64–65.

7. CIA CREST files.

8. Quoted by Wadsworth in cable to State Department, NA RG 59, 886A Z553, box 5472.

9. Lebkicher, Memorandum to file, June 16, 1954, Davies Papers.

10. Skouras biography, accessed September 1, 2018, https://www.imdb.com/name/nm0804768/bio?ref_=nm_ov_bio_sm.

11. State Department memorandum of conversation, NA RG 59, 886A Z553, box 5472.

12. Ray to Davies, June 1, 1954, Davies Papers.

13. Cable to State Department, NA RG 59, 886A Z553, box 5472.

14. Message to embassy in Jeddah and consulate in Dhahran, June 28, 1954, NA RG 59, 886A Z553, box 5472.

15. "Biggest Tanker to Be Launched," *New York Times*, June 4, 1954.

16. Current Intelligence Bulletin, August 12, 1954, CIA CREST files, italics in original.

17. Testimony before Church Committee, July 30, 1975.

18. Belmont to Boardman, June 16, 1954, FBI files, part 11.

19. Davies to Onassis, June 17, 1954, Davies Papers.

Chapter 11

1. Ray memorandum to file, June 15, 1954, Davies Papers.

2. Ray memorandum to file, June 15, 1954, Davies Papers.

3. Davies memo labeled "Confidential," June 19, 1954, Davies Papers.

4. Ray letter to Davies, June 1, 1954, Davies Papers.

5. Adam Hochschild, "The Untold Story of the Texaco Oil Tycoon Who Loved Fascism," *The Nation*, March 21, 2016, accessed September 1, 2018, https://www.thenation.com/article/the-untold-story-of-the-texaco-oil-tycoon-who-loved-fascism/. See also Anthony Sampson, *The Seven Sisters: The Great Oil Companies and the World They Made* (New York: Viking Press, 1975), 81–82.

6. Noble, "Confidential Memorandum for Files," June 23, 1954, Davies Papers.

7. Aramco shared this memo with the U.S. Embassy in Jeddah, which reported its content to the State Department, NA RG 59, 886A Z553, box 5472.

8. *Richfield Oil Corp. v. State Bd. of Equalization*, 329 U.S. 69 (1946).

9. Metzger to Eakens, July 7, 1954, NA RG 59, 886A Z553, box 5472.
10. Citino, "The Postwar Petroleum Order," 149.
11. Memorandum of conversation, July 9, 1954, NA RG 59, 886A Z553, box 5472.
12. Fraser et al., *Aristotle Onassis*, 132.
13. Memorandum of conversation, July 12, 1954, FRUS 1952–1954, vol. IX, part 1, document 348.
14. Yergin, *The Prize*, 442.
15. Citino, "The Postwar Petroleum Order," 148.
16. Reported in U.S. Embassy message to State Department, NA RG 59, 886A Z553, box 5472.
17. Byroade to Murphy, July 15, 1954, NA RG 59, 886A Z553, box 5472.
18. Memorandum of conversation, July 16, 1954, FRUS 1952–1954, vol. IX, part 1, document 350.
19. See chapter 6.
20. Message to embassy, July 16, 1954, FRUS 1952–1954, vol. IX, part 1, document 351.

Chapter 12

1. Wadsworth to secretary of state, March 15, 1954, NA RG59, 786A.11/3-1554.
2. Terzian, *OPEC: The Inside Story*, 22–35.
3. Lippman, *Inside the Mirage*, 106–109.
4. This material about Sulaiman's removal from the government is from documents and unpublished biographies in the Sulaiman family papers.
5. Aramco Memorial, annex 12, 214–219.
6. Aramco Memorial, 66.
7. Aramco Memorial, annex 12, 221–226.
8. Aramco Memorial, annex 12, 227.
9. The text of this letter is in FRUS 1952–1954, vol. IX, part 1, document 357.
10. Dorsey to Murphy, July 27, 1954, NA RG 59, 886A Z553, box 5472.
11. Wadsworth to Dulles, August 23, 1954, NA RG 59, 886A Z553, box 5472.
12. On Pacific Western, see Bailey memo, August 8, 1954, NA/UK.
13. Aramco Memorial, annex 12, 229.
14. Reported in Wadsworth cable to State Department, NA RG59, 886A Z533, box 5472.
15. Wadsworth to State, August 31, 1954, NA RG59, 2553/10-454.
16. A copy of this message is in the Sulaiman family papers.
17. Alexei Vassiliev, *King Faisal of Saudi Arabia: Personality, Faith and Times* (London: Saqi Books, 2012), 193.
18. Correspondence and Arabic-language biographies in Sulaiman family papers.

19. Author's interview, June 25, 2004; see also Brown, *Oil, God, and Gold*, 227.
20. Author's interview, September 27, 2004.

Chapter 13

1. August 27, 1954. CIA CREST files.
2. Dorsey to Murphy, October 4, 1954, NA RG59, 786A.2553/10-454.
3. See chapter 2.
4. The board members are listed in a memo in the FBI files, part 2.
5. Jernegan memorandum of conversation, September 6, 1954, FRUS 1952–1954, vol. IX, part 1, document 366.
6. Jernegan to Dorsey, September 1, 1954, NA RG 59, 886A Z553, box 5472.
7. Alexei Vassiliev, *King Faisal of Saudi Arabia: Personality, Faith, and Times* (London: Saqi Books, 2012), 145; Brown, *Oil, God, and Gold: The Story of Aramco and the Saudi Kings*, 83–84.
8. Wadsworth to State, September 2, 1954, NA RG 59, 886A Z553, box 5472.
9. Testimony before Church Committee, July 30, 1975.
10. Ray to Davies, "SAG Honor and Prestige RE Onassis Agreement," July 21, 1955, Davies Papers.
11. "U.S. Studies Aramco Monopoly For Shipping Saudi Arabia's Oil," *New York Times*, June 23, 1954.
12. "Onassis Denies It Is Monopoly," *New York Times*, June 25, 1954.
13. Memorandum of conversation, September 6, 1954, FRUS 1952–1954, vol. IX, part 1, document 356.
14. Jernegan to Brownell, September 7, 1954, NA RG 59, 886A Z553, box 5472.
15. Citino, "Defending the 'Postwar Petroleum Order,'" 153.
16. Youngdahl's order in *United States v. Onassis* is reported in 125 F. Supp. 190.
17. From the company's Web site, accessed September 18, 2018, https://www.drewry.co.uk/about-us.
18. Drewry to Dodds-Parker, September 25, 1954, NA/UK.
19. See note 16, chapter 2.
20. Benjamin Schwadran, *The Middle East, Oil, and the Great Powers*, 2nd ed. (New York: Council for Middle East Affairs Press, 1959), 343.
21. Wadsworth to State, September 19, 1954, NA RG 59, 886A Z553, box 5472.
22. Memorandum of conversation, September 24, 1954, FRUS 1952–1954, vol. IX, part 1, document 368.
23. Phillips cable to Foreign Office, September 14, 1954, NA/UK.
24. Holden and Johns, *The House of Saud*, 106.
25. Vassiliev, *King Faisal of Saudi Arabia*, 181, 193.
26. Phillips letter to Foreign Minister Eden, September 19, 1954, NA/UK.
27. Evans, *Ari*, 130. Variants of this story can be found in other narratives as well.

Chapter 14

1. Turrou's account is reported in undated memo labeled "strictly confidential," in Davies Papers. It refers to Catapodis as "Catapolis." The spelling has been changed here for consistency.

2. This letter to Alireza is in the file on the Onassis affair in NA/UK. All the files related to the Onassis matter, including the affidavit and the writing expert's statement, are in that archive.

3. NA/UK.

4. Foreign Office telegram to British Embassy, Jeddah, November 13, 1954, NA/UK.

5. Memo titled "The Saudi Arabian-Onassis Tanker Agreement," September 27, 1954, NA/UK.

6. Evans, *Ari*, 137; Fraser et al., *Aristotle Onassis*, 146.

7. Memorandum of conversation, September 25, 1957, FRUS 1952–1954, vol. IX, part 1, document 367. This document and others incorrectly give Gerrity's first name as Paul.

8. Memorandum of conversation, note 7.

9. Memorandum of conversation, note 7.

10. Testimony before Church Committee, accessed December 24, 2018, https://www.maryferrell.org/showDoc.html?docId=33943&search=Maheu#relPageId=28&tab=page.

Chapter 15

1. Foreign Office to Jeddah, November 13, 1954, NA/UK.

2. Nichols to Tolson, November 20, 1954, FBI files, part 4.

3. Testimony before Church Committee, accessed December 24, 2018, https://www.maryferrell.org/showDoc.html?docId=33943&search=Maheu#relPageId=28&tab=page.

4. Foreign Office to Jeddah, November 13, 1954, NA/UK.

5. Testimony before Church Committee.

6. *New York Times*, December 24–26, 1977. These articles appeared on the front page.

7. Joyce Battle, ed., "U.S. Propaganda in the Middle East—The Early Cold War Version," National Security Archive Electronic Briefing Book No. 78, 2002, accessed September 4, 2018, https://nsarchive2.gwu.edu//NSAEBB/NSAEBB78/essay.htm.

8. Phillips to Foreign Office, October 3, 1954, NA/UK.

9. Phillips to Foreign Office, note 8.

10. Dorsey to Murphy, October 4, 1954, NA RG59, 786A.2553/10-454.

11. See chapter 14.

12. Dulles to Wadsworth, October 4, 1954, and reply, NA RG 59, 886A Z553, box 5472.

13. Embassy in Lebanon to State Department, RG 59, 886A Z553, box 5472.

14. The *New York Times* account was published November 20, 1954, as was the *Herald-Tribune*'s. *TIME* published on November 22, *Newsweek* on November 29.

15. "Onassis Contract Payments Bared," *Journal of Commerce* (New York), November 20, 1954, 3.

16. Reported to Jeddah by British Foreign Office, NA/UK.

17. Robert Lacey, *The Kingdom* (New York: Harcourt Brace Jovanovich, 1981), 307.

18. Evans, *Ari*, 145.

19. Fraser et al., *Aristotle Onassis*, 115.

20. Evans, *Ari*, 139.

21. Fraser et al., *Aristotle Onassis*, 123; *New York Times*, November 17, 1954, 1.

22. Fraser et al., *Aristotle Onassis*, 125.

23. Hougan, *Spooks*, 298.

24. Harlaftis, "The Onassis Global Shipping Business."

25. Memorandum of conversation, NA RG 59, 886A Z553, box 5472.

26. Acting Secretary of State to embassy in Peru, FRUS 1952–1954, vol. IV, document 688.

27. Evans, *Ari*, 142.

28. See Johan Tonnesen and Arne Odd Johnsen, *The History of Modern Whaling* (Berkeley: University of California Press, 1982), 555–556; Fraser et al, *Aristotle Onassis*, 130; and Gelina Harlaftis, "Mr. Onassis and Game Theory," accessed December 24, 2018, http://aristotle-onassis.blogspot.com/2015/01/mr-onassis-business-structure-analysis.html.

Chapter 16

1. "Onassis Deal Alarms Tanker Men," *Journal of Commerce*, July 3, 1954.

2. "Onassis Defends Saudi Arabian Ship Deal," *Journal of Commerce*, August 14, 1954.

3. See chapter 12.

4. Aramco Memorial, 36.

5. Aramco Memorial, 36.

6. Wadsworth to State, October 25, 1954, FRUS 1952–1954, vol. IX, part 1, document 369.

7. Hoover to Andrews, October 19, 1954, FBI files, part 1.

8. Embassy to Fry, Eastern Department, Foreign Office, November 13, 1954, NA/UK.

9. Wadsworth to State, FRUS 1952–1954, vol. IX, part 1, document 372.

10. Aramco Memorial, 138.

11. Aramco Memorial, annex 12, 231; Phillips letter to "Dear Bunny," October 25, 1954, NA/UK.

12. Embassy to Fry, Eastern Department, Foreign Office, November 13, 1954, NA/UK.
13. Aramco Memorial, annex 12, 230.
14. Aramco Memorial, annex 12, 231.
15. Wadsworth to Dorsey, FRUS 1952–1954, vol. IX, part 1, document 372.
16. Aramco Memorial, annex 1, 12.
17. Aramco Memorial, annex 1, 12.
18. Memorandum of conversation, November 1, 1954, FRUS 1952–1954, vol. IX, part 1, document 370.
19. Simmons memo to Minnich, November 9, 1954. Eisenhower Library, Papers as President, International Series, box 46.
20. Author's interview, May 1, 2016.
21. Memorandum of conversation, November 3, 1954, FRUS 1952–1954, vol. IX, part 1, document 371.

Chapter 17

1. Saltzman to embassy in Saudi Arabia, November 27, 1954, FRUS 1952–1954, vol. IX, part 1, document 374.
2. Wadsworth's account of this conversation is in FRUS 1952–1954, vol. IX, part 1, document 375.
3. Historian's note 1 to Wadsworth cable of December 18, 1954, FRUS 1952–1954, vol. IX, part 1, document 377.
4. Wadsworth to State Department, December 18, 1954, FRUS 1952–1954, vol. IX, part 1, document 377.
5. Dulles to embassy in Saudi Arabia, December 27, 1954, FRUS 1952–1954, vol. IX, part 1, document 380.
6. Aramco Memorial, 38.
7. The article was published by many news outlets, including the *New York Times*, "Libel Suit Filed Against Onassis," December 4, 1954.
8. The case was civil action 5126-54, in the U.S. District Court for the District of Columbia. The records of the case are now at the National Archives branch in Kansas City, Mo.
9. "Onassis Disputes Charges in Paris," *New York Times*, March 27, 1955.
10. Harlaftis, "The Onassis Global Shipping Business," 115–116.
11. "Biggest Tanker Idle in Hamburg," *New York Times*, February 23, 1955.
12. Butterworth to State Department, December 24, 1954, FRUS 1952–1954, vol. IX, part 1, document 379.
13. "Onassis' Oil Tankers Boycotted; Saudi Arabian Contract Scored," *New York Times*, January 21, 1955.
14. "Denies Boycotting Ships," *New York Times*, February 24, 1955.
15. Fraser et al., *Aristotle Onassis*, 156.

Chapter 18

1. Memorandum of conversation, February 9, 1955, FRUS 1955–1957, vol. XIII, document 164.
2. "SAG Honor and Prestige re Onassis Agreement," Davies Papers.
3. "Onassis Seeks a Revised Oil Pact Making Saudi Arabia Ship Owner," *New York Times*, February 20, 1955.
4. Aramco Award Volume, ii–iii.
5. Aramco Memorial, 86–100.
6. Aramco Award Volume, iv.
7. Aramco Memorial, annex 16, 349, 368.
8. Aramco Memorial, 50.
9. Hahn, *Caught in the Middle East*, 152.
10. Madawi Al-Rasheed, *A History of Saudi Arabia* (Cambridge: Cambridge University Press, 2002), 115.
11. Allen to Murphy, March 3, 1955, FRUS 1955–1957, vol. XIII, document 165.
12. Hoover to embassy in Saudi Arabia, March 5, 1955, FRUS 1955–1957, vol. XIII, document 166.
13. Hart, *Saudi Arabia and the United States*, 65.
14. Wadsworth to State Department, July 25, 1955, FRUS 1955–1957, vol. XIII, document 169.
15. Telegram to embassy, July 25, 1955, FRUS 1955–1957, vol. XIII, document 170.
16. Surur to Aramco, June 6, 1955, Davies Papers.
17. Davies to Surur, July 24, 1955, Aramco Memorial, annex 12, 232–234.
18. Aramco Memorial, 82, italics in original.
19. Eisenhower Library, Records as President, Official File, box 732.
20. Lippman, *Inside the Mirage*, 212–226.
21. Hoover to embassy, September 7, 1955, FRUS 1955–1957, vol. XIII, document 173.
22. For details on the long-running Buraimi dispute, see Hart, *Saudi Arabia and the United States*, 66–67, and J. B. Kelly, *Arabia, the Gulf, and the West* (New York: Basic Books, 1980), 71–73.
23. Message from the Director of Central Intelligence, undated, FRUS 1955–1957, vol. XIII, document 184.
24. Consulate General to State Department, October 30, 1955, FRUS 1955–1957, vol. XIII, document 186.

Chapter 19

1. Mohamed Heikal, *The Cairo Documents: The Inside Story of Nasser and His Relationships with World Leaders, Rebels, and Statesmen* (Garden City, NY: Doubleday, 1973), 46.

2. See, for example, Guy Laron, "Cutting the Gordian Knot: The Post-WWII Egyptian Quest for Arms and the 1955 Czechoslovak Arms Deal," Woodrow Wilson Center for Scholars, Cold War International History Project, accessed August 20, 2018, https://www.wilsoncenter.org/publication/cutting-the-gordian-knot-the-post-wwii-egyptian-quest-for-arms-and-the-1955-czechoslovak.

3. Laron, "Cutting the Gordian Knot"; Robert E. Kanet, "The Superpower Quest for Empire: The Cold War and Soviet Support for 'Wars of National Liberation,'" *Cold War History* 6, no. 3 (August 2006): 331–352; Thomas W. Lippman, *Hero of the Crossing: How Anwar Sadat and the 1973 War Changed the World* (Lincoln, NE: Potomac Books, 2016), 41–46.

4. Holden and Johns, *The House of Saud*, 187.

5. Vassiliev, *King Faisal of Saudi Arabia*, 202.

6. State Department to Wadsworth, October 10, 1955, FRUS 1955–1957, vol. XIII, document 181.

7. Telegram to U.S. Embassy in Jeddah, October 17, 1955, FRUS 1955–1957, vol. XIII, document 182.

8. For a brief summary, see Bandung Conference, accessed September 9, 2018, https://www.britannica.com/event/Bandung-Conference.

9. National Intelligence Estimate 30-55, "Middle East Defense Problems and Prospects," June 21, 1955, FRUS 1955–1957, vol. XII, document 46.

10. Allen to secretary of state, January 4, 1956, FRUS 1955–1957, vol. XIII, document 203.

11. Lloyd to Dulles, January 23, 1956, FRUS 1955–1957, vol. XIII, document 209.

12. Memorandum of White House conversation, January 30, 1956, FRUS 1955–1957, vol. XIII, document 213.

13. Text of statement and details of settlement in FBI Files, part 10.

14. Harlaftis, "The Onassis Global Shipping Business."

15. "Brownell Defends Ships Settlement," *Washington Post*, July 23, 1958; "Brownell Called For as Onassis Testifies," *Washington Star*, June 24, 1958.

16. "Onassis Wins in Court," *New York Times*, March 21, 1956.

17. CIA memo, "Subject: Maheu, Robert A.," June 7, 1966, accessed September 9, 2018, www.archives.gov/files/research/jfk/releases/104-10122-10344.pdf; on the civil cases generally, see Fraser et al., *Aristotle Onassis*, 151–152.

18. *Catapodis v. Onassis*, Judge Gold's ruling granting motion to dismiss, 151 N.Y.S. 2d 39.

Chapter 20

1. Memorandum of conversation, July 2, 1956, FRUS 1955–1957, vol. XIII, document 237.

2. NA, RG 218, CCS 381 Saudi Arabia (2–7–41), sec. 11.

3. Robert Stephens, *Nasser* (Harmondsworth, U.K.: Pelican Books, 1973), 181.

4. Stephens, *Nasser*, 202.

5. FRUS 1955–1957, vol. XVI, document 5.

6. Statement of policy, July 23, 1954, FRUS 1952–1954, vol. IX, part 1, document 219.

7. Editorial note, FRUS 1955–1957, vol. XVI, document 11.

8. Telegram from U.S. delegation, FRUS 1955–1957, vol. XVI, document 95.

9. Telegram from U.S. delegation, FRUS 1955–1967, vol. XVI, document 120.

10. Many scholars and historians have described the Sevres meeting. See, for example, Stephens, *Nasser*, 223–237; and Daniel Gordis, *Israel: A Concise History of a Nation Reborn* (New York: Ecco, 2016), 230–231.

11. Radio and Television Report to the American People, October 31, 1956, Public Papers of the Presidents, accessed January 4, 2019, https://www.presidency.ucsb.edu/documents/radio-and-television-report-the-american-people-the-developments-eastern-europe-and-the.

12. Gelina Harlaftis, "Mr. Onassis and Game Theory," accessed September 10, 2018, http://aristotle-onassis.blogspot.com/2015/01/mr-onassis-business-structure-analysis.html.

13. Telegram to the president, Eisenhower Papers, Papers as President, International Series, box 46.

14. Message of November 11, 1956, Eisenhower Papers, Papers as President, International Series, box 46.

15. Letter from King Saud, December 13, 1956, Eisenhower Library, Papers as President, International Series, box 46.

16. White House press release, January 7, 1957.

17. Lacey, *The Kingdom*, 315; Holden and Johns, *The House of Saud*, 192–193.

18. "Eisenhower Greets Saud, Deplores Any Discourtesy," *New York Times*, January 31, 1957.

19. Guest list in Eisenhower Papers, Papers as President, International Series, box 46.

20. State Department memorandum of conversation, January 30, 1957, Eisenhower Papers, International Series, box 46.

21. FRUS 1955–1957, vol. XIII, document 260.

22. FRUS 1955–1957, vol. XIII, document 260.

23. FRUS 1955–1957, vol. XIII, document 261.

24. Communiqué, February 8, 1957, Eisenhower Papers, Official File, box 732.

25. Hart, *Saudi Arabia and the United States*, 68.

26. Memorandum of conversation, FRUS 1955–1957, vol. XIII, document 271.

Chapter 21

1. Stephen M. Schwebel, "The Kingdom of Saudi Arabia and Aramco Arbitrate the Onassis Agreement," *Journal of World Energy Law & Business* 3, no. 3 (November 1, 2010). Online version, accessed September 6, 2018, https://doi

Notes

.org/10.1093/jwelb/jwq012, unpaginated. On the significance of the case to Saudi law and to international businesses operating in the kingdom, see Saud Al-Ammari and Timothy Martin, "Arbitration in the Kingdom of Saudi Arabia," *Arbitration International* 30, no. 2 (August 2014): 387–408.

2. Aramco Memorial, 8, italics in original.

3. Award volume, i.

4. Davies handwritten summary of Jennings paper and Page memo in Davies Papers, summer of 1956.

5. Schwebel, "The Kingdom of Saudi Arabia and Aramco Arbitrate the Onassis Agreement."

6. Aramco Oral History, Bancroft Library, University of California, Berkeley.

7. Aramco Memorial, annex 5.

8. Aramco Memorial, annex 6.

9. Ray to Davies, April 1, 1957, Davies Papers.

10. Notes on meetings with Sultan, April 17, 1957, Davies Papers.

11. "Confidential Memorandum" from Garry Owen, May 9, 1957, Davies Papers.

12. Owen to Ray, May 11, 1957, Davies Papers.

13. Award volume, 76.

14. Award volume, English text, 96–97. For a concise summary, see Schwebel, "The Kingdom of Saudi Arabia and Aramco Arbitrate the Onassis Agreement," 8–10. A 31-page memo from Ray summarizing the arguments and outcome is in Davies Papers.

15. Award volume, English text, 102–103.

16. Award volume, French text, 132. This is the author's translation of the French text. The official English version, on pp. 102–103 of the Award volume, is less clear.

17. Wanda Jablonski, "The Sovereign 'Right' to Welch?" *Petroleum Week*, September 12, 1958.

18. Al-Ammari and Martin, "Arbitration in the Kingdom of Saudi Arabia."

19. McDonald to Davies, June 22, 1957, Davies Papers.

20. Memorandum of conversation, August 29, 1957, FRUS 1955–1957, vol. XIII, document 282.

21. "Libya Takes Over All Oil Companies Operating There," *New York Times*, September 2, 1973.

22. For a full history of these developments, see Terzian, *OPEC: The Inside Story*, chapters 3–7.

23. For the story of JECOR, see Lippman, *Inside the Mirage*, 167–177.

24. Al-Ammari and Martin, "Arbitration in the Kingdom of Saudi Arabia," 389.

25. Osborn memorandum "Robert A. Maheu and Associates," January 20, 1971, accessed September 11, 2018, https://www.maryferrell.org/archive/docs/153/153705/images/img_153705_3_300.png.

26. Evans, *Ari*, 165.

27. "Onassis Defends Deals on Tankers," *New York Times*, June 20, 1958.
28. Fraser et al., *Aristotle Onassis*, 162; Evans, *Ari*, 166.
29. Memorandum of discussion, July 7, 1960, FRUS 1958–1960, vol. VI, document 545.
30. Fraser et al., *Aristotle Onassis*, 152.
31. "Iran Maps Fleet of Own Tankers," *New York Times*, November 20, 1955.
32. "Profiling Iran's Leading Shipping Companies," *ITE Transport and Logistics*, August 28, 2016, accessed September 6, 2018, http://www.transport-exhibitions.com/Market-Insights/Iran/Profiling-Iran%E2%80%99s-leading-shipping-companies.
33. "Saudi Arabia Seeks to Create Biggest Tanker Fleet with New Fund," *Bloomberg News*, July 18, 2016, accessed September 6, 2018, https://www.bloomberg.com/news/articles/2016-07-18/saudi-arabia-seeks-to-create-biggest-tanker-fleet-with-new-fund.
34. See "2017 in Numbers" section of Saudi Aramco's Annual Review for 2017, accessed September 6, 2018, http://www.saudiaramco.com/en/home/news-media/publications/corporate-reports/2017-annual-review.html.
35. Al-Rasheed, *A History of Saudi Arabia*, 106.
36. Lacey, *The Kingdom*, 323.

Select Bibliography

Ammari, Saud al-, and Timothy Martin. "Arbitration in the Kingdom of Saudi Arabia." *Arbitration International* 30, no. 2 (2014): 387-408.

Barrett, Roby. *The Greater Middle East and the Cold War: U.S. Foreign Policy under Eisenhower and Kennedy*. London: I. B. Tauris, 2007.

Bronson, Rachel. *Thicker Than Oil: America's Uneasy Partnership with Saudi Arabia*. New York: Oxford University Press, 2006.

Brown, Anthony Cave. *Oil, God, and Gold: The Story of Aramco and the Saudi Kings*. New York: Houghton Mifflin, 1999.

Campbell, John C. *Defense of the Middle East: Problems of American Policy*. New York: Frederick A. Praeger, 1960.

Cheney, Michael Sheldon. *Big Oil Man from Arabia*. New York: Ballantine Books, 1958.

Citino, Nathan J. "Defending the 'Postwar Petroleum Order': The U.S. Britain, and the Onassis Tanker Deal." *Diplomacy and Statecraft* 11 (July 2000): 137–160.

Citino, Nathan J. *From Arab Nationalism to OPEC: Eisenhower, King Saud, and the Making of U.S.-Saudi Relations*. Bloomington: Indiana University Press, 2002.

Evans, Peter. *Ari: The Life and Times of Aristotle Socrates Onassis*. New York: Summit Books, 1986.

Eveland, Wilbur Crane. *Ropes of Sand: America's Failure in the Middle East*. New York: W. W. Norton, 1980.

Fraser, Nicholas, Philip Jacobson, Mark Ottaway, and Lewis Chester. *Aristotle Onassis*. Philadelphia: J. B. Lippincott, 1977.

Hahn, Peter L. *Caught in the Middle East: U.S. Policy toward the Arab-Israeli Conflict, 1945–1961*. Chapel Hill: University of North Carolina Press, 2004.

Harlaftis, Gelina. "The Onassis Global Shipping Business." *Business History Review* 88 (Summer 2014): 241–271.

Hart, Parker T. *Saudi Arabia and the United States: Birth of a Security Partnership*. Bloomington: Indiana University Press, 1998.

Heikal, Mohamed. *The Cairo Documents: The Inside Story of Nasser and His Relationship with World Leaders, Rebels, and Statesmen.* Garden City, NY: Doubleday, 1973.
Holden, David, and Richard Johns. *The House of Saud: The Rise and Rule of the Most Powerful Dynasty in the Arab World.* New York: Holt Rinehart and Winston, 1982.
Hougan, Jim. *Spooks: The Haunting of America—The Private Use of Secret Agents.* New York: William Morrow, 1978.
Kéchichian, Joseph A. *Faysal: Saudi Arabia's King for All Seasons.* Gainesville: University Press of Florida, 2008.
Kelly, J. B. *Arabia, the Gulf, and the West.* London: Weidenfeld and Nicolson, 1980.
Lacey, Robert. *The Kingdom.* New York: Harcourt Brace Jovanovich, 1981.
Lippman, Thomas W. *Arabian Knight: Colonel Bill Eddy USMC and the Rise of American Power in the Middle East.* Vista, CA: Selwa Press, 2008.
Mosley, Leonard. *Power Play: Oil in the Middle East.* New York: Random House, 1973.
Naimi, Ali al-. *Out of the Desert: My Journey from Nomadic Bedouin to the Heart of Global Oil.* London: Portfolio Penguin, 2016.
Primakov, Yevgeny. *Russia and the Arabs.* New York: Basic Books, 2009.
Rasheed, Madawi al-. *A History of Saudi Arabia.* Cambridge: Cambridge University Press, 2002.
Rogan, Eugene. *The Arabs: A History.* New York: Basic Books, 2009.
Sampson, Anthony. *The Seven Sisters: The Great Oil Companies and the World They Made.* New York: Viking Press, 1975.
Schwebel, Stephen M. "The Kingdom of Saudi Arabia and Aramco Arbitrate the Onassis Agreement." *Journal of World Energy Law and Business* 3, no. 3 (2010): 245–256.
Stegner, Wallace. *Discovery! The Search for Arabian Oil.* Vista, CA: Selwa Press, 2007.
Stephens, Robert. *Nasser.* Harmondsworth, U.K.: Penguin Press, 1971.
Stork, Joe. *Middle East Oil and the Energy Crisis.* New York: Monthly Review Press, 1975.
Terzian, Pierre. *OPEC: The Inside Story.* London: Zed Books, 1985.
Twitchell, Karl. *Saudi Arabia, With an Account of the Development of Its Natural Resources.* Princeton, NJ: Princeton University Press, 1947.
Vassiliev, Alexei. *King Faisal of Saudi Arabia: Personality, Faith and Times.* London: Saqi Books, 2012.
Vitalis, Robert. *America's Kingdom: Mythmaking on the Saudi Oil Frontier.* Stanford, CA: Stanford University Press, 2007.
Yergin, Daniel. *The Prize: The Epic Quest for Oil, Money, and Power.* New York: Simon & Schuster, 1991.

Index

Abdul Aziz al-Saud, King (Ibn Saud), 155; and Aramco Concession (1933), 3–4; and communism, 72; and concept of corruption, 56; creation of Council of Ministers, 133, 135; creation of Saudi Arabia, 20; and Dhahran air base, 59, 190; death of, 20; designation of Prince Saud as successor, 20; and Eisenhower, 26–27; and Gorgoni, 15, 144, 149; and Onassis tanker deal, 41; and original Aramco concession, 3–8; and Saudi-American bilateral relationship, 12, 111, 225; and Sulaiman, 27–28, 31, 140; and Yassin, 15, 149
Abdullah al-Faisal, Prince, 133
Abu Dhabi, 7, 8, 12, 24, 97, 194, 199, 208–209
Acheson, Dean, 101
Alatas, Said, 113–114
Algeria, 205, 208, 224, 228
Alireza, Abdullah, 91, 160
Alireza, Ali, 38, 39, 138, 173
Alireza, Mohammed: appointed Ministry of Commerce, 134, 160; demands of, 91–94, 113–117, 119, 124; family and background of, 38–39; role in Onassis tanker deal, 38–42, 44–45, 48–49, 55–58, 165, 171, 173, 184
Allen, George V., 189–190, 194, 198–199, 204
Ameen, Mike, 21–22, 176
American Independent Oil Company (AMINOIL), 10, 129
Anderson, Robert B., 64
Andrews, T. Coleman, 172
Anglo-American Petroleum, 19. *See also* British Petroleum (BP)
Angola, 208
Antitrust laws, 2, 99–106, 110, 117, 185; Madison Case, 54–55, 76, 100, 104
Appel, Charles A. "Uncle Charlie," Jr., 161
Arab League, 11, 119
Arabian American Oil Company (Aramco); and arbitration Tribunal, 216–223; and Article IV of Onassis contract, 170–171, 178–182, 185–188, 192–193; and Buraimi Oasis, 194–195; creation of, 5–6; Dammam No. 7, 5; first concession, 3–6; labor strikes, 23–25, 75; Saudi buyout of, 225; and Sulaiman, 133–141. *See also* Aramco Concession (1933)

Aramco Concession (1933), 3–6, 193–194; Aramco's fear of losing, 150, 173; Article 1, 120, 121, 127; Article 22, 120, 121; Article 23 (employment of Saudi nationals), 11, 18; Article 31 (arbitration), 60, 174, 176; and Onassis tanker contract, 174–176, 187–188, 192, 221–222; Tribunal's ruling on Onassis contract's violation of, 221–222
Arbenz, Jacobo, 71
Argentina, 34, 35, 37, 46, 153

Badawi, Helmy Baghat, 218, 219–220, 221
Baghdad Pact, 71, 189–192, 193, 196, 198, 205, 210
Bahrain, 5, 7, 8, 39, 55, 208
Baker, Michael, Jr., 29–31
Baksheesh, 94, 114, 141
Barastis (palm-frond huts), 17, 18
Bechtel Corp., 143
Bechtel, Stephen, 143
Beirut, Lebanon, 57, 61, 118, 138, 141, 163–165
Belmont, Alan H., 119–120
British Petroleum (BP), 2–3, 19
Bronson, Rachel, 24
Brook, John H., 98, 103
Brougham, Robert I., 94, 122
Brownell, Herbert, 47, 49–50, 146, 183, 200–201
Buraimi Oasis, 11–12, 24–26, 75, 112, 113, 130, 175, 193–195, 199, 212, 214, 216, 218, 221
Burger, Warren E., 34, 35, 47, 50, 200
Byroade, Henry A., 13, 62, 89, 101, 103, 114–116, 130–131, 138, 145, 178, 179, 182, 189

Caccia, Harold, 154
Callas, Maria, 37, 51
Caltex, 107
Carrigan, John W., 195
Cartels, 100–102, 104
Case, John E., 186, 188
Casey, Joseph E., 47
Castro, Fidel, 80, 83, 227
Catapodis, Spyridon, 49; background of, 32–33; dossier, 152–165, 176, 181; falling out with Onassis, 53, 91–94, 142; lawsuit against Onassis, 182–184, 201–202; role in Onassis tanker deal, 33–34, 38–41, 45, 115, 119, 151
Celler, Emanuel, 111–112
Central Intelligence Agency (CIA): Castro assassination plot, 80, 83, 227; and Catapodis dossier, 153–156, 161, 164, 176; and Catapodis's lawsuits against Onassis, 202; and Church Committee, 84–85, 157, 159, 230 n.9; contractors hired by, 79; creation of (National Security Act 1947), 61, 77; Current Intelligence Bulletins, 61, 98, 113, 118, 142; on FTC report, 101; functions of, 78–79; Guatemalan coup (1954), 71; and Denial Plan, 7–9; Iranian coup (1953), 19, 69–70; Maheu's contract deployment for, 79–87, 118–119, 137, 139, 141, 181; Maheu's release from CIA employment, 225–226; Office of National Estimates, 147–148; Office of Strategic Services (OSS) as precursor to, 54, 76–79; and oil industry, 61, 105; Project Twixt, 79–87, 181; "Review of the World Situation As It Relates to the Security of the United States," 77–78; Strategic War Plan (Denial Plan), 6–9, 70, 72, 119; types of deployed workers, 79; and weaponization of media, 160–161, 164, 176. *See also* Close, Ray;

Index

Dulles, Allen; Eveland, Wilbur Crane; McCone, John; Smith, Walter Bedell
Chase Bank, 26
Childs, J. Rives, 56, 233 n.32
China, 47, 52, 69, 71, 77–78, 191, 205, 227
Church, Frank, 70, 84–85
Church Committee, 84–85, 157, 159, 230 n.9
Churchill, Winston, 24, 71
Citino, Nathan J., 40, 63, 128, 146–147
Clauzel, M. Ghislain, 104
Close, Ray, 141
Coates, Charles B., 89
Coates & McCormick Inc., 89, 167
Cokkinis, Nicolas, 91, 121, 125–126, 171, 173, 223, 224
Concession system, 217–224; as anachronistic, 19; definition of concession, 3; end of, 221–224; Fifty-Fifty Agreement, 11–13, 23, 27, 148; and Saudi-Kuwaiti Neutral Zone, 9–12. See also Aramco concession (1933); Onassis tanker contract
"Coolie camps," 17
Copeland, Miles, 79
Coulsen, J. E., 108
Cunningham, Robert M., 81, 82
Czech Arms Deal, 195, 197–198
Czechoslovakia, 69, 195, 197–198

Davies, Fred J., 55, 58, 60–61, 94–95, 111, 113, 117, 119–120 220–221, 223–224
DeGolyer, Everette, 3–4
Denial Plan, 6–9, 70, 72, 119
Dhahran, Saudi Arabia, 7, 15; building of, 5; Eisenhower era, 17; King Saud's first visit to, 18
Dhahran Airfield agreement, 190–191, 211, 214

Donovan, Leisure, Newton and Irvine, 105
Donovan, William J. "Wild Bill," 54, 64, 76–77, 105
Dorsey, Richard, 162–163
Drewry, H. P., 147
Duce, Terry, 93, 117, 125, 176–177, 182, 186, 194–195
Dulles, Allen, 68, 78–79, 141, 146, 194
Dulles, John Foster, 208; and Buraimi Oasis, 24–25; and boycott of Cuba, 227; and King Saud's visit to the U.S., 211–215; and Nonaligned Movement, 198–199; and Onassis contract negotiations, 63, 64, 66–67, 85, 108, 112, 118, 131–132, 136, 138, 146, 163 191; and Red Scare, 74
Duniway, Ben G., 83

Eakens, Robert H. S., 98, 103
Eddy, William A., 15, 27, 29, 57, 61, 64, 77, 79, 105, 141, 143, 146, 233 n.32
Eden, Anthony, 199, 205–206, 208
Egypt, 141, 161, 189, 192, 195; Suez Crisis, 204–215
Eisenhower, Dwight D., 8, 17, 148, 167, 176, 179, 185, 188–189, 193, 196, 198–199, 225, 227; Buraimi Oasis policy, 24; CIA under, 78; congratulatory letter to King Saud, 175; Eden's "Dear Friend" letter to, 206; King Abdul Aziz's letter to, 25; King Saud's "Dear Friend" letter to, 210; and King Saud's visit to U.S., 210–214; meeting with NSC to discuss Onassis deal, 66–68; and "Mossadegh syndrome," 70; NSC 5428 (Near East "Statement of Policy") under, 69–72, 75, 84–85, 88, 99, 131, 135, 146, 206; and nullification of Onassis contract,

223; Prince Faisal's meeting with, 38; and Red Scare, 73–74; and Suez Crisis, 204, 206–215
Eisenhower Doctrine, 70–72, 74
Esso. *See* Standard Oil Company of New Jersey
Esso Standard, 106–107
Evans, Peter, 33, 36, 85–87, 151, 166
Eveland, Wilbur Crane, 8, 9, 26

Fahd bin Abdul Aziz, Prince, 133
Faisal bin Abdul Aziz, Prince, 20–22, 94, 99, 110, 128, 150, 155, 160, 161, 180–181, 191, 195; Awalt on, 138; and Egyptian arms purchases, 197; as minister of foreign affairs, 133; successor to King Saud, 224, 228; and Sulaiman, 27, 31, 92, 141; visit to U.S., 24, 38; and Wadsworth, 110, 112, 136–138
Federal Bureau of Investigation (FBI): and Greek network, 35, 37–38; and Onassis, 35, 37–38, 119, 172; Technical Services Laboratory, 161, 201. *See also* Hoover, J. Edgar
Federal Trade Commission (FTC), 100–105
Fifty-Fifty Agreement (Saudi Arabia), 11–13, 23, 27, 148
Fifty-Fifty Agreement (Venezuela), 11, 12
Flags of convenience, 97
Follis, R. Gwin, 62
Ford, Charlotte, 34
France, 32, 51, 69–70, 106–107, 128, 153, 158, 164, 196, 201, 202, 205–208, 210–211
Franco, Francisco, 125
Free Princes, 228

Game of Nations, The (Copeland), 79
Garbo, Greta, 166
Garrison, Jim, 80
Gay, Merrill, 131

Germany, 30, 40, 48, 50, 78, 86, 141, 144, 167. *See also* West Germany
Gerrity, John F., 154–156, 162–163
Getty, J. Paul, 9–11, 48, 58, 128–129, 131, 162, 185
Giancana, Sam, 82–83
Glubb, John Bagot, 205
Gold, Samuel, 202
Gorgoni, Khalid, 15, 57, 134, 144–145, 149, 155
GOVENCO Affair, 27–31, 133, 140, 150, 165
Gratsos, Costas, 33
Greek Network, 35–37
Gresham, Robert C., 86
Guatemala, 71
Gulf Oil, 2

Habachy, Saba, 218, 220
Hagerty, James, 73, 210
Hahn, Peter, 75
Hare, Raymond A., 14–16, 24, 103, 233 n.32
Harlaftis, Gelina, 34, 36, 47–48, 52, 166, 201, 209
Hart, Parker T. "Pete," 20–21, 103–104, 114–116, 191, 214
Hassan, Mahmoud, 221–222
Heikal, Mohamed, 196
Helms, Richard, 226
Hiss, Alger, 80
Hitler, Adolf, 40, 125, 144
Hochschild, Adam, 125
Holden, David, 21, 32, 56
Holmes, Julian C., 47
Hoover, Herbert, 89
Hoover, Herbert, Jr., 190, 194
Hoover, J. Edgar, 35, 50, 83, 85, 172
Hoover Commission (Commission on Organization of the Executive Branch of Government), 89
Hopwood, Frank, 153–155
Hougan, Jim, 82, 85, 86, 166
Houston, Lawrence R., 86

Huddleston, Walter, 157, 159
Hughes, Howard, 79, 83, 161, 225–226
Humphrey, George M., 68
Hussein, Jamal, 57
Hussein, king of Jordan, 205

Indonesia, 2, 82, 191; Bandung Conference, 198, 206
International Bank for Reconstruction and Development (World Bank), 26, 140
Iran, 6, 19–20, 25, 26, 63, 154, 208, 212, 227; and concession system, 19, 223; and FTC report, 101–102; nationalization of oil, 8, 19, 70, 101, 115, 125, 187; and Soviet Union, 19, 189; Tudeh Party (communist party), 19, 69–70; U.S. aid to, 125
Iranian National Oil Company, 8, 19, 70, 101, 115, 125, 187
Iraq, 2, 6, 14, 69, 97–98, 115, 153–154, 164, 208; Baghdad Pact, 71, 189–192, 193, 196, 198, 205, 210; U.S. invasion of, 225
Islam, 99, 149, 197; culture, 218–219; Hanbali school of Muslim law, 188; and hiring oil workers from Muslim countries, 11; holy cities of Mecca and Medina, 4; Wahhabism, 3
Israel, 13, 19, 75, 91, 92, 113; Arab boycott of, 94, 193–194; and Baghdad Pact, 189; creation of, 19, 94; and King Saud, 113; and Onassis, 163–164; raid on Gaza Strip (February 1955), 196–197; Saudi demands for Mobil to stop doing business with, 193–194; and Suez Crisis, 207–214; U.S. recognition of, 11, 24, 111, 208, 225; Zionism, 57, 72, 163–164, 209–210
Italy, 11, 23, 80–81, 107, 108, 196

Jablonski, Wanda, 25, 222
Jackson, Robert H., 54
Japan, 1, 3, 73, 76, 78, 107–108, 168, 185
JECOR (U.S.-Saudi Arabian Joint Economic Commission), 225
Jeddah, Saudi Arabia, 4, 30, 38, 49, 55, 57–59, 90–91, 98–99, 157, 160, 172, 174–176, 179, 181
Jennings, B. Brewster, 128, 217, 223
Jernegan, John, 89–90, 128, 143–148, 154–156, 167, 175, 178, 179, 182
Jiluwi, Saud bin, 195
Johns, Richard, 21, 32, 56
Johnston, Joseph J., 12–13
Jones, J. Jefferson, 99
Jordan, 199, 205
Journal of Commerce, 25, 165, 169, 176

Kéchichian, Joseph, 24–25
Kelly, J. B., 22
Kennedy, Jacqueline, 34, 227–228
Kennedy, John F., 34, 73, 80, 227–228
Kennedy, Robert F., 83
Keyes, Robert L., 117
Khayal, Abdullah Al-, 193
Khrushchev, Nikita, 196
King, W. L., 104
King Saud Foundation, 20
Klemmer, Harvey, 112
Kopper, Sam, 26
Korean War, 49–50, 52, 69, 71, 77–78, 84
Kuwait, 3, 6, 16, 20; Saudi-Kuwait Neutral Zone, 7–11, 58, 128–129, 138–139, 185, 201

Lacey, Robert, 165, 228
Laws, Bolitha J., 51–52
Lay, James S., Jr., 69
Lebanon, 14, 28, 57, 58, 97, 118, 134, 141, 163–165, 199
Lebkicher, Roy, 113–114
Lenin, Vladimir, 74

Libya, 97, 144, 224
Linder, Harold F., 102
Livanos, Stavros "Stormy Weather," 34, 35, 114
Lloyd, Selwyn, 199
Long, Augustus C., 63

Madison (antitrust) Case, 54–55, 76, 100, 104
Maheu, Robert A., 90, 143, 144, 183, 184; background and career of, 79–83; and Castro assassination plot, 80, 83, 227; and Catapodis dossier, 154–158, 159, 181; contractor for CIA, 79–87, 118–119, 137, 139, 141, 181; news media used as weapon by, 159–162, 164–165, 181; Onassis investigation for Niarchos, 84–87, 118–119, 201; Operational Security Clearance given to, 79; terminated from CIA work, 225–226
Mann Act, 82
McCarthy, Joseph, 73–74, 80
McCarthyism, 52, 73–74
McCloy, John J., 26
McCone, John, 143–144, 146
McCormick, Robert L. L., 89–90, 167
McDonald, Harry J., 223
McDougal, Myres, 218
McGhee, George, 13
McGuire, E. Perkins, 204
McGuire, Phyllis, 82–83
McLeod, Scott, 85, 154
Meader, Vaughn, 73
Mecca: *Al Bilad al-Saudiyah* (government newspaper), 90; Hajj (pilgrimage), 4, 27, 106, 192, 205; Jeddah-Mecca road, 30; King Abdul Aziz's seizure of, 20
Medina, 20
Merchant Ship Sales Act (1946), 46
Merriam, Gordon, 29, 73
Metzger, Stanley D., 127, 135–136, 176, 222

Mexico, 1
Michael Baker Jr. International (MBJI), 29–31, 143
Military Sea Transportation Service (MSTS), 64
Mishal bin Abdul Aziz, Prince, 133
Mitchell, Reginald P., 166–167
Morse, Clarence, 226
Mossadegh, Mohammed, 19, 70, 125
"Mossadegh syndrome," 70
Murphy, Robert, 64, 105, 130–131, 143, 146, 147, 162, 189–190, 199, 204
Mussolini, Benito, 125

Naimi, Ali al-, 23
Nasser, Gamal Abdel, 13, 22–23, 24, 26, 59, 219, 228; and Baghdad Pact, 189; and Czech Arms Deal, 195, 196–197; and Egyptian revolution (1952), 22; removal of British troops from Egypt, 71; and Suez Crisis, 204–215
National Security Act (1947), 77
National Security Archive, 160–161
National Security Council (NSC), 66–67, 77, 117; NSC 26/2 ("Denial Plan"), 7–9, 70, 72, 119; NSC 5428 (Near East "Statement of Policy"), 69–72, 75, 84–85, 88, 99, 131, 135, 146, 206
Nehru, Jawaharlal, 198
Nejd, 15, 21
Netherlands, 107, 108, 113, 227
Neutral Zone, Saudi-Kuwait: and AMINOIL concession, 10; bids for oil rights, 10–11; defined, 7, 10; and Onassis contract, 58, 128–129, 138–139, 185, 201; Pacific Western Oil Company concession, 10–11
Niarchos, Constantine, 89
Niarchos, Stavros, 139, 167, 175, 177, 178, 179; and Catapodis dossier, 153, 154, 165; court testimony of, 201–202; indictment against, 47;

investigating Onassis for Maheu, 84–87, 118–119; Niarchos Collection, 35; obituary for, 35; rivalry with Onassis, 34–36, 47, 51, 84–87, 118–119, 128; Royal Dutch Shell scheme, 128
Nixon, Richard M., 85, 128, 213, 225; Watergate scandal, 78, 80, 85, 227
Noble, John, 125, 126
Nonaligned movement, 198–200
Norway, 97, 106, 108, 114, 166, 168, 170

O'Connell, James P., 81–82, 86
Office of Strategic Services (OSS), 54, 76–79, 105, 143
Ohliger, Floyd, 91, 171, 219
Oil embargo (1973), 6, 224–225
Olympic Airways, 35
Oman, 24
Onassis tanker contract: Aramco response to, 59–64; Article IV, 57, 58, 64, 88, 89–91, 94–95, 110, 112, 116, 126–127, 139, 170, 174, 178, 182, 185, 187, 192–194; arbitration tribunal, 216–223; British opposition to, 97–99; Catapodis's role in, 33–34, 38–41, 45, 115, 119, 151; and CIA's Project Twixt, 79–83; contract terms, 58–59, 96–97, 99, 150, 169, 170; and disappearing ink, 53–54, 152, 161, 164, 184, 201; French opposition to, 102–105; international reactions to, 97–99, 102–108; and NSC 5428 (Near East "Statement of Policy"), 69–72, 75, 84–85, 88, 99, 131, 135, 146, 206; nullification of, 223; Saudi response to, 58–59; Sulaiman's letter notifying Aramco of, 57–58; U.S. national defense concerns, 64–65; NSC meeting with Eisenhower to discuss, 66–68; and Yassin's request for U.S. arms, 214–215

Onassis, Aristotle Socrates, 32–33, 224; arraignment of, 51; background and family of, 34; boycott of tankers owned by, 184–185; civil lawsuits against, 46, 50, 102, 147, 182–185, 201–202, 226; FBI file on, 37; and Greek network, 35–37; indicted for violating Merchant Ship Sales Act, 46–52, 88–89, 115, 121, 168, 178, 179, 200, 201; *Journal of Commerce* interview (post-contract), 169–170; and King's Saud's ratification of, 49, 53, 56–57, 89–93, 111, 117, 144, 150, 152, 169, 177, 182, 188; letter to Mohammed Alireza, 41–44; marriage to Jacqueline Kennedy, 227–228; Maheu's investigation of, 84–87, 118–119; and Niarchos's obituary, 35; and Olympic Airways, 35; rivalry with Niarchos, 34–36, 47, 51, 84–87, 118–119, 128; and Suez crisis, 208–209, 226; survivor of Smyrna massacre, 51–52; testimony before Congress, 226; whaling fleet of, 38, 49, 165–168, 176, 185, 203; and yacht for King Saud, 93–94. *See also* Onassis tanker contract
Onassis, Christina "Tina," 33, 51, 89, 153, 163, 202; *Christina* (yacht), 163; *Tina Onassis* (tanker), 49, 167
Organization of Petroleum Exporting Countries (OPEC), 22, 134, 224
Owen, Garry, 114, 161–162, 172, 221
Owen, William, 54–55, 58, 60, 63, 105, 130, 139, 218

Pacific Carriers Inc., 143
Pacific Western Oil Co. (PacWest), 10, 58, 128–131, 138–139, 162, 182, 185
Page, Howard, 217
Pahlavi, Mohammed Reza Shah, 19, 101
Pakistan, 11, 189

Pappas, Thomas, 114
Payne, P. R., 153
Pelham, Clinton, 20, 27, 37
Peron, Eva, 37
Peru, 165–168, 176
Pétroles d'Atlantique, 107
Phillips, Horace, 150, 162, 172–173
Point Four technical assistance program, 11, 24, 75, 134, 191, 193, 225; King Saud's withdrawal from, 113, 138, 213
Primakov, Yevgeny, 72
Project Twixt, 79–83
Pulaski, Count Maximilian de, 39

Qatar, 3, 7, 8–9, 16
Quinn, Anthony, 37
Quwatli, Shukri al-, 213

Radford, Arthur W., 67–68
Radio Free Europe, 160
Railroad (Dammam–Riyadh), 12, 18, 150, 191
Ras Tanura, Saudi Arabia, 5, 23, 58, 64–65, 95, 97, 107, 118, 128–129
Rasheed, Madawi al-, 228
Rathbone, Monroe J., 62, 63
Ray, George W., Jr., 54–55, 60, 117, 121, 124–127, 178, 186–187, 218–223
Reagan, Ronald, 26
Red Scare, 73–75
Rieber, Torkild "Cap," 122–126, 143
Riyadh, Saudi Arabia, 57, 102, 129, 157, 221; accessibility of, 4, 12, 18; Nixon's visit to, 225; royal permission required for visits from foreigners, 172
Robinson, Edward G., 34–35
Roosevelt, Franklin D., 26
Roselli, Johnny, 80
Ross, Edward J., 183–184, 200–201
Rowan, Dan, 82–83
Royal Dutch Shell, 2, 128, 153
Russia and the Arabs (Primakov), 72

Sadat, Anwar, 228
Saud bin Abdul Aziz, King, 63–67, 225, 227; Aramco-Saudi committee ordered by, 172; delivery of Catapodis dossier to, 155, 161, 162, 181; denunciation of Baghdad Pact, 71; first visit to Dhahran, 18; influence of Id bin Salem, 21; meeting with Onassis, 171; and ratification of Onassis tanker contract, 49, 53, 56–57, 89–93, 111, 117, 144, 150, 152, 169, 177, 182, 188; removal of, 228; succession to throne, 20–26, 41; and Soviet and Suez Crisis, 204–205, 209–215; and Sulaiman, 26–28, 56; visit to United States (1957), 210–214; and Wadsworth, 57; withdrawal from Point Four technical assistance program, 113, 138, 213
Saudi Arabian American Development Co. (SAADCO), 28–29, 59, 155
Saudi Arabian Tankers Company Limited (SATCO), 53, 55, 57–59, 75, 96–97, 103, 150, 169, 170, 179, 192. *See also* Onassis tanker contract
Schacht, Hjalmar, 40–41
Schwebel, Stephen M., 216–217, 218
September 11, 2001, terror attacks of, 225
Seven Sisters, 2, 102. *See also* British Petroleum (BP); Gulf Oil; Royal Dutch Shell; Socony-Vacuum Co. (Mobil); Standard Oil Company of California (Chevron); Standard Oil Company of New Jersey (later Exxon); Texaco
Shakir, Ibrahim, 29
Skouras, Spyros, 114, 145–146, 148–149, 154
Smith, Walter Bedell, 24, 145–149, 154
Smyrna massacre, 51–52

Socony-Vacuum Co. (Mobil), 2, 5, 11, 102, 104–105, 128, 186–188, 193–194, 217, 223

Soviet Union: arms sales, 196–197, 210, 212; and Baghdad Pact, 189; and beginning of Cold War, 77–78; and CIA, 77–79; and communist activity in Arab states, 75, 225; and Denial Plan, 6–9, 119; desire to re-establish diplomatic relations with Saudi Arabia, 191–192; dissolution of, 228; and Fifty-Fifty Agreement, 13; and Iran, 19, 189; nationalization of oil, 102; and NSC 5428, 69–70, 72; and Red Scare, 73–75; and Suez Crisis, 207, 208

Spain, 107, 125, 196

Spanish Civil War, 125

Spooks (Hougan), 82, 85, 166

Stalin, Joseph, 72, 74, 196

Standard Oil Company of California (Chevron), 2, 3, 4, 5, 11, 27, 54, 59, 62, 107, 108, 124

Standard Oil Company of New Jersey (later Exxon), 5, 11, 62, 107, 217

Stassen, Harold, 84–85

Stegner, Wallace, 4, 5, 11

Stephens, Robert, 206

Stevenson, Adlai, 26, 81

Suez Canal, 42, 69, 118, 129

Suez Crisis, 70, 204–215, 221, 223, 226; and King Saud, 204–205, 209–215; Onassis's benefits from, 208–209, 223

Sukarno, 82, 191

Sulaiman, Abdullah (Abdullah Sulaiman al-Hamdan), 18, 23, 26–30; and Aramco Concession (1933), 4; and Aramco, 133–141; and death of King Abdul Aziz, 31; dismissed from government, 139, 157, 160, 162, 175; Eddy on, 15, 61; and Neutral Zone concessions, 9–14; as only non-royal member of 1954 cabinet, 133; role in Onassis tanker deal, 40–41, 44–45, 48–49, 53, 55–58, 60, 88, 90, 111, 120, 126; succeeded by Surur, 139–140, 162

Sultan bin Abdul Aziz, Prince, 31, 133

Sultan, Hamed, 219–221

Sulzberger, C. S., 145

Sunni Islam, 3

Surur, Mohammed, 57, 134, 144–145, 156, 171, 226; advisor to Nasser, 219; and arbitration, 174–176, 187, 192, 214, 219, 220–224; successor to Sulaiman, 139–140, 162; Wadsworth on, 140

Sweden, 107, 108, 196

Switzerland, 182, 188, 195, 196, 215, 218–223

Syria, 14, 21, 26, 57, 199, 210, 213, 225

Talal bin Abdul Aziz, Prince, 133, 228

Tanker ships: *Al-Malik Saud Al-Awal (King Saud I)*, 118, 123, 129, 167, 169, 172, 182, 185; *Lake George*, 48; owned by Seven Sisters, 2; and Suez Crisis, 208–209; *Tina Onassis*, 49, 167; *World Glory*, 118. *See also* Onassis tanker contract

Tariki, Abdullah, 22, 23, 134, 140, 224

Texaco, 2, 3, 5, 11, 54, 63, 107–108, 122–125, 143

Thomas, Evan, 50

Tito, Josip Broz, 198

Trans World Airlines (Transcontinental and Western Air Co.), 59

Trans-Arabian Pipeline Co. (Tapline), 15, 58, 97, 125

Tripartite Aggression, 205–208

Trudeau, Arthur, 119

Truman, Harry S., 57, 143, 146; and Attorney General's List of Subversive Organizations, 73; Denial Plan, 6–9, 70, 72, 119; and

dissolution of the Office of Strategic Services (OSS), 76; election of 1948, 1; Point Four technical program, 11, 24, 75, 113, 134, 138, 191, 193, 213, 225; recognition of Israel, 11, 24, 111, 208, 225; Strategic War Plan, 7
Trump, Donald, 225
Turrou, Leon, 48–49, 53, 92–94, 119, 122, 152, 184
20th Century Fox, 114
Twitchell, Karl, 28–29, 33, 59, 115, 155–157, 172

Ulmer, Alfred C., 86
United Arab Emirates, 12, 199. *See also* Abu Dhabi
United States Export-Import Bank (Ex-Im Bank), 30
United States Information Agency, 160
United States Petroleum Carriers Inc., 46
U.S.-Saudi Arabian Joint Economic Commission (JECOR), 225

Vassiliev, Alexei, 140, 149, 197
Venezuela, 2, 23, 67, 102; Fifty-Fifty agreement, 11, 12
Vertical integration of oil companies, 2
Very Large Crude Carriers, 227
Victory Carriers Inc., 46
Vlachos, Helen, 36
Voss, J. M., 107

Wadmond, Lowell, 127, 218
Wadsworth, George, 61, 66–67, 88, 93, 108, 130–131, 171–176, 179–182, 190–191, 194, 204, 205; and arms sales, 197–198; background of, 57; conversation with Gorgoni, 144–145, 155; and court cases against Onassis, 200; guest at royal dinner for Sukarno, 191; letter to Crown Prince Faisal, 136–138; meeting with Crown Prince Faisal, 112–113; meetings with King Saud, 63–65, 103, 110, 130–131, 142, 162–163; on Onassis, 175; at state dinner for King Saud, 211; on Surur, 140
Wagner, Marcel, 28–29
Wagner, Robert F., 210
Wahhabism, 3
Watergate scandal, 78, 80, 85, 227
West Germany, 26, 51, 66
Whaling ships, 38, 49, 165–168, 176, 185, 203
White & Case, 126
Williams, Edward Bennett, 50, 80–81, 83, 182–183
Wilson, Charles E., 64, 67
Withrow, James R., 102, 105
World Bank, 26, 140

Yassin, Yusuf, 18, 103, 134, 191; and Fifty-Fifty Agreement negotiations, 15–16; and Onassis tanker contract, 149–150, 154, 155, 179–181, 187; and Saudi request for U.S. arms, 214–215
Yergin, Daniel, 6, 10, 102, 104, 129
Youngdahl, Luther, 147, 201

Zelenko, Herbert, 49, 226
Zionism, 57, 72, 163–164, 209–210

About the Author

Thomas W. Lippman is an author and journalist who has been writing about U.S. policy in Saudi Arabia and the greater Middle East for 40 years. A former Middle East bureau chief at the *Washington Post*, he covered foreign policy and national security throughout the 1990s. He is author of seven previous books, including *Saudi Arabia on the Edge: The Uncertain Future of an American Ally*. Lippman is an adjunct scholar at the Middle East Institute in Washington, D.C., where he serves as the principal media contact on Saudi Arabia and U.S.-Saudi relations.

www.ingramcontent.com/pod-product-compliance
Lightning Source LLC
Chambersburg PA
CBHW050627300426
44112CB00012B/1686